The International
Political System:
Introduction and Readings

The International Political System: Introduction & Readings

edited by
Romano Romani
Indiana State University

John Wiley & Sons, Inc.
New York • London • Sydney • Toronto

Library of Congress Cataloging in Publication Data

Romani, Romano, 1942-   comp.
  The international political system.

    1. International relations—Addresses, essays,
lectures. I. Title.

JX1395.R55   327'.08   77-39012
ISBN 0-471-73200-1 (pbk.)

Printed in the United States of America

10 9 8 7 6 5 4 3 2 1

In memory of my father

Acknowledgments

Since this volume grew out of my own efforts to offer an effective and challenging course in international politics, it owes much to those students whose reactions, both positive and negative, helped steer me in what I hope has been the right direction. My greatest debt is, of course, to those authors and publishers who so graciously consented to the inclusion of their work.

Although a modest undertaking, a reader nonetheless reflects the ideas and assistance of many people. The theoretical framework was inspired by the writings of Oran R. Young of Princeton University—to whom I apologize in advance for any misrepresentations. Samuel Huntington of Harvard University, Richard Rosecrance of Cornell University, and Steven L. Spiegel of UCLA read and made suggestions concerning all or part of the book, many of which were incorporated. Among my colleagues in the department, our chairman, Paul C. Fowler, encouraged the project and made both funds and personnel available for its execution; Robert C. Puckett offered a number of valuable suggestions; and J. L. Bonham, a dear friend, was a constant source of ideas and gave freely of his time and considerable talents. Carl E. Beers of John Wiley & Sons made the experience of publishing a book a pleasurable one. Finally, a word of thanks to the unsung heroines of this venture, Karen Johnson, Sue Herlitz, and most of all my wife, Yara.

R. R.

Contents

Contributors

David Baldwin
Associate Professor of Government at Dartmouth College, and the author of *Economic Development and American Foreign Policy.*

Louis J. Cantori
Assistant Professor of Political Science at the University of California at Los Angeles. He is the coauthor (with Steven L. Spiegel) of *The International Politics of Regions: A Comparative Approach.*

William D. Coplin
Associate Professor of Political Science and Director of the International Relations Program at Syracuse University. *The Functions of International Law* and *Introduction to International Politics: A Theoretical Overview* are among his numerous publications.

Carol Ann Cosgrove
Lecturer in Politics at the Aberdeen College of Education and a frequent contributor to scholarly journals, including *Orbis* and *Political Student.*

Karl W. Deutsch
Professor of Government at Harvard University. His many works include *Nationalism and Social Communication* and *The Nerves of Government.*

Carl J. Friedrich
Eaton Professor of the Science of Government at Harvard University. Among his numerous publications are *Man and His Government* and *The Philosophy of Law in Historical Perspective.*

Harold Guetzkow
Fulcher Professor of Decision-Making at Northwestern University. His many works include *Simulation in International Relations* and *A Social Psychology of Group Processes for Decision-Making.*

Morton Grodzins
Late Professor of Political Science at the University of Chicago, and the author of *Americans Betrayed* and *Government and Housing in Metropolitan Areas.*

Ernst B. Haas
Professor of Political Science at the University of California at Berkeley. He is best known for *The Uniting of Europe* and *Beyond the Nation-State.*

Morton H. Halperin
Senior Fellow at the Brookings Institution, and the author of *Limited War in the Nuclear Age* and *Contemporary Military Strategy*.

Wolfram F. Hanrieder
Associate Professor of Political Science at the University of California at Santa Barbara. His latest book in international politics is *The Stable Crisis: Two Decades of German Foreign Policy*.

John H. Herz
Professor of Political Science and Chairman of the Graduate Program in International Relations at the City University of New York. *Political Realism and Political Idealism* and *International Politics in the Atomic Age* are among his publications.

Stanley Hoffmann
Professor of Government at Harvard University, and the author of the widely used *Contemporary Theory in International Relations* as well as *Gulliver's Troubles or the Setting of American Foreign Policy*.

K. J. Holsti
Associate Professor of Political Science at the University of British Columbia. He has written numerous works in international politics, including the textbook, *International Politics: A Framework for Analysis*.

Samuel P. Huntington
Professor of Government at Harvard University, and the author of *The Soldier and the State: The Theory and Politics of Civil-Military Relations* and *The Common Defense: Stategic Problems in National Politics*.

Fred Charles Iklé
Head of the Social Science Department of the Rand Corporation. His books include *How Nations Negotiate* and *Every War Must End*.

Morton A. Kaplan
Professor of Political Science at the University of Chicago. *System and Process in International Politics* and *The Political Foundations of International Law* (with Nicholas Katzenbach) are among his many publications.

Klaus E. Knorr
William Stewart Tod Professor of Public Affairs and Professor of Economics at Princeton University. His works include *On the Uses of Military Power in the Nuclear Age* and *Military Power and Potential*.

Werner Levi
Professor of Political Science at the University of Hawaii. His publications include *Modern China's Foreign Policy* and *The Australian Outlook on Asia*.

George Liska
Professor of Political Science at Johns Hopkins University. Among his books on international politics are *International Equilibrium* and *Nations in Alliance.*

Robert E. Osgood
Professor of International Politics and Director of the Washington Center for Foreign Policy Research at the Johns Hopkins University School of Advanced International Studies. His contributions to the field include *Limited War* and *NATO: The Entangling Alliance.*

Terence H. Qualter
Professor of Political Science and Chairman of the Department at the University of Waterloo. *Propaganda and Psychological Warfare* and *The Election Process in Canada* are among his publications.

Richard N. Rosecrance
Walter S. Carpenter, Jr. Professor of International and Comparative Politics at Cornell University. He is the author of *Action and Reaction in World Politics: International Systems in Perspective* and *Defense of the Realm: British Strategy in the Nuclear Epoch.*

James N. Rosenau
Professor of Political Science at Ohio State University. He is the author of *National Leadership and Foreign Policy* and the editor of *International Politics and Foreign Policy.*

Bruce M. Russett
Professor of Political Science at Yale University, and the author of *Trends in World Politics* and *What Price Vigilance? The Burdens of National Defense.*

Jack Sawyer
Associate Professor of Psychology at Northwestern University, and is a frequent contributor to numerous scholarly journals, including *American Sociological Review, American Political Science Review,* and the *Psychological Bulletin.*

Steven L. Spiegel
Assistant Professor of Political Science at the University of California at Los Angeles. He is coauthor (with Louis J. Cantori) of *The International Politics of Regions: A Comparative Approach.*

Harold and *Margaret Sprout*
Research Associates at the Center of International Studies of Princeton University. Harold Sprout is also Professor Emeritus of International Relations. Their various joint publications include *The Foundation of International Politics* and *Toward a Politics of the Planet Earth.*

Robert W. Tucker
Professor of Political Science at Johns Hopkins University, and the author of *The Just War* and coauthor (with Robert E. Osgood) of *Force, Order and Justice.*

Kenneth J. Twitchett
Lecturer in International Relations at the University of Aberdeen, and is the coeditor (with Carol Ann Cosgrove) of *The New International Actor: The U.N. and the E.C.C.*

Kenneth Waltz
Adlai E. Stevenson Professor of International Politics at Brandeis University. Included among his publications are *Man, the State, and War* and *Foreign Policy and Democratic Politics.*

Arnold Wolfers
Late of the Johns Hopkins University School of Advanced International Studies and Professor Emeritus at Yale University. He wrote *Britain and France Between the Two Wars* and numerous essays, some of which have been collected in *Discord and Collaboration.*

The International
Political System:
Introduction and Readings

INTRODUCTION

I

A survey of the principal works in the field of international affairs reveals the interesting fact that the terms "international relations" and "international politics" are used almost interchangeably. Textbooks and readers usually bear one of the terms in their title (lately, "world politics" has also come into vogue). Before proceeding to discuss more important matters, this question of terminology merits a few brief remarks.

Without getting into the etymology of the terms, the denotation as well as the connotation of the two is palpably different. Logic suggests that the term international relations refers to *all* interactions at the international level of contact. In other words, it encompasses all relations between what we refer to as international actors. There is nothing in the term to suggest limits of any sort; all international interactions are ipso facto part of international relations. In practical terms, this means that such diverse phenomena as international trade, diplomatic relations, world health problems, and matters pertaining to international postal service are all included. In no way does the term seem to imply that it is limited to relations that are predominantly political.[1] Yet curiously enough, most of the books that include international relations as part of the title are decidedly political in orientation.[2]

If international relations denotes all interactions between international actors (or, alternatively, between members of the international system), then it is clear that political behavior is also included. An analysis of the term international politics suggests a concept of more limited applicability. It specifically refers to and isolates those relations between international actors which are predominantly political. Therefore, international politics is logically a subcategory of international relations. The latter term encompasses all relations between members of the international system, while the former focuses only on that subset of relations which are political in purpose or result. In this book, we will be dealing exclusively with international politics; that is, our attention will focus on those interactions between international actors which are essentially political. This assumes that we are capable, both conceptually and empirically, of differentiating between political and nonpolitical behavior.

The difficulties involved in isolating political from other types of behavior are eloquently attested to by the manifold efforts of political scientists over the years to devise a completely acceptable formula. In the field of international affairs, probably the most well-known definition of the discipline was offered by Professor Hans J. Morgenthau. "International politics," he argued, "is a *struggle for power;*" furthermore, "power is *always* the immediate aim [of international politics]."[3] This now classic statement is derived philosophically from the teachings of Hobbes and historically from the relations between states in the eighteenth and nineteenth centuries.

---

[1] The term "world politics" suggests a field of inquiry even less differentiated than international relations. Although the latter term at least limits itself to relations between international actors, world politics would appear to encompass *all* political relations in the world, whether international, national, or subnational.

[2] In fact, I was unable to discover discussions in any textbook (regardless of the terms used in the title) that did not focus exclusively on political matters, that is, on topics such as war, peace, strategy, decision making, power, alliance, change, international organization, etc.

[3] Hans J. Morgenthau, *Politics Among Nations: The Struggle for Power and Peace* (4th ed., New York: Alfred A. Knopf, 1967), p. 25. Emphasis added.

Only in recent years has Professor Morgenthau's conception of international politics come under serious attack.[4] His "Realist" approach has been chided for its narrowness and lack of flexibility. All relations or behavior that do not manifest the "struggle for power" are automatically excluded from consideration on the grounds that they do not constitute political behavior. But many scholars have suggested that politics is a great deal more subtle than Morgenthau would allow, and that interactions which involve no apparent "struggle for power" are nonetheless both political and important. The Realists have also been taken to task for not defining their central concept, that is, power, with any degree of precision.[5] The critics argue that not only is power hazy conceptually but also that it is almost impossible to apply empirically. On the positive side of the ledger, however, there is virtual unanimity that relations which *do* manifest a struggle for power are assuredly political.

Professor Stanley Hoffmann has also suggested a definition of international politics,[6] one that has found favor among many current scholars. He asserts that we ought to be concerned with "the factors and the activities which affect the external policies and the power of the basic units into which the world is divided."[7] Although Professor Hoffmann's definition is clearly broader and more reasonable than Morgenthau's, it is not without certain inherent limitations. First, the concept of power, with all its ambiguities, remains. Second, Hoffmann's formula presupposes a vast amount of information *before* an action can be accepted as political. To classify an event as political, we must be able to ascertain that the action has either changed the configuration of power or that it has affected the foreign policy of one or more of the actors in the international system. It is perhaps not an overstatement to suggest that this formu-

[4] For excellent critical discussions of Morgenthau's approach, see two essays by Arnold Wolfers, "The Pole of Power and the Pole of Indifference," and "Power and Influence: The Means of Foreign Policy," both of which appear in *Discord and Collaboration* (Baltimore: Johns Hopkins Press, 1962) and Robert W. Tucker, "Professor Morgenthau's Theory of Political Realism," *The American Political Science Review*, XLVI (1952).

[5] See K. J. Holsti, "The Concept of Power in the Study of International Relations," *Background*, VII (1964). Reprinted in this volume.

[6] Although Professor Hoffmann speaks of a definition of international relations, it is clear from the context that he is referring to international politics, at least as that term has been used in this work.

[7] Stanley H. Hoffmann (ed.), *Contemporary Theory in International Relations* (Englewood Cliffs, N. J.: Prentice-Hall, Inc., 1960), p. 6.

lation concentrates primarily on the effects of behavior rather than on its purpose. It seems more than likely that some actions designed to change the power and/or policy of others will fail. Does this mean that the action was less political than one that succeeded? At best, Hoffmann's definition of international politics is ambiguous on this point.

A third and final objection can be raised against the adoption of Professor Hoffmann's definition. The concept of international actor is unnecessarily rigid. According to the formulation, international actors are the "basic units into which the world is divided." This clearly implies that while types of actors have changed over the years, being variously empires, kingdoms, city-states, and nation-states, the critical element common to each is territoriality.[8] Regardless, in other words, of nomenclature or number, international actors are the territorial units into which the world is divided. We can readily accept the overwhelming importance of territorial actors, but at least three significant types of international actor[9] that are *not* territorial can be identified—*supra*national, *inter*national, and *trans*national actors. Organizations such as the European Common Market (EEC), Euratom, and the European Coal and Steel Community are representative of *supra*national actors. These actors can, within their limited areas of competence, make binding decisions for national actors. The major *inter*national actors are the NATO and Warsaw Pact alliance systems, the United Nations, and lesser regional organizations. These actors are composed of national actors that perform in unison on a more-or-less voluntary basis. The third category, *trans*national actors, would be represented by such organizations as the International Red Cross and the International Communist Party. As a rule, they represent groups of private citizens rather than governments.

In our search for useful definitions of international politics, it might be profitable to consider conceptions developed in the context of intranational or domestic politics. There is no sound reason why a definition of politics, if it is generally accepted as useful, cannot be

[8]For a fascinating discussion of the idea of "territoriality," see John Herz, "The Rise and Demise of the Territorial State," *World Politics*, IX (1957). Reprinted in this volume.

[9]For a discussion of international actors, see Arnold Wolfers, "The Actors in International Politics," in William T. R. Fox (ed.), *Theoretical Aspects of International Relations* (Notre Dame, Ind.: Notre Dame University Press, 1959), reprinted in this volume, and Fred W. Riggs, "International Relations as a Prismatic System," in Klaus Knorr and Sidney Verba (eds.), *The International System: Theoretical Essays* (Princeton, N. J.: Princeton University Press, 1961).

applied to international political phenomena. Apparently, the main objection to such a procedure—at least intellectually—is that intranational and international politics differ in that the former is usually characterized by a government, while the latter is "stateless." Stanley Hoffmann's strong plea for the erection of disciplinary boundaries between the two is based precisely on that distinction. "International relations," he argues, "owe their distinctive character to the fact that power has been fragmented into competing or independent groups throughout the world's history. . . . It is the very lack of a supreme and generally accepted authority [government] which explains why the rules of the game in world politics differ so sharply from the rules of domestic politics."[10] The same basic argument in slightly different form is expressed by Morton Kaplan. He states that a political system—a term that he uses almost synonymously with government—is the arbiter of jurisdictional disputes, and since the international system lacks such an arbiter, it "may be characterized as a null political system."[11]

Not all scholars are so impressed with the differences between intranational and international politics. In his well-known article comparing the international system to various primitive political systems, Roger Masters[12] suggests that insights gained in the study of one set of phenomena might lead to a greater understanding of the other. His discussion of various "stateless" societies is, in fact, designed to shed light on the international system. Reversing perspectives, the anthropologist Paul Bohannan, in attempting to explain the functioning of these same "stateless" societies, relies on such concepts as international law and international politics. He refers to the " 'international law solution' to political problems . . . [which] depends on an arrangement of power reminiscent of what used to be called the 'balance' of power,"[13] as the means whereby political decisions are made and implemented in societies that lack formal governmental institutions.

Chadwick Alger, in an article designed to explore the implications for international politics of concepts developed in the context of intranational politics, argues that "the lack of 'governments' in inter-

[10] Hoffmann, *Contemporary Theory*, pp. 1-2.

[11] Morton Kaplan, *System and Process in International Politics* (New York: John Wiley, 1957), p. 14.

[12] "International Politics as a Primitive International System," *World Politics*, XVI (1964).

[13] Paul Bohannan, *Africa and Africans* (Garden City, N. Y.: The Natural History Press, 1964), p. 196.

national systems does not preclude wider application of knowledge and concepts from intranational politics to the study of international politics."[14] He also examines the feasibility of applying such things as functional analysis to international politics. The thrust of Alger's argument is that there can be fruitful reciprocal relationships between domestic and international political analysis and theory. Although the distinction between the two levels on the basis of the existence/nonexistence of governmental structures is obvious, it is *not* controlling. The importance we attach to the notion of government or governmental institutions is closely related to our general orientation toward political phenomena.

Insofar as the analyst identifies politics with government (and by government I mean more or less formal institutions that can formulate and apply rules with a better than 50% rate of compliance),[15] even if the identification is not overt, the more he will tend to be impressed by the differences between intranational and international politics. I am not suggesting that this variance is not important. It is perfectly legitimate to argue as Hoffmann does.[16] This should not obscure the fact, however, that it is also perfectly possible to adopt an alternate perspective which may, in some cases, shed a new and suggestive light on the subject. It is possible to think not in terms of governments and institutions, but in terms of political processes that occur either with or without formal structures.

It is revealing that quite a number of political scientists and international relations specialists have discussed the similarities between the so-called "stateless" societies and the international system.[17] The point that strikes most of these observers is that neither the "stateless" societies nor the international system have any formal governmental institutions. This isomorphism serves as the basis for comparison, and suggests the relevance of insights gained in each arena for the other. Implicitly, these analyses are placing three types

[14]Chadwick F. Alger, "Comparison of Intranational and International Politics," *The American Political Science Review*, LVII (1963), p. 414.

[15]Karl Deutsch discusses the level of compliance in "The Concepts of Politics and Power," *Journal of International Affairs*, XXI (1967). Reprinted in this volume.

[16]In fact, Hoffmann undoubtedly represents the view of the majority of scholars in international relations.

[17]Among the most important of these attempts are the previously cited articles by Masters and Alger, and the book by Bohannan. To this list we might add David Easton, "Political Anthropology," in Bernard J. Siegel (ed.), *Biennial Review of Anthropology 1959* (Stanford: University Press, 1959), and F. H. Hinsley, *Sovereignty* (New York: Basic Books, 1966), especially Chapter I.

of systems on a two-dimensional scale. The three systems are primitive-stateless, national-developed, and international. On one dimension, the international and the primitive are at opposite ends with the nation-developed system occupying a midway position. On the other, however, the primitive-stateless and the international are at one pole, while the national-developed is at the other. The second of these two implicit scales is easy to name; it is clearly a scale that represents the degree or level of political integration. The first scale is a bit more difficult, but I think it is largely a combination of size and comprehensiveness criteria supported by a sort of developmental logic which holds that primitive-stateless groups eventually amalgamate into more sophisticated political communities, represented ultimately by the nation-state; the nation-states together form a still broader community, the international system.

All comparisons of the international system with stateless societies bear traces of this ambiguity concerning the relationship between these three systems. Rarely is it noted that the general thrust of contemporary comparative politics is in the direction of developing concepts (and conceptions of politics itself) that allow the least and most "developed" political systems to be compared and analyzed. To do this it has been necessary, in effect, to replace earlier notions of politics which were wedded to the idea of government with more flexible ideas. As Almond and Powell point out, "The focus [of comparative politics] tended to be on institutions (primarily governmental ones) and their legal norms, rules, and regulations, or on political ideas and ideologies, rather than on performance, interaction, and behavior."[18] Given this sort of bias, it was literally impossible to adequately study most non-Western political systems. Concepts, approaches, and theories had to be developed that were capable of penetrating the largely formalistic aspects of politics and uncovering the elements that *all* political systems have in common.

If the orientation of contemporary political science is in the direction of finding the common denominator between primitive-stateless and national-developed systems, and international relations specialists (not to mention some anthropologists) have already noted the striking similarities between the primitive-stateless systems and

[18]Gabriel A. Almond and G. Bingham Powell, Jr., *Comparative Politics: A Developmental Approach* (Boston: Little, Brown, 1966), p. 3. For further discussion of the new orientation of political science, see, for example, Heinz Eulau, *The Behavioral Persuasion in Politics* (New York: Random House, 1963), and Gabriel A. Almond and James S. Coleman, *The Politics of Developing Areas* (Princeton, N. J.: Princeton University Press, 1960).

the international system, then it should be clear that a strong basis
already exists for comparing the national-developed system and the
international system. Alger and others have pursued some of the
possibilities inherent in such a comparison, but there has been considerable resistance to this approach. However, these developments
point to an emerging (if as yet unstated) theoretical consensus which
makes it possible to argue that the same (roughly) conception of
politics that is applicable at the intranational level will also be
applicable at the international level.

Politics at the Intranational Level

Asked to identify the manifestations of political behavior, few of
us would experience much difficulty. Activities such as running
for office, legislative debates, patronage, party caucuses, voting,
campaigning, and the passage of laws would come readily to mind. If,
however, we were asked to translate this intuitive appreciation of
political phenomena into a precisely articulated statement that
defined the nature of politics, it is more than likely that we would be
incapable of doing so. In frustration, we might answer that politics is
government. This, in fact, was the answer given by political thinkers
until fairly recently. But close scrutiny of the statement forces us to
the conclusion that it is not compatible even with our intuitive
appreciation of political events. The identity between politics and
government leads to the determination that political behavior exists
only in the context of government; alternatively, we would be forced
to argue that governmental activity exhausts all forms of political
behavior. This would have the effect of definitely excluding activities
engaged in by political parties and pressure groups (lobbies), as well
as interpersonal behavior such as exchanging or arguing about
political beliefs. The stateless societies referred to earlier would be, in
effect, devoid of political activity since they are characterized by a
lack of government.

Where formal definitions are so patently at variance with observation and experience, intellectually the situation becomes intolerable. Such situations are, according to Thomas Kuhn, "anom-
alies."[19] If they persist, scientific revolutions are likely to be the
result. The anomaly we have just alluded to did indeed cause in
political science what is often referred to as the "behavioral revolution." This "revolution" changed the perspective of the discipline

---

[19]Thomas S. Kuhn, *The Structure of Scientific Revolutions* (Chicago: University of Chicago Press, 1962), p. 52 ff.

away from the oneness of politics and government; it was replaced by a conception of politics which held that governmental activity was *only one* manifestation of political activity. It further recognized that much—in some cases, most—political behavior occurred outside the formal institutions of government. This newly developed conception of the discipline allowed cross-cultural comparative analyses that were previously impossible, while it broadened the horizons of all political scientists, opening such fields as political sociology, political psychology, small group behavior, game theory, and so on.[20]

A widely accepted definition of politics spawned by the "behavioral revolution" was developed by Professor David Easton.[21] Political behavior, Professor Easton contends, is that aspect of human behavior which is "primarily oriented toward the *authoritative allocation of values.*"[22] Every society—every group, in fact—needs to develop means for the making of decisions that will be accepted fairly regularly as binding by its members. The Eastonian view of politics holds that political behavior is the sum total of all those acts performed by individuals or groups which are relevant to the process of allocating values among the members of a group.[23]

As it stands, Easton's view of politics is broad, too broad in fact to be very useful as a guide for political scientists anxious to undertake serious research. At its most comprehensive, the formula suggests, for example, that the processes by which a local labor union distributes values among its membership are as political as the activities of the U. S. Senate. Conceptually, of course, this is quite true: all processes that authoritatively allocate values for a group are political. For practical purposes, however, Easton decided to limit relevant interactions

[20] Almond and Powell, *Comparative Politics*, pp. 7-15.

[21] For a discussion of the considerations that led Easton to develop his particular conception of politics, see David Easton, *The Political System: An Inquiry into the State of Political Science* (New York: Alfred A. Knopf, 1953), especially Chapters IV and V. More important from the point of view of spelling out the implications of the approach is the sequel, *A Framework for Political Analysis* (Englewood Cliffs, N.J.: Prentice Hall, 1965), Chapter IV.

[22] Easton, *Political Analysis*, p. 50.

[23] The extent to which Easton's definition of politics has been accepted in the discipline is reflected in its adoption by two new major introductory textbooks: Karl W. Deutsch, *Politics and Government: How People Decide Their Fate* (Boston: Houghton Mifflin, 1970), and Joyce M. Mitchell and William C. Mitchell, *Political Analysis and Public Policy: An Introduction to Political Science* (Chicago: Rand McNally, 1969).

to those involved in the process of allocating values *for the society as a whole.*[24] This modification of the basic definition is useful for political scientists concerned primarily with the investigation of intranational politics; for our own purposes, however, the more comprehensive view of politics will be more expedient.

"Value" is a concept which refers to anything that is valued or desired by individuals or groups. This means that the number of specific values, that is, things which people want, is practically limitless. Specific values can range from television sets to religious freedom to abortion laws. Given such a bewildering variety of values, it is helpful to organize specific values into classes or types of values. One typology that has proven quite useful to political scientists over the years was advanced by Harold Lasswell: "Available values," he stated, "may be classified as *deference, income, safety.*"[25] Were it not for the basic scarcity of these values, either absolutely or relatively, there would be no need to allocate them. In actual fact, however, each of these types of values is more or less in short supply. The most obvious example is income; whatever the particular distribution of income within a society, there are bound to be differentials that favor one group or another, or demands on the part of some groups to enjoy a greater share of the total available. Deference is a value that is scarce by definition since it can only exist where there are differences in status. Total equality would mean the complete absence of deference. Recent "law and order" political campaigns reaffirm both the importance and scarcity of safety. In sum, politics is the process of making authoritative decisions concerning which groups or individuals will enjoy—and to what extent—the values of income, safety, and deference.[26]

Modern Western societies have evolved very elaborate procedures and institutions that enable them to allocate the values of safety,

[24]See, for example, the distinction that Easton draws between "political" and "parapolitical" systems, *Political Analysis,* pp. 50-56.

[25]Harold Lasswell, *Politics: Who Gets What, When, How* (Cleveland: World Publishing Company, 1936), p. 13. For the evolution and modification of Lasswell's ideas concerning a typology of available values, see his later work, *The Analysis of Political Behavior: An Empirical Approach* (London: Routledge & Kegan Paul, 1948). It ought to be noted that the author considers his typology "representative" and not necessarily "definitive."

[26]For excellent case studies of the process of allocating various values, see Mitchell and Mitchell, *Political Analysis and Public Policy,* especially Chapters III, IV, V, and VI.

deference, and income in a relatively orderly and peaceful fashion. These societies are characterized by what political scientists are wont to call a very high level of "structural differentiation." Translated, this means that these political systems have highly developed and complex governmental structures. Given this sort of environment, it is understandable that there is a tendency to equate government and politics. It is important to recall, however, that even in these systems much political behavior occurs outside governmental structures, and many societies manage to accomplish these same ends (albeit somewhat less efficiently) with few, if any, formal political institutions.

Politics of the International System

The position I am espousing in this essay is that politics is relatively immutable in its essential characteristics regardless of the context within which it occurs or the types of actors involved in the process. If national or subnational politics is defined as the authoritative allocation of values, it is not unreasonable to argue that international politics can be viewed as those processes and interactions which tend to more or less authoritatively allocate values for the members of the international system. This approach not only allows us greater insight into the activities of international actors, but also clarifies the relative position of international politics, placing it squarely within the orbit of political science. International politics must be regarded as but one (among many) manifestation of political behavior.

Most societies—with the exception of those previously designated as "stateless"—have governments of one sort or another, ranging from tribal chiefs and councils to our own complex institutional arrangements. For all intents and purposes, the governmental agency or structure(s) is the "allocator" of values for the members of a particular political community. Allocations or binding decisions are concentrated in a few, usually highly visible, organizations (for example, the U. S. Congress or a seventeenth-century monarch). Given this type of experience, it requires some effort to conceive of the allocating process as being diffused throughout the community.[27] Diffuseness, however, is a chief characteristic both of international politics and the politics of "stateless" societies. No in-

[27]Even Easton, whose avowed purpose is to develop a conception of politics that is behavioral rather than institutional in orientation, finds it difficult not to equate politics and government.

ternational government, or central allocator of values, presently exists; this does not deny the possibility that an organization such as the United Nations might not so evolve in the future.[28]

Currently, there is no central body, group, or institution that makes decisions binding on the members of the international system. Instead, binding decisions are made through the bilateral or multilateral interactions of members. Actors might bargain with each other over the disposition of a particular piece of real estate; alternatively, they might, through the dispensation of various forms of economic aid, attempt to draw other actors into their own sphere of influence or dominance. Regardless of the specific form that interactions take, the overall political process consists of the total of these separate encounters. Each of these "transactions" generally results in some sort of agreement or, at least, temporary understanding between the parties. Duress is often a significant component of the outcome.[29] The aggregate of these individual decisions is, from the systemic point of view, the authoritative allocation of values for the international system.

The aggregation of diffuse interactions and their consequent outcomes to obtain a comprehensive view of the functioning of a system is a relatively common technique. Classical economics epitomizes this approach. Within the free market economy, allocations are not centrally planned (although at present they may be centrally influenced); it is the independent action of individual buyers and sellers that determines price, output, and rate of growth. In the free market model, no individual is able to set, for example, price. This model does not allow for an actor comparable to that of government

[28]A number of studies recently have attempted to apply categories of political analysis—especially those developed in the context of structural-functional theory—to such international bodies as the United Nations. Although these are useful exercises that yield some interesting results, the authors are not taking the position that these organizations are in any real sense international governments. See, for example, Robert W. Gregg and Michael Barkun (eds.), *The United Nations System and Its Functions: Selected Readings* (Princeton, N. J.: D. Van Nostrand, 1968).

[29]That an agreement, such as one embodied in a treaty, is legitimate even if one or more of the parties was "forced" to consent is a long-standing principle of international law. See, for example, J. L. Brierly, *The Law of Nations: An Introduction to the International Law of Peace* (5th ed., New York: Oxford University Press, 1955), p. 244, and William W. Bishop, Jr., *International Law: Cases and Materials* (2nd ed., Boston: Little, Brown, 1962), pp. 114-116. The sagacity of forcing a defeated actor to endure a harsh and humiliating treaty is, of course, an altogether different question. Many diplomatic historians regard the Versailles settlement which ended World War I as a direct cause of World War II.

in the sense of being able to make systemwide decisions or allocations. The individual firm is usually not even concerned with the systemic implications of its actions; this is directly analogous to the position of the international actor, looking out for its own interests, rarely, if ever, considering the ramifications of its behavior for the entire system.[30] Some international actors, like some firms, are oligopolistic in the sense that their decisions carry an inordinate amount of weight in some segments of the system. But even the superpowers are unable to allocate values authoritatively for the entire international system.

Diffuse political processes are also characteristic of "stateless" societies. The more extreme of this group lack any form of organized political activity; not even such rudimentary structures as the "chief" exist.[31] From one point of view these societies are nothing more than conglomerates of extended families, that is an elder male, his sons and their wives and children, and his unmarried daughters. In many ways the group is autonomous, but incorporated into the larger society through the invisible bonds of common blood. Each extended family shares a direct common ancestor with two or three other similar extended families. Together these families form a bloc which is, in turn, related to two or three other similar blocs. This progressive grouping continues until it embraces all members of the society. Most important decisions are made in the context of the extended family by the elder male. This does not mean, however, that allocations are not made which affect all or most members of the society; in many cases, they are. Without any centralized "allocator," each extended family (or bloc to which it belongs) must rely on its own resources and influence.[32]

If, for example, one extended family comes into conflict with

[30]The analogy between international politics and economics has been successfully employed by a number of authors, most notably, Kenneth E. Boulding, *Conflict and Defense: A General Theory* (New York: Harper & Row, 1962), and Kaplan, *System and Process.*

[31]For a general discussion of "stateless" societies, see Meyer Fortes and E. E. Evans-Pritchard (eds.), *African Political Systems* (London: Oxford University Press, 1940), and John Middleton and David Tait (eds.), *Tribes Without Rulers* (London: Routledge & Kegan Paul, 1958).

[32]This discussion is based on one particular "stateless" society, the Tiv of central Nigeria. My account relies on the extensive fieldwork of Paul and Laura Bohannan. See, for example, their monograph, "The Tiv of Central Nigeria," *Ethnographic Survey of Africa* (London: International Institute, 1953). Also Laura Bohannan, "A Genealogical Charter," *Africa*, XXII (1952) and *Return to Laughter* (London: Readers Union, Victor Gollancz, 1956) under the pseudonym, Elenore Smith Bowen.

another over land rights, the difficulty may be resolved by negotiation or sporadic, semiorganized violence. If a settlement is not reached, one family is likely to call upon the other members of the bloc for assistance, and its adversary is apt to do the same. At some point, there will be a "balance of power" standoff, and a resolution of the conflict will occur. It is not at all inconceivable that before this point is reached the entire society, through the progressive entrance of larger groups or blocs, may be involved. A similar process occurs with regard to external relations. Not only is it possible for societies organized in this manner to effectively meet external threats but in some cases they also actually adopt an aggressive stance and mount relatively successful expansionary campaigns.[33]

The very existence of "stateless" societies is prima facie evidence that it is possible to have politics (the authoritative allocation of values for a group) without government (structures organized for the purpose of allocating values). The earlier analogy between economics and international politics merely suggests that the idea of aggregating numerous independent decisions, arrived at between bargaining partners, is capable of yielding a comprehensive view of the decision-making process of a system, and that this is not a particularly new or extraordinary way of proceeding.

A dual purpose is served by the definition of international politics which I suggested earlier—that is, that international politics consists of all those processes and interactions that tend to more or less authoritatively allocate values for members of the international system. First, it is above all else a way of thinking about international politics and the international system which, in a broad sense, serves to give meaning to the empirical data. Second, it does what any definition ought to be capable of doing—distinguishing between those sets of phenomena that we wish to include in a system and those that are part of the system's environment. In other words, it provides us with a guide as we approach the arena of international relations, differentiating between the field in general and international politics per se. At the beginning of this essay I summarized the definitions of international politics offered by Professors Morgenthau and Hoffmann. Each was found wanting in a number of respects. The Eastonian definition, I believe, is not subject to these deficiencies and may enable us to more accurately and easily single out international political phenomena.

[33]For the expansion of the "stateless" society, especially the Tiv, see Marshall D. Sahlins, M. D., "The Segmentary Lineage: An Organization of Predatory Expansion," *American Anthropologist*, LXIII (1961), and Paul Bohannan, "The Migration and Expansion of the Tiv," *Africa*, XXIV (1954).

The elimination of the concept "power" and the even more ambiguous notion of a "struggle for power" is the most obvious advantage of the new definition.[34] It hardly seems reasonable to peg the entire area of international politics onto a concept that cannot (at least not without a great deal of difficulty) be defined or given clear empirical referents. International politics both gains flexibility and is broadened by doing away with the limitation that only those interactions that display elements of a "struggle for power" can be regarded as political. It is considerably easier to determine whether behavior is oriented toward the allocation of values. To do so requires considerably less information; for example, it does not matter whether an actor was successful in changing the policy of another. It is the process of trying to do so that is important. The definition is equally capable of handling the past as it is the present. No particular types of interactions or values are either included or excluded. Specific typologies can be developed according to the exigencies of the period being examined. But regardless of either types of values or types of processes, the definition clearly distinguishes between political and nonpolitical phenomena.

Conceptually, the values allocated by the international political process are the same as those allocated at other levels of political interaction. To conceive of the primary international values as safety, income, and deference requires only a modicum of imagination and very slight modifications of the concepts.[35] The terminology is somewhat foreign to scholars in international politics—those things over which empires and nations disagree, and sometimes fight, are

[34]The fact that we have eliminated "power" from our definition of international politics should not lead to the conclusion that power is unimportant or even impossible to study. It remains a concept of very great importance and (unfortunately) very great complexity and ambiguity. Three of the selections in this volume deal specifically with one or more aspects of power. See K. J. Holsti, "The Concept of Power," Karl Deutsch, "On the Concepts of Politics and Power," and Klaus Knorr, "The Concept of Military Potential," in *Military Power and Potential* (Lexington, Mass.: D. C. Heath, 1970).

[35]Although international and national political values may be identical at the level of general concepts, they are obviously quite different empirically. A shack and a mansion may both be conceptually homes, but their observable similarities are rather limited. Therefore, we should not be surprised to find that under safety we would need to list such things as crime prevention legislation and international disarmament agreements, or that under income we would list national health service and international tariff agreements. In both cases, however, the political process (whether at the national or international level) resulted in a particular distribution of the value—a distribution that was to some degree disputed by members of the particular system.

usually referred to as national security, territorial or economic aggrandizement, and power or prestige.[36] The connotations of the typologies, however, are practically the same: national security corresponds to safety; territorial or economic aggrandizement to income; power and prestige, finally, are the international equivalents of deference. The purpose served in adapting Lasswell's tripartite division of values to international politics is to reemphasize the links between all forms of political behavior, regardless of where or how that behavior is manifested.

So far, our approach has concentrated on the homologous nature of political interactions whether they occur between individuals, groups, or corporate national actors such as nation-states. The fact that intranational and international politics are conceptually similar has been a major point of departure. As valuable as such an orientation is, however, it should not obscure the many important differences that clearly exist. The distinctiveness of international politics will become apparent in our discussion of the actors, structure, processes, and environment of the international political system.

II

The aim of the preceding section was to provide the reader with a general orientation toward international politics and the international system. At this juncture it becomes appropriate, however, to examine the underlying analytic-organizational structure of the book which consists, essentially, of a set of interrelated concepts designed both to organize the data of international politics and to investigate the functioning of the system.

The term "analysis" refers to the process of disassembling a system into its component parts.[37] In chemistry, for example, a substance is analyzed by breaking it down into its constituent elements, that is, its atomic structure. The chemist uses the atom as

---

[36] For example, most diplomatic histories are no more than chronicles of shifts in the distribution of international values through processes such as war making and treaty making. A classic example of this genre (and invaluable to the student of international politics) is A. J. P. Taylor, *The Struggle for Mastery in Europe: 1848-1918* (London: Oxford University Press, 1954).

[37] An excellent discussion of "analysis" in international politics will be found in David V. Edwards, *International Political Analysis* (New York: Holt, Rinehart and Winston, 1969), p. 34 ff.

his basic analytic unit because the guiding paradigm of his discipline is atomic theory; if atomic theory were not generally accepted among scientists, however, different chemists might use different analytic units or concepts. In all scientific endeavor, research and analysis is directed by general theories. In the social sciences—as opposed to the "hard" sciences such as chemistry and physics—there is very little consensus with regard to either the general theories that define the disciplines or the more important or relevant analytic units. The situation is much more fluid, allowing both for great diversity and innovation, but also creating the often perplexing problem of multiple approaches to the same body of data. In effect, there are a number of different analytic frameworks all designed to "break down" and study the same phenomena. To further complicate the matter, none of these differing approaches is demonstrably "right" or "wrong." Approaches (like theories)[38] are only more or less useful—a purely operational criterion which is itself subject to considerable debate and controversy.

The approach employed here is but one of many.[39] It organizes and interprets the data of international politics differently than its alternatives; in the process it forces the knowledgeable to reevaluate and reconceptualize, while the neophyte is provided with a fairly comprehensive and challenging introduction to the discipline. The

[38]In this sense, "approaches" are being treated in much the same manner as "theories." Theories are, properly speaking, neither true nor false; they are more or less useful, and more or less capable of explaining a particular body of data. It is even possible for competing theories to coexist in the scientific community. With time, one will tend to be discarded or a synthesis will emerge. Theories are, however, rarely absolute—even in the hardest of the "hard" sciences. There are many discussions of science, theory, and their collateral dimensions. A few of the most useful would include the previously cited Easton, *The Political System* and Kuhn, *The Structure of Scientific Revolutions,* as well as Fred M. Frohock, *The Nature of Political Inquiry* (Homewood, Ill.: The Dorsey Press, 1967); Ernest Nagel, *The Structure of Science* (New York: Harcourt, Brace & World, 1961); W. G. Runciman, *Social Science and Political Theory* (Cambridge: Cambridge University Press, 1963); Arnold Brecht, *Political Theory: The Foundations of Twentieth-Century Political Thought* (Princeton, N. J.: Princeton University Press, 1959); and Abraham Kaplan, *The Conduct of Inquiry: Methodology for Behavioral Science* (San Francisco: Chandler Publishing Company, 1964).

[39]The simplest way for the student to inform himself of the competing analytic approaches is to peruse the table of contents of the various texts and readers in the discipline. Generally, this will provide clues to the major elements of the discipline as viewed by the particular author. A less than exhaustive, but

author, of the approach is Professor Oran R. Young,[40] and its intellectual lineage can be traced back to "general systems theory."[41] All systems, according to Professor Young, are composed of four clusters or sets of variables which he labels *actors, structure, processes,* and *environment.*[42] The exploration of the various dimensions of each of these four aspects of the international political system will yield a comprehensive view of that system. Each chapter of this book is devoted to the examination of one of the four main variables.

A system, in its most elementary sense, refers to a set of interrelated variables. Each member of the group, in other words, can be affected by the actions or changes generated by the other members. Mutual interdependence is most easily observed in a physical system

noteworthy cross section of currently employed approaches to international politics will be found in Morgenthau, *Politics Among Nations*; Hoffmann, *Contemporary Theory*; A. F. K. Organski, *World Politics* (2nd ed., New York: Alfred A. Knopf, 1968); John G. Stoessinger, *The Might of Nations* (3rd ed., New York: Random House, 1969); W. W. Kulski, *World Politics in a Revolutionary Age* (Philadelphia: J. B. Lippincott, 1964); James N. Rosenau (ed.), *International Politics and Foreign Policy* (rev. ed., New York: The Free Press, 1969); William D. Coplin and Charles W. Kegley, Jr. (eds.), *A Multi-Method Introduction to International Politics* (Chicago: Markham Publishing Company, 1971); George S. Masannat and Gilber Abcarian, *International Politics: Introductory Readings* (New York: Charles Scribner's Sons, 1970); K. J. Holsti, *International Politics: A Framework for Analysis* (Englewood Cliffs, N. J.: Prentice-Hall, 1967); Herbert J. Spiro, *World Politics: The Global System* (Homewood, Ill.: The Dorsey Press, 1966); Keith R. Legg and James F. Morrison, *Politics and the International System: An Introduction* (New York: Harper & Row, 1971); and Andrew M. Scott, *The Functioning of the International Political System* (New York: Macmillan, 1967).

[40] See Oran R. Young, "A Systemic Approach to International Politics," Research Monograph No. 33, Princeton Center of International Studies, 1968, especially pp. 27-35.

[41] Although I intend both for the sake of brevity and simplicity to avoid any discussion of the basic concepts and orientations of "general systems theory," the reader is urged to consult Oran R. Young, *Systems of Political Science* (Englewood Cliffs, N. J.: Prentice-Hall, 1968), pp. 14-20 for a cogent analysis of the subject. Other works by Professor Young dealing with the same topic, but in more detail, are "A Survey of General Systems Theory," *General Systems*, IX (1964) and "The Impact of General Systems Theory on Political Science," *General Systems*, IX (1964).

[42] Young, "A Systemic Approach to International Politics," p. 27 ff. It should be noted that while Professor Young uses the term "context," I have opted for the more conventional, "environment." The difference in terms is simply that, and does not imply any substantive variations.

where changes are usually capable of being measured in a fairly un-ambiguous manner through the use of gauges, thermometers, oscilloscopes, and the like.[43] If the analyst decided to examine a system which he determined was composed of three variables, but found that after repeatedly altering the value of one (while controlling for extraneous influences) that no changes were produced in the values of the remaining two, he would be forced to reevaluate his initial decision to include the first variable in the system. The problems facing the political scientist are less amenable to solution since he is rarely in the position of being able to manipulate his variables. To determine the membership of a system, he must rely more heavily on his judgment—which, in turn, is formed by his experience, common sense, and even some intuition.[44]

Since it is impossible to create, for example, a governmental crisis in Tanzania to see what effects it will have on the other members of the international system, the analyst must use his judgment that given certain types of conditions, change originating there will have perceptible effects on the system. The political scientist, then, must think in terms of the *potential* for changing when he makes decisions regarding the membership of a system. There is an additional problem as well. In the typical physical system, each member is equally capable of generating change; this is not so in the international system. Although it may be true that under very extreme conditions Tanzania will be able to generate major changes in the

[43]Much thinking and writing about systems in the social sciences was stimulated by Ross Ashby's seminal work, *Design for a Brain: The Origin of Adaptive Behavior* (2nd ed., New York: John Wiley, 1960). The reader will find in Ashby's work rigorous definitions of basic systemic concepts such as "variable," "stability," "homeostasis," etc., as well as an abundance of examples drawn from the physical and biological sciences.

[44]The question of system membership is one to which scholars have devoted considerable attention. In the social sciences, there are basically two positions. According to the first, systems exist in reality and merely need to be identified. While logical, this involves the analyst in a seemingly endless debate as to whether or not his set is actually a system (it is difficult to test interaction when variables cannot be manipulated), or whether this or that variable ought to be included. The alternative approach, dubbed by Easton as "constructivist," merely asserts that the analyst ought not to worry about demonstrating the interrelatedness of his variables during the first stages of research. In effect, he should treat any group of variables which, on the basis of common sense and experience, he feels will yield useful results. In the social sciences the latter approach not only makes more sense but is the one adopted by most systems analysts. See on this question Easton, *A Framework for Political Analysis*, pp. 27-34.

system, normally it would tend to be affected by changes originating elsewhere. In social systems, therefore, the capacity to engender system changes is asymmetrical. Given these two types of qualification, the determination of a system's membership is not a straightforward proposition; the task must be approached with a certain degree of sensitivity.

The international system is constantly changing. These changes are the result of variations and modifications in each of the four essential variables. For example, the membership of the system is likely to vary over time—since World War II, over 50 new members have arisen. We might say, then, that between 1940 and 1970 the "value" of the variable denoting number of members (a subclass of the actor variable) has changed. In terms of a physical system, this would be the same as saying that the variable temperature or length had changed its value. Assuming that this variation is important, it can be expected to have repercussions with regard to the three other major variables, that is, for the system as a whole. A significant change in the actor variable is likely to produce some changes in the process, structure, and environment variables. This might be comparable to a physical system composed of a heating element, a container, and liquid; if changes were registered in the heating element (i.e., if its value changed), it is likely that there would be changes in the rate of contraction/expansion/conduction of the container as well as changes in the rate at which the liquid was transformed into vapor, etc.

The four central variables of the international political system— actors, structure, processes, and environment—themselves constitute a system: significant changes in any one will tend to displace the value of the others. Much of systems analysis and theory is concerned with the relationships that obtain between the "analytic" variables[4][5] of a system and the attendant problem of system transformation. In this book, however, the general emphasis is far more narrow. The major goal is to sketch a relatively accurate and comprehensive picture of the present international system by examining (in a sense, attaching values to) the various dimensions of each of the

[45]Another question that I am avoiding is the difficult distinction between analytic and physical systems. The matter involves varying levels or degrees of abstraction of the units of the system. For a discussion of this problem, see Easton, *A Framework for Political Analysis*, pp. 26-27; Young, *Systems of Political Science*, pp. 16-17; and Young, "A Systemic Approach to International Politics," pp. 20-22.

four main variables. The residual of this process, however, will be a framework with which the reader will be able to analyze both future and past international systems.

Actors in the International Political System

The logical place to begin any discussion of a system is with the actors that comprise it. The concept "actor" is adopted rather than more familiar terms, such as "nation" because it lacks the connotations with which these other concepts abound.[46] Actor denotes an entity that behaves in interrelationship with other members of a system. In the international system, the characteristics or types of actors may vary over time, and a number of different types may coexist simultaneously. It helps, therefore, to clarify our thinking if we utilize a term that is essentially neutral; it also adds a dimension of "timelessness" to the conceptual framework since we find we are not tied to any one historical period. Projecting into the future, it is possible to argue with some confidence that as long as an international system can be identified, the concept international actor will remain a useful analytic unit.

The types of actors that dominate the present international system have emerged only relatively recently.[47] Although for certain purposes it might be useful to regard tribes and bands of food gatherers as proto-international actors, the first recognizable units were the great empires of the Nile, Tigris, and Euphrates River

---

[46]The concept "actor" does have one connotation that is misleading. It suggests a person, since in common parlance we associate it with the theater. In international politics, however, the term is meant to have no such implication. The actors are formally organized entities (composed, ultimately, of course, of human beings) which affect and are affected by the international system. There are a number of approaches to international politics that tend to focus on the individual, especially the official decision maker. See Richard C. Snyder, H. W. Bruck, and Burton Sapin, *Decision-Making as an Approach to the Study of International Politics* (Foreign Policy Analysis Series No. 3; Princeton, N. J., 1954); Richard C. Snyder, "A Decision-Making Approach to the Study of Political Phenomena," in Roland Young (ed.), *Approaches to the Study of Politics* (Evanston, Ill.: Northwestern University Press, 1958); and Richard C. Snyder and Glenn D. Paige, "The United States Decision to Resist Aggression in Korea: The Application of an Analytical Scheme," *Administrative Science Quarterly*, III (1958). For a discussion of the benefits and limitations of this approach, see Hoffmann, *Contemporary Theory in International Relations*, pp. 50-53, and Wolfers, "The Actors in International Politics."

[47]See Herz, "The Rise and Demise of the Territorial State."

valleys: the Egyptian, Chaldean, Hittite, and Assyrian. During a slightly later period of world history, the city-state as developed on the Greek Peninsula emerged as an important, if not the dominant type of international actor. The imperial order of Rome and Carthage succeeded the city-state, only to collapse into the chaos of the Middle Ages where the number of actors—mostly feudal barons and independent cities—rose into the thousands. By the beginning of the sixteenth century, new organizational forms were emerging (at least in Europe); strong central governments under kings armed with mercenary armies and legions of tax collectors slowly replaced the innumerable tiny principalities. The Thirty Years' War ended by the signing of the Treaty of Westphalia, a moment in history which scholars regard as the formal beginning of the modern state system.

Secular monarchies created strong, independent states in Europe. Their distinguishing feature was their "impermeability"—as Professor John Herz has pointed out[48]—resulting from both a particular level and type of technology and a set of shared values regarding the legitimacy of the monarch. But the "patrimonial" state (i.e., the state that was regarded more or less as the personal patrimony or property of the monarch) was fundamentally different than our own "nation-state," even though territorial distributions have remained relatively stable since Westphalia. The mere act of centralizing political decision making and administration did not immediately result in the dissolution of parochial loyalties and orientations.[49] The process was a slow one. It took the convulsions and agonies of the French Revolution and Napoleonic Wars to crystallize the sense of national identity that had been gestating for generations. But the birth of modern nationalism dramatically and profoundly changed the nature of international actors. Dead was the ideal of a monarch divinely ordained to rule over a supplicant population; the relationship between individual and state became immediate and reciprocal.[50] The new order of things was with equal logic able to

[48]Ibid.

[49]I do not mean to imply that parochial loyalties and nationalism are incompatible. In fact, they coexist. The point is, however, that prior to the development of nationalism most men did not feel part of a community larger than their immediate village or town. Consciousness of being French, for example, is typically a product of the nation-state.

[50]For an excellent discussion of the psychological dimensions of the relationship between individual and state, see Morton Grodzins, "The Basis of National Loyalty," *The Bulletin of the Atomic Scientists*, VII (1951). Reprinted in this volume.

lead to liberal democracy or what we now refer to as totalitarianism. The patrimonial state was limited in countless ways, not least of which was its ability to command and mobilize resources. The unleashing of nationalism brought with it a new level of actual and potential violence, a process which through the agency of a rapidly accelerating rate of technological change continues into the present.

The "nation-state" is, unquestionably, the most significant type[51] of actor in the present international system. It is not altogether clear, however, what exactly is embraced by the term. There are a number of interpretations,[52] all of which vary as to what characteristics an entity must possess before it can properly be referred to as a nation-state. Six properties, argued the former Secretary of State John Foster Dulles, typified the "true" nation-state: (1) laws reflecting the mores of the community; (2) political structures and processess capable of changing the law; (3) the administrative organization necessary to apply the law; (4) a judicial system capable of settling disputes arising under the law; (5) the capacity to deter violence by enforcing the law upon those who resist it; and (6) a level of material well-being sufficient to dissuade the resort to violence.[53] Under the conditions of the Dulles formula, few members of the present system would qualify as nation-states. At a minimum, the formula suggests that there may be degrees of being a nation-state; and that within the same general category there is the possibility of wide variations.

Even admitting that it is possible for an actor to be more or less of a nation-state, it is still necessary to differentiate the various sub-types. Classificatory schemes abound, however, and ultimately the analyst must choose the one(s) most congruent with his own conception of international politics. During the heyday of the Cold War, for example, the most popular typology of nation-states was a simple dichotomy: communist versus noncommunist. This reflected an overwhelming concern with the ideological variable. A more complex, and presumably more valuable approach would be to organize

[51] For other types of actors in the present system, see pp. 47-66.

[52] For an alternative approach to the meaning of the nation-state, see Karl Deutsch, *Nationalism and Social Communication* (2nd ed., Cambridge, Mass.: MIT Press, 1966) and "The Growth of Nations: Some Recurrent Patterns of Political and Social Integration," *World Politics*, V (1953), reprinted in this volume.

[53] Dulles' statement of the characteristics of the nation-state is discussed in Riggs, "International Relations as a Prismatic System," p. 144.

nation-state actors according to their social, economic, and political structures. This might result in such categories as developing-socialist-authoritarian, industrial-capitalist-totalitarian, industrial-socialist-democratic, and so on. Kaplan, on the other hand, finds the degree of vertical organization to be the most salient feature of actors; accordingly, he divides them into hierarchical and non-hierarchical. Further distinctions of possible importance which cut across those already mentioned might include orientations of actors toward the system[54] such as isolation versus participation, and satiated versus nonsatiated.

There are other dimensions of the actor variable that are of consequence in an analysis of the international system. The overall number of actors in the system is relevant, as well as the breakdown of actors into major, minor, and intermediate powers. If one actor is significantly more influential and able to marshal substantially greater resources than its closest competitors, the general complexion of the system is likely to be much different than if five or six roughly equal actors dominate the system. In other words, the level and distribution of political capabilities would be vital aspects of the actor variable. Equally important in understanding and interpreting the system is the extent to which the major actors are all of the same general type, or whether there is considerable diversity. For example, a system consisting of nation-states might display behavior patterns dissimilar to one composed of mercantile city-states (e.g., Republic of Venice), multinational empires, patrimonial states, and a significant international actor.

Structure of the International Political System

The structure of a system inheres in the pattern of inter-relationships among its most important elements. This holds true regardless of whether the system is biological, physical, or social. For example, the size, general appearance, and physical attributes of animals are, in large measure, a function of their skeletal structure. Buildings offer another area of obvious examples of the relationship between structure and the other properties of a system: the steel infrastructure fairly well determines both a building's appearance and function. Conceptually, social structure is no different; in practice, however, both the identification of the major elements and their characterization present real difficulties.

Every social system consists of a set of roles; examples in the

[54]See Young, "A Systemic Approach to International Politics," pp. 28-30.

family setting are the roles of "mother" and "father." Structure, in the context of the family system, refers to the more or less enduring relationships between these roles. The Western family system is generally characterized as patriarchal because the role of father dominates the role of mother; were the situation reversed, the term matriarchal might more adequately summarize the structure of the family system. At any rate, it is the long-term relationship between roles that is important.

In international politics, structure consists of the "characteristic relationships among actors in international systems over time."[55] Moving from a general definition to the delineation of an actual international system's structure, however, involves a number of problems. Most important is the selection of criteria to assess what relationships are fundamental or "characteristic." This question is logically prior to all others, and is likely to be critical in determining how the structure of the system is ultimately characterized. The mere fact that members of the international system interact with one another does *not* constitute structure any more than would a family argument. In fact, structure may be usefully construed as the framework within which the members of a system conduct their relationships. The typical classroom situation, for example, is made up of (a) the roles of "student" and "professor" and their essential relationship; and (b) processes occurring within that framework designed to increase learning or (and, unfortunately, this is more often the case) influence the distribution of grades. The basic student-professor relationship structures the situation for all parties concerned: each role player has certain expectations concerning the behavior of others, feels strong compulsions to act in accordance with the expectations of others, and understands the pattern of authority that obtains between the roles. The various classroom processes or specific transactions will be consistent with the basic role relationships, although within those limitations they will vary widely according to the proclivities of the individual role players.

Implicit in these two examples (the family and the classroom) is the notion that the characteristic or fundamental relationship between roles involves differentials in the relative authority and/or power that each commands. In the determination of the structure of an international system, a similar logic applies. The criteria of structure center on the distribution of power and resources among the

<hr />

[55]Young, "A Systemic Approach to International Politics," p. 30.

actors.[56] For example, one type of international structure that has tended to emerge from time to time has been labeled "imperial" or "unifocal," and is characterized by the preponderance of one actor over all others in "size, scope, salience, and sense of task," as well as in territory and material resources. In such a system, "order rests in the last resort on the widely shared presumption of the ultimately controlling power of the imperial state."[57] It is, then, the dominant position of the "imperial" role player that structures the situation and establishes the boundaries for the interactions among all members of the system.

It is possible, through historical analysis, logical deduction, or a combination of both, to construct typologies of international structures.[58] Logically, each type would be defined according to a set of roles, the relationships between roles, and a specification of the role functions. Besides the previously mentioned imperial or unifocal type, there is, for example, the familiar "bipolar" model.[59] In this system there are two essential roles, superpowers and others.

---

[56]The choice of the distribution of power as the key to structure was specifically suggested by Kenneth N. Waltz in "International Structure, National Force, and the Balance of World Power," *Journal of International Affairs*, XXI, No. 2 (1967). Reprinted in this volume.

[57]The "imperial" model is developed by George Liska in *Imperial America* (Baltimore: Johns Hopkins Press, 1967), p. 37 ff. Reprinted in this volume.

[58]Most attempts to develop typologies of international systems have been backward-oriented; that is, they have focused almost exclusively on the analysis of past international systems. Two of the best examples of this genre are Richard N. Rosecrance, *Action and Reaction in World Politics* (Boston: Little, Brown, 1963) and Liska, *Imperial America*. Morton Kaplan is the only scholar who has seriously attempted to develop types of systems that have *no* historical counterparts. He presumably relied on imagination and logic in constructing his "possible" types. The reader can trace the development of Professor Kaplan's ideas on this matter by consulting the following: "Balance of Power, Bipolarity, and Other Models of International Systems," *The American Political Science Review*, LI, No. 3 (1957), which is reprinted in this volume; *System and Process in International Politics;* "Some Problems of International Systems Research," in *International Political Communities* (Garden City, N. Y.: Doubleday, 1966); and "The Systems Approach to International Politics," in *New Approaches to International Relations* (New York: St. Martin's Press, 1968).

[59]See Kaplan, "Balance of Power, Bipolarity, and Other Models of International Systems," for a complete catalogue of the attributes of the bipolar system. In actual fact, Kaplan distinguishes between the "loose" and "tight" bipolar systems, the distinction resting, essentially, on the degree to which the nonsuperpowers have the ability to maintain a more or less neutral stance vis-a-vis the bipolar conflict.

The two actors that play the role of superpower are relatively equal in terms of capabilities, and absolutely superior to all other members of the system. Obviously, no real international system will conform in all ways to these abstract models, even though the model may have originally been inspired by an actual system. If they have no other purpose, models serve as the starting point in the analysis of real international systems; for at the very least, the structure of a particular system can be viewed in terms of the degree to which it conforms or diverges from the relationships specified in the model.

The international political system and the global system are coterminous; this, however, is a relatively recent phenomenon. Prior to advances made in communications and transportation beginning in the latter part of the nineteenth century, the world was effectively divided into a number of different, largely independent international systems. The understandable ethnocentrism of Western historians has tended to obscure the basically separatist nature of international politics by implicitly identifying them with the European state system. Until relatively recently, however, large portions of the world were as little influenced by or interested in the West as it was of them. The integration of regional international systems into one global system has proceeded to the point where it is an incontestable fact that no region of the world is either too small or too remote to be relevant to the international distribution of values. Continual crises and conflicts surrounding such areas as Korea, the Congo, and Tibet are prima facie evidence of both the globalization of international politics, and its unpleasant consequences.

Up to this point we have been concerned solely with the structure of the international system *as a whole*. This is not, however, the only important level of analysis. Regional systems—more accurately, "subsystems"—continue to be important arenas of international activity, in spite of their integration into the global system.[60] In fact, a regional subsystem is defined as a group of actors that have proportionately more interactions among themselves than with others. This

[60]There are a number of excellent works on regional sub-systems, including Louis J. Cantori and Steven L. Spiegel, "The International Relations of Regions," *Polity*, II, No. 4 (1970), reprinted in this volume, and the authors' fuller treatment of the subject in *The International Politics of Regions: A Comparative Approach* (Englewood Cliffs, N. J.: Prentice-Hall, 1970), especially pp. 1-40. Also of interest are Michael Brecher, "The Subordinate State System of Southern Asia," *World Politics*, XV (1963), and William I. Zartman, "Africa as a Subordinate State System in International Relations," *International Organization*, XXI (1967).

suggests that in terms of the international allocation of values, the region may be of paramount importance in the sense that most of the actor's immediate interests are tied to it. The situation is somewhat analogous to the American political system where broad, and often symbolic, issues are processed at the national level, while immediate "bread and butter" issues (patronage, property taxes, school control, zoning, etc.) are resolved in the context of state and local politics. The analysis of regional subsystems, therefore, is almost certainly going to yield depth to our understanding of international politics.

In like manner, another level of analysis can be identified—that is, functional and regional international organizations. These are groupings of international actors that have banded together for specific purposes, ranging from mutual defense to economic development. An examination into the structure of these organizations—that is, the set of roles and the relationships between them—will serve to round out our picture of the international system.[61]

Processes in the International Political System

Structure, it has been noted, refers to the characteristic relationships between actors in a system; process, on the other hand, is a concept that embraces the typical modes of interaction between those actors. For example, the family structure may involve a degree of male dominance, but within that framework the female may have any number of means at her disposal to persuade or cajole the male into making decisions that she favors. Whether she chooses to be nagging, quarrelsome, or seductive, she is involved in a species of political process. In like manner, the ultimate law-making power in the United States rests with Congress, and the decisions of that body are binding on the community. But both organized groups and individuals employ a vast array of techniques—ranging from the writing of letters to out-and-out attempts at bribery—to influence and mold the decisions of that body. All of these activities are part and parcel of the political process.

International politics, like all other politics, also involves the making of more or less binding decisions. Processes are the means employed by international actors to achieve their objectives, that is,

---

[61]See, for example, Herbert S. Dinerstein, "The Transformation of Alliance Systems," *The American Political Science Review*, LIX, No. 3 (1965); Robert E. Osgood, *NATO: The Entangling Alliance* (Chicago: University of Chicago Press, 1962); and George Modelski, *SEATO: Six Studies* (Melbourne: F. W. Cheshire, 1962).

the most favorable distribution of safety, income, and deference. These may and do run the gamut from peaceful discussion to violent conflict. During any one historical period, actors are likely to engage in a variety of political processes; certain types, however, will tend to be more in evidence in one period than another. This is largely because of the greater affinity that some structures have for particular processes. In other words, a particular international structure is more likely to be associated with certain types of processes than with others. The relative prominence of particular processes is also dependent upon such factors in the environment as technology, ideological cleavage, domestic opinion, and the level of international consensus.

Granted that each set of interactions between members of the international system is, in a sense, unique, it is both possible and profitable to speak of "types" of processes or interactions. This allows us the freedom of generalization: we need not be bound to specific historical instances, and can speak, for example, of "economic interactions" in a general sense. Even this economy, however, is not sufficient to allow a complete catalogue of the possible types of processes. As a result, I have chosen a few representative categories that I consider the most important under contemporary conditions. Each type might be further divided into subtypes. For example, under economic processes I have restricted the discussion to foreign aid; undoubtedly, other types of economic process are important and should have been included, such as international trade. But the types of processes chosen for inclusion should enable the reader to develop the beginnings of a systematic understanding of international interrelationships.

Bargaining and negotiation are probably the most prevalent types of international interaction.[62] Because of the many forms this

[62]There are a number of excellent works on bargaining and negotiation in international relations. A good starting point is Thomas Schelling's seminal work, *The Strategy of Conflict* (New York: Oxford University Press, 1963), as well as his article, "Bargaining, Communication, and Limited War," *Journal of Conflict Resolution*, I (1957). Fred C. Iklé, *How Nations Negotiate* (New York: Harper & Row, 1964) applies many of Schelling's insights to the actual process of international negotiations. A highly stimulating analysis of the sociological and psychological factors involved in negotiating is to be found in Jack Sawyer and Harold Guetzkow, "Bargaining and Negotiation in International Relations," in Herbert C. Kelman (ed.), *International Behavior: A Social-Psychological Analysis* (New York: Holt, Rinehart and Winston, 1966), also reprinted in this volume.

process takes, however, generalizations are both dangerous and difficult. Bargaining and negotiation involve, at a minimum, two or more actors in exchanges or transactions designed—at least at the outset—to maximize the value situation of at least one party. As in the case of all processes, they are only political insofar as they concern the allocation of income, safety, or deference; this qualification effectively excludes purely technical negotiations related to such matters as the Anglo-French development of the Concorde, unless it can be shown that these do have political implications. Negotiations may involve any number of actors, and may cover an infinite variety of specific matters. Negotiations may be either overt or covert, the Paris peace talks being an example of the former, and the famous "secret treaties" prior to World War I being an example of the latter. Normally, bargaining parties communicate with one another explicitly, but this is not essential as many important agreements are reached "tacitly."[63]

The present international system has given rise to two processes that are relatively unique in the history of international politics. The first of these, foreign aid, was not unknown in prior historical periods;[64] its form, scope, and importance account for its novelty. The emergence of foreign aid as a technique employed by actors to change and/or maintain particular distributions of values is the result of the intersection of a variety of factors. Most important among these is the structure of the present system which Kaplan has labeled "loose bipolar." In such a system, there is a sizeable group of actors not part of either major bloc. These "uncommitted" actors become—almost automatically—the objects of the bipolar struggle. And since bipolarity suggests relative stalemate, at least in terms of the all-out use of force, the utility of economic incentives and penalties is fairly obvious. Foreign aid is an instrument that can be used to bolster blocs as well as to gain influence among the uncommitted. As in the case of bargaining and negotiation, all foreign aid is not automatically political: it must be undertaken to affect the distribution of values.[65]

[63] For a discussion of "tacit" bargaining (that is, bargaining without formal communication), see Schelling, "Bargaining, Communication, and Limited War."

[64] For an excellent discussion of the various dimensions of foreign aid, including its history as a political instrument and its uses in the context of the Cold War, see George Liska, *The New Statecraft: Foreign Aid in American Foreign Policy* (Chicago: The University of Chicago Press, 1960), especially Chapters II and V.

[65] Although it may not be immediately obvious, it is quite possible for an actor to extend foreign aid without any political intent. In fact, a number of

The second set of processes that distinguishes the modern from previous periods are those we normally refer to as propaganda and psychological warfare. The essential idea involved in these two processes is not particularly new, but the extent to which they have been used is.[66] Previously, their use was almost exclusively restricted to wartime when it was deemed advantageous to attempt to sap the morale of the enemy's forces and affect his willingness to fight. Today, we tend to think of propaganda and psychological warfare as inevitable components of the relations between states, especially the superpowers.[67] In large measure, this reflects the extent to which the major powers engage in symbolic rather than physical combat. Gaining political objectives seems to dictate demonstrating (in word, if not in deed) the superiority of one's socio-economic-political organizational forms. And large amounts of resources are spent fomenting internal dissatisfactions and disaffections, supporting indigenous revolutionary groups, and disseminating antigovernment information.

---

scholars have strongly urged the U. S. to embark upon such a policy. Because it is recognized that any aid given by one national actor to another will invariably produce either expectations of gratitude (on the part of the donor) or dissatisfactions arising from interference (on the part of the recipient), the usual solution for those who wish to "depoliticize" foreign aid is to put the resources in the hands of an impartial international actor (e.g., an organ of the United Nations) and allow it to make decisions concerning its distribution. The best statement of this position is by M. F. Millikan and W. W. Rostow, *A Proposal: Key to an Effective Foreign Policy* (New York: Harper & Row, 1957). Hans J. Morgenthau's article, "Preface to a Political Theory of Foreign Aid," in Robert A. Goldwin (ed.), *Why Foreign Aid?* (Chicago: Rand McNally, 1962), takes the opposite tack, arguing that foreign aid ought to serve the political ends of a state.

[66] According to Sir Harold Nicolson, the Byzantine emperors employed propaganda and psychological warfare in ways similar to those employed today. They attempted to convert the barbarians to Christianity, and thereby undermining their political and social system and, in a sense, defusing them as a threat. *Diplomacy* (New York: Oxford University Press, 1963), p. 11.

[67] The history and meaning of propaganda and psychological warfare are discussed in Terence Qualter's excellent study, *Propaganda and Psychological Warfare* (New York: Random House, 1965), a portion of which is reproduced in this volume. Also of interest is William E. Daugherty and Morris Janowitz, *A Psychological Warfare Casebook* (Baltimore: Johns Hopkins Press, 1958), and Robert T. Holt and Robert W. van de Velde, *Strategic Psychological Operations and American Foreign Policy* (Chicago: The University of Chicago Press, 1960).

With the development of nuclear technology and sophisticated delivery systems, a major war between the superpowers has become dysfunctional in terms of real political objectives.[68] In fact, it can be convincingly argued that even before Hiroshima, war between the major actors was no longer a useful political process: conventional warfare had become too destructive to be useful, and victory a hollow phrase founded on a technicality but without substance.[69] However, *before* the marriage of modern industrial techniques to the military establishment,[70] war was the *ultima ratio* of international politics, and was undertaken with relative equanimity. Prior to our own century (with the possible exception of the Napoleonic Wars), war did not involve the survival of major actors; it was rather the means of last resort for the resolution of otherwise irresolvable conflicts.[71] In some ways, war performed a function similar to that of general elections, palace revolts, or even civil wars in domestic society. Karl von Clausewitz, whose writings on military strategy and tactics represent the quintessence of eighteenth- and nineteenth-century thinking, observed that "War is not merely a political act, but also a political instrument, a continuation of political relations, a carrying out of the same by other means."

War in the traditional sense is but one of many manifestations of processes involving the use or threatened use of force. Under that general heading, we would have to include such concretely diverse phenomena as limited war, conventional war, nuclear war, limited

---

[68] That war can no longer be rational is not a universally accepted opinion. See, for example, Herman Kahn's well-known works, *Thinking About the Unthinkable* (New York: Horizon Press, 1962) and *On Thermonuclear War* (Princeton, N. J.: Princeton University Press, 1960). Henry Kissinger considered the possibility of the use of tactical nuclear weapons in a war between the U. S. and U. S. S. R. in *Nuclear Weapons and Foreign Policy* (New York: Harper and Brothers, 1957).

[69] For excellent discussions of the evolution of military technology, see Robert E. Osgood and Robert W. Tucker, *Force, Order, and Justice* (Baltimore: Johns Hopkins Press, 1967), Chapter II, and F. H. Hinsley, *Power and the Pursuit of Peace: Theory and Practice in the History of Relations between States* (Cambrdige: Cambridge University Press, 1967), Chapters VIII, IX, X, and XI.

[70] A most interesting and informative case study of the "marriage" between industry and government is William Manchester, *The Arms of Krupp: 1587-1968* (Boston: Little Brown, 1968).

[71] The best discussion of the role of force and war is Osgood and Tucker, *Force, Order and Justice,* Chapter I, reprinted in this volume.

nuclear war, guerrilla war, revolutionary war, unconventional war, cold war, threats of war, and arms races. Technology may have made all-out war among the major actors irrational, but it has certainly not eliminated force and coercion as international processes. In fact, the threat of nuclear war itself remains important, as the Cuban missile crisis amply demonstrated. It is equally difficult to deny that guerrilla war and arms races do not serve the ends of states.[72] It is unlikely, in other words, that the major actors in the system will engage each other directly in any way because of the fear of escalaction; it is equally true, however, that the use of force—either indirectly through proxies or in the form of threats and arms races—continues to be crucial in affecting the distribution of values in the international political sytem.

Setting of the International Political System

All systems exist and function in a setting or environment. One of the premises of general systems theory is that systems can be distinguished from their settings; this makes it possible to think in terms of system boundaries.[73] The task of constructing boundaries, that is, differentiating between a system and its environment, is far easier to accomplish with regard to physical systems than social systems. The latter are composed not of tangible, physical elements, but of units of behavior or interaction between the actors. This means, in effect, that the analyst must abstract from the totality of behavior only that portion relevant to his needs; from this he conceives a system, such as the international political system, which represents only a portion of all the behavior of international actors.[74] Once distinguished from its environment, a system may be regarded either in isolation or in relationship with that environment, depending upon the objectives of

[72] A good account of the various techniques utilized by the U. S. government which fall short of war, but involve the use of force to one degree or another is given in H. Bradford Westerfield, *The Instruments of America's Foreign Policy* (New York: Thomas Y. Crowell, 1963).

[73] A most thorough discussion of the concept of "boundary" and its implications for systems theory is found in Easton, *A Framework for Political Analysis*, pp. 59-68. A further discussion, at the level of general systems theory, can be found in A. D. Hall and R. E. Fagen, "Definition of System," *General Systems*, I (1965), pp. 19-20.

[74] Again, the best discussion of the "analytic" nature of systems is in Easton, *A Framework for Political Analysis*, Chapter III.

the observer. The present approach focuses on the interaction between system and setting, arguing, in effect, that setting is an important independent variable; its importance lies both in aiding in the understanding of the system as well as in providing a source of system change. But the relationship between system and setting is not necessarily unidirectional: the international system may have substantial effects on its environment (this is particularly evident in the case of the domestic setting).

It is relatively easy to demarcate a biological system from its environment, and to suggest the nature of their relationship. An individual, for example, comes upon a rattlesnake (an environmental factor); this is likely to have quite measureable effects on the system: rapid pulse and breathing rates, increased hormonal secretions, perspiration, and the general psychological state of fear and anxiety. The system may then react or at least adapt to these changes in the setting: an attempt to kill the snake would be a response designed to eliminate the source of change; alternatively, the system might react by shifting its location relative to the snake (flight), or by standing quite still until the danger passes. Regardless of alternative chosen, the system has in some ways changed because of the outside influence.

There is a world of difference between biological and social systems. These differences, however, should not be allowed to obscure the fact that at certain levels of abstraction both types of systems exhibit similar structural and behavioral characteristics.[75] It is possible to isolate the international political system from its environment, that is, to abstract from the total universe of elements and behavior those interactions involving the distribution of safety, income, and deference. To do so, of course, requires a greater intellectual output than it would if the system were more palpable. It is likewise possible to investigate the impact which changes in the environment have on the international system, and its responses to those changes.[76]

System is a limited and positively defined concept. It consists of a

---

[75]The theoretical perspective that, at certain levels of analysis, very different concrete systems exhibit very similar or homologous structures and processes is the core of systems theory. This position is forcefully argued by one of the founders of modern systems theory, Ludwig von Bertalanffy in "General System Theory," *General Systems*, I (1956).

[76]As in the case of the three previous variables, the reader is urged to consult Young's "A Systemic Approach to International Politics," pp. 33-35.

set of identified (or identifiable) variables that stand in some relationship of mutual interdependence. Setting, on the other hand, is a concept that is neither limited nor specific, being, roughly speaking, the converse of system. Anything not specifically included in a system is automatically part of the system's total setting. At the extreme, the environment of a system includes the entire universe. Such a gross notion is in need of considerable refinement before it can serve any useful analytic purpose. Decisions must be made limiting the scope of environment by creating categories of environment deemed relevant for the particular investigation at hand. Unfortunately, there is no automatic or foolproof way of doing this; choices are made largely on the basis of the observer's experience and common sense. Validation is dependent upon the dual tests of time and the continual scrutiny of the academic community. However, there is no reason to suppose that particular categories of environment will be relevant in the future simply because they have been so in the past. The typology of setting in Part Four is suggestive of those categories which scholars have consistently viewed as important.

The international political system has been previously defined as consisting of all those interactions among international actors involving the distribution of national security, international economic benefits, and power. It therefore follows that the activities normally characterized as "domestic" politics are *not* part of international politics proper. On the other hand, it is obvious that such things as domestic political structure(s), public opinion, foreign policy decision-making structures and processes, and characteristics of elites are extremely important to the understanding of international politics.[77] Insofar as this represents a dilemma, it is easily resolved if we regard domestic politics as part of the environment or setting of the international political system. This allows the simul-

[77] One of the pioneering efforts examining the relationship between domestic politics and foreign policy is Gabriel A. Almond, *The American People and Foreign Policy* (New York: Harcourt, Brace, 1950). A leading scholar in this area today is James N. Rosenau. See especially, *Domestic Sources of Foreign Policy* (New York: The Free Press, 1967) and "Pre-Theories and Theories of Foreign Policy," in R. Barry Farrell (ed.), *Approaches to Comparative and International Politics* (Evanston, Ill.: Northwestern University Press, 1966). Also see Bernard C. Cohen, *The Press and Foreign Policy* (Princeton: Princeton University Press, 1963), and Henry A. Kissinger, "Domestic Structure and Foreign Policy," *Daedalus* (Spring, 1966).

taneous achievement of two goals. First, the traditional distinction between international politics and foreign policy and foreign policy making is maintained. Second—and more important—it puts us in the position of being able to focus our attention on the effects of domestic politics on international politics. In other words, we are more strategically located conceptually in terms of explaining and/or understanding changes in the international system by reference to changes in the domestic political environment.

Another category of the setting of the international political system is that of international law and morality.[78] It may, on the face of it, seem strange to regard these phenomena as environmental factors; however, the same logic that was used above is applicable. In general, law and morality (in international politics they often are indistinguishable) are not part of the political process itself. Rather, they may function to limit the nature and extent of political processes. In the context of domestic politics, the term law usually denotes the output of the political process; internationally, however, it is more of a reflection of the degree of consensus among international actors over the legitimate areas of conflict, the goals of politics, and the proper means to achieve them. In this sense, therefore, law and morality are conceptually exterior to international politics but influential in shaping them. For example, during the eighteenth century there was a relatively high degree of agreement

---

[78]The literature on international law is vast. Most approaches, however tend to isolate law from the dynamics of the political process. A notable exception is Morton A. Kaplan and Nicholas deB. Katzenbach, *The Political Foundations of International Law* (New York: John Wiley, 1961). Another interesting work consists of a series of case studies, each focusing on a particular international crisis and examining the role played by international law. The rather pessimistic conclusions tend to give a somewhat misleading impression. By isolating crises, the authors are examining situations in which much—perhaps everything— is at stake. Under such extreme conditions even law in domestic political systems tends to break down. The day-to-day functioning of international law and the conditioning effect it has on the behavior of actors is left unexamined. The study is still quite valuable in suggesting the limits of international consensus in the present international system. See Lawrence Scheinman and David Wilkinson (eds.), *International Law and Political Crisis* (Boston: Little, Brown, 1968). For an analysis of international morality, see Hans J. Morgenthau, "The Twilight of International Morality," *Ethics*, LVIII (1948), and Werner Levi, "The Relative Irrelevance of Moral Norms in International Politics," *Social Forces*, XLIV (1965), reprinted in this volume.

among actors concerning the proper limits of political conflict. Wars, as a consequence, were fought for quite limited objectives, using equally limited means. During the 1962 Cuban missile crisis, the Kennedy administration reportedly rejected proposals to mount a surprise air attack on the missile bases on the grounds that such an action would outrage both American and world opinion[79]—an example of the effects of international morality on politics.

Possibly the most obvious aspect of the setting of international politics is the physical-technological. Concepts like milieu, environment, and setting immediately suggest physical and spatial relationships. This is buttressed by a strong "geopolitical" tradition in the discipline which still conditions much of our thinking. Geographical factors do play a significant role in shaping international politics, although this influence is by no means constant.[80] In previous eras, insularity provided security, a fact that explains a good deal about the British and American behavior in the international system. However, neither the English Channel nor the Atlantic Ocean provide immunity from attack today. Geography, therefore, must be considered in conjunction with technology, as the former is much influenced by the latter. No survey of this or any international system would be complete without reference to the state of technology in the areas of transportation, communications, and weapons.[81] The present international system would hardly be intelligible without reference to nuclear weapons and their delivery systems. Not only does technology help to explain a particular system but it is also an extremely important source of system change. John Herz, for example, has argued that the transition from feudalism to the

[79] There are many accounts of the deliberations surrounding the Cuban missile crisis. Among the best are Elie Abel, *The Missile Crisis* (Philadelphia: J. B. Lippincott, 1966), and Robert F. Kennedy, *Thirteen Days: A Memoir of the Cuban Missile Crisis* (New York: W. W. Norton, 1969).

[80] One of the most sophisticated analyses of environment or setting in international politics is Harold and Margaret Sprout, "An Ecological Paradigm for the Study of International Politics," Research Monograph No. 30, Princeton Center of International Studies, 1968. Also see by the same authors, "Geography and International Politics in an Era of Revolutionary Change," *Journal of Conflict Resolution*, IV (1960), reprinted in this volume.

[81] There are a number of excellent analyses of the impact of weapons on the international system. Especially good are Osgood and Tucker, *Force, Order, and Justice*, Chapter II, and Walter L. Dorn, *Competition for Empire, 1740-1763* (New York: Harper & Bros., 1940).

modern state was, in large measure, a product of the "gunpowder revolution."[8][2]

III

In the preceding pages, I have tried to deal with two related problems. First, I examined the tendency among political scientists to treat international politics as conceptually distinct from other political phenomena. This approach is largely a function of the often unstated assumption that politics and government are much the same thing; lacking a government—at least in any meaningful sense—international politics is regarded as substantively different, requiring, at the extreme, a completely independent discipline to study it. Clearly visible, formalized governmental structures and/or institutions are *not*, however, part of the experience of all societies. Indeed, some cultures possess no recognizable institutions of government. This apparent contradiction disappears once politics is conceived of in terms of *processes* rather than institutions or formal structures. The concentration on process enables us to emphasize the basic unity of all political manifestations, regardless of the arena in which they occur: subnational, national, or international. It also provides a very simple (but fundamental) intellectual perspective as a point of departure in our attempt to more clearly understand international politics. According to this perspective, international politics is viewed as a process or set of processes that result in the distribution of values for the members of the international system. It might be added that this is neither the only nor the necessarily correct way of thinking about the subject. Competing perspectives can and do exist side by side; the inconveniences and possible confusions they create are more than offset by the variety, richness, and dimension that they bring to the study of international political phenomena. Poor, indeed, would be the intellectual discipline able to muster energy and imagination enough for only one view of itself.

The second problem involved the development of a specific analytic framework, not only consistent with my basic view of international politics but also capable of organizing the data in a useful and enlightening manner. The resulting framework is a distillation of general systems theory, but should not be confused with the theory itself. Although related, theories and frameworks perform rather different functions: the former explain reality, while the latter

[8][2]Herz, "Rise and Demise of the Territorial State," pp. 475-477.

merely organize the data systematically, making it easier for the analyst to perceive possibly relevant relationships. In all, four categories or key sets of variables have been suggested. Each deals with one aspect of international politics, and collectively they represent a fairly exhaustive view of the subject. The actor variable focuses on the members of the international system, indicating the predominant types, their evolution, basic socioeconomic and psychological characteristics, and capabilities. Structure concentrates on the fundamental relationships among the actors that result from the prevailing distribution pattern of power and authority. Within the parameters of structure, the process variable refers to the means by which actors actually distribute values among themselves. Finally, setting or environment includes those factors, both tangible and intangible, that affect the actors, their structural relationships, and the political process.

Each of the four major variables has been further subdivided. Although it is possible to argue that the four major categories represent a fairly exhaustive and logically exclusive view of the discipline, no such claim can be made for the manner in which each was subdivided. The choices made are largely idiosyncratic; any number of very important topics that might have been included have been disregarded, others perhaps disproportionately emphasized. In part this represents purely personal bias, and in part is a reflection of the exigencies of time and space. Boundaries must be drawn and discussions ended somewhere, however uncomfortable it makes one feel. But if the framework has any instrinsic value, the reader will expand, modify, and use it to pursue the study of international politics well beyond the limited purposes of this introductory volume.

part one

Actors in the International Political System

Introductory Note

The concept, "system" with its emphasis on the mutuality and interdependence of its elements is like a circle when it comes to finding a suitable starting point. But practicality demands that we begin somewhere, and of the four sets of variables being considered (actors, structure, processes, and setting), actors strikes me as the most logical point of departure. They are the doers, and without them there can be no system. It is their interactions—in the aggregate—with which we are ultimately concerned.

Before proceeding, a note on terminology seems in order. Why use a term like actor instead of more conventional nomenclature such as nation or state? The answer lies in our desire to convey two things. First, we do not wish to restrict ourselves to any particular type of actor (nation, state, or nation-state all refer to a specific type of actor). The term, in other words, is flexible enough to accommodate a variety of political organizations. Second, the emphasis throughout this book is on behavior, and actor conveys the idea of an agent performing an action.

The selections of Chapter One are largely concerned with the problem of determining which types of political organization are relevant to the present international system. The late Professor Arnold Wolfers lists a number of possible international actors that might merit serious consideration. He concludes, however, that the nation-state is still by far the most important type of actor; he then raises some rather thorny conceptual problems involved in its study. In the brief excerpt from Professors Carol Ann Cosgrove and Kenneth Twitchett's work, they set out to demonstrate the theoretical and practical efficacy involved in regarding both the United Nations and the European Economic Community as independent national actors. Although it is probably safe to generalize that the majority of scholars regard all but the nation-state as relatively unimportant international actors, the Cosgrove and Twitchett analysis alerts us to the fact that political forms are constantly evolving. The historical curiosity we reserve for such interesting social experiments as the Greek city state or the Holy Roman Empire may be the manner in which our own nation-states will be regarded in a generation or two.

In fact, Professor John Herz's article on the historical evolution of the nation-state, which comprises Chapter Two, questions the continued viability of that particular type of political organization in light of contemporary developments.* The interesting and suggestive relationship between the development of the nation-state and technological change that he postulates is also quite relevant to Chapter Fourteen. The selections of Chapter Three deal with more abstract dimensions of the nation-state. Professor Karl Deutsch, for example, focuses on patterns of growth, and the ability of national actors to integrate successively larger groups of people into the economic and social system. The psychological bond between the individual and the state is examined in the article by the late Professor Morton Grodzins. He argues that there are at least two patterns of loyalty that characterize the individual-state relationship, and both have resulted in the ability of the state to mobilize resources, human and material, on an unprecedented scale.

The three selections of Chapter Four all deal with what is unquestionably one of the most difficult concepts in all social science, "power." Writers in international politics have used and abused this concept to such an extent that only the most careful explication of

*In a later work, Professor Herz revises his estimate of the viability of the nation-state. See Herz, "The Territorial State Revisited: Reflections on the Future of the Nation-State," *Polity, The Journal of the Northeastern Political Science Associations,* I, i (1968).

its meaning and implications can save it from being useless for the purposes of serious discussion. This is precisely the task that Professors K. J. Holsti and Deutsch set for themselves in their respective articles. Both explore the meaning, uses, and limitations of power in the context of international political phenomena. Professor Klaus Knorr, on the other hand, deals with power at a more concrete level. Military power and potential are critical to a nation's ability to act, and he examines the physical, organizational, and psychological factors that affect it.

chapter one
TYPES OF
INTERNATIONAL
ACTORS

The Actors in International Politics

Arnold Wolfers

In theorizing about almost any feature of international politics, one soon becomes entangled in a web of controversy. Even the identity of the "actors"—those who can properly be said to perform on the international stage—is a matter of dispute which raises not unimportant problems for the analyst, for the practitioner of foreign policy, and for the public. If the nation-states are seen as the sole actors, moving or moved like a set of chess figures in a highly abstract game, one may lose sight of the human beings for whom and by whom the game is supposed to be played. If, on the other hand, one sees only the mass of individual human beings of which mankind is composed, the power game of states tends to appear as an inhuman interference with the lives of ordinary people. Or, take the diplomat who sees himself as accredited to an entity called Indonesia or

SOURCE: From William T. R. Fox (ed.), *Theoretical Aspects of International Relations.* Copyright (c) 1959 by the University of Notre Dame Press. Reprinted and abridged by permission of the University of Notre Dame Press.

France: he may behave quite differently from the diplomat who considers his mission addressed to specific individuals or to ruling groups or to a people. A statesman accustomed to an analysis of international politics in terms of state behavior alone will treat the United Nations differently from one who believes in the rise of international organizations to a place of independent control over world events similar to that exerted by states.

Until quite recently, the "states-as-the-sole-actors" approach to international politics was so firmly entrenched that it may be called the traditional approach. After the Napoleonic wars, nation-states, particularly the European "Great Powers," as they were called, replaced the image of the princes or kings of former centuries as the sovereign, independent, single-minded actors, the movers of world events. To "nation-states" were ascribed the acts that accounted for changes in the distribution of power, for alignments and counter-alignments, for expansion and colonial conquest, for war and peace—the chief events in international affairs whenever a multitude of sovereigns have been in contact with one another. The concept of a multi-state system composed of entities of strikingly similar character and behavior appeared realistic to observers and analysts.

Starting in the period between the two world wars and gaining momentum after World War II, a reaction set in against the traditional states-as-actors approach. This reaction has taken two distinct forms: one new theory has placed individual human beings in the center of the scene that had previously been reserved to the nation-states; the other emphasized the existence, side by side with the state, of other corporate actors, especially international organizations. Both reactions have led to valuable new insights and deeper understanding of the dynamics of world politics, but they are in fact supplements to the traditional theory rather than substitutes for it.

I

. . .

The reaction to the once firmly established states-as-actors theory . . . implies a shift of attention to individuals and groups of individuals as the true actors. It has taken the form of what is properly called the "decision-making" approach, since it is concerned with decisions, with the way they are made, and with the men who make them. What interests us here is the role that this approach assigns to identifiable human beings and their predispositions. Although the emphasis on the decision-makers, like the emphasis on the minds of men, developed in protest against the states-as-actors theory, it was not also a reaction born of humanitarian or social considerations; it was provoked, instead, by the sweeping, seemingly over-simplified psychological and anthropological presuppositions on which the traditional theory rests.

If nation-states are conceived as the sole actors, it is inevitable that they be treated as if endowed, like human beings, with wills and minds of their own that permit them to reach decisions and to carry them out. Moreover, if state behavior is to be intelligible and to any degree predictable, states must be assumed to possess psychological traits of the kind known to the observer through introspection and through acquaintance with other human beings. States must be thought capable, for example, of desires and preferences, of satisfaction and dissatisfaction, of the choice of goals and means.

Actually, the states-as-actors theory postulates a limited number of such traits which, moreover, all states are assumed to have in common. States are presumed to possess a will to survive and a will to power; they live in fear of losing their possessions to others and are tempted by opportunities of acquiring new possessions. Because these basic traits are shared by all states, the exponents of the traditional approach can afford to treat these psychological presuppositions in a cavalier fashion. Little attention need be given to traits that, because they are constants or invariants, are incapable of helping to explain any differences in state behavior.

. . .

The decision-making approach questions the possibility of reaching realistic conclusions from any such crude and generally applicable psychological presuppositions. Its exponents insist that decisions and actions taken in the name of the state cannot be understood unless one penetrates to the individuals from whom they emanate. In contrast to what is implicit in the views of the opposing school, the basic hypothesis here is that all acts of states, as we are used to calling them, are vitally affected or determined by the particular predispositions of particular decision-makers or of particular groups of participants in the decision-making process. Thus, differences in such individual psychological traits as motivation, value preferences, temperament, and rationality are considered essential variables, and so are differences arising from affiliation of individuals with particular parties, agencies within the state, or with peoples of different culture.

One can illustrate the contrast between the two hypotheses by means of important past decisions in international politics.

According to the states-as-actors theory, the American employment of the A-bomb over Hiroshima, or the American intervention in the war in Korea, could have been foreseen—to the extent to which foresight is possible at all—on the basis of the supposed common psychological disposition of states, coupled with an analysis of the existing circumstances which were external to the actors. Those who hold to the decision-making approach, on the contrary, consider it necessary to probe into the personal events that took place within the psyches of men like Stimson, Truman, and Acheson—and perhaps also of their advisors, backers, and opponents—and led them to choose one particular course of action rather than some alternative course.[1]

. . .

At first glance, it would seem as if the actual performance of a particular state could conform only by sheer coincidence with expectations based on extremely crude generalizations about the way "states" tend to act under given circumstances. Why should the particular individuals responsible for United States policy in 1945 or 1950, men differing from others by a multitude of psychological features—motivations, idiosyncrasies, preferences, temperament—reach decisions of the kind the states-as-actors theory deduces from its abstract model? Yet a correlation in many instances between the predictions of theory and actual behavior is not accidental. It may be expected if two assumptions on which the theory rests are justified by the circumstances prevailing in the real world.

There is, first, the assumption mentioned above, that all men acting for states share the same universal traits of human nature. Specifically, these men are expected to place exceedingly high value on the so-called core possessions of the nation—above all, on national survival, national independence, and territorial integrity—and to react in fear against any threats to these possessions. It is also assumed that they share a strong inclination to profit from opportunities for the acquisition or re-acquisition of cherished national possessions, with national power as the chief means of preserving or acquiring national values. To the extent to which these traits are shared and have a decisive effect on the actions or reactions of statesmen and peoples, they create conformity as if by a kind of inner compulsion.

---

[1] See Richard C. Snyder and Glenn D. Paige, "The United States' Decision to Resist Aggression in Korea: The Application of an Analytical Scheme," *Administrative Science Quarterly*, Vol. 3, No. 3, December 1958, especially pp. 348 and 374.

The second assumption concerns the environment in which governments are required to act. If it is true that the anarchical multistate system creates a condition of constant danger to national core possessions—specifically, to national survival—and, at the same time, provides frequent opportunity for new acquisitions, the actors can be said to act under external compulsion rather than in accordance with their preferences.

It is easy to see that both these sweeping assumptions are not the products of unrealistic fantasies. Attachment to possessions, fear, and ambition—though they vary in degree from man to man and from people to people—can properly be called "general traits of human nature," which are likely to operate with particular strength in men who hold positions of authority and national responsibility. That the condition of multiple sovereignty is one in which states "live dangerously" is also a matter of common experience and knowledge. The real question is whether internal and external pressures are strong enough everywhere and at all times to transform the actors into something like automatons lacking all freedom of choice. Certainly, to the degree that these compulsions exist in the real world, the psychological peculiarities of the actors are deprived of the opportunity to express themselves and can therefore be discounted as irrelevant to an analysis of international politics.

. . .

Yet, if one considers the conditions of danger and opportunity, of fear and appetite that have to exist in order to produce anything approaching inexorable compulsion, one will see that the highly abstract model used by the exponents of the states-as-actors theory cannot offer more than a first approximation to reality. Certainly, the employment of the states-as-actors theory in predicting the outcome of a crisis in which less than extreme compulsions were operative would prove dangerously unreliable and would need to be strictly qualified.

. . .

Where less than national survival is at stake, there is far less compulsion and therefore a less uniform reaction. It is hard to predict the course that Nehru will follow as a consequence of the rather remote threats of the Cold War to India. On the other hand, any serious threat to India's control of eastern Kashmir can be expected to result in Indian military action, despite Nehru's alleged pacifist inclinations.

The differences in behavior arising from variations in the internal pressures are no less great. While a propensity for fear and an appetite for gain may be universal, men's reactions to danger and opportunity are far from identical and vary even among those who are responsible for the fate of their nation. Complacency no less than hysteria, and willingness to demand sacrifices no less than desire for popularity, affect the interpretation men give to what the "necessity of state" requires. Moreover, the "exits" are not clearly marked, with the result that some statesmen seek safety in military preparedness while others expect to find it in appeasement. Although statesmen who are entirely indifferent or blind to serious national danger and opportunity are the exception that proves the rule, it is hard to conceive of situations that leave no room at all for choice and thus for the expression of differences in psychology. While Eden believed Nasser's nationalization of the Suez Canal Company endangered Britain's economic lifeline and required military action, most other British statesmen would have reacted differently, and no one could have said with certainty at the time what course of action would have been the most rational under the circumstances. If Nasser had attacked the British homeland, thereby really "setting the house on fire," the reaction of any British government, whatever the personal traits of its members, could have been predicted.

From what has been said, it seems proper to conclude that the closer nations are drawn to the pole of complete compulsion, the more they can be expected to conform in their behavior and to act in a way that corresponds to the deductions that can be made from the states-as-actors model.

It is worth noting that a similar degree of conformity may be found where danger and compulsion are at a minimum. When not more than minor values are threatened by international discord, governments usually find it expedient to act according to established rules, since their interest in seeing others do likewise exceeds their interest in winning an occasional and minor advantage. Under these circumstances, they may forfeit an immediate national gain for the sake of sustaining the rule of law and its long-run benefits.

In war, compulsiveness and conformity are usually at a maximum, with the result that all nations feel compelled, for example, to employ the most effective weapons at their disposal. Hiroshima, as we said earlier, requires little if any decision-making analysis to explain the American action. Such an analysis might prove useful as a means of throwing light on varying attitudes of men or groups within the American government, some of whom opposed the use of the bomb on the grounds that victory was already assured and that there existed, therefore, no external compulsion requiring the application of the strongest weapon.

The American failure in the Korean War to use atomic bombs against tempting military targets north of the Yalu River is a far more promising area of decision-making analysis, because it represents a deviation from the practices one generally associates with warfare. The explanation may lie in a particularly high degree of foresightedness, or, as others believe, in an unusual degree of compliance with the wishes of friends and allies. In any case, General MacArthur, whose inclinations differed from those of the men charged with the final decision, might well have felt "compelled" to pursue the opposite course.

While there may be leeway for choice, and thus for the impact of psychological factors which distinguish individuals rather than abstract "states," it is by no means useless or misleading to take the relatively simple and very abstract states-as-actors model as an initial working hypothesis. Thus, in formulating expectations, it is possible and helpful to assume that no state will voluntarily make unilateral concessions to an opponent if these would seriously affect the existing distribution of power. When an exception to this general proposition is encountered, it calls for special analysis: for example, as a "deviationist" move, France's initiation of discussions on the Saar in 1949, pointing toward French withdrawal before West Germany itself had raised any such demand.

. . .

These illustrations indicate the particular services that the two theories on the "actors" are able to render. By establishing the "normal" actions and reactions of states in various international situations, the states-as-actors model sets a standard on which to base our expectations of state behavior and deviations. At the same time, a far more complex model is required if our expectations are to become sufficiently refined and realistic to take at least the predispositions of typical categories of decision-makers into account. There is no reason why intensive and comparative study of actual decisions should not, in time, provide much needed insight into the peculiarities in the behavior of such types of countries as those with dictatorial or democratic governments, with Asian or Western, Bolshevik or bourgeois elites, with predominantly military or civilian regimes, with a fanatical or a complacent public.[2] While it may be impractical to aim at knowledge about the decision-making of individual actors—if only because it is hard to foresee who will be the

---

[2]Morton A. Kaplan, *System and Process in International Politics* (John Wiley & Sons, New York, 1957), pp. 54 ff., calls for a typology of national actors.

future decision-makers—it may prove useful to analyze the approach and behavior of certain "subnational" actors such as the business community, the trade union leaders, the Christian Democrats, or the American political parties. Only if it becomes possible to understand and predict typical kinds of nonconformist behavior can theory hope to approach reality. Moreover, because different degrees of compulsion will be operating at different times, it is not enough to know how states tend to act in situations of extreme danger or extreme temptation; one must also know what action to expect when the actors are relatively free to choose among alternative courses.

. . .

II

Up to this point, the discussion has been devoted to criticizing the states-as-actors theory for its neglect of the individuals as actors. Another kind of objection to the theory has been raised on the ground that it fails to allow for the possibility of corporate actors other than the nation-states. It is asked whether a realistic image of the contemporary international scene should not include such non-state corporate actors as the United Nations or the Communist International. If it should, the term multi-state system would no longer be fully adequate to describe the environment in which statesmen and other actors operate in the world today.

The "billiard-ball" model of the multi-state system which forms the basis for the states-as-actors theory leaves no room for corporate actors other than the nation-state. By definition, the stage is pre-empted by a set of states, each in full control of all territory, men, and resources within its boundaries. Every state represents a closed, impermeable, and sovereign unit, completely separated from all other states. Since this is obviously not an accurate portrait of the real world of international politics, one can say that reality "deviates" in various ways from the model, because corporate bodies other than nation-states play a role on the international stage as co-actors with the nation-states. To the extent that these corporate bodies exert influence on the course of international politics, knowledge about them and about the deviations that permit them to operate becomes indispensable to the development of a well-rounded theory.

More even than in the case of the individual actors, one is justified in using the term "deviation" here to indicate that any important impact of non-state corporate actors constitutes the exception rather than the rule. As things stand today—and are likely to remain for an indefinite period—there can be no serious doubt about the paramount position of the nation-state or about the superiority of its influence and power. Even enthusiastic supporters of the UN can hardly fail to realize that there can be no UN action of any consequence if a single great power refuses to permit it. To date, no non-state corporate actor has been able to rob a nation-state of the primary loyalty of more than a small fraction of its people. If this should ever occur—if, for example, a Communist International could persuade a state's soldiers and workers to refuse obedience to their own national government—the state in question would prove an empty shell when put to the test of war. Occurrences of this kind were well-known in medieval times, before the age of nation-state predominance, when excommunication by the Pope, a supranational actor, could deprive a king of control over his people.

There is no lack of a suitable vocabulary to identify a set of nonstate corporate actors, but it is not without significance that all the terms refer to something called "national" which is the characteristic feature of the nation-state. One distinguishes between international, supranational, transnational, and subnational corporate bodies as potential co-actors on the international stage. Some have criticized this terminology on the very ground that it creates a prejudice in favor of the nation-state as the center of things and have suggested that the term "international" politics be replaced by the term "world" politics. However, one is hard put to define where "world" politics begin and domestic politics end, unless the former is designed to comprise acts that transcend national boundaries—which brings one back to the nation-state with its territorial borders.

It is not hard to see what kinds of deviations from the billiard-ball model of a multi-state system are possible, or to see that certain types of deviations facilitate the operations and increase the influence of non-state corporate actors.

If the states of today are not monolithic blocs—and none but the totalitarian states are—groups, parties, factions, and all sorts of other politically organized groups within such states can take a hand in matters transcending national boundaries. They may do so directly, in negotiating and dealing with similar groups abroad or even with the governments of other states, or they may exert their influence as domestic pressure groups so effectively that foreign statesmen would be ill-advised to ignore them. Some democratic states have exhibited such pluralistic tendencies that they offer to the world a picture of

near-anarchy. They seem to speak to the world with many and conflicting voices and to act as if one hand—one agency or faction—does
not know what the other hand is doing. One can also point to states,
some of them new states in the process of consolidation, where
integration is so poor that other states must deal with parts, rather
than with a fictitious whole, if diplomacy is to be effective.

Another deviation bears on the degree of separateness or, if one
prefers, of cohesion between nations. Here, too, one can visualize a
wide gamut of gradations. Since World War II, for example, West
Germany and France have at times been close to the pole of
complete and even hostile separateness; but at other times they have
been drawn so closely together that a merger of the two into a single
European Union appeared as a practical possibility. While such a
union might have become a new super-state, it might instead have
remained a more loosely-knit international organization, like the
British Commonwealth which can exert considerable influence on
the behavior of its members.

Then, again, there are deviations from the complete impermeability of the nation-states envisaged in the billiard-ball model.[3] Some
peoples today are shut off from contact with the rest of the world by
an Iron Curtain, but the boundaries of most states are permeable,
leaving the inhabitants relatively free to organize into groups transcending national boundaries. If they desire, they can do so even for
the purpose of exerting international influence. One need only think
of the international Communist movement, of international Socialist
groups, or of international cartels which have, at times, been able to
perform as transnational actors.

Finally, sovereignty, in the political sense of the term, is not everywhere and always as undivided and total as the legal concept would
indicate. The behavior of the satellite states within the Soviet orbit,
legally recognized as sovereign, can be understood only if the role of
the Soviet Union is taken into account, either as a co-actor in the
background or as the master actor. Another case of divided sovereignty is presented by the European Coal and Steel Community
which can act with considerable independence within the field of its
competence.

Whether the United Nations has become a center of decision and

---

[3]In *International Politics in the Atomic Age* (Columbia University Press, New
York, 1959), John H. Herz uses the term "impermeability" to indicate the protection that the classical nation-state was able to provide until, with the advent
of the air and missile age, "the roof blew off the territorial state" (p. 104).

action in its own right is a *quaestio facti,* as it is in the case of all the competitors of the state. Theoretically, there is no reason why the real world should not "deviate" from the condition of complete nation-state sovereignty to the point of permitting an international organization, such as the UN, to become a relevant actor. It would have to be recognized as such if resolutions, recommendations, or orders emanating from its organs should, for all practical purposes, compel some or all member governments to act differently than they would otherwise do.

A theoretical discussion of the actors is not the place to answer the question whether non-state corporate actors are presently gaining or losing ground in their competition with the nation-state. But because there has been much speculation about an alleged trend away from the state system and toward an ever-increasing role of international bodies, if not of a single supranational world government, it is worth noting that two sharply conflicting tendencies can be detected in the world today: one toward the enhancement, the other toward the diminution of the paramount position of the nation-state. Which of the two tendencies will gain the upper hand in the end depends on so many factors that a reliable prediction seems impossible.[4]

In recent times, the nation-state has been gaining much ground geographically. There is hardly a region left in the world where nation-states are not either already functioning or in process of being established. There has also been a marked increase in the power over men that can be exercised in the name of the state. Never before has the state achieved so complete a monopoly of control within large areas as is enjoyed today by the totalitarian Soviet Union with its Iron Curtain and its ability to radiate ideologically far beyond its own borders. Satellitism and international Communism represent more of a triumph of the Russian state than of a break with the traditional multi-state system.[5]

However, there are other developments, too, which point in the opposite direction. It is not enough, obviously, to point to the

[4]John H. Herz, *ibid.*, sees two "blocs" replacing the now obsolete nation-state.

[5]George Liska, in *International Equilibrium* (Harvard University Press, Cambridge, Mass., 1957) points out that "the trend to horizontally expanding functionalism has been at least equalled by the drive to enlarge the vertical power structures of major states by the addition of dependable allies and dependent satellites" (p. 132).

impressive array of international and other non-national organizations that have mushroomed in recent years; these organizations may constitute or develop into mere instruments of national policy. Nor is it enough to prove on rational grounds that the nation-state is becoming increasingly less fit to satisfy the needs for security and economic development. However, there is ample evidence to show that the United Nations and its agencies, the Coal and Steel Community, the Afro-Asian bloc, the Arab League, the Vatican, the Arabian-American Oil Company, and a host of other non-state entities are able on occasion to affect the course of international events. When this happens, they become actors in the international arena and competitors of the nation-state. Their ability to operate as international or transnational actors may be traced to the fact that men identify themselves and their interests with corporate bodies other than the nation-state.

Here, there appears a connection between the phenomenon of non-state corporate actors and the individuals-as-actors approach. No deviations from the states-as-actors or billiard-ball model are conceivable unless it is unrealistic to assume that men identify themselves completely and exclusively with their respective nation-states, an assumption that excludes the possibility of non-state corporate actors exerting any influence of international significance. But in order to discover how men in the contemporary world do in fact identify themselves . . . when they speak of the "we" in international affairs—attention must be focused on the individual human beings for whom identification is a psychological event.[6] If their loyalties are divided betweeen the nation and other political organizations, such subnational bodies as a domestic political party, such international bodies as the UN, and such transnational bodies as a Communist International can, in principle, become significant factors in the shaping of world events. Tito's actions are often unintelligible if it is forgotten that he identifies himself not only with Yugoslavia but with some loose grouping he calls the Socialist camp. What Arab leaders mean when they speak from the point of view of their primary corporate interest may be a purely national interest or instead a changing composite of national, Pan-Arab, and Pan-Islamic interest. Whether the Pope merits recognition as an actor in world affairs cannot be determined merely by reference to the fact that he lacks the military power states are able to muster. If nations and

[6]In Kaplan's words, "Individuals, after all, have no biological ties to the nation" (*ibid.*, p. 157).

statesmen do, in fact, act differently when under the impact of orders or admonitions from the Vatican, to disregard the Pope as an actor would mean overlooking a significant aspect of international politics. Similarly, the actor capacity of the United Nations depends on whether the policies of national statesmen are affected by resolutions of the General Assembly, by reprovals of the UN Secretary General, or by orders of the Security Council.

One may conclude, then, that only an empirical analysis, penetrating to the minds of men and to their manner of choosing one course of action over another, can throw light on the role of non-state corporate actors and thus supplement a possibly oversimplified and unrealistic concentration on the nation-states as sole corporate actors. While it would be dangerous for theorists to divert their primary attention from the nation-state and multi-state systems which continue to occupy most of the stage of contemporary world politics, theory remains inadequate if it is unable to include such phenomena as overlapping authorities, split loyalties, and divided sovereignty, which were pre-eminent characteristics of medieval actors. These phenomena, which indicate serious deviations from the billiard-ball model, also deserve attention from the analyst today. Here, too, then, the states-as-actors and the individuals-as-actors theories must supplement each other. If they can be made to do so, they will contribute to the development of a theory that can rightly claim to be "realistic" since it will throw light on all the chief aspects of the realities of contemporary international politics.

International Organizations as Actors

Carol Ann Cosgrove and Kenneth J. Twitchett

INTRODUCTION

Since the Second World War international organisations have become integral features of the international scene. Only two of them, however, have emerged as significant international actors in their own right: the United Nations and the European Economic Community. They can and do exert influence on a similar scale to that of many medium-sized powers and are certainly more influential internationally than most newly independent, small underdeveloped states.

. . .

The usual, somewhat facile image of an international system activated solely by sovereign states, all equal in terms of international

SOURCE: From Carol Ann Cosgrove and Kenneth J. Twitchett (eds.), *The New International Actors: The U.N. and the E.E.C.* Copyright (c) 1970 by St. Martin's Press, Inc., Macmillan & Co., Ltd. Reprinted and abridged by permission of the publisher.

law, is, to say the least, misleading. For instance, it does not take into consideration the capacity or ability of states to lead a viable international existence as autonomous units. Sovereign independence does not guarantee an ability to act in the international arena. Many small ex-colonial states consider U.N. membership to be both the definitive expression of sovereign independence and symbolic of an ability to undertake meaningful international actions. Such membership, however, imposes duties and obligations which even the U.N. Secretary-General apparently recognises that some micro-states cannot perform. U Thant upheld the smallest colony's right to independence, but suggested placing a limit on their right to U.N. membership:

> ... it appears desirable that a distinction be made between the right to independence and the question of full membership in the United Nations. Such membership may ... impose obligations which are too onerous for the "micro-states" and ... may lead to a weakening of the United Nations itself.[1]

International organisations as such cannot become U.N. members and are perhaps no more than the sum of their member states, but they can develop an international character which impinges on the international milieu in its own collective right. To contend that some have more meaningful international roles than many states is not to advocate federalism, international integration, or world government. Neither does it imply that international organisations could or should replace states as the basic units of the global political system. As international bodies they are not analogous to states, do not possess sovereignty, and do not necessarily perform similar roles. Nevertheless, they can be endowed with an international legal personality and undertake binding international contracts. Moreover, while the U.N. cannot be a disputant before the International Court of Justice, the E.E.C. within its sphere of activity possesses similar rights before the Court of the European Communities to those of the member states, and can sue them. The U.N. and the E.E.C. coexist with sovereign states and in varying degrees most of their members have come to expect if not rely upon their existence and services. A similar statement could perhaps be made regarding some regional bodies like the O.A.U., but these do not possess the quality of *actorness* in the same degree as the U.N. and the E.E.C. The two

---

[1] See U Thant's report to the Twenty-Third Session of the General Assembly on *The State of the World.*

organisations, however, cannot be viewed in identical terms. The U.N. is an actor more by virtue of its pervading global influence whereas the E.E.C. has had a direct impact on many aspects of European and international affairs.

There are three mutually interdependent tests, or rather guide lines, for determining an international organisation's capacity to act on the global scene. The first is the degree of autonomous decision-making power embodied in its central institutions. The second is the extent to which it performs significant and continuing functions having an impact on inter-state relations. The third, and most important, is the significance attached to it in the formation of the foreign policies of states, particularly those of its members. No international organisation completely fulfils all these conditions all of the time; yet elements of all three must be present in some degree for most of the time. Whether they are or not is, of course, a matter of judgement. The tests themselves are not clear cut and have a close functional relationship with each other: which comes first or is of primary significance is difficult, if not impossible, to gauge.

While the second and third tests are self-explanatory, it is helpful to explain more precisely what is understood by autonomous decision-making power. The degree to which this exists can be identified in the first instance in the constitutional provisions and institutional structure of an international organisation. Are these such that it possesses the right to take meaningful decisions which are binding on its members? Have its institutions been given a supranational capacity in the sense of a decision-making authority empowered to make decisions independently of and separately from the member states? Is such a capacity exercised jointly with the member states or does it rest solely with the latter? Whatever the answers to these questions, the greater the degree of integration between the member states, the more significant the autonomous decision-making capacity and the more notable the organisation's institutional impact within its sphere of competence.

Autonomous decision-making capacity is meaningless if not sufficiently exercised by those entrusted with it. The capacity may be developed from a minimal constitutional base through the organisation's day-to-day operations: the member states and the relevant international secretariat, either individually or acting together, can acquire as well as be given responsibility for operating the decision-making process. Similarly, they can be given or develop a decision-making ability both by virtue of initiative or merely through the preparation of documentation on which others might base their decisions. The latter role can be crucial in determining an international secretariat's ability to influence; much depends on the personal characteristics of the senior international civil servants and the general environment in which their functions are undertaken.

Whether organisations have *de jure* or attain *de facto* decision-making capacities or abilities, much depends on the controls over them. These may rest with the member states, other institutions within the organisational framework, or a mixture of both. For instance, the Commission of the European Communities is controlled in three ways: in practice by the member states acting individually, in theory and practice by the corporate actions in the Council of Ministers, and by the Communities' Court of Justice. Controversy surrounds the European Parliament as a possible fourth agency of control. If an inter-state assembly—either directly elected from the member states, elected from their parliaments, selected by their governments, or a mixture of all three—is given or acquires meaningful powers of control, exercised independently of and even against the wishes of the member governments, then a definite step towards the formation of a new sovereign corpus will have been taken. This phenomenon, however, does not and for many years probably will not exist on the international scene either at the global or regional levels. The powers of the European Parliament in this respect are limited and latent to say the least. This point is well illustrated by the 1965 decision-making crisis in the E.E.C. The Commission's proposal that the European Parliament's voice in the allocation of the Community budget be marginally increased was a factor precipitating the French six-month-long boycott of the Community institutions.

. . .

CONCLUSIONS

The U.N. and the E.E.C. fulfil the three conditions necessary for consideration as viable international actors. They represent important centres of activity alongside states, and as centres of decision-making have an impact on the international system coincidental with them. There is a distinct difference between the two organisations, however, in that the U.N.'s impact is primarily a function of its all-pervading role, while the fact that it is essentially a collectivity of relatively important industrialised states assists in giving the E.E.C. a more precise impact.

The U.N.'s autonomous decision-making capacity is less definite, less utilised, and more dependent on the member states than that of

the E.E.C., where the international civil servants have more significant roles to perform. In both organisations, however, the international civil servants' roles depend on the acquiescence of the
member states, and to have viable functions the U.N. Secretariat and
the E.E.C. Commission respectively must exercise self-restraint lest
their initiatives unduly antagonise the *amour propre* of national
governments. For the U.N. Secretariat especially self-control is vital,
as its powers and autonomous functions, *de jure* and *de facto*, are
easily curtailed by the member states. For instance, an excessive use
of the Secretary-General's right under Article 99 of the Charter to
bring before the Security Council disputes he considers threaten international peace could result in continuous rebuff, thereby undermining and diminishing the Secretariat's international status. While
the E.E.C. Commission must also exercise a similar element of self-
control, there is an important difference. As well as formulating
package deals embodying the Community and the six separate
national interests, the Commission must be prepared to take the
initiative in every sphere of Community activity. This is its primary
function under the Rome Treaty formula and a failure to do so
would jeopardise the E.E.C. Whereas the U.N. could exist with a very
truncated and restricted Secretariat, the E.E.C. as we know it today
could not.

The League of Nations and the U.N. were originally conceived as
instruments for preserving the international *status quo*. In practice,
however, the U.N.'s impact, especially regarding decolonisation, has
been as an instrument of evolutionary but not revolutionary change.
Regarding the U.N.'s peace-keeping role, there is also an implicit
assumption of a rudimentary international concern that events
should not be left to run their *natural* course or be unduly subjected
to the whims and interests of the great powers. As an instrument for
changing the *status quo*, the U.N.'s impact is a function of the contemporary international system—in an age of rapid, revolutionary
technological innovations the international system must be dynamic
compared with the relatively static international system of, say, the
eighteenth century.

The integration objectives of the E.E.C. are designed to alter the
existing situation and ultimately to change it beyond recognition.
Nevertheless there is some attachment to the *status quo* in so far as
one of the E.E.C.'s objectives is to preserve and even extend its
members' economic strength relative to that of the rest of the world,
particularly the super powers. But this is to be undertaken through
collective rather than individual action. This collective function gives

the Commission a greater role in determining the form and incidence of the Community's impact than is so with the U.N., where the emphasis lies primarily with the member states alone.

The U.N. and the E.E.C. command important priorities in the foreign policy formation of states. In the case of the U.N., however, lack of consensus and deep cleavages among the member states regarding beliefs, values and interests diminish its role. The relatively high degree of consensus between the E.E.C.'s members underlies their willingness to make the Community's preservation a major foreign policy objective. Important non-governmental groups, moreover, endeavour to persuade the Six to allow the Community interest to take precedence over the separate national ones. This form of Community consciousness is not found within the U.N., although some Western European League of Nations societies and prominent individuals unsuccessfully endeavoured to persuade national governments to formulate foreign policy in the light of Covenant principles. Growing concern with the twin human predicaments of war and poverty, combined with recognition that these might be ameliorated with a world-wide harnessing of the technological and scientific knowledge at mankind's disposal, could result in the U.N. or a future global organisation embodying the necessary core of community feeling. The aforementioned knowledge has its roots, albeit accidentally, in the European experience of the last two centuries or so. At the present time it underlies the E.E.C., but a universal development of a core area similar to that of the E.E.C. appears unlikely from the perspective of the contemporary age. Thirty years ago, however, few if any observers foresaw the E.E.C., and sixty years ago it appeared unlikely that nation states would attempt to justify their actions before other nation states in a permanent international forum like the U.N.

Finally it should be emphasised that the objective of this exposition of the U.N. and the E.E.C. as international actors has been to examine both the factors underlying these roles and some of the ways in which they impinge on the working of the international system. It is not suggested that their roles are always similar in type and impact, or that their actor functions are desirable and ought to be developed. The objective has merely been to state how and why they are international actors. David Mitrany's comments on the arguments put forward are a useful corrective against over emphasising the U.N.'s and the E.E.C.'s common characteristics and potential roles. While not necessarily agreeing with all his underlying sentiments and reasoning, both editors are convinced that they deserve serious consideration. Professor Mitrany pointed out that it is reasonable to compare their roles at the institutional level, but that the comparison should not be pushed too far:

> *A central, and vital difference is inherent, and ineradicable, in their very nature: the U.N. has internationally a* unifying *role (however imperfectly achieved so far), whereas the E.E.C. or any other regional union while having a unifying role* locally *has of necessity a* divisive *role internationally. In fact, the more effective the first, the sharper the second. [Regarding] 'the twin human predicaments of war and poverty', the E.E.C. might contribute something towards the second, but regionalism, as such, has nothing to contribute towards the nuclear nightmare, much less towards the new space problems.*
>
> *Beyond a certain point the comparison between an egocentric regional unit and the grand limitless purpose of a universal body becomes meaningless. The 'actor roles' become so different and distant in scope that they no longer belong to the same world of organisation and policy—and of possibilities. One can admire the E.E.C., but as students we cannot overlook that, internationally speaking, its limits are also its limitations.*

In the long run there probably will be an ineradicable conflict. In the short run, however, the goals of universal and regional co-operation do not necessarily conflict. If and when they do, moreover, the conflict itself may be both necessary and desirable.

chapter two
THE NATION-STATE: DEVELOPMENT AND PROSPECTS

Rise and Demise
of the
Territorial State
John H. Herz

Students and practitioners of international politics are at present
in a strange predicament. Complex though their problems have been
in the past, there was then at least some certainty about the
"givens," the basic structure and the basic phenomena of international relations. Today one is neither here nor there. On the one
hand, for instance, one is assured—or at least tempted to accept
assurance—that for all practical purposes a nuclear stalemate rules
out major war as a major means of policy today and in the foreseeable future. On the other hand, one has an uncanny sense of the
practicability of the unabated arms race, and a doubt whether
reliance can be placed solely on the deterrent purpose of all this
preparation. We are no longer sure about the functions of war and
peace, nor do we know how to define the national interest and what
its defense requires under present conditions. As a matter of fact, the
meaning and function of the basic protective unit, the "sovereign"

SOURCE: From *World Politics*, Vol. IX, No. 4 (1957). Copyright © 1957
by Princeton University Press. Reprinted and abridged by permission of the
author and Princeton University Press.

nation-state itself, have become doubtful. On what, then, can policy
and planning be built?

In the author's opinion, many of these uncertainties have their
more profound cause in certain fundamental changes which have
taken place in the structure of international relations and, specifically, in the nature of the units among which these relations occur.
This transformation in the "statehood" of nations will be the subject
of this article.

I. BASIC FEATURES OF THE MODERN
STATE SYSTEM

Traditionally, the classical system of international relations, or the
modern state system, has been considered "anarchic," because it was
based on unequally distributed power and was deficient in higher—
that is, supra-national—authority. Its units, the independent,
sovereign nation-states, were forever threatened by stronger power
and survived precariously through the balance-of-power system.
Customarily, then, the modern state system has been contrasted with
the medieval system, on the one hand, where units of international
relations were under higher law and higher authority, and with those
more recent international trends, on the other, which seemed to
point toward a greater, "collective" security of nations and a "rule of
law" that would protect them from the indiscriminate use of force
characteristic of the age of power politics.

From the vantage point of the atomic age, we can probe deeper
into the basic characteristics of the classical system. What is it that
ultimately accounted for the peculiar unity, compactness, coherence
of the modern nation-state, setting it off from other nation-states as
a separate, independent, and sovereign power? It would seem that
this underlying factor is to be found neither in the sphere of law nor
in that of politics, but rather in that substratum of statehood where
the state unit confronts us, as it were, in its physical, corporeal
capacity: as an expanse of territory encircled for its identification
and its defense by a "hard shell" of fortifications. In this lies what
will here be referred to as the "impermeability," or "impenetrability," or simply the "territoriality," of the modern state. The
fact that it was surrounded by a hard shell rendered it to some extent
secure from foreign penetration, and thus made it an ultimate unit of
protection for those within its boundaries. Throughout history, that
unit which affords protection and security to human beings has
tended to become the basic political unit; people, in the long run,
will recognize that authority, any authority, which possesses the
power of protection.

Some similarity perhaps prevails between an international structure consisting of impenetrable units with an ensuing measurability of power and comparability of power relations, and the system of classical physics with its measurable forces and the (then) impenetrable atom as its basic unit. And as that system has given way to relativity and to what nuclear science has uncovered, the impenetrability of the political atom, the nation-state, is giving way to a permeability which tends to obliterate the very meaning of unit and unity, power and power relations, sovereignty and independence. The possibility of "hydrogenization" merely represents the culmination of a development which has rendered the traditional defense structure of nations obsolete through the power to by-pass the shell protecting a two-dimensional territory and thus to destroy—vertically, as it were—even the most powerful ones. Paradoxically, utmost strength now coincides in the same unit with utmost vulnerability, absolute power with utter impotence.

This development must inevitably affect traditional power concepts. Considering power units as politically independent and legally sovereign made sense when power, measurable, graded, calculable, served as a standard of comparison between units which, in the sense indicated above, could be described as impermeable. Under those conditions, then, power indicated the strategic aspect, independence the political aspect, sovereignty the legal aspect of this selfsame impermeability. With the passing of the age of territoriality, the usefulness of these concepts must now be questioned.

Thus the Great Divide does not separate "international anarchy," or "balance of power," or "power politics," from incipient international interdependence, or from "collective security"; all these remain within the realm of the territorial structure of states and can therefore be considered as trends or stages *within* the classical system of "hard shell" power units. Rather, the Divide occurs where the basis of territorial power and defensibility vanishes. It is here and now. But in order to understand the present, we must study more closely the origin and nature of the classical system itself.

II. THE RISE OF THE TERRITORIAL STATE

The rise of the modern territorial state meant that, within countries, "feudal anarchy" of jurisdictions yielded to the ordered centralism of the absolute monarchy, which ruled over a pacified area with the aid of a bureaucracy, a professional army, and the power to levy taxes, while in foreign relations, in place of the medieval hierarchy of power and authority, there prevailed insecurity, a disorder only slightly attenuated by a power balance that was forever being threatened, disturbed, and then restored. Such has been the customary interpretation.

It is possible to view developments in a somewhat different light. Instead of contrasting the security of groups and individuals within the sovereign territorial state with conditions of insecurity outside, the establishment of territorial independence can be interpreted as an at least partially successful attempt to render the territorial group secure in its outward relations as well. Especially when contrasted with the age of anarchy and insecurity which immediately preceded it, the age of territoriality appears as one of relative order and safety.

· · ·

The idea that a territorial coexistence of states, based on the power of the territorial princes, might afford a better guarantee of peace than the Holy Roman Empire was already widespread at the height of the Middle Ages when the emperor proved incapable of enforcing the peace.[1] But territoriality could hardly prevail so long as the knight in his castle (that medieval unit of impermeability) was relatively immune from attack, as was the medieval city within its walls. Only with a developing money economy were overlords able to free themselves from dependence on vassals and lay the foundations of their own power by establishing a professional army. Infantry and artillery now proved superior to old-style cavalry, firearms prevailed over the old weapons.

As in all cases of radically new developments in military technology, the "gunpowder revolution" caused a real revolution in the superstructure of economic, social, and political relationships because of its impact on the units of protection and security. A feeling of insecurity swept all Europe.[2] Though a Machiavelli might establish

---

[1] F. A. von der Heydte, *Die Geburtsstunde des souveränen Staates,* Regensburgh, 1952, pp. 103ff., 277, 293ff.

[2] Ariosto expressed the feeling of despair which invaded the "old powers" of chivalry when gunpowder destroyed the foundations of their system, in terms reminding one of present-day despair in the face of the destructive forces loosed upon our own world:

> *"Oh! curs'd device! base implement of death!*
> *Framed in the black Tartarean realms beneath!*
> *By Beelzebub's malicious art design'd*
> *To ruin all the race of human kind."*

Quoted from *Orlando Furioso* by Felix Gilbert, in Edward M. Earle, ed., *Makers of Modern Strategy,* Princeton, N. J., 1943, p. 4.

new rules as to how to gain and maintain power, there still followed more than a century of unregulated, ideological "total" wars inside and among countries until the new units of power were clearly established. Before old or new sovereigns could claim to be recognized as rulers of large areas, it had to be determined how far, on the basis of their new military power, they were able to extend their control geographically.[3]

The large-area state came finally to occupy the place that the castle or fortified town had previously held as a unit of impenetrability. But the new unit could not be considered consolidated until all independent fortifications within it had disappeared and, in their place, fortresses lining the circumference of the country had been built by the new central power and manned by its armed forces.[4] If we contrast our present system of bases and similar outposts surrounding entire world regions with what are today small-scale nation-states, perhaps we can visualize what the hard shell of frontier fortifications consolidating the then large-scale territorial states meant by way of extending power units in the age of absolutism. They became, in the words of Frederick the Great, "mighty nails which hold a ruler's provinces together." There now was peace and protection within. War became a regularized military procedure; only the breaking of the shell permitted interference with what had now become the internal affairs of another country.

In this way was established the basic structure of the territorial state which was to last throughout the classical period of the modern state system. Upon this foundation a new system and new concepts of international relations could arise.

. . .

IV. THE TERRITORIAL STATE IN INTERNATIONAL RELATIONS

From territoriality resulted the concepts and institutions which characterized the interrelations of sovereign units, the modern state system. Modern international law, for instance, could now develop. Like the international system that produced it, international law has often been considered inherently contradictory because of its claim to bind sovereign units. But whether or not we deny to it for this

[3]On this, see Garrett Mattingly, *Renaissance Diplomacy*, Boston, 1955, pp. 59ff., 121ff., 205ff.

[4]See Friedrich Meinecke, *Die Idee der Staatsraison in der neueren Geschichte*, Munich and Berlin, 1925, pp. 241ff.

reason the name and character of genuine law, it is important to see it in its connection with the territorial nature of the state system that it served. Only then can it be understood as a system of rules not contrary to, but implementing, the sovereign independence of states. Only to the extent that it reflected their territoriality and took into account their sovereignty could international law develop in modern times. For its general rules and principles deal primarily with the delimitation of the jurisdiction of countries. It thus implements the *de facto* condition of territorial impenetrability by more closely defining unit, area, and conditions of impenetrability. Such a law must reflect, rather than regulate. As one author has rightly remarked, "International law really amounts to laying down the principle of national sovereignty and deducing the consequences."[5] It is not for this reason superfluous, for sovereign units must know in some detail where their jurisdictions end and those of other units begin; without such standards, nations would be involved in constant strife over the implementation of their independence.

But it was not only this mutual legal accommodation which rendered possible a relatively peaceful coexistence of nations. War itself, the very phenomenon which reflected, not the strength, but the limitations of impermeability, was of such a nature as to maintain at least the principle of territoriality. War was limited not only in conduct but also in objectives. It was not a process of physical or political annihilation but a contest of power and will in which the interests, but not the existence, of the contestants were at stake. Now that we approach the era of absolute exposure, without walls or moats, where penetration will mean not mere damage or change but utter annihilation of life and way of life, it may dawn on us that what has vanished with the age of sovereignty and "power politics" was not entirely adverse in nature and effects.

Among other "conservative" features of the classical system, we notice one only in passing: the balance of power. It is only recently that emphasis has shifted from a somewhat one-sided concern with the negative aspects of the balance—its uncertainty, its giving rise to unending conflicts and frequent wars, etc.—to its protective effect of preventing the expansionist capacity of power from destroying other power altogether.[6] But at the time of its perfection in statecraft and

---

[5] Francois Laurent, as quoted by Walter Schiffer, *The Legal Community of Mankind*, New York, 1954, p. 157.

[6] See my *Political Realism and Political Idealism*, Chicago, 1951, pp. 206-21.

diplomacy, there were even theories (not lived up to in practice, of course) about the *legal* obligations of nations to form barriers against hegemony power in the common interest.[7]

More fundamental to the conservative structure of the old system was its character as a community. Forming a comparatively pacified whole, Europe was set off sharply against the world outside, a world beyond those lines which, by common agreement, separated a community based on territoriality and common heritage from anarchy, where the law of nature reigned and no standards of civilization applied. Only recently have the existence and role of so-called "amity lines" been rediscovered, lines which were drawn in the treaties of the early modern period and which separated European territories, where the rules of war and peace were to prevail, from overseas territories and areas.[8] There was to be "no peace beyond the line"; that is, European powers, although possibly at peace in Europe, continued to be *homo homini lupus* abroad. This practice made it easier for the European family of nations to observe self-denying standards at home by providing them with an outlet in the vast realm discovered outside Europe. While the practice of drawing amity lines subsequently disappeared, one chief function of overseas expansion remained: a European balance of power could be maintained or adjusted because it was relatively easy to divert European conflicts into overseas directions and adjust them there. Thus the openness of the world contributed to the consolidation of the territorial system. The end of the "world frontier" and the resulting closedness of an interdependent world inevitably affected this system's effectiveness.

Another characteristic of the old system's protective nature may be seen in the almost complete absence of instances in which countries were wiped out in the course of wars or as a consequence of other power-political events. This, of course, refers to the territorial units at home only, not to the peoples and state units beyond

[7] J. von Elbe, "Die Wiederherstellung der Gleichgewichtsordnung in Europa durch den Wiener Kongress," *Zeitschrift für ausländisches öffentliches Recht und Völkerrecht*, IV (1934), pp. 226ff.

[8] See Carl Schmitt, *Der Nomos der Erde*, Cologne, 1950, pp. 6off.; also W. Schoenborn, "Über Entdeckung als Rechtstitel völkerrechtlichen Gebietserwerbs," in D. S. Constantinopoulos and H. Wehberg, eds., *Gegenwartsprobleme des internationalen Rechts und der Rechtsphilosophie*, Hamburg, 1953, pp. 239ff.

the pale abroad; and to the complete destruction of a state's independent existence, not to mere loss of territory or similar changes, which obviously abounded in the age of power politics.

. . .

What, in particular, accounts for this remarkable stability? Territoriality—the establishment of defensible units, internally pacified and hard-shell rimmed—may be called its foundation. On this foundation, two phenomena permitted the system to become more stable than might otherwise have been the case: the prevalence of the legitimacy principle and, subsequently, nationalism. Legitimacy implied that the dynasties ruling the territorial states of old Europe mutually recognized each other as rightful sovereigns. Depriving one sovereign of his rights by force could not but appear to destroy the very principle on which the rights of all of them rested.

With the rise of nationalism, we witness the personalization of the units as self-determining, national groups. Nationalism now made it appear as abhorrent to deprive a sovereign nation of its independence as to despoil a legitimate ruler had appeared before. States, of course, had first to become "nation-states," considering themselves as representing specific nationality groups, which explains why in the two regions of Europe where larger numbers of old units stood in the way of national unification their demise encountered little objection. In most instances, however, the rise of nationalism led to the emergence of *new* states, which split away from multinational or colonial empires. This meant the extension of the European principle of "non-obliteration" all over the world. It is perhaps significant that even in our century, and even after the turmoil of attempted world conquest and resulting world wars, a point has been made of restoring the most minute and inconsiderable of sovereignties, down to Luxembourg and Albania.[9]

. . .

V. THE DECLINE OF THE TERRITORIAL STATE

Beginning with the nineteenth century, certain trends became visible which tended to endanger the functioning of the classical system. Directly or indirectly, all of them had a bearing upon that feature of the territorial state which was the strongest guarantee of

[9] Cf. also the remarkable stability of state units in the Western Hemisphere *qua* independent units; unstable as some of them are domestically, their sovereign identity as units appears almost sacrosanct.

its independent coexistence with other states of like nature: its hard shell—that is, its defensibility in case of war.

Naturally, many of these trends concerned war itself and the way in which it was conducted. But they were not related to the shift from the limited, duel-type contests of the eighteenth century to the more or less unlimited wars that developed in the nineteenth century with conscription, "nations in arms," and increasing destructiveness of weapons. By themselves, these developments were not inconsistent with the classical function of war. Enhancing a nation's defensive capacity, instituting universal military service, putting the economy on a war footing, and similar measures tended to bolster the territorial state rather than to endanger it.

Total war in a quite different sense is tied up with developments in warfare which enable the belligerents to overleap or by-pass the traditional hard-shell defense of states. When this happens, the traditional relationship between war, on the one hand, and territorial power and sovereignty, on the other, is altered decisively. Arranged in order of increasing effectiveness, these new factors may be listed under the following headings: (a) possibility of economic blockade; (b) ideological-political penetration; (c) air warfare; and (d) atomic warfare.

(a) *Economic Warfare.* It should be said from the outset that so far economic blockade has never enabled one belligerent to force another into surrender through starvation alone. Although in World War I Germany and her allies were seriously endangered when the Western allies cut them off from overseas supplies, a very real effort was still required to defeat them on the military fronts. The same thing applies to World War II. Blockade was an important contributing factor, however. Its importance for the present analysis lies in its unconventional nature, permitting belligerents to by-pass the hard shell of the enemy. Its effect is due to the changed economic status of industrialized nations.

. . .

(b) *Psychological Warfare.* The attempt to undermine the morale of an enemy population, or to subvert its loyalty, shares with economic warfare a by-passing effect on old-syle territorial defensibility. It was formerly practiced, and practicable, only under quite exceptional circumstances. Short periods of genuine world revolutionary propaganda, such as the early stages of the French Revolution,[10] scarcely affected a general practice under which dy-

---

[10]See my article, "Idealist Internationalism and the Security Dilemma," *World Politics*, II, No. 2 (January 1950), pp. 157ff.; in particular, pp. 165ff.

nasties, and later governments, fought each other with little ideological involvement on the part of larger masses or classes. Only in rare cases—for instance, where national groups enclosed in and hostile to multinational empires could be appealed to—was there an opening wedge for "fifth column" strategies.

With the emergence of political belief-systems, however, nations became more susceptible to undermining from within. Although wars have not yet been won solely by subversion of loyalties, the threat involved has affected the innner coherence of the territorial state ever since the rise to power of a regime that claims to represent, not the cause of a particular nation, but that of mankind, or at least of its suppressed and exploited portions. Bolshevism from 1917 on has provided the second instance in modern history of world revolutionary propaganda. Communist penetration tactics subsequently were imitated by the Nazi and Fascist regimes and, eventually, by the democracies. In this way, new lines of division, cutting horizontally through state units instead of leaving them separated vertically from each other at their frontiers, have now become possible.

(c) *Air Warfare and* (d) *Nuclear Warfare.* Of all the new developments, air warfare, up to the atomic age, has been the one that affected the territoriality of nations most radically. With its coming, the bottom dropped out—or, rather, the roof blew off—the relative security of the territorial state. True, even this new kind of warfare, up to and including the Second World War, did not by itself account for the defeat of a belligerent, as some of the more enthusiastic prophets of the air age had predicted it would. Undoubtedly, however, it had a massive contributory effect. And this effect was due to strategic action in the *hinterland* rather than to tactical use at the front. It came at least close to defeating one side by direct action against the "soft" interior of the country, by-passing outer defenses and thus foreshadowing the end of the frontier—that is, the demise of the traditional impermeability of even the militarily most powerful states. Warfare now changed "from a fight to a process of devastation."[11]

. . .

The process has now been completed with the advent of nuclear weapons. For it is more than doubtful that the processes of scientific invention and technological discovery, which not only have created and perfected the fission and fusion weapons themselves but have

[11]B. H. Liddell Hart, *The Revolution in Warfare*, New Haven, Conn., 1947, p. 36. Suspicion of what would be in the offing, once man gained the capacity to fly, was abroad as early as the eighteenth century. Thus Samuel Johnson re-

brought in their wake guided missiles with nuclear warheads, jet aircraft with intercontinental range and supersonic speed, and the prospect of nuclear-powered planes or rockets with unlimited range and with automatic guidance to specific targets anywhere in the world can in any meaningful way be likened to previous new inventions, however revolutionary. These processes add up to an uncanny absoluteness of effect which previous innovations could not achieve. The latter might render power units of a certain type (for instance, castles or cities) obsolete and enlarge the realm of defensible power units from city-state to territorial state or even large-area empire. They might involve destruction, in war, of entire populations. But there still remained the seemingly inexhaustible reservoir of the rest of mankind. Today, when not even two halves of the globe remain impermeable, it can no longer be a question of enlarging an area of protection and of substituting one unit of security for another. Since we are inhabitants of a planet of limited (and, as it now seems, insufficient) size, we have reached the limit within which the effect of the means of destruction has become absolute. Whatever remained of the impermeability of states seems to have gone for good.

. . .

VI. OUTLOOK AND CONCLUSION

It is beyond the compass of this article to ask what the change in the statehood of nations implies for present and future world relations; whether, indeed, international relations in the traditional sense of the term, dependent as they have been on a number of basic data (existence of the nation-state, measurable power, etc.) and

marked: "If men were all virtuous, I should with great alacrity teach them all to fly. But what would be the security of the good, if the bad could at pleasure invade them from the sky? Against an army sailing through the clouds, neither walls, nor mountains, nor seas, could afford security" (quoted in J. U. Nef, *War and Human Progress*, Cambridge, Mass., 1952, p. 198). And Benjamin Franklin, witnessing the first balloon ascension at Paris in 1783, foresaw invasion from the air and wrote: "Convincing Sovereigns of folly of wars may perhaps be one effect of it, since it will be impracticable for the most potent of them to guard his dominions. . . . Where is the Prince who can afford so to cover his country with troops for its defense, as that ten thousand men descending from the clouds, might not in many places do an infinite deal of mischief before a force could be brought together to repel them?" (from a letter to Jan Ingelhouss, reproduced in *Life Magazine*, January 9, 1956).

interpreted as they were with the aid of certain concepts (sovereignty, independence, etc.), can survive at all; and, if not, what might take their place.[12]

. . .

Hardly has a bipolar world replaced the multipower world of classical territoriality than there loom new and unpredictable multipower constellations on the international horizon. However, the possible rise of new powers does not seem to affect bipolarity in the sense of a mere return to traditional multipower relations; since rising powers are likely to be nuclear powers, their effect must be an entirely novel one. What international relations would (or will) look like, once nuclear power is possessed by a larger number of power units, is not only extremely unpleasant to contemplate but almost impossible to anticipate, using any familiar concepts. Or, to use another example: We have hardly drawn the military and political conclusions from the new weapons developments, which at one point seemed to indicate the necessity of basing defense on the formation and maintenance of pacts like NATO and the establishment of a network of bases on allied territory from which to launch nuclear weapons "in case" (or whose existence was to deter the opponent from doing so on his part), and already further scientific and technological developments seem to render entire defense blocs, with all their new "hard shells" of bases and similar installations, obsolete.

. . .

One radical conclusion to be drawn from the new condition of permeability would seem to be that nothing short of global rule can ultimately satisfy the security interest of any one power, and particularly any superpower. For only through elimination of the single competitor who really counts can one feel safe from the threat of annihilation. And since elimination without war is hardly imaginable, destruction of the other power by preventive war would therefore seem to be the logical objective of each superpower. But—and here the security dilemma encounters the other great dilemma of our time—such an aim is no longer practical. Since thermonuclear war would in all likelihood involve one's own destruction together with the opponent's, the means through which the end would have to be

[12]Some of the pertinent questions are discussed in a more comprehensive manuscript, "Reflections on International Politics in the Atomic Age," from whose initial chapters the preceding pages were adapted.

attained defeats the end itself. Pursuance of the "logical" security objective would result in mutual annihilation rather than in one unit's global control of a pacified world.

If this is so, the short-term objective must surely be mutual accommodation, a drawing of demarcation lines, geographical and otherwise, between East and West which would at least serve as a stopgap policy, a holding operation pending the creation of an atmosphere in which, perhaps in consequence of a prolonged period of "cold peace," tensions may abate and the impact of the ideologies presently dividing the world diminish. May we then expect, or hope, that radically new attitudes, in accordance with a radically transformed structure of nationhood and international relations, may ultimately gain the upper hand over the inherited ones based on familiar concepts of old-style national security, power, and power competition? Until recently, advocacy of policies based on internationalism instead of power politics, on substituting the observance of universal interests for the prevalence of national interests, was considered utopian, and correctly so. National interests were still tied up with nation-states as units of power and with their security as impermeable units; internationalist ideals, while possibly recognized as ethically valid, ran counter to what nations were able to afford if they wanted to survive and prosper. But the dichotomy between "national self-interest" and "internationalist ideals" no longer fits a situation in which sovereignty and ever so absolute power cannot protect nations from annihilation.

What used to be a dichotomy of interests and ideals now emerges as a dichotomy between two sets of interests. For the former ideal has become a compelling interest itself. In former times, the lives of people, their goods and possessions, their hopes and their happiness, were tied up with the affairs of the country in which they lived, and interests thus centered around nation and national issues. Now that destruction threatens everybody, in every one of his most intimate, personal interests, national interests are bound to recede behind—or at least compete with—the common interest of all mankind in sheer survival. And if we add to this the universal interest in the common solution of other great world problems, such as those posed by the population-resources dilemma (exhaustion of vital resources coupled with the "population explosion" throughout the world), or, indeed, that of "peacetime" planetary pollution through radio-active fallout, it is perhaps not entirely utopian to expect the ultimate spread of an attitude of "universalism" through which a rational approach to world problems would at last become possible.

chapter three
THE NATION-STATE: SOCIOECONOMIC AND PSYCHOLOGICAL CHARACTERISTICS

The Growth of Nations:
Some Recurrent Patterns
of Political
and Social Integration*
Karl W. Deutsch

At many places and times, tribes have merged to form peoples; and peoples have grown into nations. Some nations founded empires; and empires have broken up again into fragments whose populations later attempted again to form larger units. In certain respects, this sequence appears to describe a general process found in much of history. This process shows a number of patterns which seem to recur, and which to a limited extent seem to be comparable among different regions, periods, and cultures.

Such recurrent patterns of integration, like other relative uniformities in history, raise the problem of the comparability or uniqueness of historical events. Yet the search for such relative uniformities in politics and history is essential to the pursuit of knowledge in these fields. No historical or political analysis can be written without the use of general concepts in which some notions of

*The substance of this paper was read at the Annual Meeting of the American Historical Association at New York, December 28, 1951.

uniformity are necessarily implied.[1] Indeed, such recurrent patterns offer a background of similarities against which differences can stand out, and against which investigators can evaluate the specific and perhaps unique aspects of each particular case of national or supra-national integration.

At the same time, the study of the growth of nations may reveal cumulative change. It may suggest that the present period is unique in respect to both the extent of nationalism and the potentialities for supra-national organization. To the student of contemporary politics, it may further suggest specific problems of research and policy in the on-going process of social and political integration on the national as well as the international level.

Before discussing the recurrent problems of national integration, it may be well to note the use of a few terms. For the purposes of our discussion, a distinction is made between a *society*, which is defined as a group of persons who have learned to work together, and a *community*, which is defined as a group of persons who are able to communicate information to each other effectively over a wide range of topics.[2] A similar distinction is adopted between a *country*, which denotes a geographic area of greater economic interdependence and thus a multiple market for goods and services, and a *people*, which is a group of persons with complementary communications habits. A

[1] The alternative views that all history is random, or that all important historical events are unique, involve grave philosophic difficulties. Historians who criticize the search for certain historical uniformities by their colleagues use in effect other uniformities which they prefer. Similar considerations apply to much of the debate about uniformities in other fields of social science. All knowledge involves the matching of patterns, and thus requires at least some similarities between some aspects of the events or processes studied. It thus requires some degree of relative uniformity among the processes to be investigated, in order to enable each science to proceed beyond the relatively simple and the relatively uniform to the recognition and study of those situations which are relatively complex and unique. Simplicity and uniformity, in this view, are not sweeping metaphysical assumptions about all aspects of all processes. They are properties of those aspects of processes which were first selected for investigation, or first investigated with success. With the growth of each science, this concern with the simple and the uniform reveals itself as a steppingstone to the study of more difficult matters. Cf. H. T. Pledge, *Science Since 1500*, New York, 1947, which supersedes, in this respect, the view of E. A. Burtt, *The Metaphysical Foundations of Modern Physical Science*, London, 1932, and J. H. Randall, Jr., *The Making of the Modern Mind*, 2nd ed., Boston, 1940, pp. 227-29.

[2] Cf. K. W. Deutsch, *Nationalism and Social Communication*, Cambridge, Mass., and New York, 1953 (in press).

nation is then a people which has gained control over some institutions of social coercion, leading eventually to a full-fledged *nation-state;* and *nationalism* is the preference for the competitive interest of this nation and its members over those of all outsiders in a world of social mobility and economic competition, dominated by the values of wealth, power, and prestige, so that the goals of personal security and group identification appear bound up with the group's attainment of these values.[3]

While peoples are found at almost any period in history, nationalism and nations have occurred during only a few periods. A nation is the result of the transformation of a people, or of several ethnic elements, in the process of social mobilization. Thus far, however, the processes of social mobilization and communication have at no time included all mankind. The "universal states" listed by A. J. Toynbee as stages in the disintegration of particular civilizations[4] were superficial short-cuts, rather than solutions to the problem of the unity of mankind.

Periods of "universal states" have left behind them, however, a number of widespread languages, such as Latin, Greek, or Arabic; and a measure of cultural assimilation among certain social groups such as the nobility, town population, or the clergy of some "universal church."[5] The results have somewhat resembled a *layer-cake pattern,* with a high degree of cultural assimilation and participation in extended social communication among the top layers of society; a lesser degree on the intermediate levels; and little or no assimilation or participation among the mass of the population at the bottom.[6]

[3]*Ibid.*; and "Nationalism and the Social Scientists," in L. Bryson, *et al.*, eds., *Foundations of World Organization: A Political and Cultural Appraisal*, New York, 1952, pp. 9-20, 447-68. On recent studies in this field, cf. K. W. Deutsch, *An Interdisciplinary Bibliography on Nationalism, 1935-1951*, Boston, 1953 (in press).

[4]*A Study of History*, London, 1939, IV, pp. 2-3.

[5]For examples of such limited assimilation during and after the expanding phase of certain civilizations or universal states, see *ibid.*, Vols. I-VI, *passim*, and the appendix on "Lingue Franche" in Vol. V, pp. 483-526. Cf. also A. C. Woolner, *Languages in History and Politics*, London, 1938; and H. A. Innis, *Empire and Communication*, Oxford, 1950, and *The Bias of Communications*, Toronto, 1952. On particular languages, see Woolner, *op.cit.*, pp. 109-48, 156-67; H. A. R. Gibb, *The Arabs*, Oxford, 1940; George Antonius, *The Arab Awakening*, Philadelphia, 1939, p. 16; P. K. Hitti, *History of Syria Including Lebanon and Palestine*, New York, 1951, pp. 483-89.

[6]Cf. Royal Institute of International Affairs, *Nationalism*, London, 1939, p. 9; A. P. Usher, *Economic History of England*, Boston, 1920, pp. 20-21.

In several parts of the world, the cycle—from local isolation to "universal" empire and back to a new age of localism[7]—has been traversed more than once. Yet the cycle has usually shown a net gain, in the sense that there has been a gain in man's technological and scientific command over nature,[8] and that some of the most important cultural, intellectual, moral, and spiritual traditions of the earlier civilization have tended to survive that civilization in which they arose, and continue, often as a "universal church" or religion to influence the development of new peoples and new regions.[9]

. . .

The processes of partial social mobilization and of nation-building have been recurrent phenomena in history, at least in certain general characteristics. What uniformities can we find in this growth of nations in the past? And in what ways is our own age different in respect to the growth of nations from any age that has gone before?

SOME POSSIBLE SPECIFIC UNIFORMITIES

Uniformities which have been found in the growth of nations include the following:

1. The shift from subsistence agriculture to *exchange economies.*
2. The social mobilization of rural populations in *core areas* of denser settlement and more intensive exchange.
3. The growth of *towns,* and the growth of social mobility within them, and between town and country.
4. The growth of *basic communication grids,* linking important rivers, towns, and trade routes in a flow of transport, travel, and migration.
5. The differential accumulation and *concentration of capital* and skills, and sometimes of social institutions, and their *"lift-pump" effect* on other areas and populations, with the successive entry of different social strata into the nationalistic phase.

[7] For a discussion of the chances of linguistic disintegration following upon the dissolution of a universal empire, see Ramón Menéndez Pidal, *Castilla, la tradición, el idioma,* Buenos Aires, 1945, pp. 191-94.

[8] For the Graeco-Roman and medieval civilizations, this point has been stressed by Gordon Childe, *What Happened in History,* Harmondsworth, Eng., Penguin Books, 1950, pp. 279-82.

[9] Toynbee, *op.cit.,* V, p. 79, and *passim.*

6. The rise of the concept of *"interest"* for both individuals and groups in unequal but fluid situations, and the growth of *individual self-awareness* and awareness of one's predispositions to join a particular group united by language and communications habits.

7. The awakening of *ethnic awareness* and the acceptance of *national symbols,* intentional or unintentional.

8. The merging of ethnic awareness with attempts at *political compulsion,* and in some cases the attempt to transform one's own people into a privileged class to which members of other peoples are subordinated.

Some of these similarities may be discussed briefly.

The Shift to Exchange Economies

The shift from subsistence agriculture to an exchange economy seems to have characterized all cases of wider national integration which I have been able to find. Where the exchange economy came to embrace the bulk of the population and to bring many of them into direct contact with each other in the interchange of a wider variety of goods and services, there we find a tendency to "national" or at least regional, linguistic, and cultural "awakening," provided only that sufficiently large numbers of individuals enter the exchange economy and its more intensive communication *faster* than they can be assimilated to another "alien" language or culture.

Where these shifts take place, the ethnic and in part the linguistic situation becomes, as it were, loosened or softened, and capable of settling again into new and different molds. The awakening of the Slavic population of the Balkans, and the rise of regions of greater intensity of trade and exchange around which the revived Serbian and Bulgarian languages and nationalities were constituted, may perhaps serve as illustrations.[10]

[10]By the end of the [eighteenth] century many village notables (*knez*) began to come into contact as hog exporters with foreign lands, especially with the supply services of the Austrian armies. Among this class the leaders of the Serbian uprising of 1804 were found . . . [who] started the movement for Serbian independence and beyond that for Southern Slav unification . . ." (Hans Kohn, *The Idea of Nationalism,* New York, 1944, p. 549). Cf. also S. Mladenov, *Die Geschichte der Bulgarischen Sprache,* Berlin, 1929; Alfred Fischel, *Der Panslawismus bis zum Weltkrieg,* Stuttgart, 1919; etc. For some general social and political aspects of the shift to an exchange economy, see Karl Polanyi, *The Great Transformation,* New York, 1944.

Further Social Mobilization
and Integration in Core Areas

The shift to an economy and culture based on wider interchange takes place at different times and different rates of speed in different regions. The result is often the existence of more "advanced" regions side by side with more "undeveloped" ones. The former are then often in a position to function as centers of cultural and economic attraction for some of the populations of the latter, and thus to become nuclei of further integration. The "when" is thus often as important and sometimes more important than the "where," and the processes of social mobilization and partial integration are truly historical in the sense that each step depends to a significant extent on the outcome of the step that went before.

Political geographers have sought to identify *core areas* around which larger states were organized successfully in the course of history. Characteristic features of such core areas are unusual fertility of soil, permitting a dense agricultural population and providing a food surplus to maintain additional numbers in nonagricultural pursuits; geographic features facilitating military defense of the area; and a nodal position at an intersection of major transportation routes. Classic examples of such core areas are the Ile de France and the Paris basin, or the location of London.[11]

It should be noted that the density that makes a core area is one of traffic and communication rather than mere numbers of passive villagers densely settled on the soil. Thus the dense population of the Nile valley seems to have been less effective as a wider center of integration than the sparse population of the Arab territories beyond Mecca and Medina, who more than compensated for their smaller numbers by their proportionately far greater mobility, activity, and traffic.

The theory of core areas, however, cannot account for the persistence of some states and the failure of others. What counts for more may well be what happens within each core area, and perhaps particularly what happens in its towns.

The Growth of Towns, Mobility,
and Ties Between Town and Country

There is no developed nation, it appears, without towns which have or have had a period of considerable growth, of mobility within

[11] For core areas and population clusters, see D. Whittlesey, *The Earth and the State*, New York, 1939, pp. 11-12, 142-52; and Preston James, *Latin America*, New York, 1942, pp. 4-8. For the nodal location of London, see Sir Halford Mackinder, *Britain and the British Seas*, New York, 1902.

the towns, and of increasing ties of social mobility, communication, and multiple economic exchange between town and country.

There have been towns, of course, where one or more of these conditions did not exist, and to that extent national development has been incomplete, absent, halted, or retarded. On the other hand, to the extent that there was such growing mobility and communication within towns and between town and country, national development was accelerated.

The Growth of Basic Communication Grids

Most nations do not seem to have grown from single centers. Many nations have had several capitals and have shifted their central regions several times in the course of their history. Even the classical example of growth around one center, France, has long had two capital cities, Paris and Orleans; and some significant phases of the unification of the French language took place at the Champagne fairs and along the trade routes leading through that region—not to mention the role of the North-South routes and connections in helping the North to consolidate its victory over separatist and Albigensian elements in the Midi during the religious wars of the thirteenth century.[12]

. . .

The same notion of a basic grid seems to be applicable to the unification of China, Russia, Switzerland, Canada, and the United States.[13] It would be interesting to investigate the relationship of such a grid to the incomplete unification and more recent separation of the areas that now comprise India and Pakistan.

[12]D. Whittlesey, *The Earth and the State, op. cit.,* pp. 138-39, 151. Cf. W. von Wartburg, *Evolution et structure de la langue francaise,* Leipzig, 1934, and *Les origines des peuples romans,* Paris, 1941.

[13]Cf., on China, G. B. Cressey, *The Geographic Foundations of China,* New York, 1934; Percy M. Roxby, "China as an Entity: The Comparison with Europe," *Geography,* XIX, No. 1 (1934), pp. 1-20; John de Francis, *Nationalism and Language in China,* Princeton, N.J., 1950; etc. On Russia, see Robert Kerner, *The Urge to the Sea: The Role of Rivers, Portages, Ostrogs, Monasteries and Furs,* Berkeley, Calif., 1942; V. O. Kluchevskii, *A History of Russia,* Vol. 1, New York, 1911; J. W. Thompson, *Economic and Social History of the Middle Ages, A.D. 300-1300,* New York, 1931; etc. On Switzerland, see Aloys Schulte, *Geschichte des mittelalterlichen Handels und Verkehrs Zwischen Westdeutschland und Italien,* Vol. I, Leipzig, 1900; Lüdtke und Mackensen, *op.cit.;* Hans Nabholz, *Geschichte der Schweiz,* Vol. I, Zürich, 1932; C. Englert-Faye, *Vom Mythus zur Idee der Schweiz,* Zurich, 1940; Richard Weiss, *Volkskunde der Schweiz,* Zurich, 1946; etc.

It is not suggested that a grid in itself can make a nation. Also necessary, as a rule, are a minimum of cultural compatibility and, in many cases, sufficient similarity between spoken dialects to permit the emergence of a common language for large sections of the population. The cultural and linguistic data in themselves are given by history, of course, at each stage of the process. Yet we know how much of a difference in language or culture has been bridged successfully in the emergence of such nations as the Swiss, the British, or the Canadians, provided that enough tangible and intangible rewards and opportunities were present, ranging from greater wealth, security, freedom, and prestige to the subtler attractions of new common symbols, dreams, and ways of life.

The Differential Concentration of Capital, Skills, and Social Institutions

A major factor in national differences and national pride today are the differences in the general standard of living. To some extent such differences tend to cut across the differences between social classes; there is a social, moral, or traditional component in what is considered "bare subsistence" in a given community, or in what counts as "luxury" in another; and a significant part of what is considered the poor population in a relatively wealthy community may be appreciably better off in terms of physical goods and services than even many of the relatively well-off members of a poor or economically backward people. This difference between the generally prevailing standards of wealth, comfort, and opportunity among different regions or peoples has sometimes been called the *Kulturgefälle* ("the drop in the level of culture") by German writers who have employed this concept to bolster claims to German supremacy or exclusiveness vis-à-vis the populations of Eastern Europe and the Balkans.

Behind the differences in the standards of living lie differences in levels of productivity and in the supply of factors of production, that is, in the material means to pursue any one of a wide range of conceivable ends regardless of the difference in importance assigned to some of these ends relative to others in some particular culture. These differences in productivity may involve geographic factors such as soils, water supplies, forests, mineral deposits, and the absence of obstacles to transportation. All such geographic factors, however, depend on specific technologies to give them significance. Every concentration of natural resources requires, therefore, a concentration of productive skills and knowledge if men are even to know how to use them; and resources as well as skills require a concentration of invested *capital* if they are to be used in fact.

It should be clear that, as technology progresses, the relative importance of the man-made factors of production, such as capital and skills, has tended to increase relative to the importance of the few natural facilities which once were the only ones that more primitive technologies could exploit. There is reason to believe that present-day differences in living standards are due far less to differences in natural factors of production, and far more to differences in the supply of skilled labor, schools, housing, and machinery.

Particular peoples and nations may then tend to crystallize, as it were, around particular concentrations of capital and technology, or of particular social institutions which offer individuals greater opportunities for the pursuit of the goods or factors which they have learned to desire.

. . .

The effects of differential standards of living and of productivity operated long before the Industrial Revolution, but they were increased by its coming. Where large economic or industrial developments have taken place, they have had a "lift-pump" effect on the underlying populations. They have induced migrations of populations to the regions of settlement, employment, and opportunity, and put these newcomers into intensive economic and political contact with the locally predominant peoples, and with each other. This physical, political, and economic contact had one of two cultural and linguistic consequences: either it led to national assimilation, or, if national assimilation to the dominant group could not keep pace with the growing need for some wider group membership for the newcomer, then the "lift-pump" effect would tend to lead eventually to a new growth of nationalism among the newly mobilized populations. Eventually, it might result in the assimilation of some previously separate groups, not to the still-dominant minority, but to the "awakening" bulk of the population.

. . .

Both national assimilation and national resurgence thus respond in a "lift-pump" situation to the power of the "pump." The intensity and appeal of nationalism in a world of sharply differentiated income and living standards perhaps may tend to be *inversely proportional to the barriers to mobility between regions and classes,* and *directly proportional to the barriers against cultural assimilation, and to the extent of the economic and prestige differences between classes, cultures, and regions.*

Seen in this light, the rise of nationalism and the growth of nations have some semi-automatic features, even though they have other features which are by no means automatic. As the distribution of scarce rewards is made unequal by economic or historic processes; as men learn to desire the same kinds of rewards; as they fail to be assimilated to the language and culture of the dominant group; and as they succeed in becoming assimilated with other men who possess cultural and language habits more compatible with their own—as all these processes go on, situations conducive to nationalism are created without anyone's deliberate intention.

The Concept of Self-Interest and the Experience of Self-Awareness

The concept of a nation is bound up with that of a national interest. Already the non-national or proto-national institutions of the city-state and the princely state imply the notion of group interests and interests of state, and all these notions of national, state, or city interests imply in turn the interests of individuals. But this concept of individuals with interests has itself gained its present importance only gradually in the course of certain developments of history.[14] Even today different regions and civilizations ascribe to it different degrees of significance, and it may lose again in the future much of its present importance.

At bottom the notion of interest perhaps implies a situation in which men are pitted against each other in a competitive situation in which some of them can improve or even maintain their positions only at the expense of others. The word "interest" denotes then the ensemble of an individual's chances for improving or maintaining his position against all competitors, and thus, indirectly, the amount and effectiveness of disposition of his resources applicable to the competitive situation in which he finds himself. Such competitive situations may be relatively vague and unpredictable, or they may be formalized and hence in part predictable to a more or less high degree. The more predictable they are, the more easily can they be recognized as competitive by the participants.

. . .

As men leave the relative security of villages and folk cultures for the mobility and uncertainty of travel, towns, and markets, and for the competition of wealth-getting, politics, and warfare, they may

[14]Cf. Charles A. Beard, *The Idea of the National Interest*, New York, 1934, pp. 22-25. I am indebted to Professor Hans Kohn for valuable suggestions on this point.

find greater opportunities and rewards for aggressiveness and self-assertion; and at the same time they may come to feel more poignantly the loneliness, the loss of security, and the loss of context and meaning in their lives which the transition to the new ways of life entails.

Nationalism is one peculiar response to this double challenge of opportunity and insecurity, of loneliness and power. Men discover sooner or later that they can advance their interests in the competitive game of politics and economics by forming coalitions, and that they stand to gain the firmer these coalitions can be made, provided only that they have been made with individuals and groups who have to offer in this game the largest amount of assets and the least amount of liabilities. To form the firmest possible connections with the most promising group of competitors would seem to be sound long-run strategy. With which group such firm connections can be formed is by no means arbitrary: in politics and economics such coalitions will depend to a significant degree on social communication and on the culture patterns, personality structures, and communications habits of the participants. Their chances of success will thus depend to some degree on the links that make a people, the ties of nationality.

. . .

Organization along ethnic or national lines is by no means the only type of alignment which may be tried in the competitive game. Yet of all these probable patterns of organization, ethnic or national alignments often combine the greatest strength and resilience with the greatest adaptability to a competitive world. So long as competitive institutions continue to prevail, nationalism can mobilize more people and organize them more firmly than can many competing types of organization. The potential rewards of nationalism then grow in proportion to the potential resources of wealth and power to which members of a particular people have, or can gain, access on preferred terms.

To develop thus the economic, intellectual, and military resources of a territory and a population, *and to knit them together in an ever tighter network of communication and complementarity based on the ever broader and more thorough participation of the masses of the populace*—all this is sound power politics; and those who carry out such policies tend to be rewarded by the long-run outcome of this contest.

What may fit the necessities of the competitive game may also fit some inner needs of its participants. Ages of social mobilization, of rapid changes in the traditional social contexts, tend to be ages of increasing self-doubt and self-awareness for the individuals who live in them. The questions: Who am I? Whom do I resemble? In whom can I trust?—are asked with a new urgency, and need more than a traditional answer.

As a man seeks answers to these questions he must try to take stock of himself, of his memories, his preferences, and his habits, of the specific images and indeed of the specific words in which they were conveyed and in which they are now stored in his mind. As old cultural or religious patterns, beliefs, and ceremonies become questionable, self-searching must lead back to the childhood memories and the mother tongue, in terms of which so many experiences have been acquired, and out of which, in a sense, the individual's character and personality have been built up. When men seek for themselves, they thus may come to find their nationality; and when they seek the community of their fellows, they may discover once again the connection between ethnic nationality and the capacity for fellowship. Instances of this process can be found even in antiquity: it is well known that Socrates enjoined upon his pupils the imperative, "Know thyself," and that Socrates' pupil, Plato, proposed that all Greeks should henceforth cease to plunder or enslave their fellow Greeks, but should rather do these things to the barbarians.[15]

. . .

Our hypothesis finds some confirmation in a well-known pattern in the history of nationalism and the biographies of nationalist leaders. Many emotionally, culturally, and politically sensitive individuals react to a sojourn abroad, i.e. away from their native region or culture, with a far stronger assertion of nationalism and of allegiance to their own language, culture, and people. This precipitating crisis in the lives of many nationalists has been dubbed the *Fremdheitserlebnis* ("the experience of strangeness"), and it has been described repeatedly in the literature of nationalism.[16]

[15] ". . . our citizens should . . . deal with foreigners as Greeks now deal with one another" (Plato, *Republic*, v, 469-70, Cornford trans., New York, 1945, p. 174). Cf. also Glenn R. Morrow, *Plato's Law of Slavery in Its Relation to Greek Law*, Urbana, Ill., 1935.

[16] Hans Kohn, *The Idea of Nationalism, op. cit.*, pp. 98, 601 (Petrarch); p. 127 (Machiavelli); pp. 239, 659 (Rousseau); p. 294 (Jefferson). On the problem of individual self-awareness and identification with groups, cf. also Chr. Bay, I. Gullavg, H. Ofstad, and H. Toenessen, *Nationalism: A Study of Identification with People and Power: I. Problems and Theoretical Framework*, Oslo, Institute of Social Research, 1950, mimeographed.

From Group Awareness to the Nation-State

Individual awareness of one's language and people may appear to be a matter of personal psychology, even though there are social situations which make such awareness more probable. Group awareness, on the other hand, seems clearly a matter of social institutions. Some secondary symbols are attached to some aspects of group life and are repeated and disseminated over and over again by an organization or institution, often for a purpose that has nothing to do with nationality, or which might even be opposed to it. After a time, the institution may change or disappear, the organized repetition of the symbols may cease—but if there were enough of a primary reality capable of being symbolized, *and if there had been going on that basic process of social mobilization* which has been described earlier, then the results of the dissemination of those symbols may well prove irreversible.

. . .

Given these underlying conditions, symbols and institutions of group awareness may be produced quite unintentionally. A process of social mobilization may even transform the function of existing symbols or institutions so as to turn them into agencies of group awareness, regardless of their original purposes.

. . .

Once the process of group consciousness has started, however, there appear also the deliberate pioneers and leaders of national awakening. There appear grammarians who reduce the popular speech to writing; purifiers of language; collectors of folk epics, tales, and songs; the first poets and writers in the revised vernacular; and the antiquarians and historians who discover ancient documents and literary treasures—some genuine, some forged, but all of them tokens of national greatness.

Side by side with the awakeners of national pride and fashioners of symbols appear the first organizers. There arise the first social circles and literary societies where the formerly despised native language is read or spoken. There follow the first benevolent societies, fraternal orders, credit cooperatives, and all the devices of mutual credit, support, or insurance, which now begin to collect the financial resources of the awakening nationality. There appear the organizers of the first schools, singing societies, athletic organizations, agricultural colleges, which herald the array of all the organizations for cultural, physical, and technological improvement which characterize every full-fledged modern nation.

Together with all this activity we find the gradual acceptance, or the deliberate proposal, of national symbols, of national colors, flags, animals, and flowers, of anthems, marches and patriotic songs, from the "Rule Britannia" and the "Marseillaise" of the eighteenth century to the *"Nkosi sikelel i Africa"*—"God Save Africa"—of today's nationalist South African Negroes.[17] How all these symbols, maps, anthems, flags, and flag-salutes are then taught and impressed upon the populations and their children by informal group pressure and the media of mass communication as well as by all the coercive powers of the state and its system of compulsory public education—this is a story that has been told often and well by students of these late stages of the nation-building process.[18]

What does this process accomplish, and what does it aim at? When a nation has been built up, and when it has been reinforced finally by the full compulsive power of the state, then four things have been accomplished.

1. A relatively large community of human beings has been brought into existence who can communicate effectively with each other, and who have command over sufficient economic resources to maintain themselves and to transmit this ability for mutual communication to their children as well. In other words, there has been brought into being a large, comprehensive, and very stable human network of communication, capable of maintaining, reproducing, and further developing its channels.
2. There has been both an effective accumulation of economic resources and a sufficient social mobilization of manpower to permit the social division of labor necessary for this process and to permit its continuation.
3. There has been a social accumulation and integration of memories and symbols and of individual and social facilities for their preservation, transmission, and recombination, corresponding to the level of mobilization and integration of material and human resources, or even pointing beyond it.

[17] Detailed documentation here would be unnecessary. On the Swiss symbols, see Englert-Faye, *op.cit.* For a novelist's description of the singing of the Negro anthem in South Africa, cf. Alan Paton, *Cry the Beloved Country: A Story of Comfort in Desolation*, New York, 1948.

[18] Cf. Carlton H. Hayes, *Essays on Nationalism*, New York, 1926, and *The Historical Evolution of Modern Nationalism*, New York, 1931; F. L. Schuman, *International Politics*, 3rd ed., New York, 1941, pp. 300-65; etc.

4. There has been at least some development of the capacity to redirect, re-allocate, or form a new combination of economic, social, and human resources as well as of symbols and items of knowledge, habit, or thoutht—that is to say, of the capacity to learn. Some of the social *learning capacity* is developed invisibly in the minds of individuals; some of it can be observed in the habits and patterns of culture prevailing among them; some of it finally is embodied in tangible facilities and specific institutions. Together, all these constitute the community's capacity to produce and accept new knowledge or new goals, and to take the corresponding action.

On all four counts, it should be evident, the nation represents a more effective organization than the supra-national but largely passive layer-cake society or the feudal or tribal localisms that preceded it.

On all these counts, there may be considerable contrasts between different nations. The social models accepted for imitation, the established institutions, the economic practices, and the methods of compulsion within each nation are all intimately connected with the cultural traditions and leading social classes currently prevailing there. Whether a leading class of businessmen or farmers or wage earners will prove more hospitable to accumulation of resources and to efficient dynamic innovation in their use may depend not merely on the general outlook to be found prevailing in each particular stratum, but also—and perhaps sometimes crucially—on the particular cultural goals and traditions which have become accepted by that particular class in that particular nation.[19] Yet, the impression remains that even the worst-led nation represents, relative to its numbers of population, a greater amount of social communication facilities, of economic resources, and of social learning capacity than any pattern of ethnic or social organization preceding it.

[19] For some problems of conservative aristocratic leadership in undeveloped nations, cf., for the Arabs, the writings of H. A. R. Gibb; for an example from Tibet, Nicholas Mansergh, "The Asian Conference, 1947," in *The Commonwealth and the Nations*, London, 1948, pp. 115-16; and for Southeast Asia, Cora Du Bois, *Social Forces in Southeast Asia*, Minneapolis, Minn., 1949, pp. 33-36, 59. On the contrast, e.g., between French and American business investment policies, cf. David S. Landes, "French Entrepreneurship and Industrial Growth in the Nineteenth Century," *Journal of Economic History*, IX (May 1949), pp. 45-61.

Where does this process aim? The nation has been valued as a means of social advancement. In a world of extreme differences between living standards, men have tended to use the nation as an instrument to improve their own standards relative to those of their neighbors. The intrinsic bias of this process has been, where the opportunity offered itself, to produce in the temporarily most successful nation a sociological pattern reminiscent of a *mushroom cloud*. The stem of this social mushroom was formed by the "national solidarity" between the poorest and the lower-middle strata of the nation; the poorest strata, both rural and urban, however, tended to be somewhat less in relative numbers, and offered their members greater chances for "vertical mobility" than was the case in other less "successful" nations. The middle and upper strata, on the other hand, tended to form the crown of the mushroom; they tended to be somewhat larger in number than the corresponding group in other nations, with a greater propensity to spread out horizontally into new positions of privilege or control over new territories, populations, or capital resources, and correspondingly with at least somewhat greater opportunities to accept in their midst newcomers from the less favored strata of their own nation.

It is perhaps this sociological explosion into a mushroom cloud that has been at the heart of the transitory popularity of empire-building. Nationalism typically has led to attempts at empire or at least at establishing privileges over other peoples. The essence of this empire-building has been perhaps the attempt at ruling without sharing, just as the essence of nationalism has been the attempt at improving the position of one's "own" group without any sharing with "outsiders." To the extent that this process was successful it could only tend ultimately to transform the whole nation into a privileged class, a *Herrenvolk* lording it over servant peoples, as the Nazis dreamed of it, or a small, select population monopolizing vast natural resources or accumulations of technological equipment regardless of the fate of the rest of mankind. In reality, this state has probably never been achieved; and where it was even partially approximated, the results in the long-run were anything but lasting. Invariably, thus far, the same nation-building process which had permitted one nation to get temporarily on top of its neighbors subsequently raised up other nations to weaken or destroy it.

From this it might seem at first glance that the whole process of the rise and decline of nations has been cyclical, with only the names of the actors changing in an endlessly repeated drama. Closer scrutiny may show that this is not the case, and that some tentative inferences may be drawn from the events and processes surveyed.

THE UNIQUENESS OF THE
PRESENT PERIOD

Our survey offers no support for the belief of many nationalists that nations are the natural and universal form of social organization for mankind. But neither does it confirm entirely the opposite view held by many thoughtful and distinguished observers—the view that nations are exclusively the product of the modern period and of Western civilization.[20] Perhaps the impression that remains might be summed up by saying that the West has gone much farther on a road which all the world's great civilizations have traveled to some extent.

. . .

[20]Cf. Toynbee, *op. cit.*, *passim;* Kohn, *op. cit.*, *passim;* Carlton H. Hayes, "Nationalism," *Encyclopedia of the Social Sciences;* etc.

The Basis of
National Loyalty

Morton Grodzins

It is a contradiction in terms to speak of a man without loyalties. He does not exist. The human qualities that differentiate man from other mammals are the products of his social life. One with all the attributes of man, including his brain, is in isolation not a man. He is a beast.

This only says that when you scratch man you touch loyalty. For man means society. And society—social structures of every sort—rests upon loyalties: upon systems of mutual rights and duties, common beliefs, and reciprocal obligations. To accuse one of being devoid of loyalty can have only one meaning. His loyalties are antagonistic to your own.

SOURCE: From *Bulletin of the Atomic Scientists,* Vol. VII (1951). Copyright © 1970 by the Educational Foundation for Nuclear Science. Reprinted and abridged by permission of Science and Public Affairs, the *Bulletin of the Atomic Scientists.*

The basic objective of this article[1] is twofold: to show how factors of life situation tend to bind men's loyalty to their *nation;* and to apply this general analysis to the situation of physical scientists. My current research is concerned with the social and psychological correlates of national loyalty and disloyalty. I have not studied physical scientists, as such. Therefore, my primary emphasis must be a general, though partial, statement of theory. The concluding remarks on the situation of scientists are simply deduced from that theory. The entire statement is a preliminary one, a report on a larger work in progress, subject to correction on the basis of later evidence and reflection.

FUNCTION OF LOYALTIES

Loyalties are a part of every individual's life because they serve his basic needs and functions. They are a part of his indispensable habit patterns. Loyalties provide him with a portion of that framework through which he organizes his existence. In the absence of such a framework, he could establish no easy, habitual responses. He would be faced with the endless and hopelessly complicated task of making fresh decisions at each moment of life. He would soon degenerate into wild and random inconsistencies or into a brooding state of confusion and indecisiveness, conditions that soon merge into the psychotic.

The propensity of man to organize the structure of his activities is apparent in every phase of his life. His very perceptions are so organized. Even what a man sees or smells or hears is determined in very large part by predisposing frameworks. This has been demonstrated in laboratory experiments, and the experiments are duplicated daily in ordinary life situations. Drivers of cars which have collided have very different stories to tell. Two readers of the same book derive from it support for widely divergent points of view. Chinese music and Mohammedan paintings are displeasing or unintelligible to those who have not acquired the framework necessary to make them beautiful and meaningful.

This "structuring" of life's enormous range of potentialities begins from the very moment of birth. For the first years of life, when the

---

[1] The substance of this paper was first presented at a conference on "What is Loyalty for the Scientist?" at Roosevelt College, Chicago, on May 18, 1951.

plasticity of individuals is very great, the family is the dominant molding agency. Later, play groups, school, church, job, social class, government, all take important, sometimes parallel, sometimes conflicting, roles in shaping an individual's career, attitudes, and personality.

These groups that so crucially affect existence are the groups that demand and receive loyalty. They become the eye-pieces through which a person views his life and its relation to society. They actually and literally determine what he does and does not see, what he does and does not like, what he does and does not consider his life goals. Without the aid and comfort of these group ties, an individual would find existence impossible.

Loyalties are thus the source of great personal gratification. They contribute to making life satisfying. They protect the individual, reducing the area of his uncertainty and anxiety. They allow him to move in established patterns of interpersonal relations with confidence in the action expected of him and of responses that his action will evoke. By serving the group to which he is loyal, he serves himself, what threatens the group, threatens the self. There is no self outside group activity. "In so far as one identifies himself with a whole, loyalty to that whole is loyalty to himself; it is self-realization, something which one cannot fail without losing self respect."[2]

Complete identification between individual and group does not often exist. Totalitarian governments attempt to accomplish this end by destroying all intermediary loyalties, or by fusing the activities of all other groups with those of the state.

In the Western democracies the case is different. Except in periods of extreme crisis, freedom to form and maintain group ties is cherished and encouraged, and individuals preserve strong loyalties to numerous non-national groups. These loyalties are given to family, friends, neighborhood, church, ethnic society, job, class, and to a host of other institutions, groups, and idea systems. They exist most frequently in situations that bring the individual face-to-face with others who share his views and situation; they may also exist where this immediate human contact does not exist. The relative strength and weakness of these numerous loyalties change with age, with

[2] C. H. Cooley, *Social Organization: A Study of the Larger Mind* (New York: C. Scribner's Sons, 1909), p. 38.

shifts in life situation, with new experience, and especially under stress of crisis. They change as old relationships no longer serve biological needs or as they no longer supply satisfaction and security to the individual in the total network of his social existence.

TWO STRANDS OF
NATIONAL LOYALTY

Individual satisfactions are related to *national* loyalty in an infinite number of ways. Almost the entire social structure is organized to promote and sustain this relationship. One of the prime reasons for the strength and universality of national loyalties is the virtuosity and deftness with which the connection between nation and happiness can be established. For convenience, one can distinguish between two broad strands which together tend to bind human satisfaction to national welfare.

Direct Nation-Person Tie

Patriotism as a Religion. On one plane the relationship between individual and nation is direct. Satisfaction springs from immediate identification with nation, from the acceptance of national symbols, the internalization of national ideals. There is delight in attaching oneself to a larger cause. Inner doubts are dissipated: the cause gives purpose and direction to life. The meanness and pettiness of everyday existence become unimportant; the nation is the dominant power unit in the modern world and it is involved in enterprises of grandeur. In this way, the nation acts to dissipate actual and imagined discontents and weaknesses; it simultaneously crystallizes the common faith which philosophers and politicians, sociologists and seers have argued is essential to any successful group life.

The world is organized territorially, and to some extent functionally, into national units. This very organization permits a complex flow of simple emotions to be woven into the sentiment of national loyalty. National states and the institutions within them conspire to promote and to sustain this loyalty.

Ethnocentrism: Death to the Porpoises. The tendency of man to prefer the familiar to the unfamiliar is a universal social phenomenon. The search for new experience and delight in the exotic must largely be understood in terms of the reassurance of the familiar and the habitual. As the world is presently organized, the familiar and the habitual are principally equated with the national. In this way affection for the scenes and experiences of childhood becomes identified with the nation. The familiar language, the familiar inter-personal responses—including, as Kipling wrote, the familiar lies—all are affectionately related to the nation.

Familiar misery is frequently more attractive than promised or actual, but unfamiliar, bliss. This is a function of what social anthro-pologists call ethnocentrism, the practice of judging foreign customs by familiar standards. Even the mean and savage regard their own way of life as the best and all others as sub-human or at least distinctly inferior. This mechanism has been described and documented in many ways. A classic example is in Anatole France, whose Penguin cottager affirms:

> "He who says neighbours says enemies. . . . Don't you know what patriotism is? For my part there are two cries that rise to my lips: Hurrah for the Penguins! Death to the Porpoises!"

The modern network of world-wide communications and other technological factors tend to weaken the force of ethnocentrism. But it remains potent because it lives on difference, real or imagined. It is strengthened by the structual qualities of the nation-state system. The great hostilities generated within nations are suppressed to every extent possible; they find outlets in bursts of patriotic fervor directed against other national units.[3] Man's love of community—his aim-inhibited libido, in Freud's term—is thus encouraged to stop at national boundaries. The ills of one's own person and one's own culture are projected outward: we are peaceful, they are aggressive; we are kind, they cruel; we aim for justice, they for conquest.

These mechanisms prompted the sardonic Sumner to comment that "the masses are always patriotic." They inspire the antagonisms and animosities that are basic to most patriotic endeavor. The process is self-generating and circular. National boundaries and patriotism to the nation establish convenient ethnocentric battle lines; the belligerencies so evoked add to patriotic fervor; the heightened patriotism produces new belligerencies. Thus patriotism can pour meaning into otherwise empty lives. The price may be individuality itself; but this seems cheap to those glorying in and suffering for great causes.

The Conspiracy of Institutions. The nation is not the only focal point for mass loyalties. Just as loyalty to a nation competes with

[3]See Talcott Parsons, "Certain Primary Sources and Patterns of Aggression in the Social Structure of the Western World," *Psychiatry*, X (May, 1947), 167-81.

loyalty to family, job, and friends, so it must compete with loyalty to race, religion, and class. The nation's advantage is based not only on the psychological processes just described: to some degree those energies are also available to other causes. The strength of national, rather than other, loyalties is also partly the result of objective facts: common language, common historical traditions, a definable territory. Finally, national loyalty is built strong as the result of the active role taken by social institutions in building a firm direct tie between individual and nation. The institution of government is of first importance in this effort.

Government is a powerful agency in setting up norms of behavior. By laws establishing limits of freedom and control, government defines general guidelines for life activities. Through control of the schools, government has a crucial lever for inculcating habits of thought, for encouraging some character traits and discouraging others, and for molding individuals to standards of thought and action. Through its multitude of substantive programs, the state purchases conformity and allegiance. By enforcing service in the armed forces, the state transforms citizens into soldiers and in the process brings about similarly striking changes in attitude and outlook. As the source of major news developments, government commands a large portion of the words and symbols transmitted to the public by press, radio, television, and film. By the encouragement of national holidays and festivals, government pounds home myths of national might and images of national glory. By fostering patriotic organizations and activities, government enlists citizens in active demonstrations of patriotism.

There are tremendous variations in the extent and manner that governments utilize the power they possess for building patriotism. There are even greater variations in the size and composition of the groups to which governments are responsible and thus in the final ends for which patriotism is utilized.

Democratic values and traditions do not countenance the ruthless exploitation of people by the state for the state. The power structure within democracies makes such exploitation impossible; it occurs only at the price of changing the character of the state itself. And in the United States, government power is further dispersed as the result of the federal system. Nevertheless, even in the United States, the patriotic theme is an essential ingredient of all public activity, even that at the state and local level.

Public education, for example, has been least affected in the United States by the insistent trend toward national financing and supervision. Yet, as the studies of Charles Merriam and Bessie Pierce have shown, the themes of patriotism and national service are consistently and insistently pursued.[4]

The total impact of the schools is designed certainly, if unwittingly, to conform· to Rousseau's dictum: that education should direct the opinion and tastes of men so that they will be "patriots by inclination, by passion, by necessity."

This is true for all nations. Naturally enough, the truth has been demonstrated most graphically and most bleakly by the totalitarian governments. The Nazis showed that a state-operated educational system could be even more powerful than the family as a molder of attitudes and personality, supplanting or destroying the family's influence to a large measure.

The Nazis attempted to create a situation in which individuals received all their cues for action from a state or party agency. They did this by capturing or destroying all other institutions and groups—religious, professional, and social—that guide and control human action. The terrible efficiency of this fully mobilized state-controlled education cannot be doubted. It drastically altered the direction of the culture and the temper, the very personality of the people.

In the United States and other Western democracies, one does not find this total mobilization of state resources and state institutions for the purpose of constructing strong national allegiance. Yet state activities, with minor exceptions, move strongly toward cementing loyalty to the nation. Only a small portion of these activities aim at building direct emotional ties between individual and state. School programs illustrate this attempt, as do bond drives, ceremonies dramatizing the might of armed forces, the display and symbolic care of the flag. But in the democracies, unlike the totalitarian nations, the major impact of state activities is an indirect one: it strengthens national loyalties by strengthening the numerous voluntary groups through which so much of the life and politics of democratic people is organized and directed.

The effects of these programs do not, of course, stop with the voluntary groups. The groups have a vitality of their own. They, in turn, direct the emotions of group members toward the nation. In this circular fashion, virtually all groups contribute to national allegiance. Their members minimize or efface any antagonisms be-

[4]Charles Edward Merriam, *The Making of Citizens* (Chicago: The University of Chicago Press, 1931); Bessie L. Pierce, *Civic Attitudes in American School Textbooks* (Chicago: The University of Chicago Press, 1930).

tween their own group and the nation. They identify group and national welfare. "What is good for business is good for the nation," trumpets the National Association of Manufacturers. "High wages mean national health," responds the Congress of Industrial Organization.

The voices and forces all pushing in the same direction produce the religious quality of patriotism. It is a quality for which totalitarian nations strive continuously but which is known to democracies largely in periods of crisis—"an element of worship, of willing sacrifice, of joyful merging of the individual in the life of the nation."[5] Here the direct nation-individual linkage is most graphically expressed.

Indirect Nation-Person Tie

Non-National Loyalties as Filters of National Loyalty. The second strand relating individual to nation is an indirect one. Here satisfactions are experienced in the face-to-face relations of everyday living, in pleasurable interpersonal experiences, warm friends, sympathetic neighbors, the achievement of expectations in marriage and career. One's relationships to the nation are transmitted, or filtered, through these experiences. To the extent that they produce a satisfactory life situation, the individual's identification with his nation is positive. His loyalty may be presumed, though it is a loyalty different in kind from the loyalty fostered by direct ties with the state. Where a life situation does not produce a balance of gratifications, the individual's identification with the nation wavers. His loyalty may be more easily eroded.

Until the advent of modern totalitarianism, it is doubtful if the direct nation-person tie could have been built strong enough to sustain national loyalties over long periods of time. It involves, ultimately, the destruction of all privacy. Only with the techniques of modern political exploitation does this seem possible.

For the Western democracies, at least, patriotism cannot be maintained over long periods of time. No one has expressed this idea more clearly than George Washington, who wrote from Valley Forge in April, 1788:

> *Men may talk of patriotisms; they may draw a few examples from ancient story, of great achievements performed by its influence; but whosoever builds upon it, as a sufficient Basis for*

---

[5]Bertrand Russell, *Why Men Fight* (New York: The Century Company, 1917), p. 55.

conducting this Bloody war, will find themselves deceived in the end. . . . I do not mean to exclude altogether the Idea of Patriotism. I know it exists, and I know it has done much in the present Contest. But I venture to assert, that a great and lasting War can never be supported on this principle alone. It must be aided by a prospect of Interest or some reward.

Washington's concept of "interest" was largely a commercial one. The definition need not be so narrow. But Washington's point is basic.

Democratic nations cannot exist unless the "interests"—the life goals—of its citizens are at least approximately achieved. And these achievements are in areas where there is little or no direct nation-person relationship. National loyalty here becomes a by-product of satisfactions achieved in non-public spheres of activity.

Indeed, from this view a generalized national loyalty is a misnomer. It does not exist. Loyalties are to specific groups, specific goals, specific programs of action. Populations are loyal to nation only because the nation is believed to symbolize and sustain these values.

Leon Trotsky once remarked that revolutions were not caused by the poor. If they were, he said, there would be revolutions going on all the time. This is one way of expressing the important fact that "life expectations" or "life goals" are not fixed or static concepts. Individuals define these terms in various and divergent fashions; their definitions are influenced in many ways, not least of all by parents, profession, sex, and social class.

To say that loyalty is dependent upon the achievement of life satisfactions is therefore not to say that the poor are the disloyal, the rich, loyal. The individual's own definition of satisfaction is of crucial importance. The fat men who do not make easy converts are those fat in satisfactions, not necessarily in body or other material possessions. A subtle tool to measure these satisfactions would be an index of the discrepancy, if any, between life expectancy and life achievements, as defined by the individual. Where the spread is a big one deprivations are experienced and loyalty to the nation (not considering direct nation-person ties) is presumably less strong than where expectations are actually or approximately achieved.

This variety in definition of life satisfactions is crucial to understanding the interplay between those satisfactions and national loyalty.

A second general consideration is also of great importance. Life goals are achieved and life satisfactions are pursued within the framework of groups. The happy man in isolation does not exist. He may—and most frequently does—take his terms of reference, his cues for action, his definitions of the good and desirable from the small face-to-face groups with which he comes into most intimate contact: family, friends, business associates, professional colleagues, fellow-workers. Or these cues for life may be influenced by larger, less visible groups with which he identifies himself: social class, the universal church, the international workers. In these latter cases and even in those cases where frames of reference are derived from such apparent abstractions as "the good of mankind," there is usually a face-to-face group in existence, functioning to define and to clarify abstract goals in terms of day-to-day activity.

The principal loyalties of men in democratic states are directed toward these non-national groups and interests. Their very existence provides possibilities for sharp clashes between national and other loyalties. But these other loyalties are also the most important foundation of national loyalty.

Why this is so has already been suggested. The nation is the most important group with which all persons in a given geographic area are associated. It gives all citizens a common point of reference. It sustains their groups. A threat to a nation is interpreted as a threat to all groups within the nation and to the gratifications derived from those groups. The satisfactions springing from smaller groups are thus related to the nation and to national loyalty.

But in times of crisis, the national demands may easily conflict with the demands of non-national groups. Family welfare, professional status, career and job stability may be threatened or thwarted by governmental policy. In such circumstances, clean choices need not always be made. When they do, national loyalty may mean family or professional disloyalty. Where loyalty to family or to career or to profession is held foremost, then the result is national disloyalty.

The total configuration is a fine paradox: non-national loyalties are the bricks from which national loyalty is constructed; they are also the brickbats by which national loyalty is destroyed.

SOCIAL IMPEDIMENTS TO DISLOYALTY

Many people do not react positively to national symbols. And many do not achieve a balance of satisfactions through participation in non-national groups. There are, nevertheless, potent social forces that push them in the direction of loyal conduct and just as strongly repel them from disloyal acts.

Protest Is Easy. Many acts of social protest and adjustment, short of disloyalty, are readily available. Within the framework of national groups, there are a great number of attachments available to man in democratic states. If he does not like one lodge, there are others. If he is dissatisfied with his neighbors, he can move. If marriage palls, divorce is easy. If pastor or church become distasteful, other leaders and other denominations exist in great number.

Even in the political sphere, democratic society allows for easy protest. The existence of political parties channels discontents into socially approved forms. Inside and out of the formal party structure, special interest groups offer numerous activities in a wide spectrum of political beliefs.

These avenues to sense and satisfaction in life are not only readily available. They are, just as importantly, prescribed and accepted social processes. They are carried on within the nation, not against it.

Some protests against a life situation are neither easy nor socially acceptable. They run the whole gamut of deviant behavior: alcoholism, arson, bank robbery, embezzlement, promiscuity or perversion, hoboing. In the extreme, the individual may withdraw himself from all meaningful human contact. Eventually, he may find himself under the wheels of a street car or, escaping or denying the psychiatrist's skills, in an institution for the mentally ill.

These deviant methods for seeking integration and meaning for life meet with the highest social disapproval. Yet many of them, especially within the great urban centers, are available. They are utilized without discovery and therefore without social sanction. They may result in intense guilt feelings that frustrate their aim, though men have infinite abilities to appease their conscience and to rationalize their behavior. And even if brought to public light, the community wrath aroused hardly compares with that called down upon the head of the traitor.

The very ambiguity of what constitutes disloyal acts in a democratic state widens the area of permissible acts of public protest. No such ambiguity exists in the totalitarian states. But every culture must provide methods of easing tensions and discharging aggression. Where they are not available in the public sphere, they express themselves privately; or they may be mobilized against an external foe.

Whatever the type of state, the disloyal act must compete with all the other socially disapproved means by which individuals seek to express dissatisfaction and to achieve integration and satisfaction. But the disloyal act is the least likely way.

Disloyalty Is Difficult. There are few available alternatives to national loyalty. This is true on a relative scale: the very multiplicity of other available opportunities for deviant behavior makes the disloyal act less enticing. It is also true on a positive scale: the traitorous act usually requires a combination of circumstances not easily achieved. Confederates are usually necessary, and they are not always available. The necessary joint activity involves ideological and personal demands that are often extreme. Foresight and planning may be necessary. The time must be propitious.

A related factor discouraging acts of disloyalty is their lack of relevance to the frustrations and deprivations that individuals commonly face. Relationships between deprivation and protest are not always clear: witness the man who kills his cat because he cannot kiss his wife. Usually, however, the connection is more apparent. And only as the state increases its functions and demands more and more from its citizens do acts of disloyalty become immediately pertinent. The very increase in state functions thus provides new opportunities for disloyalty. If national conscription did not exist, there would be no draft dodgers. Historically, state programs of the Western democracies have been relatively light in their impact upon the lives of citizens. Only within recent years have government programs made the disloyal act a relevant protest for many people for many reasons.

Even where government programs might realistically inspire protest, other considerations become potent. Satisfactions in the nonpublic spheres of life—on the job, in the home—constitute a powerful deterrent. He who is completely involved in his job, for example, may find no time to become sensitive to political effrontery. This is an ignorance imposed by limitations of time and energy. Most people are "too busy" to acquaint themselves with matters they might find distasteful. Even awareness of the displeasing situation is followed only infrequently by protest so strong that it is disloyal. The penalties for such action strike at the very roots of happiness. Job, family, friends, and comfortable existence are in this sense all hostages insuring loyalty.[6]

Indeed, it is often more attractive to join your enemies than to fight them, especially if they occupy the benches of legality and the seats of power. The most recent striking illustration of this occurred

[6]I am indebted to Louis Kriesberg for suggestions incorporated in this and the preceding paragraph.

during the Nazi regime. Those abandoning protest may solace themselves with the thought of achieving reform more effectively from within. In the interim, they do not jeopardize many spheres of happiness and need not surrender their hostages.

The scales are thus heavily weighted against disloyalty. Even under the darkest circumstances, individuals can always look to better things in the future. They can channelize their protests within the institutionalized processes, however narrow they may be, and believe with fullest sincerity that no more is possible. And they rationalize their inaction in terms of higher loyalties: the nation must be preserved for all time, the current government must therefore be suffered; socialism (or Mother Russia) must triumph. Stalinism is therefore a temporary evil.

Finally, disloyalty is rare because of the stigma attached to it. Dante placed the traitor in the lowest pit of hell. In the eyes of his contemporaries, the traitor is more corrupt than even the murderer and the rapist. He runs the risk of losing his place in all social life. Since one depends upon society for sustenance in no less certain a manner than he depends upon food, this risk is one that few are willing to take. If he takes it, he has found a new social environment in which to act.

The alternatives to national loyalty increase with advances in levels of education and communication. But it remains true that these alternatives are relatively limited. Traitorous acts stand in a poor competitive position with all the other opportunities for deviant behavior.

In sum, the state has become modern man's largest point of reference. It supplies him with psychic security. Whatever his objective maladjustment to life conditions, he is molded to conformity by the forces of ethnocentrism, by the powerful antagonisms of the strange and unknowable, by the satisfactions that even suffering sometimes brings, by the utilization of patriotic activity as a substitute for other satisfactions, by the relative absence of alternatives to national conformity, and by the social vengeance that follows the traitorous act. To these factors must be added all the positive steps taken by society to identify the individual with his nation. Government, family, neighborhood, church, school, and business, all push under most circumstances in the direction of strong national loyalties. Life may be hell. But disloyalty is the last way out.

. . .

CONCLUDING REMARKS

The view presented here rejects the contention that national allegiance is a simple conditioned response to political symbols. It equally rejects the idea that loyalty is a cool and rational choice of one way of life over another. It emphasizes that loyalty can be explained, like other social phenomena, in terms of life situation (discussed here) and personality attributes (neglected here).

This view also recognizes how ambiguous the concept of national loyalty is in Western democracies. Does "nation" means administrative programs or national ideology or a specific leader or a system of government? The variety in answers to this question makes it possible for traitors to act in the name of patriotism and patriots to perform the role of traitors. Traitors, for example, can wreck great programs of government in the service of lofty slogans and honored principles; and the patriot can subvert principle while honoring program.

This ambiguity becomes crucial when linked to the tendency, already mentioned, of all groups to validate their conduct in terms of national values. This is a near-universal phenomenon. Klu Klux Klansmen and racial equalitarians, high tariff and low tariff proponents, management and labor, all link their efforts to national welfare. Even traitors do the same.

Disloyalty to the nation therefore does not emerge as a simple act of rejection. With rare exception it also requires a positive act of identification, sometimes identification with the nation itself, though in one of the meanings not recognized as valid by others. Despite the many social impediments discussed above, people thus slip into disloyal action. A new loyalty becomes primary: to family, to labor union, to profession, to Marxist study club. What sense of evil or betrayal they may feel as the result of subordinating national to other demands becomes overshadowed by the positive values of serving a cause.

This is so even for the most blatant traitor. He regards his acts as an expression of loyalty to, not disloyalty against. He is almost always supported by some group with which he is in intimate, daily, face-to-face contact. There are few Iagos who glory in villainy. "No man at bottom means injustice," Carlyle said. "It is always for some distorted image of a right that he contends."

And this leads to a final observation. This is in the nature of opinion, not directly a part of the analysis presented here but growing out of that analysis.

I have tried to indicate, in a most general and incomplete way, how democracy, to attract the loyalty of men, must provide them with satisfactions that spring from the ordinary round of their life.

The loyalty thus engendered is different from the religious-like quality of direct nation-person relationships, those dominant in totalitarian states. In the latter case, loyalty emerges from the poverty or absence of participation in voluntary groups. It is mobilized by state leaders, and it is marked by a high emotional content. In democracies national loyalties are largely by-products of participation in voluntary groups. They do not emerge as a consequence of manipulation from above. They are not submissive. They are more studied, less emotional; more qualified, less completely mobilized at any given moment.

This explains the greater intensity of totalitarian loyalties, in comparison with democratic ones. It also suggests the greater duration and stability of democratic loyalties. They are based upon human satisfactions derived from numerous overlapping but independent group contacts. Barring complete social catastrophe, no single cause can bring widespread dissatisfaction, widespread disloyalty.

To sustain such loyalties, democracies in practice must supply some achievement of the expectations promised in the democratic creed. The danger, among scientists as well as others, is not that of individual persons becoming disenchanted and turning to disloyal acts. Nor is the danger that democracy will fail because it is inherently unable to supply the immediate life satisfactions that, indirectly but solidly, lead to strong national allegiance. The danger is that democracy may fail, not on its merits, but because it fails to be democratic.

chapter four
THE NATION-STATE: CAPACITY TO ACT

The Concept of Power
in the Study
of International
Relations

K. J. Holsti

Students of international politics have for years argued that the concept of power can be used as a fruitful approach in studying processes in international systems. Unfortunately, there has been little systematic examination of the concept so that, like the balance of power, its meaning has remained ambiguous. Some have claimed that the concept can be used to analyze every major phenomenon in international politics. Others have defined power roughly as a means to an end. Some use the term to denote a country's military forces, but when used in this way they are really discussing only a country's military capability and not the amount of influence the country wields in the system.

Hans Morgenthau (1960) is the foremost advocate of the concept of power as the theoretical core of international politics. In his view, all politics is a struggle for power. He derives this dictum from the

SOURCE: From *Background*, Vol. VII, No. 4 (1964), pp. 179-194. Copyright © 1964 by Sage Publications, Inc. Reprinted by permission of the author and Sage Publications, Inc.

assumption that the desire to dominate is "a constitutive element of all human associations." Thus, regardless of the goals and objectives of government, the immediate aim of all state action is to obtain and to increase power. Since by definition all states seek to maximize their power, international politics can be conceived of and analyzed as a struggle between independent units seeking to dominate others.

Professor Morgenthau unfortunately fails to submit the concept of power to further examination so that some ambiguity remains.[1] He implies, for example, that power is also a major goal of policy or even a determining motive of any political action. Elsewhere, however, he suggests that power is a relationship and a means to an end. Because of this ambiguity, we do not know what the concept explains or fails to explain in international politics. Does the term "struggle for power" shed light on the many processes that go on within an international system? The word "struggle" certainly does not tell us much about the relations between Norway and Sweden or between Canada and the United States. Does the term "power," defined as the immediate goal of all governments, explain the major external objectives of Nicaragua or Chad or Switzerland?

In contrast to the "struggle for power" concept is the "anti-power theory" of international relations. The proponents of this theory (including Woodrow Wilson) claim that there is a distinction between "power politics" and some other kind of politics. Not pessimists regarding human nature, they assume that man is essentially tolerant and pacific and that the human community is united through many bonds. Statesmen, they claim, have a choice between practicing "power politics" and conducting foreign relations by some other means. Wilson and others made the further assumpsion that there is a correlation between a nation's social and political institutions and the way it conducts its foreign relations. To them, autocracies which did not consult "the people" usually engaged in deception, duplicity, and saberrattling. Democracies, on the other hand, displayed tolerance, morality, and justice, and sought only peace and stability. In the new order which they envisaged for the post World War I period, negotiations would replace threats of war, and world-wide consensus on the desirability of peace would sustain democratic statesmen. In other words, power politics was synonymous with autocracy. But how democratic governments were supposed to achieve their objec-

---

[1] Other noteworthy proponents of the "power" theory of international relations are Kalijarvi (1953), and Strausz-Hupé and Possony (1950).

tives is left unexplained.[2] This view is also of limited use because it is mostly prescriptive: it enunciates how international processes *should* be carried on, but it fails to help us understand what actually occurs.

A third view of power is found in past and contemporary texts on international relations. Authors present the student with a brief and formal definition of power, often equating power with the physical assets a nation possesses. Most texts, in fact, concentrate on the analysis of these assets (often called the "elements of national power") without discussing the actual relations between governments and the techniques by which these assets are brought to bear on the pursuit of national objectives.

Should we not, however, define power in a way which best clarifies what we observe and what we wish to know? A definition should suggest areas of inquiry and reality, though no definition is likely to account for the totality of the subject. Thus, one definition of the concept may be useful for describing and analyzing social relations within a political party or within a family, but it may not be useful for studying international relations. Let us first describe an *act* which we conceive to be central to the process of international politics; that is, the act or acts that A commits toward B so that B pursues a course of behavior in accordance with A's wishes. The act can be illustrated as follows:

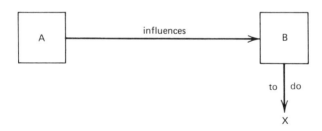

<hr>

[2]There is room for disagreement on this characterization of the Wilsonian theory of power. Wilson was obviously aware of the role of power as military force and as public opinion. His concept of collective security, where all peaceful nations would band together to enforce the peace, implies that democracies no less than autocracies, should use force when necessary.

A seeks to influence B because it has established certain goals which cannot be achieved (it is perceived) unless B (and perhaps many other actors as well) does X. If this is an important act in international political processes, we can see that it contains several elements:

1. Influence (an aspect of power) is essentially a *means* to an end. Some governments or statesmen may seek influence for its own sake, but for most it is instrumental, just like money. They use it primarily for other goals, which may include prestige, territory, souls, raw materials, security, or alliances.

2. The act also implies a base of capabilities which the actor uses or mobilizes to use in his efforts to influence the behavior of B. A capability is any physical or mental object or quality available as an instrument of inducement. The concept of capability may be illustrated in the following example. Suppose an armed man walks into a bank and asks the clerk to give him all her money. The clerk observes clearly that the man has no weapons and refuses to comply with his order. The man has sought to influence the behavior of the clerk, but has failed. The next time, however, he walks in armed with a pistol and threatens to shoot if the clerk does not give him the money. This time, the clerk complies. In this instance the man has mobilized certain resources or capabilities (the gun) and has succeeded in influencing the clerk to do as he wished. The gun, just like a nation's military forces, *is not synonymous with the act of influencing,* but it is the instrument that was used to induce the clerk to change her behavior to comply with the robber's objectives.

3. The act of influencing B obviously involves a *relationship* between A and B, though as we will see later, the relationship may not even involve communication. If the relationship covers any period of time, we can also say that it is a *process.*

4. If A can get B to do something, but B cannot get A to do a similar thing, then we can say that A has more power than B *vis a vis* that action. Power, therefore, is also a *quantity*. But as a quantity it is only meaningful when compared to the power of others. Power is therefore relative.

To summarize, then, power may be viewed from several aspects: it is a means, it is based on capabilities, it is a relationship, and a process, and it can also be a quantity.

But for purposes of analyzing international politics, we can break down the concept of power into three separate elements: power is (1) the act (process, relationship) of influencing other factors; (2) it includes the capabilities used to make the wielding of influence successful; and (3) the responses to the act. The three elements must be kept distinct.[3] However, since this definition may seem too abstract, we can define the concept also in the more operational terms of policy makers. In formulating policy and the strategy to achieve certain goals, they would explicitly or implicitly ask the four following questions:

1. Given our goals, what do we wish B to do or not to do? (X)
2. How shall we get B to do or not to do X? (implies a relationship and process)
3. What capabilities are at our disposal so that we can induce B to do or not to do X?
4. What is B's probable response to our attempts to influence its behavior?

Before discussing the problem of capabilities and responses we have to fill out our model of the influence act to account for the many patterns of behavior that may be involved in an international relationship. First, as Singer (1963) points out, the exercise of influence implies more than merely A's ability to *change* the behavior of B. Influence may also be seen where A attempts to get B to *continue* a course of action or policy which is useful to, or in the interests of, A. The exercise of influence does not always cease, therefore, after B does X. It is often a continuing process of reinforcing B's behavior. Nevertheless, power is "situational" to the extent that it is exercised within a framework of goals.[4]

Second, it is almost impossible to find a situation where B does not also have some influence over A. Our model has suggested that influence is exercised only in one direction, by A over B. In reality, however, influence is multilateral. State A, for example, would seldom seek a particular goal unless it had been influenced in a particular direction by the actions of other states in the system. At a minimum, there is the problem of feedback in any relationship: if B complies with A's wishes and does X, that behavior may subsequently prompt A to change its behavior, perhaps in the interest of B. Suppose, for example, that state A, after making threats, persuades B to lower its tariffs on the goods of state A. This would seem to be influence travelling only in one direction. But where state

_____

[3]The recent texts of Stoessinger (1961) and Schleicher (1962) distinguish between the act and the capabilities involved in the act.

[4]State A might also wish state B to do w, y, and z, which may be incompatible with the achievement of X.

B does lower its tariffs, that action may prompt state A to reward state B in some manner. The phenomenon of feedback may be illustrated as follows:

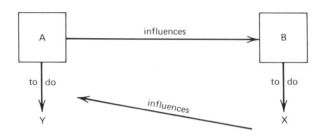

Third, the number of times a state becomes involved in acts of influence depends upon the general level of involvement of that particular actor in the system. The first requisite for attempting to wield influence is a perception that somehow state B (or any other) is related to the achievement of state A's goals and that there is, or will be, some kind of relationship of interdependence. If the relationship covers only inconsequential matters, few acts of influence may be necessary; but the greater the involvement of an actor in the system, the greater the necessity to wield influence over other actors. For example, except for limited trade relations, there is little perception of interdependence between Iceland and Uganda, hence little need for the government of Iceland to attempt to influence the domestic or external policies of the African country.

Fourth, there is the type of relationship which includes what Herbert Simon (1953) has called "anticipated reaction." This is the situation, frequently found in international relations, where A might wish B to do X, but does not try to influence B for fear that B will do Y instead, which is an unfavorable response from A's point of view. In a hypothetical situation, the government of India might wish to obtain arms from the United States to build up its own defenses, but it does not request such arms because it fears that the United States would insist on certain conditions for the sale of arms which might compromise India's neutrality. This "anticipated reaction" may also be multilateral, where A wishes B to do X, but will not try to get B to do it because it fears that C, a third actor, will do Y, which is unfavorable to A's interests. India wants to purchase

American arms, but does not seek to influence the United States to sell them for fear that Pakistan (C) will then build up its own armaments and thus start an arms race. In this situation, Pakistan (C) has influence over the actions of the Indian government even though it has not deliberately sought to influence India on this particular matter or even communicated its position in any way. The Indian government has simply perceived that there is a relatively high probability that if it seeks to influence the United States, Pakistan will react in a manner that is contrary to India's interests.

Fifth, power and influence may be measured quite objectively by scholars and statesmen, but what is important in international relations is the *perceptions* of influence and capabilities that are held by policy-makers. The reason that governments invest millions of dollars for the gathering of intelligence is to develop or have available a relatively accurate picture of other states' capabilities and intentions. Where there is a great discrepancy between perceptions and reality, the results to a country's foreign policy may be disastrous. To take our example of the bank robber again, suppose that the man held a harmless toy pistol and threatened the clerk. The clerk perceived the gun to be real and hence complied with his demand. In this case the robber's influence was far greater than the "objective" character of his capabilities, and the distorted perception by the clerk led her to act in a manner that was unfavorable to her and her employers.

Finally, as our original model suggests, A may try to influence B *not to do* X. Sometimes this is called "negative" power, where A acts in a manner to *prevent* a certain action it deems undesirable to its interests. This is a very typical relationship and process in international politics. By signing the Munich treaty, for example, the British and French governments hoped to prevent Germany from invading Czechoslovakia: the Soviet government by using a variety of instruments of foreign policy, has sought to prevent West Germany from obtaining nuclear weapons; by organizing the Marshall Plan and NATO, the United States sought to prevent the growth of communism in western Europe and/or a Soviet military invasion of this area.

CAPABILITIES

The second element of the concept of power consists of those capabilities that are mobilized in support of the act of influencing. It is difficult to understand how much influence an actor is likely to wield unless we also have some knowledge of the capabilities that are involved.[5] Nevertheless, it should be acknowledged that social scientists do not understand all the reasons why some actors—whether people, groups, governments, or states—wield influence successfully, while others do not.

It is clear that in political relationships not everyone possesses equal influence. We frequently use the terms "great powers" and "small powers" as a shorthand way of suggesting that some actors make commitments abroad and have the capacity to meet them that others lack. The distinction between the "great powers" and the "small powers" is usually based on some rough estimation of tangible and intangible factors which we have called capabilities. In domestic politics it is possible to construct a lengthy list of those capabilities and attributes which seemingly permit some to wield influence over large numbers of people and over important public decisions. Dahl (1961) lists such tangibles as money, wealth, information, time, political allies, official position, and control over jobs, and such intangibles as personality and leadership qualities. But not everyone who possesses these capabilities can command the obedience or influence the behavior of other people. What is crucial in relating capabilities to influence, according to Dahl, is that the person *mobilize these capabilites for his political purposes,* and that he possess skill in mobilizing them. A person who uses his wealth, time, information, friends, and personality for political purposes will likely be able to influence others on public issues. A person, on the other hand, who possesses the same capabilities but uses them to invent a new mousetrap is not likely to be important in politics.

The same propositions also hold true in international politics. Capabilities may also be tangible or intangible. We can predict that a country in possession of a high Gross National Product, a high level of industrial development, sophisticated weapons systems, and a large population will have more influence and prestige in the system than a state with a primitive economy, small population, and old fashioned armaments. And yet, the intangibles are also important. In addition to the physical resources of a state, such factors as leadership and national morale have to be assessed. We could not, for example, arrive at an estimation of India's influence in world politics unless we regarded the prestige and stature of its leadership abroad.

Moreover, the amount of influence a state wields over others can be related, as in domestic politics, to the capabilities that are

[5]We might assess influence for historical situations solely on the basis of whether A got B to do X, without having knowledge of either A's or B's capabilities.

mobilized in support of foreign policy objectives. Or, to put this proposition in another way, we can argue that a capability does not itself determine the uses to which it will be put. Nuclear power can be used to provide electricity or to coerce and perhaps to destroy other nations. The use of capabilities depends less on their quality and quantity than on the external objectives that a government formulates for itself.

However, the *variety* of foreign policy instruments available to a nation for influencing others is partly a function of the quantity and quality of capabilities. What a government will seek to do, and how it attempts to do it will depend at least partially on the resources it finds available. A country such as Thailand which possesses relatively few and underdeveloped resources cannot, even if it desired, construct nuclear weapons with which to intimidate others, or establish a world-wide propaganda network, or dispense several billion dollars annually of foreign aid to try to influence other countries. And in other international systems, such as in the ancient Hindu interstate system, the level of technology limited the number of capabilities that could be used for external purposes. Kautilya suggested in the *Arthasastra* that only seven elements made up the capability of the state: the excellence (quality) of the king and the ministers, and the quality and quantity of the territory, fortresses, treasury, army, and allies (Law, 1920; Ghoshal, 1947). In general, advanced industrial societies are able to mobilize a wide variety of capabilities in support of their external objectives. We can conclude, therefore, that how states *use* their capabilities depends on their external objectives, but the choice of objectives and the instruments to achieve those objectives are limited or influenced by the quality and quantity of available capabilities.

THE MEASUREMENT OF CAPABILITIES

For many years students of international politics have made meticulous comparisons of the mobilized and potential capabilities of various nations. Comparative data relating to the production of iron ore, coal, hydroelectricity, economic growth rates, educational levels, population growth rates, military resources, transportation systems, and sources of raw materials are presented as indicators of a nation's power. Unfortunately, few have acknowledged that in making these comparisons they are not measuring a state's power or influence, but only its base. Our previous discussion would suggest that such measurements and assessments are not particularly useful unless they are related to the foreign policy objectives of the various states. Capability is always the capability to do something; its assessment, therefore, is most meaningful when carried on within a framework of certain goals and foreign policy objectives.

The deduction of actual influence from the quantity and quality of potential and mobilized capabilities may, in some cases, give an approximation of reality, but historically there have been too many discrepancies between the basis of power and the amount of influence to warrant adopting this practice as a useful approach to international relations. One could have assumed, for example, on the basis of a comparative study of technological and educational level, and general standard of living in the 1920's and 1930's that the United States would have been one of the most influential actors in the international system. A careful comparison of certain resources, called by Simonds and Emeny (1939) the "great essentials," revealed the United States to be in an enviable position. In the period 1925 to 1930, it was the only major country in the world that produced from its own resources adequate supplies of food, power, iron, machinery, chemicals, coal, iron ore, and petroleum. If actual influence had been deduced from the quantities of "great essentials" possessed by the major actors the following ranking of states would have resulted: (1) United States, (2) Germany, (3) Great Britain, (4) France, (5) Russia, (6) Italy, (7) Japan. However, the diplomatic history of the world from 1925 to 1930 would suggest that there was little correlation between the capabilities of these countries and their actual influence. If we measure influence by the impact these actors made on the system and by the responses they could invoke when they sought to change the behavior of other states, we would find for this period quite a different ranking, such as the following: (1) France, (2) Great Britain, (3) Italy, (4) Germany, (5) Russia, (6) Japan, (7) United States.

Other historical discrepancies can also be cited. How, for example, can we explain the ability of the French after their defeat in the Napoleonic wars to become, within a short period of time, one of the most influential members in the Concert of Europe? More recently, how could such figures as Dr. Castro, Colonel Nasser and Marshal Tito successfully defy the pressure of the great powers? The answer to these questions lies not solely in the physical capabilities of states, but partly in the personalities and diplomacy of political leaders, the reactions of the major powers, and other special circumstances. Hence, the ability of A to change the behavior of B is enhanced if it possesses physical capabilities which it can use in the influence act; but B is by no means defenseless because it fails to own a large army, raw materials, and money for foreign aid. Persuasiveness is often related to such intangibles as personality, perceptions, friendships, traditions, and customs, all of which are almost impossible to measure accurately.

The discrepancy between physical capabilities and actual influence can also be related to credibility. A nuclear capability, for example, is often thought to increase radically the diplomatic influence of those who develop it. Yet, the important aspect of a nuclear capability is not its possession, but the willingness to use it if necessary. Other actors must know that the capability is not of mere symbolic significance. Thus, a leader like Dr. Castro possesses a particular psychological advantage over the United States (hence, influence) because he knows that in almost all circumstances the American government would not use strategic nuclear weapons against his country. He has, therefore, effectively broken through the significance of the American nuclear capability as far as Cuban-American relations are concerned.

Finally, discrepancies between actors' physical capabilities and their actual influence can be traced to the habit of analyzing capabilities only in terms of a single state. The wielding of influence in modern international politics is, however, seldom a bilateral process. In a system where all states perceive some involvement and relationship with all other actors, governments seek to use the capabilities and diplomatic influence of other actors by forming diplomatic or military coalitions. Indeed, modern diplomacy is largely concerned with eliciting support of friends and neutrals, presumably because widespread diplomatic support for an actor's policies increases the legitimacy of those objections, thereby increasing the influence of the actor. "Small" states in particular can increase their influence if they can gain commitments of support from other members of the system.[6] If there are so many factors which distort the relationship between physical capabilities and actual influence, how do we proceed to measure influence? Assessment of physical capabilities may be adequate for rough estimations of influence or war potential and in some circumstances it may suffice to rely on reputations of power. But for precise knowledge, we have to refer to the actual processes of international politics and not to charts or indices of raw materials. We can best measure influence, according to

---

[6]This is one reason why international conflicts seldom remain confined to the original disputants. Recognizing the dangers of increasing the number of parties to a dispute, the United Nations has sought to "isolate" conflicts as much as possible.

Dahl (1957), by studying the *responses* of those who are in the influence relationship. If A can get B to do X, but C cannot get B to do the same thing, then in reference to that particular action, A has more influence. Or, if B does X despite the protestations of A, then we can assume that A, in this circumstance, did not enjoy much influence over B. It is meaningless to argue that the Soviet Union is more powerful than the United States unless we cite how, for what purposes, and in relation to whom, the Soviet Union and the United States are exerting influence. We may conclude, then, that capabilities themselves do not always lead to the successful wielding of influence and that other variables have to be considered as well. In general, influence varies with (1) the type of goals an actor pursues, (2) the quality and quantity of capabilities (including allies and intangibles) at its disposal, (3) the skill in mobilizing these capabilities in support of the goals, and (4) the credibility of threats and rewards.

HOW INFLUENCE IS EXERCISED

Social scientists have noted several fundamental techniques that individuals and groups use to influence each other. In a political system which contains no one legitimate center of authority (such as a government, or a father in a family) that can command the members of the group or society, bargaining has to be used among the sovereign entities. A. F. K. Organski (1958), Charles Schleicher (1962), and Quincy Wright (1951) suggest four typical bargaining techniques in international politics[7] : persuasion, offering rewards, threatening punishments, and the use of force. These categories are very useful for analyzing the wielding of influence in the system, but they can be expanded and refined to account for slightly different forms of behavior. Recalling that A seeks one of three courses of conduct from B (e.g., B to do X in the future, B not to do X in the future, and B to continue doing X) it may use six different tactics.

---

[7] Francois de Callieres, a renowned French diplomat of the eighteenth century, also suggested these techniques when he wrote: "Every Christian prince must take as his chief maxim not to employ arms to support or vindicate his rights until he has employed and exhausted the way of reason and persuasion. It is to his interest also, to add to reason and persuasion the influence of benefits conferred, which indeed is one of the surest ways to make his own power secure, and to increase it. *On The Manner of Negotiating with Princes,* trans. by A. F. Whyte, p. 7 (1919).

1. *Persuasion.* Persuasion may include threats, rewards and actual punishments, but we will mean here those situations in which an actor simply initiates or discusses a proposal or situation with another and elicits a favorable response without explicitly holding out the possibility of rewards or punishments. We cannot assume that the exercise of influence is always *against* the wishes of others and that there are only two possible outcomes of the act, one favoring A, the other favoring B. For example, state A asks B to support it at a coming international conference on the control of narcotics. State B might not originally have any particular interest in the conference or its outcome, but decides, on the basis of A's initiative, that something positive might be gained not only by supporting A's proposals, but also by attending the conference. In this case there might also be the expectation of gaining some type of reward in the future, but not necessarily from A.

2. *The offer of rewards.* This is the situation where A promises to do something favorable to B if B complies with the wishes of A. Rewards may be of almost any type in international relations. To gain the diplomatic support of B at the narcotics conference, A may offer to increase foreign aid payments, to lower tariffs on goods imported from B, to support B at a later conference on communications facilities, or it may promise to remove a previous punishment. The latter tactic is used often by Soviet negotiators. After having created an unfavorable situation, they promise to remove it in return for some concessions by their opponents.

3. *The granting of rewards.* In some instances, the credibility of an actor is not very high and state B, before complying with A's wishes, may insist that A actually give the reward in advance. Frequently in armistice negotiations neither side will unilaterally take steps to demilitarize an area or to demobilize troops until the other shows evidence of complying with the agreements. One of the cliches of cold war diplomacy holds that deeds, not words, are required for the granting of rewards and concessions.

4. *The threat of punishment.* Threats of punishment may be further subdivided into two types:

   (a) positive threats, where, for example, state A threatens to increase tariffs, to cut off diplomatic relations, to institute a boycott or embargo against trade with B, or to use force.

(b) threats of deprivation, where A threatens to withdraw foreign aid or in other ways to withhold rewards or other advantages that it already grants to B.

5. *The infliction of non-violent punishment.* In this situation, threats are carried out in the hope of altering B's behavior which, in most cases, could not be altered by other means. The problem with this tactic is that it usually results in reciprocal measures by the other side, thus inflicting damage on both, though not necessarily bringing about a desired state of affairs. If, for example, A threatens to increase its military capabilities if B does X and then proceeds to implement the threat, it is not often that B will comply with A's wishes because it, too, can increase its military capabilities easily enough. In this type of a situation, then, both sides indulge in the application of punishments which may escalate into more serious form unless the conflict is resolved.

6. *Force.* In previous eras when governments did not possess the variety of foreign policy instruments that are available today, they had to rely frequently in the bargaining process upon the use of force. Force and violence were not only the most efficient tactics, but in many cases they were the only means possible for influencing. Today, the situation is different. As technological levels rise, other means of inducement become available and can serve as substitutes for force.[8]

PATTERNS OF INFLUENCE IN THE INTERNATIONAL SYSTEM

Most governments at one time or another use all of these techniques for influencing others, but probably over ninety per cent of all relations between states are based on simple persuasion and deal with relatively unimportant technical matters. Since such inter-actions seldom make the headlines, however, we often assume that most relations between states involve the making or carrying out of threats. But whether a government is communicating with another

---

[8]Presumably, therefore, disarmament and arms control would become more feasible because other instruments of policy can be used in the influence act. In previous eras, to disarm would have led to the collapse of the most important—if not only—capability that could be mobilized for foreign policy purposes.

over an unimportant technical matter or over a subject of great consequence, it is likely to use a particular type of tactic in its attempts to influence, depending on the general climate of relations between those two governments. Allies, for example, seldom threaten each other with force or even make blatant threats of punishment. Similarly, governments which disagree over a wide range of policy objectives are more likely to resort to threats and to the imposition of punishments. We can suggest, therefore, that just as there are observable patterns of relations between states in terms of their foreign policy strategies (alliances, isolation, neutrality, etc.), there are also general patterns of relations between actors with reference to the methods used to influence each other. The methods of exerting influence between Great Britain and the United States are typically those of persuasion and rewards, while the methods of exerting influence between the Soviet Union and the United States in the early post World War II era were typically those of threatening and inflicting punishments of various types. Since such typical patterns exist, we can then construct rough typologies of international relationships as identified by the typical techniques used in the act of influence.

1. *Relations of consensus.* Relations of consensus would be typical between actors that had few disagreements over foreign policy objectives, and/or had a very low level of interaction and involvement in each other's affairs. An example of the former would be Anglo-American relations, and of the latter, the relations between Thailand and Bolivia. In the relations of consensus, moreover, influence is exercised primarily by the technique of persuasion and through the subtle offering of rewards. Finally, since violence as a form of punishment is almost inconceivable between two countries, the military capabilities of neither actor are organized, mobilized, and "targeted" toward the other.

2. *Relations of overt manipulation.* Here, there may be some disagreement or conflict over foreign policy objectives, or state A might undertake some domestic policy which was disapproved by state B, such as a form of racial discrimination. Since there is some conflict, there will also be at least a modest degree of involvement between the two actors, or a perception that A and B are in some kind of a relationship of interdependence. The techniques used to influence will include, if normal persuasion fails, (a) offers of rewards, (b) the granting of rewards, (c)

threats to withhold rewards (e.g., not to give foreign aid in the future), or (d) threats of non-violent punishment, including, for example, the raising of tariffs against B's products. Militarily, in relations of overt manipulation, there is still no mobilization or targeting of military capabilities toward state B. Examples of overt manipulation would include the relations between China and the Soviet Union, 1960-1963, and the relations between France and the United States during this same period.

3. *Relations of coercion.* In relations of coercion, there are fundamental disagreements over foreign policy objectives. Almost all actions that A takes externally are perceived by B to be a threat to its own interests. Involvement is, therefore, high. A seeks to influence B's behavior typically by (a) threatening punishments, (b) by inflicting non-violent punishments and under extreme provocation, (c) by the selective and limited use of force as, for example, in a peace-time blockade. Military capabilities, finally, are likely to be targeted towards each other. Examples would include the Soviet Union and the western coalition for most of the period since 1947, Cuba and the United States between 1960 and 1963, Nazi Germany and Czechoslovakia between 1937 and 1939, and Egypt and Israel since 1948.

4. *Relations of force.* Here, there is almost total disagreement on foreign policy objectives and the areas of consensus are limited to a few necessities such as communications. The degree of involvement is obviously extremely high. The typical form of exercising influence is through the infliction of violent punishment, though in some instances rewards (e.g., peace offers) might be offered. National capabilities are mobilized primarily with a view to conducting the policy of punishment. However, the quantity of military capabilities that is used will vary with the geographic and force-level boundaries which the disputants place on the conflict.

Though most relations between states could be placed in one of the previous categories, it should also be apparent that under changing circumstances, governments are required to resort to techniques of influence toward others that they would normally avoid. However, the cold war represents a curious phenomenon in the history of international politics because in the relations between east and west *all* of the techniques of influence are being used simultaneously. There are several areas of policy where consensus exists between the Soviet Union and the leaders of the west and where agreements—either in treaties or through "understandings"—can be reached without making threats or imposing punishments.[9] There are also areas of great controversy where the antagonists commit military capabilities and seek to influence each other's behavior most of the time by making threats and carrying out various forms of punishment.

To summarize this analysis of power, we can suggest that power is an integral part of all political relationships, but in international politics we are interested primarily in one process: how does one state influence the behavior of another in its own interests. The act of influencing becomes, therefore, a central focus for the study of international politics and it is from this act that we can best deduce a definition of power. If we observe the act of influencing, we can see that it is a process, a relationship, a means to an end, and even a quantity. Moreover, we can make an analytical distinction between the act of influencing, the basis, or capabilities, upon which the act relies, and the response to the act. Capabilities are an important determinant of how successful the wielding of influence will be, but they are by no means the only determinant. The nature of a country's foreign policy objectives and the skill with which an actor mobilizes its capabilities for foreign policy purposes are equally important.

The act of influencing may be carried out by a variety of means, the most important of which are the offer and granting of rewards, the threat and imposition of punishment, and the application of force. The choice of means used to induce will depend, in turn, upon the general nature of relations between two governments and on the degree of involvement among actors in the system.

This formulation of the power concept will not, of course, be useful for all aspects of the study of international relations. The categories are mental constructs imposed upon reality for the purpose of clarifying certain aspects of reality. They cannot be expected to cover all international relationships, however. They fail to account for such questions as the determination of national goals or governmental decision-making processes. They will not alert the investigator or student to certain processes in bilateral or multilateral systems that contain complex patterns of economic, technical, and military relations. Questions dealing with trade relations, export

[9] Areas of agreement between the Soviet Union and the west which have resulted either in treaties or "understandings" would include the cessation of nuclear tests, the demilitarization of the Antarctic and, possibly, outer space, the renouncing of nuclear war as an instrument of policy, and efforts to prevent the spread of nuclear weapons.

134 The International Political System

credits, or investment incentives—all areas of interest in the study—are often decided on the basis of technical criteria by specialists who cannot mobilize national capabilities for bargaining purposes. Power, no matter how defined, seems particularly inappropriate as a tool for analyzing relations in a highly integrated international community, such as exists in Scandinavia or North America. The concept of leadership might be more appropriate for these relations. In addition, the state A-state B relationship does not seem to account for the activities of various international functional groups (technical, scientific, and economic) which act in concert across traditional national jurisdictions. In short, the concept of power cannot serve, as many have argued, as the core of a theory of international relations. But it can indicate areas of inquiry for further research in international processes and, if formulated carefully, it may become for the first time an important teaching device as well.

REFERENCES

Dahl, Robert A. "The Concept of Power," *Behavioral Science*, 2(1957), 201-15.

———————. *Who Governs?* New Haven: Yale University Press, 1961.

de Callieres, Francois. *On the Manner of Negotiating with Princes.* trans. A. F. Whyte; Boston: Hougton Mifflin Co., 1919.

Ghoshal, U. N. "The System of Inter-State Relations and Foreign Policy in the Early Arthasastra State," *India Antiqua.* Leyden: E. J. Brill, 1947.

Kalijarvi, Thorsten V. *Modern World Politics.* New York: Thomas Y. Crowell, 1953.

Law, Narandra Nath. *Inter-state Relations in Ancient India.* London: Luzac, 1920.

Morgenthau, Hans. *Politics Among Nations.* New York: Alfred A. Knopf, 1960.

Organski, A. F. K. *World Politics.* New York: Alfred A. Knopf. 1958.

Schleicher, Charles P. *International Relations: Cooperation and Conflict.* Englewood Cliffs, New Jersy: Prentice-Hall, 1962.

Simon, Herbert A. "Notes on the Observation and Measurement of Political Power," *The Journal of Politics*, 15 (1953), 500-16.

Simonds, Frank H., and Emeny, Brooks. *The Great Powers in World Politics.* New York: The American Book Co., 1939.

Singer, J. David. "Inter-Nation Influence: A Formal Model," *American Political Science Review*, 57 (1963), 420-30.

Stoessinger, John G. *The Might of Nations: World Politics In Our Time.* New York: Random House, 1961.

Strausz-Hupé, Robert, and Possony, Stefan. *International Relations.* New York: McGraw-Hill, 1950.

Wright, Quincy. "The Nature of Conflict," *The Western Political Quarterly*, 4 (1951), 193-209.

On the Concepts
of Politics
and Power
Karl W. Deutsch

SOME CONCEPTS ABOUT POLITICS

Among the vast number of human relations, which ones are *political?* What does politics do that other human activities and institutions do not do?

Politics consists of the more or less incomplete control of human behavior through voluntary habits of *compliance* in combination with threats of probable *enforcement*. In its essence, politics is based on the interplay of these two things: habits and threats.

The *habits* of behaving, cooperating, obeying the law, or respecting some decision as binding tend to be voluntary for most people. For habits are part of our nature and of the way we more or less automatically act. Without these habits, there could be no law and no government as we know them. Only because most drivers stick to the right-hand side of the road and stop at red lights can the traffic code be enforced at a tolerable cost. Only because most people do not steal cars can the police protect our streets against the

SOURCE: From *Journal of International Affairs*, Vol. XXI, No. 2 (1967), pp. 232-41. Copyright © 1967 by the Board of Editors of the *Journal of International Affairs*. Reprinted by permission of the author and the *Journal*.

135

few who do. If a law is not obeyed voluntarily and habitually by, say, at least 90 per cent of the people, either it becomes a dead letter, or it becomes very expensive to enforce, or it becomes a noble but unreliable experiment like Prohibition. The voluntary or habitual compliance of the mass of the population is the invisible but very real basis of power for every government.

Although this compliance is largely voluntary, it is not entirely so. If it were, we would be dealing not with politics but with folkways, custom, and morality. In politics, the compliance habits of the many are preserved and reinforced by the *probability of enforcement* against the few who may transgress the law or disobey the government.

Enforcement consists of the threat or the use of rewards or punishments. In practice, punishments are used more often than rewards. Punishments are usually cheaper; some people enjoy applying them under an ideological pretext, such as Communism or anti-Communism; and many people think they are more reliable. Clearly, where most people are in the habit of obeying the law anyhow, it would seem costly and needless to offer them rewards for it; it seems cheaper and more efficient to threaten penalties for the few who disobey. Punishments may deter some transgressors from repeating their offense, but it is more important that they deter others from following their example.

Enforcement usually is not certain; it is only probable. But ordinarily the likelihood of enforcement, together with the compliance habits of most of the population, is enough to keep the proportion of serious transgressions down to a tolerable level. The punishment of nine out of ten murderers might be enough to deter a good share of those who might otherwise commit premeditated murder. And convictions in only one-fourth of the automobile-theft cases might suffice, together with the law-abiding habits of most people, to prevent most automobile thefts.

Even the most certain or most cruel punishments, of course, do not deter those murderers who are too thoughtless, too confident, or too passionately excited to care or think realistically about the chance of getting caught. This fact points up one of the weaknesses of deterrence, whether against murder or war.

The conditions that determine the effectiveness of enforcement are much the same as those that determine the frequency of obedient or law-abiding behavior. Most significant among these are the strength of the compliance habits of the bulk of the people, and their willingness to give active support to the government in upholding its commands and laws. Next in importance are all the other conditions that influence the relative probabilities of law-abiding vs. law-breaking behavior to which the threat of enforcement is being applied. (E.g., if there is hunger among the poor, more people are likely to steal bread.) The size and efficiency of the enforcement apparatus ranks only third in importance. Least important are the processes of changing rules, passing new laws, or threatening more severe punishments.

However, mass habits of compliance and general social conditions, the most powerful long-run influences on the behavior of the population, are the most difficult to manipulate. Even the size, training, equipment, and morale of the enforcement personnel—the armed forces, police, judiciary, and to some extent the civil service—can be changed only slowly and at great cost. The weakest lever of control· thus becomes attractive because it is the easiest to use. Passing another law, threatening a more severe penalty, or relaxing the standards of legal justice are much cheaper and quicker, and hence often more attractive than the longer and harder task of effecting more fundamental changes in the situation.

Politics, then, is the interplay of enforcement threats, which can be changed fairly quickly, with the existing loyalties and compliance habits of the population, which are more powerful but harder to change. Through this interplay of habitual compliance and probable enforcement, societies protect and modify their institutions, the allocation and reallocation of their resources, the distribution of values, incentives, and rewards among their population, and the patterns of teamwork in which people cooperate in the production of goods, services, and offspring.

Rule or Dominion. With this concept of politics clearly in mind, we can readily understand the two related concepts of *rule* or *dominion.* By the rule or dominion of a leader, the German sociologist Max Weber meant the chance or probability of his being obeyed. Of two leaders or governments, according to Weber's reasoning, the one more likely to be obeyed by a given population has more dominion over them.

If we carry this reasoning a little further, we recognize what T. W. Adorno once called "the implicit mathematics in Max Weber's thought."[1] A probability, strictly speaking, is a number denoting the frequency, usually expressed as a percentage, with which events of a certain type (in this case acts of obedience to the commands of the ruler) occur within a larger ensemble of events (in this case the

[1] T. W. Adorno, "Oral Communication," 15th German Congress of Sociology (Max Weber Centenary), Heidelberg, May 1964.

general behavior of the population). Weber's concept of rule can therefore be expressed as a number. At least in principle, it can be measured in quantitative terms.

At the same time, we can see the close relationship between Weber's idea of the chance or frequency of acts of obedience and our own concept of the rate of compliance. The latter concept is somewhat broader, in that it includes passively compliant behavior as well as the more positive acts of obedience emphasized by Weber, whenever such behavior significantly influences the outcome of the political process.

Our concept of *habitual* compliance, however, is somewhat narrower than Weber's "chance of being obeyed," excluding as it does acts of submission to the immediate threat of naked force. People obey a gunman in a holdup or a foreign army of occupation so long as they have guns pointed at them. Weber's concept of "rule" or "dominion" covers such cases of obedience under duress. But it should be noted that the obedience is exacted through processes of force, not of politics. They become political only insofar as the obedient behavior continues after the gunman's or the invader's back is turned. Only then, in the interplay of remembered fear and continuing compliance, are we dealing with politics.

When we say that politics is that realm of human affairs where domination and habitual compliance overlap, we are implying that politics, owing to its double nature, is apt to be an area of recurrent tension between centralization and decentralization. For domination or rule usually can be exercised more easily by centralized organizations; threats of enforcement, too, can be manipulated more effectively from a single center. But the dependable habits of large numbers of people can be created rarely, if ever, through a single center of command; nor can they be created quickly. Habits more often develop from a multitude of different experiences repeated over time in many ways. The centralized use of threats or force rarely creates, therefore, a durable community of politically relevant habits; it is much more often such a community of habits that provides the possibilities for the exercise of centralized power.

THE CONCEPT OF POWER

Recognizing the dual nature of politics also helps us to see the limits of the concept of political power. Some brilliant writers have tried to build a theory of politics, and particularly of international relations, largely or entirely upon the notion of power. This is the approach of classical theorists like Machiavelli and Hobbes, as well as of contemporary theorists like Morgenthau and Schuman. The notion of power as the basis of international politics is also widespread in the popular press and even in the foreign services and defense establishments of many countries. What is the element of truth contained in this notion, and what are its limits?

Power, put simply and crudely, is the ability to prevail in conflict and to overcome obstacles. It was in this sense that Lenin, before the Russian Revolution, posed to his followers a key problem of politics with the question, "Who Whom?" Who was to be the master of actions and events, and who was to be their object and victim? In the 1932 depression, a German protest song called up a related image: "We shall be hammers, not anvils," it announced. Who is stronger and who is weaker? Who will get his way and who will have to give in?

Such questions as these, when asked about actual or possible encounters among a limited number of competitors, lead to rank lists, such as the rankings of baseball clubs in the pennant races, of chickens in the pecking order, and of great powers in world politics. The fewer actual encounters that have occurred, of course, the more such rank lists must be built up from hypotheses based upon the past performance and the existing or potential resources of the contestants.

POTENTIAL POWER, AS INFERRED
FROM RESOURCES

An example of the relative power potential of two coalitions of nations appears in Table 1.[2] Here the power of the Allied and Axis countries in World War II is measured, or at least suggested, by the millions of tons of munitions that each side produced each year.

The table reveals that the Axis powers produced far more munitions than the Allies in 1938, 1939, 1940, and 1941, but that their lead diminished in 1942 and was decisively lost in 1943, the year Winston Churchill aptly dubbed "the hinge of fate." After this turning point, the Axis powers fell ever further behind until their collapse in 1945.

Table 2 provides a hypothetical ranking of the power potential of the major nations for the period 1960 to 1963 and projects another one for 1980.[3]

---

[2]Klaus E. Knorr, *The War Potential of Nations* (Princeton: Princeton University Press, 1956), p. 34.

[3]From data in Wilhelm Fuchs, *Formeln zur Macht: Prognosen über Völker, Wirtschaft, Potentiale* (Stuttgart: Deutsche Verlagsanstalt, 1965), figs. 37-38, pp. 129-31.

TABLE 1 Combat-Munitions[a] Output of the Main Belligerents, 1938-1943 (percentage of total)

Country	1938	1939	1940	1941	1942	1943
United States	6	4	7	14	30	40
Canada	0	0	0	1	2	2
Britain	6	10	18	19	15	13
U.S.S.R.	27	31	23	24	17	15
Total, United Nations	39	45	48	58	64	70
Germany[b]	46	43	40	31	27	22
Italy	6	4	5	4	3	1
Japan	9	8	7	7	6	7
Total, Axis Countries	61	55	52	42	36	30
Grand Total	100	100	100	100	100	100

[a]Includes aircraft, army ordnance and signal equipment, naval vessels, and related equipment.
[b]Includes occupied territories.

TABLE 2 Some Hypothetical Rank Orderings of the Power Potential of Major Countries, 1960-63 and 1980 (Based on Energy Production, Steel Output, and Population)

Index Values: U.S. 1960 = 100			
Computed from:			
Actual Figures for 1960-63 Rank		Projections for 1980	
1. U.S.	100	1. China	250
2. U.S.S.R.	67	2. U.S.	160
3. China	41	3. U.S.S.R.	120
4. German Federal Republic	15	4. Japan	39
5. Japan	14	5. German Federal Republic	25
6. Britain	12	6. Britain	19
7. France	7	7. France	11
Total	256	Total	624

The 1980 estimates are based on projected increases in per-capita steel and energy production and total population in each country. (E.g., for China an annual per-capita steel output of about 400 lbs., or roughly one-half the 1963 level of the U.S.S.R. and of Japan, and a population of about 1,100 million are projected.) No one, of course, can yet be sure whether these projections are realistic. In any case, it seems noteworthy that the power of the strongest single country in both periods is rated at well below one-half of the total power of the first seven countries.

THE WEIGHT OF POWER, AS INFERRED FROM RESULTS

Power potential is a rough estimate of the material and human resources available for power. Indirectly, it can be used to infer how successful a country should be in a contest of power, if it uses its resources to advantage. Conversely, the *weight* of an actor's power can be inferred from his success at influencing outcomes in the international system.

The weight of an actor's power or influence over some process is the extent to which he can change the probability of its outcome. This can be measured most easily when we are dealing with a repetitive class of similar outcomes, such as votes in the UN General Assembly. Suppose, for instance, that in the Assembly motions supported by the United States pass on the average of three times out of four, or with a probability of 75 per cent, while those motions not supported by the United States pass only 25 per cent of the time. We then might say that U.S. support can shift a motion's chances of success on the average of from 25 to 75 per cent, that is, by 50 percentage points. These 50 percentage points then would be a rough measure of the average weight of U.S. power in the General Assembly. (The measure is a rough one, and it may understate the real influence of the United States, since anticipated U.S. opposition may be enough to discourage many motions from even being proposed.)

Estimating the weight of power is more difficult when we are dealing with a single event. How much power did the dropping of an atom bomb on Hiroshima, for example, exert in terms of its influence on the Japanese decision to surrender? An outstanding expert on Japan, former Ambassador Edwin O. Reischauer, concludes that the bomb shortened the war by only a few days.[4] To make such a judgment, it is necessary to imagine that the unique event—the attack on Hiroshima at a time when Japan was exhausted and seeking a way to surrender—had occurred many times. One would then try to imagine the average outcome for two sets of

[4]Edwin O. Reischauer, *The United States and Japan*, rev. ed. (Cambridge: Harvard University Press, 1957), p. 240.

hypothetical cases: those in which a bomb was dropped, and those in which it was not.

This might seem farfetched, but it is not. Indeed, it is not very different from the reasoning of an engineer trying to determine why a bridge collapsed, or of a physician trying to determine why a patient died. In order to estimate the effect of what was done, and perhaps to estimate what should have been done, we convert the unique event into a member of a repetitive class of similar hypothetical events. We then try to estimate the extent and probability of alternative outcomes in the presence and in the absence, respectively, of the action or condition whose power we wish to gauge. Finally, we infer the power of the actor in the situation from the power of the act or the condition he controls. Power considered in this way is much the same thing as causality; and the weight of an actor's power is the same as the weight of those causes of an outcome that are under his control.

Modern governments have greatly increased the weight of their power over their own populations. Taxes are collected, soldiers drafted, laws enforced, and lawbreakers arrested with a much higher probability than in the past. By the same token, the weight of government power in industrially advanced countries usually is much greater than that in the developing nations, although there are wide variations among the latter.

In world politics, on the contrary, the weight of the power of most governments, and particularly of the great powers, has been declining ever since 1945. No government today has as much control over the probable outcome of world affairs as had Great Britain, say, between 1870 and 1935. At present Britain cannot control India, Pakistan, Nigeria, or Rhodesia; the United States cannot control Cuba, and certainly not France; the Soviet Union cannot control Albania, Yugoslavia, or China; and China cannot control Indonesia or Burma.

At a closer look, the weight of power may actually include two different concepts. The first deals with the ability to *reduce* the probability of an outcome *not* desired by an actor. In domestic politics we sometimes speak of "veto groups" that can prevent or make unlikely the passage of some piece of legislation they dislike. In international politics, we find a very considerable veto power of the five permanent members of the UN Security Council formally embodied in the UN Charter. Less formally, we may speak of the power of a government to deny some territory or sphere of influence to some other government or ideological movement. Thus the United States in the 1950's successfully denied South Korea to its North

Korean attackers, and it is currently denying much of South Vietnam to the Viet Cong.

It should be easy to see why this is so. The specific outcome that we may wish to prevent may not be very probable in the first place. Suppose that Communist guerrillas in an Asian or African country had roughly one chance in three (33 per cent) of establishing a stable Communist regime. In that case, an anti-Communist intervention carried out with limited power—say with a weight of about 28 per cent—could reduce the guerrillas' chances of success from 33 per cent to only 5 per cent. In other words, the probability of their failure would be 19:1. Outcomes that are already moderately improbable thus can be made highly improbable by the application of a relatively limited amount of power. In such situations, the change in the probabilities of a particular outcome will seem quite drastic. The limited use of power will seem to have changed great uncertainty into near certainty and thus to have produced spectacular results.

The same weight of power produces far less impressive results, however, when it is used to promote an outcome that is fairly improbable in the first place. Suppose we wish to produce a stable constitutional, democratic regime in that strife-torn Asian or African country of our example. With the knowledge that only about one out of every twenty of the developing countries has a stable democratic government, we can estimate that such a venture will have about a 5 per cent chance of success. Thus, applying power with a weight of 28 per cent would still only produce a 33 per cent probability that a democratic regime could be established. We would still be left with a 2:1 chance for its failure.

Even this calculation is far too optimistic. For it has unjustifiably assumed that power to promote one outcome can be transformed without loss into the same amount of power to produce another. We all know every well that this is not true. The power to knock a man down does not give us the power to teach him to play the piano. The power to bomb and burn a village cannot be completely or easily transformed into the power to win the sympathies of its inhabitants, to govern it with their consent, or even less to produce among them the many skills, values, and freely given loyalties that are essential to democratic government.

The more specific a desired positive outcome is, the more alternatives are excluded by it. Hence, it usually is less probable; and moreover, the application of limited power cannot ordinarily make it highly probable. Limited power is most effective when used negatively to veto or deny some specific outcome. Such a use of power increases the already considerable probability of an entire range of possible alternatives to it, with little or no regard as to which particular alternative happens to materialize.

The power to increase the probability of a specific positive outcome is the power of *goal attainment* and of *control* over one's environment. Like all goal attainment and control, it implies a high degree of self-control on the part of the actor. A charging elephant can smash down a large obstacle, but he cannot thread a needle. Indeed, he cannot make a right-angled turn within a three-foot radius. The greater the brute power, mass, speed, and momentum of the elephant, the harder it is for him to control his own motions, and the less precise his control becomes. Driving offers a similar illustration. The bigger, heavier, faster, and more powerful the car, the harder it is to steer. An attempt to measure its power in terms of its performance would give us, therefore, at least two different ratings: a high one for its power to accelerate and a low one for its power to stop or turn.

Does something similar hold for the power of governments and nations? The larger a country is, the more numerous its population, and the larger the proportion of its population and resources mobilized for the pursuit of some policy (and, we may add, the more intense and unreserved their emotional commitment to that policy), the greater is likely to be its power to overcome any obstacles in its path. But national policies usually require more than surmounting obstacles. Often they aim at specific positive results. They may require, therefore, the pursuit of a constant goal through a sequence of changing tactics, or even the preservation or enhancement of a basic value through a succession of changing goals. The more people and resources have been committed to the earlier tactics, policies, or goals, however, and the more intensely and unreservedly this has been done, the more interests, careers, reputations, and emotions have become committed to the old policy, and the harder it may be for any member of the government, or even for the entire government, to propose a change. Unless substantial and timely precautions are taken, therefore, governments may become prisoners of their past policies and power may become a trap.

This danger tends to grow with the amount of national power and with the breadth and intensity of efforts to increase it. Ordinarily, therefore, the danger of losing self-control is greater for large nations than for small ones, for dictatorships than for democracies, and in wartime—hot or cold—than in peacetime. If this danger is not guarded against, the weight of power in the long run may become self-defeating, self-negating, or self-destructive.

The Concept of
Military Potential

Klaus Knorr

The military potential of states is one of the bases of military power. This potential is equal to the national resources available for producing and maintaining armed forces. Whenever a nation creates or expands military forces in peace or war, it mobilizes military potential. The concept is concerned with an input-output relationship. Available and suitable resources are the input; military forces, or strength, are the output.

Although the focus of this chapter is on national military potential as preliminarily defined—that is, on factors available for *producing* military strength—it will also be concerned throughout with national potential for *employing* military strength, since many of the factors determining the one potential also determine the other.

SOURCE: From Klaus Knorr, *Military Power and Potential.* Copyright © 1970 by D.C. Heath and Company. Reprinted and abridged by permission of the author and D.C. Heath and Company.

POTENTIAL FOR WHAT?

The study of military potential is a kind of capability analysis. As has been rightly observed, capabilities can be sensibly estimated only with reference to particular objectives, strategies and contingencies.[1] The relevant questions are: what is to be accomplished, by which courses of action, and under what circumstances? Throughout this study the reader should keep in mind this element of conditionality in the evaluation of military potential. However, this does not mean that goals, strategies and contingencies must be precisely predicted prior to utilizing capability analysis. Planners of foreign and military policy would be paralyzed if this were so. In fact, there are types of objectives, strategies and contingencies which can be analyzed and projected. Furthermore, the observed relationship is reciprocal. It is not only that capabilities are meaningful merely with reference to objectives, strategies and operational conditions. National capabilities also have a bearing on the choice of objectives and strategies, and through these choices they influence the probability with which some contingencies will arise. Certainly, historical experience with contests of military forces makes it plain that future contingencies are not predictable with any degree of confidence. It is nevertheless possible and useful to conjecture about kinds of contingencies.[2] Indeed, in view of the inevitable intrusion of uncertainties about the future, their rational consideration and the provision for flexibility is an important part of overall capability. . . .

A HISTORICAL NOTE ON
"WAR POTENTIAL"

During the latter part of the nineteenth century, concern with military potential was focused on the narrower concept of *war potential;* this concept remained in use through World War II and continues in more limited use up to the present time. As the words imply, the concept concerns economic resources available for mobilization in time of war. It was important especially during the

---

[1] *Cf.* Harold and Margaret Sprout, *An Ecological Paradigm for the Study of International Politics,* Princeton University, Center of International Studies, Research Monograph No. 30 (1968), p. 35.

[2] *Cf.* Klaus Knorr and Oskar Morgenstern, *Political Conjecture in Military Planning,* Princeton University, Center of International Studies, Policy Memorandum No. 35 (1968).

sixty-year period from the 1880's to the 1940's, after industrialization had begun greatly to increase the productive power of the
technologically more advanced nations. During this period states did
not normally maintain in peacetime the size of military forces which
they were capable of mobilizing in wartime. For example, in 1939,
Germany produced only 20 percent of the volume of combat
munitions which it manufactured in 1944. Similarly, the United
Kingdom turned out in 1940 one third of the combat munitions it
was to produce in 1944; and the United States and Japan produced
as late as 1942 a mere half of their munitions output in 1944.[3]

In peacetime, nations naturally preferred to limit military expenditures in order to employ more resources for consumption and
investment; and they were able to do so for two reasons. First, they
all adhered to the same practice, which reduced the risk of insufficient mobilization for any single nation. To be sure, occasional
arms races would lead to an additional mobilization of resources, but
even then outlays on military strength stayed usually far short of the
level feasible in time of war. Second, nations could usually afford to
follow this practice without assuming undue risk because, given the
state of military technology during these sixty years, governments
could count on ample time for the mobilization of potential
strength. This process often began when severe international crises
occurred, and it could be completed after the outbreak of hostilities
as long as the ready military forces on hand could prevent a quick
military decision favoring the opponent. Under these circumstances,
when statesmen resorted to estimates of military power, as they were
often forced to do in the pursuit of foreign policy, or when military
staffs prepared war plans for likely contingencies, they obviously had
to reckon with more than the national military forces on hand. War
potential could not be neglected. It was recognized to be part of a
state's military power.

War potential played a crucial part in the outcomes of World Wars
I and II, for these were essentially wars of attrition. In both
instances, the coalition with inferior manpower and industrial
capacity lost to the coalition with superior resources. Indeed, World
War II is especially interesting in this respect since Germany, having
mobilized before the war substantially more resources than its future
enemies, began hostilities with a considerable advantage. From 1935
to 1939, the volume of combat munitions (measured in U.S. dollars

[3] R. W. Goldsmith, "The Power of Victory: Munitions Output in World War
II," *Military Affairs*, X (1946), p. 72.

at 1944 munitions prices) produced by the main countries was: Germany $12.0 billion, Soviet Russia $8.0 billion, Britain $2.5 billion, Japan $2.0 billion, and the United States $1.5 billion.[4] Since war is fought on the basis of accumulated as well as currently produced munitions, Germany had clearly a great advantage at the outset, and this fact may account in part for her early victories. . . . While in 1939 the Axis countries still accounted for 55 percent of the total output of combat munitions, four years later their share had dropped to 30 percent. In that year, the United States alone outproduced Germany, Italy and Japan together by a third. This gradual change in munitions production parallels closely the changing turn in the fortunes of war.

· · ·

Shortly after the events of World War II had strikingly emphasized the importance of war potential, and particularly industrial war potential, as a base of military strength, the advent of the nuclear bomb led many observers to question, if not deny outright, the future usefulness of the concept. Since a small number of nuclear bombs could cripple, if not completely destroy, any country, and since no effective defense existed against delivery vehicles, it was inferred that a war between nuclear powers, or perhaps even a war involving one nuclear power, would be over in a matter of days or weeks. Obviously there would be no time for nations to mobilize their war potential once nuclear war had broken out. All that counted, therefore, were nuclear forces entirely ready in time of peace in order to deter a hostile strike, including a surprise attack.

· · ·

Nevertheless, the thesis that war potential has become obsolete has only limited application. First, there are many non-nuclear states capable of waging war among themselves, and for them war potential has not, in principle, lost significance even though the wars between such states since World War II have actually been short or limited, or both (e.g., the border war between China and India in 1962, the war between India and Pakistan in 1965, the fighting between Indonesia and Malaysia in 1963-66, and the Israeli-Arab war of 1967). Surely, Arab leaders are interested in Israel's war potential, and vice versa.

Second, there can be sizable conventional wars between a nuclear power and a non-nuclear one. This happened in the Korean War and in American fighting in South Vietnam and, in the air, against North Vietnam. The United States was unable to fight either war with

[4]*Ibid.*, p. 71.

forces and equipment in being at the outset; it proceeded to considerable mobilization of war potential although not, of course, to the degree required in World War II.[5] . . . A widely diffused revulsion to nuclear weapons has attached a powerful stigma to their employment; the resulting expectation of opprobrium will keep any nuclear-weapon states from using these arms against a non-nuclear opponent, except perhaps under the most challenging circumstances, and even then presumably with great restraint. It seems conceivable, therefore, that a nuclear power could become involved in large-scale and protracted warfare against a non-nuclear state.

. . .

MILITARY POTENTIAL VERSUS WAR POTENTIAL

In any case, in appreciating the phenomenon of military power, it is not the limited concept of *war* potential, but the broader concept of *military* potential which is indispensable, and this concept has lost none of its significance on account of the new military technology. Nations differ greatly at all times in the resource base which they could mobilize to varying degrees in order to produce and maintain the armed services on which military power in large part rests. Viewed from this perspective, the dividing line between formal peace and war becomes immaterial except insofar as nations may, at a time of sharp diplomatic crisis, or engaged in an arms race with another power or powers, or in time of war, increase the rate of mobilization. Whether a state can afford to develop and deploy nuclear capabilities for the purpose of deterring any nuclear opponent at all times, and what magnitude and kind of such forces it can afford, depends upon its military potential. So does the generation of all other types of military capabilities: for tactical nuclear war, for conventional war, or for armed intervention in the civil strife of other countries. Moreover, the significance of military potential is not confined to the production of the national military forces of the state concerned. It also affects its ability to export arms and military instruction to allies

[5]Thus, the national security expenditures of the United States mounted from $18.5 billion in 1950 to $37.3 billion in 1951, and $48.8 billion in 1952. Similarly, the armed forces expanded from 1,650,000 men in 1950 to 3,098,000 in 1951 and 3,594,000 in 1952. Defense expenditures, which had amounted to about $50 billion a year in 1962-65, rose to $60.5 billion in 1966, and $72.6 billion in 1967.

and other countries. In 1967-68, when the military potential of the United States was in part mobilized for conducting war in Vietnam, the Soviet potential was taxed for sending a large volume of arms to North Vietnam to be used in its fighting against the United States, and to the Arab states whose inventory had been depleted by Israeli military action. In large part and indispensably, nations become military powers of consequence, globally or within a region, because they have a superior military potential, which even with a moderate rate of mobilization generates commanding ready military strength, or because, though endowed with a moderate potential in terms of manpower and other resources in terms of manpower and other resources, they mobilize to a greater extent than do states of comparable military potential.

Military potential has a bearing on a nation's putative military power. This power . . . results from ready military forces, from the ability to augment these forces, and from a nation's reputation for employing military force in the event of a serious international dispute. The first two factors—ready, mobilized forces and military potential—may be regarded as a nation's military strength which figures in the equation of putative military power. Indeed, military potential may be a factor even in actualized military power. Although battles can be won only with mobilized strength—many a state has lost a war because it failed to mobilize more of its potential strength in time—the expectation of a belligerent that its adversary can mobilize further resources for future battles may influence his decision to terminate a military conflict on tolerable terms.

THE SINEWS OF MILITARY STRENGTH

In practice, the concept of military potential has been employed mostly with reference to *economic* potential. This focus is not surprising for two reasons. First, as will be demonstrated below, it is much easier to study, measure and compare economic military potential than political, administrative and psychological factors that have a bearing on the amount of military strength a nation-state can generate. Second, the concept of potential acquired considerable currency *after* World War I, and the statesmen, soldiers and scholars of this period were deeply impressed by what we have called the "industrialization" of warfare, that is, by the critical importance of industrially produced equipment in the fighting ability of modern military forces. However, the observed fact that the nations with the superior supply of manpower and industrial capacity vanquished their enemies in World Wars I and II does not prove that these two factors will prove equally decisive in any future wars, and especially not in wars of a type quite different from these two prolonged wars of attrition. Nor is economic potential crucial in brief conflicts, or in encounters which, though prolonged, do not involve men and materiel in large numbers, or in routine peacetime maintenance of armed forces at a modest level to which a nation has become adjusted. The importance of economic potential is proportional to the demands on economic resources made by military exigencies.

In order to elucidate the problem of comparing the military potential of states, one may begin by noting the difficulties encountered in comparing their *mobilized* military strength, that is, in comparing their combat power. There are neither theoretical guidance nor empirical apparatus for measuring and comparing, and essentially predicting, the combat strength of the mobilized forces of different states.[6] The only known measurement test which is accurate is the test of battle. Of course, quantitative comparisons of infantry divisions, aircraft wings, naval vessels, missile launchers and military personnel can be made. *The Military Balance* published each year by the Institute for Strategic Studies in London provides much of the data, and more of this kind of information can be assembled from other public sources. But if we had taken *The Military Balance, 1966-67,* and studied the fairly detailed entries on the armed services of Israel and the United Arab Republic, we would have noted an appreciable degree of U.A.R. superiority (*e.g.,* about 550 military aircraft for the U.A.R. versus 350 for Israel). Such a comparison would have left us completely unprepared for the outcome of the Israeli-Arab war in 1967, which was determined largely, and probably decisively, by Israel's surprise air strike which destroyed the bulk of the U.A.R.'s airpower on the ground. Every war knows its surprises and is conditioned by special circumstances that render it more or less unique. But the main problem arises from the fact that the presence of qualitative factors makes quantitative comparisons often inconclusive. In the Israeli-Arab war, important qualitative differences, in addition to the sweeping air superiority gained by an audacious surprise attack, were superior Israeli tactics especially in the use of armored motorized forces, facilitated by great speed of

---

[6]This does not mean that military intelligence services are not busy to undertake such comparisons. But this involves a great deal of guesswork. The results are more or less impressionistic and justify only low confidence.

movement at night as well as by day, superior communication of commands, superior skill of the Israeli soldier in operating complicated equipment—especially superb gunnery from aircraft, tanks and artillery—and also the superior morale and élan of Israeli forces, which were basically a citizen's army fired by the knowledge that it was fighting for national survival.[7] This broad intrusion of qualitative differences is not at all unusual. It would have been equally difficult to compare, before the event, the fighting strength of North Vietnamese regulars and U.S. marines south of the Demilitarized Zone along the Seventeenth Parallel.

The main qualitative differences result from the following factors: (1) different composition of national forces as among (and within) the army, navy, air force and various special forces; (2) different composition and qualitative differences of weaponry and other military materiel; (3) differences in military strategy, doctrine, tactics and other components of military leadership; (4) differences in military communications and control systems; (5) differences in military intelligence; and (6) differences in troops in terms of skill and training, physical stamina, ability to endure various deprivations, morale, valor, etc.

Even if we assume that superior industrial capacity is mobilized for generating combat power and reflects itself in qualitative as well as quantitative superiority of weapons (which is not a necessary inference) and in superior skill and discipline associated with their use, marked deficiencies in other qualitative factors might still eventuate in inferior combat power. We do not have sufficient knowledge for suggesting exact and invariable relationships between these several factors, so that it would become apparent how much superiority in some factors would offset how much inferiority in others; nor are many of the qualitative factors tangible enough to allow measurement. But there are numerous historical examples which caution against accepting the power of sheer numbers. To cite one example from World War II, the German conquest of France was achieved despite the fact that the Germans were inferior in numbers of men and tanks, though superior in aircraft. They won by dint of strategic surprise (e.g., invasion through an area suspected to be

---

[7] Cv. General Beaufre, "Une guerre classique moderne: la guerre israelo-arabe," and "Les enseignements operationnels de la guerre israelo-arabe," *Strategie* (Paris, Institut Francais d'Etudes Stategiques), No. 13 (1967), pp. 7-25, 27-36; Brigadier General S. L. A. Marshal, "The Army of Israel," *Military Review*, April 1968, pp. 3-9.

virtually impenetrable by armored forces), by superior tactics and probably also by superior morale.[8]

. . .

Two recent developments have made qualitative differences more complex than they were before. One is the increasing technical complexity of particular weapons. Thus, modern aircraft carriers and fighter planes are much more complex machines than the battleships and military aircraft of World War II vintage; and there is no earlier counterpart to the intercontinental ballistic missile and its nuclear warhead. The other development parallels the increasing trend toward specialization observed in all technology. There are now many more specialized forces, weapons and gear than there were some decades ago. Both developments make for potentially large differences in qualitative performance.

THE COMPONENTS OF
MILITARY POTENTIAL

The qualitative conditions of combat power result from factors which—to the extent that they do not originate in short-run or ephemeral conditions—belong properly to a nation's military potential; and so do a great many other conditions which are non-economic and nontechnological, and are often hard to measure or unmeasurable. Morale and skill in blending the mix of weapons for various missions are obvious examples. The daunting fact is that there are few characteristics of a society which do or may not affect, directly or indirectly, its ability to generate and employ military power. Its political system, social structure and culture patterns are as relevant, though not necessarily as weighty, as its economic and technological resources and sheer numbers of population. Surely, political, social and cultural factors give Israel and the U.A.R. very different military potentials.

This broader approach to military potential is not meant to suggest that economic and technological factors and numbers of men are generally overrated as determinants of national military potential. The weight of these factors is undeniable. After all, in the late 1950's, all the states in the world together spent roughly $120 billion annually on military account, a figure equivalent to between 8 and 9 percent of world annual production of goods and services; and armed

[8] Cf. L. F. Ellis, *The War in France and Flanders, 1939-1940*, History of the Second World War, United Kingdom, Military Series (London, H.M.S.O, 1953), *passim.*

forces in the world numbered about 20 million persons.[9] The purpose of this discussion is only to draw attention to other important determinants of military potential.

Unfortunately, the present state of the social sciences does not permit a proper consideration and ordering of all these elements of national life that bear on a state's military potential. The obstacles stem from the facts that most of the social sciences have not progressed as far as economics has, that, regarding many aspects of social reality, available conceputalizations and empirical work have not been undertaken from the viewpoint relevant to the focus of this study, and that, though interesting information and hypotheses are scattered over the vast literatures of the social sciences and history, no one person commands enough expertise and time to gather these fragments together. These discouraging conditions force the present study to be more modest even though it will go far beyond analyzing economic war potential. This is a conceptual study which is meant to include what seem on intuitive grounds the most relevant constituents of national military potential. But little attention will be given to some factors, and some will be ignored altogether, especially those cultural conditions that impinge on such characteristics of military personnel as physical stamina, fortitude in the face of adversity, and military courage.

We distinguish between three broad categories of factors which together are largely determinant of a state's military potential. These are economic and technological capacity, administrative skill, and political foundations of military power.[10] These three components will be briefly described in the following paragraphs. . . .

ECONOMIC AND TECHNOLOGICAL CAPACITY

A nation's ability to mobilize and deploy military forces and supplies is determined in large part by its capacity to produce various goods and services, that is, by its labor force, raw materials, certain

---

[9] United Nations, *Economic and Social Consequences of Disarmament* (New York, 1962), p. 3.

[10] In my earlier book *The War Potential of Nations*, I made the same distinctions but used somewhat different terms to refer to the three classes of factors. The terms preferred in the present study should prove less ambiguous than those employed in the earlier one. The structuring of factors within the categories is also different in the present book.

financial resources (e.g., financial claims on foreigners); and the technical military effectiveness of its armed forces and supplies is also dependent on its technological resources. Mobilization in peace or war means that a proportion of these resources is diverted from other employment, or from idleness, to the production of ready military strength. Since a nation must subsist and carry on most of its non-military activities at all times, even in time of war, not all of this capacity is available for military purposes. But any military strength which is mobilized must be derived from this capacity except to the extent that a state is given military supplies, on credit or as a gift, from other states. Economic and technological capacity then depends on the size and structure of the population, that nation's territory with its land, water and mineral resources, the economic productivity of its labor force, its capital equipment, and the stage of its economic and technological development.

ADMINISTRATIVE SKILL

Administrative skill determines the efficiency with which economic and technological resources once diverted to the military sector are transformed into effective military forces. This transformation is a function of government and the military which must decide how manpower and equipment is to be combined in the armed services; it must decide on the composition of military output, that is, on the quantity, variety and quality of weapons and other materiel, and the size and structure of the armed forces themselves; it must decide on the training and indoctrination of military personnel, the development of military strategy, doctrine and tactics with reference to different contingencies, and all other conditions, subject to its control, which impinge on ready military strength. For example, a government, or its delegated military leaders, must choose the size of the army versus that of other armed services; their equipment; the number, kinds and deployment of nuclear arms (if a nuclear power is involved); the provision of military personnel with the necessities and amenities of life; the means of transporting troops to various possible theaters of war; the education of commanding and staff officers; and numerous other matters. Obviously, the more efficiently these decisions are made, the more military strength will be derived from any given allocation of men and other economic and technological resources. Moreover, not only is administrative skill important in converting economic and technological resources into mobilized strength of the right kind; it also determines the uses of this strength, efficiently or inefficiently, in time of peace or war.

POLITICAL FOUNDATIONS OF
MILITARY POWER

Unlike economic and technological capacity, and administrative skill, which are readily understood and whose contribution to national military potential is immediately apparent, the political bases of military strength are less obvious and more difficult to identify and describe. Moreover, care must be taken in distinguishing between the determinants of potential military power and those factors which determine the mobilization of this potential; that is, *antecedent* conditions must be separated from *situational* factors.

The proportion of economic, technological, and administrative resources which a nation will actually allocate to producing military capabilities and the readiness with which it will support the international use of its military power depend upon a motivation—represented in its leadership and, to the extent it is politically effective, also in the rest of the population—which competes and sometimes conflicts with motivations to expend resources for other purposes, for instance consumption. The more strongly leaders and other groups are motivated to reduce or forego the satisfaction of interest and preferences that conflict with a large commitment to provide and employ military forces, the larger those forces and the greater the readiness to use them are likely to be.

This motivation to supply and apply military strength has several components and sources. Motivations favoring military power certainly depend upon the perceived need to resist military aggression or the perceived opportunities for employing military power aggressively, that is, on behalf of internationally acquisitive ends. The decision of a government to augment military forces or to use them, and the support of interested and influential publics depend clearly on perceptions and evaluations of the international situation existing at a particular time, and on cost-gain calculations concerning the usefulness of military power in that situation. Thus, the United States increased its military capabilities in the early 1950's when its government assumed that it faced the possibility of a powerful Soviet military challenge to the status of Berlin and the security of western Europe.

However, while a government's decision to increase military strength or to put it to international use is obviously governed by its reaction—and the reaction of other interested and politically influential groups—to the external situation, it is also influenced by various conditions prevailing in the political community of which it is the authoritative head. Its ability to increase military strength or to employ it internationally depends on public support, or perhaps even demands, especially those from the politically influential public. This mobilizability of the nation depends in part, as already indicated, on the situational factors mentioned above, but it rests also on conditions which are antecedent to the external situation.

The public support potential depends mainly on four distinguishable antecedent factors. First, there is the nation's propensity to mobilize and use military power internationally.

. . .

Second, there is the predisposition to support the national community. This attitude is based on a sense of solidarity, that is, an attachment which—notwithstanding political, social and cultural cleavages—ties citizens to a nation-state.

. . .

The third factor is the public disposition to support the foreign and military policy of the government or to accept it as authoritative and hence binding, on other grounds than the two attitudes already identified, and also on other grounds than the assessment by members of the public of the immediate external situation which poses the question of increasing or employing military strength.

. . .

The fourth factor is support for a government's foreign and military policy coming from members of the public because they have a direct and specific personal interest in the mobilization and use of military strength.

. . .

These several factors which have been singled out as political foundations of military power represent a nation's basic mobilizability for purposes of sustaining and using military strength internationally. They preexist the situations in which military questions become acute; they are a mobilization potential. If nations differ in this potential, they tend to react differently to the same kind of external situation that raises the problem of employing military strength.

It should be noted that a nation's entire motivation to support a military buildup or to apply its military power against other states, including the situational factors which are not part of military potential as defined, is a phenomenon of keen interest to statesmen and military leaders. Understanding the entire structure of motivation, which necessarily differs for each situation, is a prerequisite to attempts at predicting a nation's military response to a particular international crisis.

. . .

MILITARY POTENTIAL FOR
DIFFERENT TYPES OF CONFLICT

Different uses of military power make demands for different kinds of military forces and, hence indirectly, make different demands on the military potential of states. Deploying a nuclear capability for deterrence, preparing for conventional war, near the state's boundaries or in distant places, possessing capabilities for fighting guerrillas in foreign countries, require different amounts and combinations of economic and technological resources, administrative skills, and also put different burdens on a nation's political foundations of military power. Thus, no states possess now, and only few are able to develop, the scale and kinds of scientific, technological and industrial resources for producing a capacity for nuclear deterrence similar in scale and sophistication to those of the United States and the Soviet Union. The degree of technological and industrial development of states strongly affects the kinds of equipment they can provide for conventional conflict, although imports can to some extent substitute for deficiency in indigenous resources. Conventional forces are ill adapted in terms of weapons, other equipment and training for combatting guerrillas. The need to make a nuclear deterrent threat credible calls for special administrative skills. Employing conventional forces for coercive threats calls for skills different from those involved in the sheer forcible seizure or defense of objects of international contention. Military intervention in foreign civil wars demands different administrative skills, if only because of the high political content of such conflicts, than does the conventional defense of the homeland. Different uses of military power engage the national propensity to mobilize and use military power in different ways. This predisposition may be high for defensive, but low for offensive war, and lower for distant or short wars than for wars close by or for protracted conflict. It may favor the deployment and use of large conventional forces but impede the development and deployment of nuclear arms. The difference in these demands explains why the United States, the world's most powerful country, was in 1967 and 1968 able to deter any nuclear attack, had the capability to wage sizable conventional wars far from its shores, and yet found itself ill-prepared to cope with relatively small numbers of modestly equipped Vietcong in South Vietnam. They also explain why some states did not decide, in the middle 1960's, to develop nuclear weapons even though they were credited with the technological ability to do so.

part two
Structure of the International Political System

Introductory Note

All the readings in Part Two converge, in various ways, on the concept "structure" as it relates to the international political system. In the Introduction, I discussed what was meant by structure, and why this variable merited such close attention. At this point, let me simply reiterate that structure provides the framework within which international interaction occurs. Not only is the structure of a system interesting in itself but also knowledge of it allows us to formulate fairly accurate expectations regarding the system's behavior. Other things being equal, only certain patterns of interaction are consonant with particular structures.

The international political system is dynamic and infinitely complex. Few tasks are as intellectually challenging or inherently controversial as that of conceptualizing the overall structure of the system. In the selections that follow (especially those in Chapter Six), the reader will note the wide range of conclusions reached by scholars in dealing with this problem. Insofar as any communality is evident, it is in the recurrence of "bipolarity" as an idea associated with the present system. But heterogeneity reigns again in the their appraisal and understanding of that notion.

159

Professor Morton Kaplan, one of the earliest advocates of systems theory in international relations, undertook the task of developing a typology of international systems. In Chapter Five he argues that there is a finite range of possible international systems, bounded on the one side by more or less complete anarchy (the unit-veto system), and on the other by more or less complete global integration (hierarchical system). Between these two extremes it is possible to imagine a wide variety of types. In the article, he suggests six models of which only two have historical counterparts (balance of power and loose bipolar); the remainder are hypothetical. While the six models cover the possible range, they are not necessarily exhaustive; in a later work, the author expands his list considerably.*

The reader is confronted in Chapter Six with four alternative characterizations of the contemporary international system. Each author brings to bear his own special insight into the nature of the structure of the system. And while they differ, their views are not necessarily irreconcilable. It is the task of the reader to appraise, select, and possibly integrate the various ideas presented.

Although bipolarity is a recurrent theme, it is merely a point of departure for Professor George Liska. He suggests—in striking contrast to some of the other authors—that we are moving away from bipolarity and toward what he refers to as a "unifocal" or "imperial" system. He postulates a system organized around one predominant international actor. Professor Kenneth Waltz, on the other hand, argues that not only is the present system bipolar (and presumably will remain so for the foreseeable future), but it is also very much a continuation of the classical, prenuclear system. The system is essentially balance of power in spite of nuclear technology, the absence of shifting alliance systems, and a decrease in the number of major actors from five or more to two. Professor Wolfram Hanrieder sees bipolarity as a still useful concept for describing the international system. It needs, however, to be augmented; it is more advantageous to think of the international system as consisting of layers or levels of interaction with bipolarity relevant to some, but not all. Professor Richard Rosecrance brings a somewhat different perspective to the discussion. His aim is to examine the extent to which a bipolar system is more (or less) stable than a multipolar one. (The implication is that we are moving toward multipolarity.) In the process, he presents a very lucid analysis of both concepts.

*See Morton Kaplan, *International Political Communities* (Garden City, N.Y.: Doubleday, 1966).

Chapter Seven is devoted to subsystems of the international system. While it is possible to conceive of subsystems in many ways, the idea of regional, that is, more or less geographic, subsystems is most compelling. Professors Louis Cantori and Steven L. Spiegel provide an excellent introduction to this area. They suggest means of identifying subsystems, ways of characterizing their relations, and comment on their interactions. In the course of their article, they considerably broaden our appreciation of the many different dimensions of the international system.

chapter five
THE RANGE OF INTERNATIONAL STRUCTURES

Balance of Power, Bipolarity and Other Models of International Systems

Morton A. Kaplan [1]

The postwar years have been a period of great interest in the theory of international politics. A contributor to this *Review* [2] has surveyed the state of the study of that theory and indicated the alternatives open to it. Within the last year the Institute of War and Peace Studies of Columbia University has held a series of seminars on the subject in an effort to push forward research frontiers.

Interest in theory is no reflection upon the merits of scholarly endeavors that are not oriented primarily to theoretical considerations. But it does assume the independent importance of a

SOURCE: From *The American Political Science Review*, Vol. II, No. 3 (1957). Copyright (c) 1957 by the American Political Science Association. Reprinted by permission of the author and the APSA.

[1] This article is based upon the first section of *System and Process in International Politics*, to be published in the fall of 1957 by John Wiley and Sons. In this version, definitions of precise technical terms used in the book have mostly been eliminated.

[2] Kenneth W. Thompson, "Toward a Theory of International Politics," this Review Vol 49 (September 1955), pp. 733-746.

theory of international politics. The present essay assumes the importance of theory in general, but is based upon a particular kind of theory, namely, systems theory.[3]

I

A number of theoretical considerations underlie this essay. One is that some pattern of repeatable or characteristic behavior does occur within the international system. Another is that this behavior falls into a pattern because the elements of the pattern are internally consistent and because they satisfy needs that are both international and national in scope. A third is that international patterns of behavior are related, in ways that can be specified, to the characteristics of the entities participating in international politics and to the role functions they perform there. A fourth is that international behavior can also be related to other factors such as military and economic capability, communication and information, technological change, demographic change, and additional factors well recognized by political scientists.

Just as it is possible to build alternative models of political systems, e.g., democratic or totalitarian, and of family systems, e.g., nuclear families, extended families or monogamous or polygamous families, so it is possible to build different models of international systems. The models can be given an empirical interpretation and the specific propositions of the models can be tested. In the last part of this paper, some specific tests will be suggested.

The aspiration to state testable propositions in the field of international politics is useful provided some degree of caution is observed concerning the kinds of propositions one proposes to test. For instance, can a theory of international politics yield a prediction of a specific event like the Hungarian revolution of October 1956? The answer probably must be negative. Yet why make such a demand of theory?

Two basic limitations upon prediction in the physical sciences are relevant to this problem. In the first place, the mathematics of complicated interaction problems has not been worked out. For instance, the physical scientist can make accurate predictions with respect to the two-body problem, rough guesses with respect to the

---

[3]The development of systems theory by W. Ross Ashby, *Design for a Brain* (New York, 1952), is a landmark in theoretical research.

three-body problem, and only very incomplete guesses concerning larger numbers of bodies. The scientist cannot predict the path of a single molecule of gas in a tank of gas.

In the second place, the predictions of the physical scientist are predictions concerning an isolated system. He does not predict that so much gas will be in the tank, that the temperature or pressure of the tank will not be changed by someone, or even that the tank will remain in the experimental room. He predicts what the characteristic behavior of the mass of gas molecules will be if stated conditions of temperature, pressure, etc., hold.

The engineer deals with systems in which many free variables enter. If he acts wisely—for instance, in designing aircraft—he works within certain constraints imposed by the laws of physics. But many aspects of exact design stem from experiments in wind tunnels or practical applications of past experiences rather than directly from the laws of physical science.

The theory of international politics normally cannot be expected to predict individual actions because the interaction problem is too complex and because there are too many free variables. It can be expected, however, to predict characteristic or modal behavior within a particular kind of international system. Moreover, the theory should be able to predict the conditions under which the system will remain stable, the conditions under which it will be transformed, and the kinds of transformations that may be expected to take place.

II

Six alternative models of international systems, will be presented in this paper. These models do not exhaust the possibilities for international organization but they represent positions along a scale of political organization; with the unit veto system exhibiting the smallest degree of political integration and the hierarchical system the greatest. The six international systems are the "balance of power" system, the loose bipolar system, the tight bipolar system, the universal system, the hierarchical system, and the unit veto system.

In their present stage of development the models are tentative and may be less complex than the real phenomena to which they refer. Yet, if they have some degree of adequacy they may permit a more meaningful organization of existing knowledge and more productive organization of future research.

Only two of the models—the "balance of power" system and the loose bipolar system—have historical counterparts. Greater attention will be given to these in this paper. The other four are projections based upon requirements of internal consistency and of relationships to other political and economic factors. They function both to illustrate possible transformations of the loose bipolar system and as possible predictions of the theory when the transformations are explicitly linked to the conditions that will bring them into being.

The first system to be examined is the "balance of power" international system. Quotation marks are placed around the term to indicate its metaphoric quality.

The "balance of power" international system is an international social system which does not have as a component a political subsystem. The actors within the system are exclusively national actors, such as France, Germany, Italy, etc. Five national actors—as a minimum—must fall within the classification "essential national actor"[4] to enable the system to work.

The "balance of power" international system is characterized by the operation of the following essential rules, which correspond to the elements of the characteristic behavior of the system: (1) increase capabilities but negotiate rather than fight; (2) fight rather than fail to increase capabilities; (3) stop fighting rather than eliminate an essential actor; (4) oppose any coalition or single actor which tends to assume a position of predominance within the system; (5) constrain actors who subscribe to supranational organizational principles; and (6) permit defeated or constrained essential national actors to reenter the system as acceptable role partners, or act to bring some previously inessential actor within the essential actor classification. Treat all essential actors as acceptable role partners.

The first two rules of the "balance of power" international system reflect the fact that no political subsystem exists within the international social system. Therefore, essential national actors must rely upon themselves or upon their allies for protection. However, if they are weak, their allies may desert them. Therefore, an essential national actor must ultimately be capable of protecting its own national values.

The third essential rule illustrates the fact that expansion beyond certain limits would be inconsistent with nationality. It is not

---

[4]The term "essential actor" refers to "major power" as distinguished from "minor power."

necessary to raise the question whether capabilities place limits on appetites or whether more basic national values are inconsistent with unlimited national expansion.

The fourth and fifth rules give recognition to the fact that a predominant coalition or national actor would constitute a threat to the interests of other national actors. Moreover, if a coalition were to become predominant, then the largest member of that coalition might also become predominant over the lesser members of its own coalition. For this reason members of a successful coalition may be alienated, although they may also be able to bargain for more from the threatened national actors.

The sixth rule states that membership in the system is dependent only upon behavior which corresponds with the essential rules or norms of the "balance of power" system. If the number of essential actors is reduced, the "balance of power" international system will become unstable. Therefore, maintaining the number of essential national actors above a critical lower bound is a necessary condition for the stability of the system. This is best done by returning to full membership in the system defeated actors or reformed deviant actors.

Although any particular action or alignment may be the product of "accidents," i.e., of the set of specific conditions producing the action or alignment, including such elements as chance meetings or personality factors, a high correlation between the pattern of national behavior and the essential rules of the international system would represent a confirmation of the predictions of the theory.

Just as any particular molecule of gas in a gas tank may travel in any direction, depending upon accidental bumpings with other molecules, particular actions of national actors may depend upon chance or random conjunctions. Yet, just as the general pattern of behavior of the gas may represent its adjustment to pressure and temperature conditions within the tank, the set of actions of national actors may correspond to the essential rules of the system when the other variables take the appropriate specific values.

Thus, by shifting the focus of analysis from the particular event to the type of event, the seemingly accidental events become part of a meaningful pattern. In this way, the historical loses its quality of uniqueness and is translated into the universal language of science.

The number of essential rules cannot be reduced. The failure of any rule to operate will result in the failure of at least one other rule. Moreover, at this level of abstraction, there does not seem to be any other rule that is interrelated with the specified set in this fashion.

Any essential rule of the system is in equilibrium[5] with the remaining rules of the set. This does not imply that particular rules can appear only in a particular international system. The first two rules, for instance, also apply to bloc leaders in the bipolar systems. However, they are necessary to each of the systems and, in their absence, other rules of the two systems will be transformed.

The rules of the system are interdependent. For instance, the failure to restore or to replace defeated essential national actors eventually will interfere with the formation of coalitions capable of constraining deviant national actors or potential predominant coalitions.

The equilibrium of the set of rules is not a continuous equilibrium but one that results from discrete actions over periods of time. Therefore, the possibility of some change operating to transform the system becomes great if sufficient time is allowed.

It is relatively easy to find historical examples illustrating the operation of these rules. The European states would have accepted Napoleon had he been willing to play according to the rules of the game.[6]

The restoration of the Bourbons permitted the application of rule three. Had such a restoration not been possible, the international system would immediately have become unstable. Readmission of France to the international system after restoration fulfilled rule six.

The European concert, so ably described by Mowat, illustrates rule one. The *entente cordiale* illustrates rule four and the history of the eighteenth and nineteenth centuries rule two. Perhaps the best example of rule three, however, can be found in the diplomacy of

---

[5]This kind of equilibrium is not mechanical like the equilibrium of a seesaw which reestablishes itself mechanically after a disturbance. Instead, it is a "steady state" or homeostatic equilibrium which maintains the stability of selected variables as the consequence of changes in other variables. For instance, the body maintains the temperature of blood in a "steady state" by perspiring in hot weather and by flushing the skin in cold weather. The international system is not simply stable but in Ashby's sense is ultrastable. That is, it acts selectively toward states of its internal variables and rejects those which lead to unstable states. See W. Ross Ashby, *op. cit.*, p. 99, for a precise treatment of the concept of ultrastability.

[6]It is nevertheless true that since Napoleon threatened the principle of dynastic legitimacy, the system would have been strained. The principle of legitimacy, for quite some time, reduced the suspicions which are natural to a "balance of power" system.

Bismarck at Sadowa, although his motivation was more complex than the rule alone would indicate.

It is not the purpose of this essay to multiply historical illustrations. The reader can make his own survey to determine whether international behavior tended to correspond to these rules during the eighteenth and nineteenth centuries.

Apart from the equilibrium within the set of essential rules, there are two other kinds of equilibrium characteristic of the international system: the equilibrium between the set of essential rules and the other variables of the international system and the equilibrium between the international system and its environment or setting.

If the actors do not manifest the behavior indicated by the rules, the kind and number of actors will change. If the kind or number of actors changes, the behavior called for in the rules cannot be maintained.

In addition, the essential rules of the "balance of power" international system may remain in equilibrium for a number of values of the other variables of the system. Some changes in capabilities and information for instance may be compatible with the rules of the system, while others may not.

Indeed, if the value of one variable changes—for instance the capabilities of a given coalition—the system may not maintain itself unless the information of some of the actors changes correspondingly. Otherwise a necessary "counter-balancing" shift in alignment may not take place. Some shifts in the pattern of alliance may be compatible with the rules of the system and others may not.

If the rules of the "balance of power" international system are consistent with the actions of the national actors in the eighteenth and nineteenth centuries, the system may well have appeared to be an absolute system to observers and the "balance of power" a rule of universal applicability. But since the described system is not consistent with the present bipolar international system, it is clear that the system operated only under fixed conditions. To account for the change from one system to the other, it is necessary to isolate the critical conditions for the maintenance of the "balance of power" system.

The changes in conditions that may make the "balance of power" international system unstable are: the existence of an essential national actor who does not play according to the rules of the game, such as one whose essential rules are oriented toward the establishment of some form of supranational political organization; failures of information which prevent a national actor from taking the required measures to protect its own international position; capability changes which become cumulative and which thus increase an initial disparity between the capabilities of essential national actors; conflicts between the prescriptions of different rules under some conditions; difficulties arising from the logistics of the "balancing" process, the small number of essential actors, or an inflexibility of the "balancing" mechanism.

An important condition for stability concerns the number of essential national actors. If there are only three, and if they are relatively equal in capability, the probability that two would combine to eliminate the third is relatively great. It is possible that the third actor may not be eliminated and that, after defeat, it would participate in a new coalition with the weaker of the victorious powers. But clearly the probability of such an outcome—necessary to the stability of the system—rises if the number of essential actors is greater than three. Mistakes or failures in information can be tolerated more easily if the number of actors is greater. Therefore, only some numerical lower bound will give sufficient flexibility to the "balance of power" system to permit the required shifts in alliance as conditions change.

Coalitions with many members may regard loosely attached members with equanimity. The role of the non-member of the coalition also will be tolerated. When there are a large number of loosely attached actors or non-members of an alliance, any change of alliance or addition to an alliance, can be "counter-balanced" by the use of an appropriate reward or the cognition of danger to the national interest of some actor. There are many national actors to whom these bids may be made.

When, however, there are very few loosely attached or non-member actors, a change in or an addition to an alignment introduces considerable tension into the international system. Under these circumstances, it becomes difficult to make the necessary compensatory adjustments.

For the same reasons, coalition members will have more tolerance for the role of "balancer," i.e., the actor who implements rule 4, if the international system has a large number of members and the alignments are fluid. Under these conditions, the "balancer" does not constitute a lethal threat to the coalition against which it "balances."

If, however, there are only a few essential actors, the very act of "balancing" may create a permanent "unbalance." In these circumstances the tolerance of the system for the "balancing" role will be slight and the "balance of power" system will become unstable.

Instability may result although the various national actors have no intention of overthrowing the "balance of power" system. The wars against Poland corresponded to the rule directing the various national actors to increase their capabilities. Since Poland was not an essential national actor, it did not violate the norms of the system to eliminate Poland as an actor. The Polish spoils were divided among the victorious essential national actors. Nevertheless, even this cooperation among the essential national actors had an "unbalancing" effect. Since the acquisitions of the victorious actors could not be equal—unless some exact method were found for weighting geographic, strategic, demographic, industrial, material factors, etc., and determining accurately how the values of these factors would be projected into the future—a differential factor making the system unstable could not easily be avoided.

Even the endeavor to defeat Napoleon and to restrict France to her historic limits had some effects of this kind. This effort, although conforming to rules four, five, and six, also aggrandized Russia and Prussia, and hence upset the internal equilibrium among the German actors. This episode may have triggered the process which later led to Prussian hegemony within Germany and to German hegemony within Europe. Thus, a dynamic process was set off for which shifts within alignments or coalitions were not able to compensate.

The logistical or environmental possibilities for "balancing" may be decisive in determining whether the "balancing" role within the "balance of power" international system will be filled effectively. For example, even had it so desired, the Soviet Union could not have "balanced" Nazi pressure against Czechoslovakia without territorial access to the zone of potential conflict. In addition, the intervening actors—Poland and Rumania—and possibly also Great Britain and France, regarded Soviet intervention as a threat to their national interests. Therefore, they refused to cooperate.

It is possible that a major factor accounting for British success in the "balancing" role in the nineteenth century lay in the fact that Great Britain was predominantly a naval power and had no territorial ambitions on the European continent. These facts increased the tolerance of other national actors for Britain's "balancing" role. As a preponderant maritime power, Great Britain could interfere with the shipping of other powers and could also transport its small armed forces to the zone of conflict. It could afford to maintain only a small army, because it was able to use its naval capabilities to dispel invading forces. Even so, Palmerston discovered occasions on which it was difficult to play the "balancing" role either because it was difficult to make effective use of Britain's limited manpower or because other powers displayed little tolerance for the role.

The "balance of power" system in its ideal form is a system in which any combination of actors within alliances is possible so long as no alliance gains a marked preponderance in capabilities. The system tends to be maintained by the fact that even should any nation desire to become predominant itself, it must, to protect its own interests, act to prevent any other nation from accomplishing such an objective. Like Adam Smith's "unseen hand" of competition, the international system is policed informally by self-interest, without the necessity of a political subsystem.

The rise of powerful deviant actors, inadequate counter-measures by nondeviant actors,[7] new international ideologies, and the growth of supranational organizations like the Communist bloc with its internationally organized political parties, sounded the death knell for the "balance of power" international system.

In its place, after an initial period of instability, the loose bipolar system appeared. This differs in many important respects from the "balance of power" system. Supranational actors participate within the international system. These supranational actors may be bloc actors like NATO or the Communist bloc or universal actors like the United Nations. Nearly all national actors belong to the universal actor organization and many—including most of the essential national actors—belong to one or the other of the bipolar blocs. Some national actors, however, may be non-members of bloc organizations.

In distinction to the "balance of power" international system, in which the rules applied uniformly to all national actors, the essential rules of the loose bipolar system distinguish, for instance, between the role functions of actors who are members of blocs and those who are not.

In the "balance of power" system, the role of the "balancer" was an integrating role because it prevented any alliance from becoming predominant. In the ideal form of the system, any national actor is qualified to fill that role. In the loose bipolar system, however, the integrating role is a mediatory role. The actor filling it does not join one side or the other, but mediates between the contending sides. Therefore, only non-bloc members or universal actor organizations can fill the integrative role in the loose bipolar system.

[7] Britain and France violated rules 1, 2, 4, 5, and 6 in the 1930's.

The functioning of the loose bipolar system depends upon the organizational characteristics of the supranational blocs.[8] If the two blocs are not hierarchically organized, the loose bipolar system tends to resemble the "balance of power" system, except that the shifting of alignments takes place around two fixed points. Such shifting is limited by the functional integration of facilities, since a shift may require the destruction of facilities and the reduction of the capabilities of the shifting national actor. Shifting in alignment tends also to be limited by geographic and other logistic considerations. Nevertheless, the bloc actors constitute relatively loose organizations and the international system itself develops a considerable flexibility.

If one bloc has some hierarchical organizational features and the other is not hierarchically organized, a number of consequences can be expected. The hierarchical or mixed hierarchical bloc will retain its membership, since functional integration will be so great that it would be difficult for satellite members to withdraw or to form viable national entities if they did.[9] The relative permanence of membership in the bloc constitutes a threat to non-members. Therefore, such a bloc is unlikely to attract new members except as a consequence of military absorption or political conquest by a native political party which already had associate membership in the bloc through the medium of an international party organization. The irreversible characteristics of membership in such a bloc constitute a threat to all other national actors, whether associated in a bloc or not.

The non-hierarchical bloc has a looser hold over its members but is more likely to enter into cooperative pacts of one kind or another with non-bloc members. The pressure emanating from the hierarchically organized bloc, however, is likely to force the non-hierarchically organized bloc to integrate its bloc activities more closely and to extend them to other functional areas, or alternatively to weaken and undermine the bloc.

If both blocs subscribe to hierarchical integrating rules, their memberships become rigid and only uncommitted states can, by

[8] Extensional definitions would identify NATO as relatively non-hierarchical and the Communist bloc as mixed hierarchical. If the Communist bloc were to be so integrated that national boundaries and organizational forms were eliminated, it would become fully hierarchical.

[9] In this connection, it is noteworthy that the Yugoslavs were able to resist the drastic Soviet demands for economic integration. Tito's withdrawal would have been much more difficult—and perhaps impossible—had this not been the case.

choosing an alignment, change the existing line-up. Any action of this sort, however, would tend to reduce the flexibility of the international system by eliminating nations not included in blocs. Non-bloc member actors therefore would be more likely to support one or the other of the blocs on specific issues rather than to support either in general. If both blocs are hierarchically organized, their goals are similar—hierarchical world organization—and incompatible, since only one can succeed in leading such a world system.

With only two major groupings in the bipolar system, any rapid change in military capabilities tends to make this system unstable. For this reason, possession of a larger stockpile of atomic and thermonuclear weapons by both major blocs is a factor for stability within the system.

The rules of the loose bipolar system follow:

1. All blocs subscribing to hierarchical or mixed hierarchical integrating principles are to eliminate the rival bloc.

2. All blocs subscribing to hierarchical or mixed hierarchical integrating principles are to negotiate rather than to fight, to fight minor wars rather than major wars, and to fight major wars—under given risk and cost factors—rather than to fail to eliminate the rival bloc.

3. All bloc actors are to increase their capabilities relative to those of the opposing bloc.

4. All bloc actors subscribing to non-hierarchical organizational principles are to negotiate rather than to fight, to increase capabilities, to fight minor wars rather than to fail to increase capabilities, but to refrain from initiating major wars for this purpose.

5. All bloc actors are to engage in major war rather than to permit the rival bloc to attain a position of preponderant strength.

6. All bloc members are to subordinate objectives of universal actors to the objectives of their bloc but to subordinate the objectives of the rival bloc to those of the universal actor.

7. All non-bloc member national actors are to coordinate their national objectives with those of the universal actor and to subordinate the objectives of bloc actors to those of the universal actor.

8. Bloc actors are to attempt to extend the membership of their bloc but to tolerate the non-member position of a given national actor if the alternative is to force that national actor to join the rival bloc or to support its objectives.

9. Non-bloc member national actors are to act to reduce the danger of war between the bloc actors.
10. Non-bloc members are to refuse to support the policies of one bloc actor as against the other except in their capacities as members of a universal actor.
11. Universal actors are to reduce the incompatibility between the blocs.
12. Universal actors are to mobilize non-bloc member national actors against cases of gross deviation, e.g., resort to force by a bloc actor. This rule, unless counterbalanced by the other rules, would enable the universal actor to become the prototype of a universal international system.

Unlike the "balance of power" international system, there is a high degree of role differentiation in the loose bipolar system. If any of the roles is pursued to the exclusion of others, the system will be transformed. If one bloc actor eliminates another, the system may be transformed into a hierarchical system. If the universal actor performs its function too well, the system may be transformed into a universal international system. Other variations are possible.

The tight bipolar international system represents a modification of the loose bipolar system in which non-bloc member actors and universal actors either disappear entirely or cease to be significant. Unless both blocs are hierarchically organized, however, the system will tend toward instability.

There is no integrative or mediatory role in the tight bipolar system. Therefore there will tend to be a high degree of dysfunctional tension in the system. For this reason, the tight bipolar system will not be a highly stable or well integrated system.

The universal international system might develop as a consequence of the functioning of a universal actor organization in a loose bipolar system. The universal system, as distinguished from those international systems previously discussed, would have a political system as a subsystem of the international social system. However, it is possible that this political system would be of the confederated type, i.e., that it would operate on territorial governments rather than directly on human individuals.

The universal international system would be an integrated and solidary system. Although informal political groupings might take place within the system, conflicts of interest would be settled according to the political rules of the system. Moreover, a body of political officials and administrators would exist whose primary loyalty would be to the international system itself rather than to any territorial subsystem of the international system.

Whether the universal international system is a stable system or not depends upon the extent to which it has direct access to resources and facilities and upon the ratio between its capabilities and the capabilities of the national actors who are members of the system.

The hierarchical international system may be democratic or authoritarian in form. If it evolves from a universal international system—perhaps because the satisfactions arising from the successful operation of such a universal international system lead to a desire for an even more integrated and solidary international system—it is likely to be a democratic system. If, on the other hand, the hierarchical system is imposed upon unwilling national actors by a victorious or powerful bloc, then the international system is likely to be authoritarian.

The hierarchical system is a political system. Within it, functional lines of organization are stronger than geographical lines. This highly integrated characteristic of the hierarchical international system makes for great stability. Functional cross-cutting makes it most difficult to organize successfully against the international system or to withdraw from it. Even if the constitution of the system were to permit such withdrawal, the integration of facilities over time would raise the costs of withdrawal too high.

The unit veto international system is one in which all actors possess such great capabilities that an aggressor—even if it succeeded eventually in destroying an actor—could be destroyed in return. Within this system, each actor relies upon itself exclusively for its own protection, rather than upon alliances.

The unit veto system is maintained by mutual threat. Therefore the dysfunctional tension within it is likely to be quite high. For this reason, actors may succumb to threats, i.e., they may lose nerve, or they may launch an aggressive venture simply because they cannot stand the tension. As a consequence, the unit veto international system is not likely to have a high degree of stability.

III

History will still remain the laboratory for research, since controlled experiments, for the most part, are out of the question in the field of international politics. Yet, the normal modes of historical investigation are not adequate for the confirmation of a theory of international politics.

The mere statement of the alternative models of international systems necessitates the collection of information relevant to their validation, in particular, of information dealing with the patterns of national interactions. It is significant that the simple task of counting various kinds of interactions has never been seriously attempted in the literature, and that this information is essential to the description of the international system.

Some consequences of the theory which can be empirically tested are fairly obvious. For instance, the rules of the "balance of power" system specify a great fluidity in the formation of alliances and groupings with respect to particular issues. The analysis of national interactions during the "balance of power" period should test this consequence and should also permit a more detailed specification of the characteristics of the "balance of power" system.

If the theory is correct, there should be a difference between the "balance of power" and bipolar systems with respect to the frequencies of certain groupings. For instance, in the "balance of power" system, groupings will depend primarily upon the interests of nations in particular situations. Therefore, they will tend to break up as soon as the interests are satisfied or forestalled. New groupings should continue to depend upon particular interests. Therefore, there should be great variety in the groupings.

In the loose bipolar system, on the other hand, groupings will depend upon long range rather than particular interests. Therefore, some alignments will have an extremely high probability and others an extremely low probability. The study of interaction patterns in the two systems should serve both to test these propositions and to permit a closer comparison of the characteristics of the two systems.

To be more specific, the "balance of power" system postulates that any alignment is as probable as any other alignment prior to a consideration of the specific interests which divide nations. Moreover, any particular alignment should not *a priori* predispose the same nations to align themselves with each other at the next opportunity. Was there, therefore, any period of the "balance of power" system during which the fluctuations in alignments did not shift as the theory predicts? If there were, some other factors must be located to account for the pattern of preferences.

It is also possible that the system of alignments became more rigid over time, i.e., that any one alignment increased the probability that that alignment would recur in the future. If so, an element of instability would be found within the system. Of course, the frequency of interactions is not identical with the predisposition to interact. Other variables complicate the picture. Nevertheless, if it is true historically that the frequency of interactions changed in some systematic manner, this in itself would have great importance.

If some important patterns of behavior are discovered, an effort should then be made to discover whether they are linked to internal system characteristics, e.g., increasing probability of repeating previous patterns of alignment, or whether they are linked to external factors, e.g., technological change, or to some combination of the two.

Still additional consequences may be derived from the rules of the various international systems. Although the problems involved in testing these propositions may prove difficult, the problems nevertheless arise in the area of empirical theory and are brought to attention by abstract theoretical considerations.

chapter six

STRUCTURAL CHARACTERISTICS OF THE PRESENT SYSTEM

The International System: Bipolar or Multibloc? [1]

Wolfram F. Hanrieder

Important historical data that cannot be accommodated by the theoretical concepts intended to elucidate them pose one of the most troublesome problems for the political theorist. Especially in unsettled periods of historical "transition," events have a disconcerting quality of eluding the ideal analytic types established for them. Approaches to the study of international politics which focus on the concept of system are no exception.

In what follows I shall be using the working definition of an "international system" put forth by Stanley Hoffmann (1961, p. 207): "An international system is a pattern of relations between the basic units of world politics, which is characterized by the scope of the objectives pursued by those units and of the tasks performed

SOURCE: From *Journal of Conflict Resolution*, Vol. IX, No. 3 (1965). Copyright © 1965 by the University of Michigan Press. Reprinted by permission of the author and the University of Michigan Press.

[1] For their criticism and advice I am grateful to Ernst B. Haas of the University of California (Berkeley) and to my colleagues at the Center of International Studies at Princeton University, especially Richard A. Falk and James N. Rosenau.

among them, as well as by the means used in order to achieve those goals and perform those tasks. This pattern is largely determined by the structure of the world, the nature of the forces which operate across or within the major units, and the capabilities, pattern of power, and political culture of those units."[2]

The systems approach is unusually flexible and can be adjusted to fit many and diverse analytical purposes, primarily because a broad definition of "system" allows application in a wide variety of contexts which may differ greatly in terms of unit size, type of relationship, issues, and so forth. But the *patterning* of behavioral regularities, which is at the core of systemic treatments, usually is much less adaptable because it represents, in effect, the creation of an ideal analytic type.

The formulation of typologies such as a "balance-of-power" system or a "bipolar" international system is always arbitrary in the sense that the theorist settles on system types, and the relationships they represent, either because they seem to approximate the "real" world or because they order the range of possible alternative systems in clear-cut and esthetically satisfying models. Of course, the needs of empirical investigation cannot always be met by ideal analytic types because of the kaleidoscopic complexity of empirical phenomena. Even if a systemic abstraction could adequately portray and relate the crucial phenomena of a particular historical configuration, reality, once captured, would not hold still. Thus the systemic vision is engaged in a constant tug-of-war with the dynamics of historical events, unless the purpose of the theory is heuristic or ideological.

The attempts which have been made to abstract the crucial relationships of the international system since World War II on the basis of *bipolar* images have not proven very flexible. International events of the last decade have imposed a severe strain on such summary and confining concepts. For example, a number of important relationships among nations exhibit patterns which could perhaps be labeled *polycentric*. Bipolarity is still with us, however, in such important respects as nuclear capabilities and a fundamentally tense relationship between the United States and the Soviet Union. Theoretical models based on polycentric patterns tend to neglect this fact.

In order to arrive at a more adequate "abbreviation of reality," in Cassirer's phrase, I should like to propose an alternative pattern-

[2]See also Easton (1953) and Hall and Fagen (1956). For the most consistent application of systems analysis to international politics, see Kaplan (1957) and Rosecrance (1963).

image which seems to me more adaptable to the dynamics and complexity of current events because it combines bipolar with polycentric patterns.

I. TRANSITIONS AND FUTURISTIC MODELS

The most clear-cut and consistent analytic models based on bipolar or multibloc images of the international system are the ones formulated, respectively, by Morton Kaplan (1957) and Roger Masters (1961). Masters apparently realized that the pace of events in the past ten years had strained the adequacy of bipolar concepts. When a systemic framework which may have been suitable before seems to be losing a good deal of its explanatory efficacy, an analyst may be moved to formulate another ideal type, abreast of developments, which would anchor reality analytically between an outgrown type and a futuristic one as yet only dimly perceived. Formulations of multibloc, polycentric, or biaxial patterns of the international system are attempts in this direction.

There is no logically compelling reason why the system builder should employ futuristic models unless predictability—say, on the basis of system "transformation rules"—is his chief aim.[3] Yet there are at least two other reasons which make it appear desirable.

One reason is to underscore the dynamic possibilities of the systems approach. Dissatisfied with the limitations of a single-cause approach—for example, *power* as an organizing principle—the systems analyst attempts to indicate *direction;* and the attempt is most successful when all major points of destination have already been abstracted in a complete systems cosmology, as in Kaplan's sweeping systemic vision. This is a compensating value when critics hold that the systems approach does not adequately account for the *causes* of transformation (see Hoffmann, 1960, p. 47; also Haas, 1960, p. 302).

The second reason is much more serious because it touches upon the core of the utility of model-building. Behavioral regularity, which is the basis for establishing relational patterns or structures, is an indispensable attribute of systems. This crucial empirical prerequisite, which should necessarily be reflected in the analytical model formulated, is usually abstracted by the analyst in two ways. When empirical phenomena are suspected of showing behavioral

---

[3] For a critical discussion of the relevance of prediction, see Hoffmann (1960, pp. 42-43).

regularity, the observer focuses first on the *kind* of relationships that are deemed relevant and secondly on the *patterns* that are discernible in these relationships. Function and structure are combined in a model. But if the model is constantly refined by adding *new kinds* of relationships and *more complex patterns* with which to abstract them, the model refines itself out of existence. By taking into account more and more variations of patterns and kinds of relationships—that is to say, by approximating reality—the clarity and simplicity of the model suffer correspondingly.

The systems approach of Kaplan and Masters is essentially based on relationships which are determined by the number and power of the members of the system. Since the *nature* of the relationships examined is largely settled, variations among these system types are mainly variations of *pattern*. But the more variations are formulated to accommodate historical reality, the less justification there is to consider international relations in terms of systems at all. If it were possible—and it may well be necessary—to formulate a new "sub"-typology of bipolarity every year to keep up with the pace of history, the label of "bipolarity" would embrace so many variations that each one would hardly be more than an annual appraisal of international events. Such microchronic slices of reality undermine the systems approach by splintering its time and pattern dimension.

If the systemic treatment of international politics is to occupy a middle ground between the broad brush-stroke of single-cause theories and the pointillistic, *n*-number images that emerge, for example, from case study treatments of diplomatic history, it must necessarily resist the temptation to create a large number of systemic typologies. One way to avoid this proliferation is to place events analytically *between* two already established ideal types—say, between bipolar and multibloc patterns—and treat them as transitory phenomena, with the anticipation that a futuristic model (the multibloc image) has a niche ready for them.

Another way to fracture a system image is to criticize as inadequate the *kinds* of relationships which are being patterned and to suggest, as an alternative, that systemic relationships should be considered on more than one relational level. I shall return to this point later.

II. FINDING ADEQUATE CONCEPTS FOR CONTEMPORARY SITUATIONS

Systemic treatments of international politics appear most vital and confident when they deal with the past or future situations. Confronted with a contemporary setting they become pale and reticent. This is unfortunate for a number of reasons, but especially because useful *descriptive* abstractions are not available to apply to empirical studies of contemporary politics. To call the present international constellation either bipolar or polycentric seems equally misleading, and we must ask to what sets of relationships these labels apply, for as summary descriptions they are too abstract (see Liska, 1962, part II).

One can circumvent the problem by regarding one set of variables as crucial and reserving the labels bipolar, multibloc, etc., to describe its pattern. The power relationship among actors may be used for that purpose. Or the number of actors in the system, coupled with power statements, can provide the relational pattern. When Kaplan distinguishes between "loose" and "tight" bipolarity he speaks primarily in terms of the number of actors which exist in the system besides the memberships of the two superblocs.[4] Such analytic condensations are achieved, of course, at great cost in richness of description; they address a one-dimensional relational level, and do not go much beyond stating the presence of certain actors and their role functions.

Pattern concepts can be refined and multiplied profusely to accommodate very specific empirical situations. Then, however, each event tends to become a system in itself; we are left with neither model nor theory, although each empirical situation has its own conceptual label. There is another avenue which, if followed to its extreme, could end up at the same point of irrelevance: that is to make ever-finer distinctions among the *kinds* of relationships that are treated systemically rather than among their *patterns*.

James Rosenau has suggested that systemic research be pursued not only in terms of local, national, and international systems—that is, actors and their relational pattern as a focal point—but also in terms of issue areas, such as foreign aid political systems, health and welfare political systems, and so on (Rosenau, 1963a). If not carried to an extreme, this useful proposal could break down the rigid "total-issues" image implicit in most contexts where bipolar or multibloc concepts are applied. The desirability of distinguishing more specifically between issue systems is obvious. When Kaplan postulates that reducing the number of uncommitted states in the "loose" bipolar system "tightens" bipolarity, he speaks presumably

---

[4]"The first thing to be noted about the tight bipolar system is the virtual disappearance of the category of nonmember national actors. This is tautological, for the system cannot be tightly bipolar except on the assumption that these actors cease to exist or that their role functions become nonessential for purposes of action within the system" (Kaplan, 1957, p. 44; see also pp. 43-45).

not only in terms of numbers but also, at least implicitly, in terms of power and capabilities. This oversimplification cannot account for developments which "loosen" bipolarity on one level but "tighten" it on another. For example, the superblocs may lose some allies and yet elevate their power potential vis-à-vis each other because of technological developments which reinforce their duopolistic preponderance of power in the system. Another example of discontinuity between the patterns of two relational levels is in United Nations General Assembly voting. The numerical support pattern which emerges on the basis of one-state-one-vote balloting may be at great variance with the power pattern of the voting states.

There is another reason why the judicious application of systems analysis to defined issue areas seems promising: it may provide tests to determine the degree of specificity at which systems analysis is most effective in the study of international politics. It may give us a clearer idea at what level, between the homogeneous attributes of a general theory and the heterogeneous qualities of issue-studies, the systems approach becomes most profitable.

But even on the level of a specific issue system, the *degree* of abstraction of terms like "bipolar," "polycentric," and "multibloc" seems appropriate. The question is whether these particular concepts are misleading at that level. Actually, a number of important relationships of the contemporary international system combine both bipolar and multibloc characteristics. Consequently, the terminology of Kaplan's loose bipolar system is too bipolar, while Masters' model goes to the other extreme by neglecting bipolar attributes altogether. The language of these two patterns does not allow a descriptive mix between bipolar and multibloc phenomena; the images they evoke are not easily combinable. Each concept may be useful on some relational levels—for example, bipolarity in the case of a nuclear power system and the multibloc image in the case of a UN voting system. But even in these two cases it is doubtful if the concept adequately conveys the essence of the relationship. Today almost all important systemic relationships are characterized by both a fundamental bipolar tension *and* a multicentric dimension.[5]

---

[5] In the United Nations, for example, many of the Afro-Asian countries which serve as "mediators" in the bipolar tension relationship between the United States and the Soviet Union trade their support on security issues, in which the superpowers are interested, against the superpowers' support on colonial and economic aid issues in which the mediators are interested. Obviously, this relationship is simultaneously bipolar and multibloc. (Cf. Haas, 1956; Russett, 1963.)

The conceptual framework of systems analysis can thus be improved, especially for application in an empirical setting, by re-formulations from two distinct vantage points. The first, suggested by Rosenau, would look at the international system as a multilevel aggregate of issues rather than as a single amalgam of undifferentiated issue levels. To the extent that these various issue systems can be regarded as functions of the "total" international system, this approach amounts to a *functional* breakdown of that system.

The second kind of reformulation—with which we shall be concerned here—would seek to refine *structural* concepts for the abstraction of patterns on these various issue levels.

III. FOUR TYPES OF PATTERN

For a more adequate conceptualization of patterns, I suggest the labels *symmetrical, asymmetrical, hetero-symmetrical, and hetero-asymmetrical.*

The term *symmetrical* is intended to describe a pattern where the phenomena ratio (e.g., nuclear delivery systems, intensity of ideological commitment, etc.) between two poles is roughly equal, and where the polar actors preempt "possession" of the phenomena at the expense of other possible system actors, or where they at least enjoy overwhelming preponderance. Thus the term not only implies an approximate equilibrium between the two poles but also indicates that they occupy a position of duopoly or preponderance within the system, either with reference to a specific functional area or with reference to the entire functional aggregate of the system. That is only to say, really, that the symmetrical situation is pronouncedly bipolar and carries overtones of Kaplan's "tight" bipolar system.

In an *asymmetrical* pattern the two poles are still predominant in a particular issue area, at the expense of other system actors, but one pole enjoys a position of predominance over the other. A monopoly of nuclear capabilities would be an extreme case of asymmetry. It is under an aggregate of strongly asymmetrical conditions that a bipolar system would tend to transform itself in the direction of a more hierarchical system.

Hetero-symmetrical patterns are those where a functional area is not preempted by the two poles, i.e., where third or fourth forces share in its possession, but the ratio between the two poles is still roughly symmetrical. In this case there is still symmetry with respect to the phenomena ratio with which the two poles confront each other, but it is truncated by the inclusion of other elements. (The graphical representation of the four pattern variations shown in

Figure 1 may be of aid here.) A sizable bloc of uncommitted nations, in addition to the bipolar blocs, would be an example of hetero-symmetry. In the present context the third or "hetero" element will implicitly be viewed as a homogeneous grouping. Depending on the focal point of analytical interest, presumably determined by the issue area, this assumption can readily be removed; all three groupings can then be treated as subsystems and appropriate pattern labels may be applied on the subsystemic level. These systems taxonomies may be circumscribed in the traditional language of the balance-of-power system, etc., or by the use of variations suggested by our symmetry images—e.g., "dissymmetric" for a unit-veto system (Kaplan, 1959, pp. 50-52).

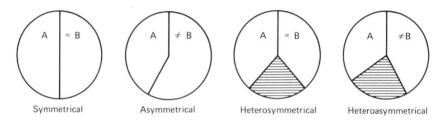

| Symmetrical | Asymmetrical | Heterosymmetrical | Heteroasymmetrical |

FIG. 1.   *Four pattern-variations for an international system.*

In a *hetero-asymmetrical* situation, significant third "hetero" forces have *upset* the equilibrium between the two poles. This pattern tends to suggest a "one-way" transformation when the term is applied to states as system actors. If most nonaligned nations in a loose bipolar system were to join one pole, this would lead not toward hetero-asymmetry but rather toward asymmetry, because the strengthening of one pole would "tighten" bipolarity at the expense of the other pole. Hetero-asymmetry would seem to result most readily from the partial breakup of one of the poles. In this case, hetero-asymmetry could conceivably lead to another bipolar con-figuration—with one bipolar bloc replaced by another bipolar bloc which had previously constituted the "hetero" element in the system. In any event, whereas asymmetrical attributes of a bipolar system carry the seed for "unipolar," hierarchical transforma-tions, hetero-asymmetrical tendencies can lead to a multibloc;

dissymmetric system where one actor tends to predominate (the unaffected pole of the disintegrated bipolar system), or to a new bipolar system if the "hetero" elements are cohesive enough.

Although these symmetry concepts can be applied to total systemic configurations, they are primarily intended for partial, functionally limited levels such as industrial capacity, conventional force levels, and so on—the assumption being, of course, that different levels exhibit different patterns. The fact that the patterns of different functional levels do not coincide, though they may overlap, points to a most interesting aspect of systemic inquiry. Thus one might examine the degree of "compatibility" which exists between functional areas which have different, noncongruous patterns. Important and recurrent incongruities arise from the troublesome decision about what to use as patterning units—the nation-states themselves, or other entities which may be equally relevant or even more so. I have already suggested that the term "bipolar" can be misleading when applied to a cohesive grouping of states in alliances, because it apparently encompasses power considerations in addition to the numerical clustering of alliance partners around two poles. "Bipolarity" conventionally implies both dimensions, and in assessing equilibria they are usually considered together.

Incongruity between the patterns of different systemic levels may be regarded as "structural distance" if recurrent patterns in a system are conceived of as structures. The degree of distance can be thought of as the degree to which patterns on different phenomenal levels do not overlap.[6] The analytic recognition of structural distance between two or more patterns can be very suggestive in getting at crucial systemic processes.

[6]In a different context, Rosenau (1963b) has introduced the concept of "functional distance" as an indicator of the degree to which a particular social situation is political or nonpolitical. "Two actors are considered to be functionally close when their responses to one another are founded on expectations that are clearly defined and are perceived to be very similar, if not identical. Conversely, they are regarded as functionally far apart when their interaction expectations are ambiguous and are perceived to be actually or potentially discrepant." This latter relationship is viewed as political. Rosenau's concept of "functional distance" is directly relevant to the present discussion when applied to the nature of the relationship between the two poles and between them and the "hetero" elements. It offers a tool to indicate relationships between system actors which range from maximum conflict to cooperation, with the possibility that these two behavioral extremes occur simultaneously on different issues.

Let us imagine a bipolar international system where there is very little structural distance and where bipolarity is "tight" on all levels. Conflict is bipolarized, nuclear power is bipolarized, conventional force levels are bipolarized, alliances are bipolarized, and so forth. Surely, the qualities of this system are different from one that exhibits a significant structural distance between the power level and the conflict level. Considerations of this nature allow a number of fruitful analytical explorations. For example, the coming-about of some measure of nuclear parity and the development of regionalism (both institutional and noninstitutional) in the 1950s have created very dissimilar patterns within the international system. There may be approximate symmetry on one level but hetero-symmetry on others. Moreover, there may be a causal connection between these disparate patterns. It was at least in part the emergence of a strongly bipolar pattern on the nuclear level which brought about divergent patterns on other levels of the international system; nuclear parity, by reducing the credibility of some types of nuclear deterrence, is said to have contributed to the loosening of the Western alliance (Osgood, 1961 and 1962). Power structures which had become more symmetrical actually loosened bipolarity and led toward a more hetero-symmetrical pattern on the level of formal and informal alignment. All this suggests the inadequacy of describing the whole system as either bipolar or multibloc.

The example of United Nations voting can be explored in more detail. The voting pattern in an international organization cannot be expected to reflect the power pattern of the membership so long as it rests on one-state-one-vote balloting. There must be significant discrepancies between the support pattern on a particular issue which emerges from counting votes and the power pattern of the voting states. Yet so long as voting behavior in international organizations matters to the superpowers, it affects bipolar equilibria. The tension between the two patterns therefore becomes an important consideration. If this tension were to become extreme and relevant—e.g., by the admission of many small nations and by an increase in the power of the organization—instability between these two functional systems is bound to result. The structural distance between the two levels may be neutralized or stabilized, of course, by third or fourth functional systems (such as nuclear bipolarity) which "hold the ring." Different patterns on different levels may have results which are contradictory, reinforcing, indifferent, etc.; this is precisely the point of seeking analytical refinements on both the functional and the structural plane.

IV. ASSIGNING RULES

In its total phenomenal aggregate, the international system of the last decade could perhaps be labeled a hetero-symmetrical bipolarity. It has symmetrical patterns too, however; to insist on hetero-symmetry as a summary label would be pointless, since my main purpose in introducing this conceptualization was to draw attention to the variety of patterns in the multiple functional layers of the system. Nuclear parity and regionalism, the major factors which transformed the international system in the 1950s, have introduced a complexity of overlapping, divergent, and at times contradictory patterns in these layers. The relationships, the scope of objectives pursued by the participating units, and the tasks performed among them differ significantly from the ones in previous systemic configurations.

The "rules" of this contemporary international system may be regarded as being different from either those postulated in Kaplan's loose bipolar system or those in Masters' multibloc system. The rules of these two models are largely stability-oriented and system-dominant; consequently they impose on the international system a teleology which has often been criticized as quasi-deterministic (see, for example, Hoffmann, 1960, pp. 40-50). Although I share some of these misgivings I do not think that they necessarily invalidate the usefulness of rules taxonomies.

It may be feasible and useful to "assign rules" to specifically identified functional layers instead of to the system as a whole. For example, rules for maintaining military-strategic stability could be distinguished from rules suggested by the nature of diplomatic activity and bargaining relationships. Discrepancies and contradictions between such rules categories would indeed be an interesting field of inquiry. Nor would this perspective necessarily be systems-teleological. Some, at least, of these rules categories would have to take into account internal predispositions of actors—for example, their willingness and capacity for rules "internalization"—and the level of analysis would therefore shift from a systemic to a sub-systemic one.[7]

Most importantly, the power patterns of a hetero-symmetrical bipolar system make it *possible* that one bipolar bloc's loss will not necessarily be the other's gain. Perhaps no political relationship is, strictly speaking, a zero-sum game; but in a confrontation of very

---

[7] For a full treatment of this problem, see Singer (1961); also Hanrieder (1965).

symmetrical powers one contestant's loss may be viewed as the other's immediate gain. The situation is different in a hetero-symmetrical pattern. So long as losses at one pole *may* be accompanied by losses at the other *and* those losses become the gains of nonaligned units, the superpowers can more easily tolerate a reduction of their power levels. The presence of nonaligned units is important; the situation just described is not analogous to partial bilateral disarmament, for example, where the losses of one superpower may be accompanied by losses of the other. For unless nonaligned third parties are present, the *structure* of bipolarity is not affected by a leveling-down of armaments—a bipolar pattern still exists, though on a lower level of power. In that sense, partial disarmament has no immediate structural effect on bipolarity, although it probably would in practice, in the long run. It is the creation of nonaligned third forces which changes the structure of bipolarity immediately and directly.

Thus bipolar actors show a relatively high degree of tolerance for hetero-symmetrical tendencies in contrast with asymmetrical ones.[8] This is a preference for a lesser evil; obviously both superpowers prefer hetero-symmetrical developments to asymmetrical developments which favor the rival bloc. But even favorable asymmetrical developments carry major risks unless they are rapid and extreme. For one thing, events apparently leading to a significant asymmetrical shift of power require an immediate and determined response by the threatened bloc, either by pressuring the opponent to retract and revert to the status quo, or through measures of compensation. Both responses amount to escalation—that is, a major international crisis or an armaments race. It is thus with a certain measure of relief, perhaps, that the superpowers view hetero-symmetrical trends. In short, for a superpower, hetero-symmetry may be preferable to symmetry and, under certain conditions, even to favorable asymmetry.

There is, however, an important exception. Symmetry with regard to nuclear capabilities, if viewed rationally, probably looks more desirable to both superpowers than either asymmetry or hetero-symmetry. This is obvious in the case of asymmetry, since it could mean nuclear preponderance for the opposing superpower. But

---

[8]See the chapter on "Limits of International Coalitions," by Deutsch and Kaplan, in Rosenau (1964); for an application of the pattern of "hetero-symmetrical multi-polarity" to a future international system, see Haas (1964, pp. 483-97).

hetero-symmetry too may be unattractive to either superpower because of the risks and potential chaos involved in the proliferation of nuclear weapons to third or nth powers. Such proliferation might approximate the dissymmetric pattern of Kaplan's "unit veto" international system. Consequently, self-interest induces the superpowers to resist nuclear hetero-symmetrical developments with respect to their own allies, the rival's allies, and nonaligned forces.

In conclusion we may point to a very specific advantage which may be gained from the application of symmetry concepts to defined functional areas of the international system. Because they are adjustable, symmetry images can provide abstractions that can be calibrated to suit the inevitably transitional (from a systems viewpoint) course of historical events. The largely ideographic and thus confining nature of bipolar and polycentric systems images is thereby avoided. Contemporary political phenomena are shifting, overlapping, and often contradictory; systems-analytic guide posts for empirical investigations must be abstractions not only of the past and future but also of the present.

REFERENCES

Easton, David. *The Political System.* New York: Knopf, 1953.

Haas, Ernst B. "Regionalism, Functionalism, and Universal International Organization," *World Politics,* 8, 2 (Jan. 1956), 238-63.

————. "The Comparative Study of the United Nations," *World Politics,* 12, 2 (Jan. 1960), 298-322.

————. *Beyond the Nation-State.* Stanford, Calif.: Stanford University Press, 1964.

Hall, A. D., and R. E. Fagen. "Definitions of a System," *General Systems,* 1 (1956), 18-28.

Hanrieder, Wolfram F. "Actor Objectives and International Systems," *Journal of Politics,* 27, 1 (Feb. 1965), 109-32.

Hoffmann, Stanley H. *Contemporary Theory in International Relations.* Englewood Cliffs, N.J.: Prentice-Hall, 1960.

————. "International Systems and International Law," *World Politics,* 14,1 (Oct. 1961), 205-37.

Kaplan, Morton. *System and Process in International Politics,* New York: Wiley, 1957.

Liska, George. *Nations in Alliance.* Baltimore, Md.: Johns Hopkins Press, 1962.

Masters, Roger. "A Multi-Bloc Model of the International System," *American Political Science Review,* 55, 4 (Dec. 1961), 780-98.

Osgood, Robert E. "Stabilizing the Military Environment," *American Political Science Review*, 55, 1 (Mar. 1961), 24-39.

—————. *NATO: The Entangling Alliance*. Chicago: University of Chicago Press, 1962.

Rosecrance, Richard N. *Action and Reaction in World Politics*. Boston: Little, Brown, 1963.

Rosenau, James N. "The Functioning of International Systems," *Background*, 7, 3 (Nov. 1963a), 111-17.

—————. *Calculated Control as a Unifying Concept in the Study of International Politics and Foreign Policy*. Research Monograph No. 15, Princeton, N.J.: Center of International Studies, Princeton University, 1963b.

—————. (ed.). *International Aspects of Civil Strife*. Princeton, N.J.: Princeton University Press, 1964.

Russett, Bruce M. "Toward a Model of Competitive International Politics," *Journal of Politics*, 25, 2 (May 1963), 226-47.

Singer, J. David. "The Level-of-Analysis Problem in International Relations," *World Politics*, 14, 1 (Oct. 1961), 77-92.

International Structure, National Force, and the Balance of World Power

Kenneth N. Waltz

Balance of power is the hoariest concept in the field of international relations. Elaborated in a variety of analyses and loaded with different meanings, it has often been praised or condemned, but has seldom been wholly rejected. In a fascinating historical account of balance-of-power concepts, Martin Wight has distinguished nine meanings of the term.[1] For purposes of theoretical analysis a tenth meaning, cast in causal terms, should be added.

Balance-of-power theory assumes that the desire for survival supplies the basic motivation of states, indicates the responses that the constraints of the system encourage, and describes the expected outcome. Beyond the survival motive, the aims of states may be

---

SOURCE: From *Journal of International Affairs*, Vol. XXI, No. 2 (1967) pp. 215-31. Copyright © 1967 by the Board of Editors of the *Journal of International Affairs*. Reprinted by permission of the author and the *Journal*.

[1] Martin Wight, "The Balance of Power," in *Diplomatic Investigations: Essays in the Theory of International Politics*, ed. by Herbert Butterfield and Martin Wight (Cambridge: Harvard University Press, 1966), p. 151.

wondrously varied; they may range from the ambition to conquer the world to the desire merely to be left alone. But the minimum responses of states, which are necessary to the dynamics of balance, derive from the condition of national coexistence where no external guarantee of survival exists. Perception of the peril that lies in unbalanced power encourages the behavior required for the maintenance of a balance-of-power system.

Because of the present narrow concentration of awesome power, the question arises whether the affairs of the world can any longer be conducted or understood according to the balance-of-power concept, the main theoretical prop of those traditionally called realists. Even many who share the realist concern with power question its present relevance. They do so for two reasons.

It is, in the first place, widely accepted that balance-of-power politics requires the presence of three or more states. Political thought is so historically conditioned that the balance of power as it is usually defined merely reflects the experience of the modern era. In Europe for a period of three centuries, from the Treaty of Westphalia to the Second World War, five or more great powers sometimes sought to coexist peacefully and at other times competed for mastery. The idea thus became fixed that a balance of power can exist only where the participants approximate the customary number. But something more than habit is involved. Also mixed into ideas about necessary numbers is the notion that flexibility in the alignment of states is a requirement of balance-of-power politics. The existence of only two states at the summit of power precludes the possibility of international maneuver and national realignment as ways of compensating for changes in the strength of either of them. Excessive concentration of power negates the possibility of playing the politics of balance.

Second, war or the threat of war, another essential means of adjustment, is said to be of only limited utility in the nuclear age. In balances of power, of course, more is placed on the scales than mere military force. Military force has, however, served not only as the *ultima ratio* of international politics but indeed as the first and the constant one. To reduce force to being the *ultima ratio* of politics implies, as Ortega y Gasset once noted, "the previous submission of force to methods of reason."[2] Insufficient social cohesion exists among states and the instruments of international control are too weak to relegate power to the status of simply the *ultima ratio*.

---

[2]Quoted in Chalmers Johnson, *Revolutionary Change* (Boston: Little, Brown, 1966), p. 13.

Power cannot be separated from the purposes of those who possess it; in international politics power has appeared primarily as the power to do harm.[3] To interdict the use of force by the threat of force, to oppose force with force, to annex territory by force, to influence the politics of other states by the threat or application of force—such uses of force have always been present at least as possibilities in the relations of states. The threat to use military forces and their occasional commitment to battle have helped to regulate the relations of states, and the preponderance of power in the hands of the major states has set them apart from the others. But, it is now often said, nuclear weapons, the "best" weapons of the most powerful states, are the least usable. At the extreme, some commentators assert that military force has become obsolete. Others, more cautious in their claims, believe that the inflated cost of using military force has seriously distorted both the balance between the militarily strong states and the imbalance between the strong and the weak ones. National military power, though not rendered wholly obsolete by nuclear weapons, nevertheless must be heavily discounted. The power of the two nuclear giants, it would seem, is then seriously impaired.[4]

A weird picture of the political world is thus drawn. The constraints of balance-of-power politics still operate: each state by its own efforts fends for its rights and seeks to maintain its existence. At the same time, the operation of balance-of-power politics is strangely truncated; for one essential means of adjustment is absent, and the operation of the other is severely restricted. In the nineteenth-century liberals' vision of a world without power, force was to be banished internationally by the growing perfection of states and their

[3]I do not mean to imply that this exhausts the purposes of power. In this essay, however, I cannot analyze other aspects of power either in themselves or in relation to the power to do harm.

[4]The point has been made most extensively by Klaus Knorr and most insistently by Stanley Hoffmann. See Knorr, *On the Uses of Military Power in the Nuclear Age* (Princeton: Princeton University Press, 1966). See also Hoffmann, "Obstinate or Obsolete? The Fate of the Nation-State and the Case of Western Europe," *Daedalus*, Vol. XCV (Summer 1965), especially pp. 897, 907; "Europe's Identity Crisis: Between the Past and America," *Daedalus*, Vol. XCIII (Fall 1964), especially pp. 1287-88; "Nuclear Proliferation and World Politics," in *A World of Nuclear Powers?*, ed. by Alastair Buchan (Englewood Cliffs, N.J.: Prentice-Hall, 1966); and two essays in *The State of War* (New York: Praeger, 1965), "Roulette in the Cellar: Notes on Risk in International Relations," especially pp. 140-47, and "Terror in Theory and Practice," especially pp. 233-51.

consequent acceptance of each other as equals in dignity. The liberal utopia has reappeared in odd form. The limitation of power—or in extreme formulations, its abolition—is said to derive from the nuclear armament of some states; for nuclear armament makes at once for gross inequality in the power of states and for substantial equality among all states through the inability of the most powerful to use force effectively. Those who love paradox are understandably enchanted. To examine the ground upon which the supposed paradox rests is one of the main aims of this essay.

I

The first reason for believing that balance-of-power politics has ended is easy to deal with, for only its relevance, not its truth, is in question.

If the balance-of-power game is really played hard it eventuates in two participants, whether states or groupings of them. If two groupings of states have hardened or if the relation of major antagonism in the world is simply between two nations, the balance-of-power model no longer applies, according to the conventional definition. This conclusion is reached by placing heavy emphasis on the process of balancing (by realignments of states) rather than on altering power (which may depend on the efforts of each state).[5] In a two-power world, emphasis must shift from the international process of balancing to the prospect of altering power by the internal efforts of each participant.

Admittedly, the old balance-of-power model cannot be applied without modification to a world in which two states far exceed all others in the force at their disposal. Balance-of-power analysis, however, remains highly useful if the observer shifts his perspective from a concentration upon international maneuver as a mode of adjustment to an examination of national power as a means of control and national effort as a way of compensating for incipient disequilibria of power. With this shift in perspective, balance-of-power politics does not disappear; but the meaning of politics changes in a manner that can only be briefly suggested here.

In a world of three or more powers the possibility of making and breaking alliances exists. The substance of balance-of-power politics is found in the diplomacy by which alliances are made, maintained,

[5]See, for example, Inis L. Claude, Jr., *Power and International Relations* (New York: Random House, 1962), p. 90; and Morton A. Kaplan, *System and Process in International Politics* (New York: John Wiley & Sons, 1957), p. 22.

or disrupted. Flexibility of alignment then makes for rigidity in national strategies: a state's strategy must satisfy its partner lest that partner defect from the alliance. A comparable situation is found where political parties compete for votes by forming and reforming electoral coalitions of different economic, ethnic, religious, and regional groups. The strategies (or policies) of the parties are made so as to attract and hold voters. If it is to be an electoral success, a party's policy cannot simply be the policy that its leaders may think would be best for the country. Policy must at least partly be made for the sake of party management. Similarly in an alliance of approximately equal states, strategy is at least partly made for the sake of the alliance's cohesion. The alliance diplomacy of Europe in the years before World War I is rich in examples of this. Because the defection or defeat of a major state would have shaken the balance of power, each state was constrained to adjust its strategy and the deployment of its forces to the aims and fears of its partners. This is in sharp contrast to the current situation in NATO, where de Gaulle's disenchantment, for example, can only have mild repercussions. Though concessions to allies will sometimes be made, neither the Soviet Union nor the United States alters its strategy or changes its military dispositions simply to accommodate associated states. Both superpowers can make long-range plans and carry out their policies as best they see fit, for they need not accede to the demands of third parties. That America's strategy is not made for the sake of de Gaulle helps to explain his partial defection.

Disregarding the views of an ally makes sense only if military cooperation is relatively unimportant. This is the case in NATO, which in fact if not in form consists of unilateral guarantees by the United States to its European allies. The United States, with a preponderance of nuclear weapons and as many men in uniform as all of the Western European states combined,[6] may be able to protect her allies; they cannot possibly protect her. Because of the vast differences in the capacities of member states, the approximately equal sharing of burdens found in earlier alliance systems is no longer conceivable. The gross inequality between the two superpowers and the members of their respective alliances makes any realignment of the latter fairly insignificant. The leader's strategy can therefore be flexible. In balance-of-power politics, old style, flexibility of alignment made for rigidity of strategy or the limitation of freedom of decision. In balance-of-power politics, new style, the obverse is

[6]See "The Text of Address by McNamara to American Society of Newspaper Editors," *The New York Times*, May 19, 1966, p. 11.

true: rigidity of alignment in a two-power world makes for flexibility of strategy or the enlargement of freedom of decision.

Those who discern the demise of balance-of-power politics mistakenly identify the existence of balances of power with a particular mode of adjustment and the political means of effecting it. Balances of power tend to form so long as states desire to maintain their political identities and so long as they must rely on their own devices in striving to do so. With shrinking numbers, political practices and methods will differ; but the number of states required for the existence and perpetuation of balance-of-power politics is simply two or more, not, as is usually averred, some number larger than two.

II

The reduction in the number of major states calls for a shift in conceptual perspective. Internal effort has replaced external re-alignment as a means of maintaining an approximate balance of power. But the operation of a balance of power, as previously noted, has entailed the occasional use of national force as a means of inter-national control and adjustment. Great-power status was traditionally conferred on states that could use force most handily. Is the use of force in a nuclear world so severely inhibited that balance-of-power analysis has lost most if not all of its meaning?

Four reaons are usually given in support of an affirmative answer. First, because the nuclear might of one superpower balances that of the other, their effective power is reduced to zero. Their best and most distinctive forces, the nuclear ones, are least usable. In the widely echoed words of John Herz, absolute power equals absolute impotence.[7] Second, the fear of escalation strongly inhibits even the use of conventional forces, especially by the United States or the Soviet Union. Nuclear powers must fear escalation more than other states do, for in any war that rose to the nuclear level they would be primary targets. They may, of course, still choose to commit their armies to battle, but the risks of doing so, as they themselves must realize, are higher than in the past. Third, in the nuclear age enormous military power no longer ensures effective control. The Soviet Union has not been able to control her Asian and European satellites. The United States has found it difficult to use military force for constructive purposes even against weak opponents in

[7] John Herz, *International Politics in the Atomic Age* (New York: Columbia University Press, 1959), pp. 22, 169.

Southeast Asia. Political rewards have not been proportionate to the strength of the states that are militarily most powerful. Finally, the weak states of the world, having become politically aware and active, have turned world opinion into a serious restraint upon the use of force, whether in nuclear or conventional form. These four factors, it is argued, work singly and in combination to make the use of force more costly and in general to depreciate its value.

Never have great powers disposed of larger national products, and seldom in peacetime have they spent higher percentages of them on their military forces. The money so lavishly expended purchases more explosive power and more varied ways of delivering it than ever before in history. In terms of world distribution, seldom has military force been more narrowly concentrated. If military force is less useful today, the irony of history will have yet another vivid illustration. Has force indeed so depreciated as to warp and seriously weaken the effects of power in international relations? The above arguments make it seem so; they need to be re-examined. The following analysis of the use of force deals with all four arguments, though not by examining them one by one and in the order in which they are stated.

E. H. Carr long ago identified the error of believing "in the efficacy of an international public opinion," and he illustrated and explained the fallacy at length.[8] To think of world opinion as a restraint upon the military actions of states, one must believe that the strong states of the world—or for that matter the weak ones— would have used more military force and used it more often had they not anticipated their condemnation. Unless in a given instance world opinion can be defined, its source identified, and the mode of its operation discerned, such a view is not plausible. To believe in the efficacy of world opinion is to endow a non-existent agent and an indefinable force with effective restraining power. Not world opinion but national views, shaped into policies and implemented by governments, have accounted for past events in international relations. Changes that would now permit world opinion, whatever that might be, to restrict national policies would have to lie not in the operation of opinion itself but in other changes that have occurred in the world. With "world opinion," as with Adam Smith's "invisible hand," one must ask: What is the reality that the metaphor stands for? It may be that statesmen pay their respects to world opinion because they are already restrained by other considerations.

---

[8] Edward Hallett Carr, *The Twenty Years' Crisis, 1919-1939,* 2nd ed. (New York: Harper & Row, 1964), p. 140.

Are such considerations found, perhaps, in changes that have taken place in the nature and distribution of force itself? If the costs of using military force have lessened its value, then obeisance paid to world opinion is merely a cloak for frustration and a hypocritical show of politeness. That the use of force is unusually costly, however, is a conclusion that rests on a number of errors. One that is commonly committed is to extend to all military force the conclusion that nuclear force is unusable. After listing the changes effected by nuclear weapons, one author, for example, concludes that these changes tend to restrict "the usability and hence the political utility of national military power in various ways."[9] This may represent merely a slip of the pen; if so, it is a telling one. A clearer and more interesting form of the error is found in the argument that the two superpowers, each stalemated by the other's nuclear force, are for important political purposes effectively reduced to the power of middle-range states. The effective equality of states apparently emerges from the very condition of their gross inequality. We read, for example, that "the very change in the nature of the mobilizable potential has made its actual use in emergencies by its unhappy owners quite difficult and self-defeating. As a result, nations endowed with infinitely less can behave in a whole range of issues as if the differences in power did not matter." The conclusion is driven home—or, rather, error is compounded—by the argument that the United States thinks in "cataclysmic terms," lives in dread of all-out war, and bases its military calculations on the forces needed for the ultimate but unlikely crisis rather than on what might be needed in the less spectacular cases that are in fact more likely to occur.[10]

Absolute power equals absolute impotence, at least at the highest levels of force represented by the American and Soviet nuclear armories. At lesser levels of violence many states can compete as though they were substantially equal. The best weapons of the United States and the Soviet Union are useless, and the distinctive advantage of those two states is thus negated. But what about American or Soviet nuclear weapons used against minor nuclear states or against those who are entirely without nuclear weapons? Here again, it is claimed, the "best" weapon of the most powerful states turns out to be the least usable. The nation that is equipped to "retaliate massively" is not likely to find the occasion to use its capability. If amputation of an arm were the only remedy available

[9] Knorr, *On the Uses of Military Power*, p. 87.
[10] Hoffmann, "Europe's Identity Crisis," pp. 1279, 1287-88.

for an infected finger, one would be tempted to hope for the best and leave the ailment untreated. The state that can move effectively only by committing the full power of its military arsenal is likely to forge the threats it has made and acquiesce in a situation formerly described as intolerable. Instruments that cannot be used to deal with small cases—those that are moderately dangerous and damaging—remain idle until the big case arises. But then the use of major force to defend a vital interest would run the grave risk of retaliation. Under such circumstances, the powerful are frustrated by their very strength; and although the weak do not thereby become strong, they are, it is said, nevertheless able to behave as though they were.

Such arguments are often made and have to be taken seriously. In an obvious sense, part of the contention is valid. When great powers are in a stalemate, lesser states acquire an increased freedom of movement. That this phenomenon is now noticeable tells us nothing new about the strength of the weak or the weakness of the strong. Weak states have often found opportunities for maneuver in the interstices of a balance of power. This is, however, only part of the story. To maintain both the balance and its by-product requires the continuing efforts of America and Russia. Their instincts for self-preservation call forth such efforts: the objective of both states must be to perpetuate an internatinal stalemate as a minimum basis for the security of each of them—even if this should mean that the two big states do the work while the small ones have the fun. The margins within which the relative strengths of America and Russia may vary without destroying the stalemate are made wide by the existence of second-strike retaliatory forces, but permissible variation is not without limit. In the years of the supposed missile gap in America's disfavor, Khrushchev became unpleasantly frisky, especially over Berlin and Cuba. The usefulness of maintaining American nuclear strength was demonstrated by the unfortunate consequences of its apparent diminution.

Strategic nuclear weapons deter strategic nuclear weapons (though they may also do more than that). Where each state must tend to its own security as best it can, the means adopted by one state must be geared to the efforts of others. The cost of the American nuclear establishment, maintained in peaceful readiness, is functionally comparable to the costs incurred by a government in order to maintain domestic order and provide internal security. Such expenditure productive in the sense that spending to build roads is, but it is not unproductive either. Its utility is obvious, and should anyone successfully argue otherwise, the consequences of accepting his argument would quickly demonstrate its falsity. Force is least visible where power is most fully and most adequately present.[11] The better ordered a society and the more competent and respected its government, the less force its policemen are required to employ. Less shooting occurs in present-day Sandusky than did on the western frontier. Similarly in international relations, states supreme in their power have to use force less often. "Nonrecourse to force"—as both Eisenhower and Khrushchev seem to have realized—is the doctrine of powerful states. Powerful states need to use force less often than their weaker neighbors because the strong can more often protect their interests or work their wills in other ways—by persuasion and cajolery, by economic bargaining and bribery, by the extension of aid, or finally by posing deterrent threats. Since states with large nuclear armories do not actually "use" them, force is said to be discounted. Such reasoning is fallacious. Possession of power should not be identified with the use of force, and the usefulness of force should not be confused with its usability. To introduce such confusions into the analysis of power is comparable to saying that the police force that seldom if ever employs violence is weak or that a police force is strong only when policemen are swinging their clubs. To vary the image, it is comparable to saying that a man with large assets is not rich if he spends little money or that a man is rich only if he spends a lot of it.

But the argument, which we should not lose sight of, is that just as the miser's money may grossly depreciate in value over the years, so the great powers' military strength has lost much of its usability. If military force is like currency that cannot be spent spent or money that has lost much of its worth, then is not forbearance in its use merely a way of disguising its depreciated value? Conrad von Hötzendorf, Austrian Chief of Staff prior to the First World War, looked upon military power as though it were a capital sum, useless unless invested. In his view, the investment of military force was ultimately its commitment to battle.[12] It may be permissible to reason in this way, but it makes the result of the reasoning a fore-

[11]Cf. Carr, *The Twenty Years' Crisis*, pp. 103, 129-32.

[12]"The sums spent for the war power is money wasted," he maintained, "if the war power remains unused for obtaining political advantages. In some cases the mere threat will suffice and the war power thus becomes useful, but others can be obtained only through the warlike use of the war power itself, that is, by war undertaken in time; if this moment is missed, the capital is lost. In this sense, war becomes a great financial enterprise of the State." Quoted in Alfred Vagts, *Defense and Diplomacy: The Soldier and the Conduct of Foreign Relations* (New York: King's Crown Press, 1956), p. 361.

gone conclusion. As Robert W. Tucker has noted, those who argue that force has lost its utility do so "in terms of its virtually un-controlled use." But, he adds, "alter the assumption on which the argument proceeds—consider the functions served by military power so long as it is not overtly employed or employed only with re-straint—and precisely the opposite conclusion may be drawn."[13]

In the reasoning of Conrad, military force is most useful at the moment of its employment in war. Depending on a country's situation, it may make much better sense to say that military force is most useful when it deters an attack, that is, when it need not be used in battle at all. When the strongest state militarily is also a status-quo power, non-use of force is a sign of its strength. Force is most useful, or best serves the interests of such a state, when it need not be used in the actual conduct of warfare. Again, the reasoning is old-fashioned. Throughout a century that ended in 1914, the British navy was powerful enough to scare off all comers, while Britain carried out occasional imperial ventures in odd parts of the world. Only as Britain's power weakened did her military forces have to be used to fight a full-scale war. By being used, her military power had surely become less useful.

Force is cheap, especially for a status-quo power, if its very existence works against its use. What does it mean then to say that the cost of using force has increased while its utility has lessened? It is highly important, indeed useful, to think in "cataclysmic terms," to live in dread of all-out war, and to base military calculations on the forces needed for the ultimate but unlikely crisis. That the United States does so, and that the Soviet Union apparently does too, makes the cataclysm less likely to occur. But not only that. Nuclear weapons deter nuclear weapons; they also serve as a means of limiting escalation. The temptation of one country to employ larger and larger amounts of force is lessened if its opponent has the ability to raise the ante. Conventional force may be used more hesi-tantly than it would be in the absence of nuclear weapons because it cannot be assumed that escalation will be perfectly regulated. But force can be used with less hesitation by those states able to parry, to thrust, and to threaten at varied levels of military endeavor.

Where power is seen to be balanced, whether or not the balance is nuclear, it may seem that the resultant of opposing forces is zero.

[13]Robert W. Tucker, "Peace and War," *World Politics,* Vol. XVII (Jan. 1965), p. 324 fn. For a comprehensive and profound examination of the use of force internationally, see Robert Osgood and Robert Tucker, *Force, Order, and Justice* (forthcoming).

But this is misleading. The vectors of national force do not meet at a point, if only because the power of a state does not resolve into a single vector. Military force is divisible, especially for the state that can afford a lot of it. In a nuclear world, contrary to some assertions, the dialectic of inequality does not produce the effective equality of strong and weak states. Lesser states that decide to establish a nuclear arsenal by slighting their conventional forces render themselves unable to meet any threat to themselves other than the ultimate one (and that doubtfully). By way of contrast, the military doctrine of the United States, to which the organization of her forces corresponds, is one of flexible response. Great powers are strong not simply because they have nuclear weapons but also because their immense resources enable them to generate and maintain power of all types, military and other, at different technological levels.

Just as the state that refrains from applying force is said to betray its weakness, so the state that has trouble in exercising control is said to display the defectiveness of its power. In such a conclusion, the elementary error of identifying power with control is evident. Absence of control or failure to press hard to achieve it may indicate either that the would-be controller noticed that, try as he might, he would have insufficient force or inappropriate types of force at his command; or it may indicate that he chose to make less than a maximum effort because imposition of control was not regarded as very important. One student of international relations has remarked that "though the weapons of mass destruction grow more and more ferociously efficient, the revolutionary guerrilla armed with nothing more advanced than an old rifle and a nineteenth-century political doctrine has proved the most effective means yet devised for altering the world power-balance."[14] But the revolutionary guerrilla wins civil wars, not international ones, and no civil war can change the balance of power in the world unless it takes place in the United States or the Soviet Union. Enough of them have occurred since the Second World War to make the truth of this statement clear without need for further analysis. Even in China, the most populous of states, a civil war that led to a change of allegiance in the cold war did not seriously tilt the world balance.

Two states that enjoy wide margins of power over other states need worry little about changes that occur among the latter. Failure to act may then not betray the frustrations of impotence; instead it

[14]Coral Bell, "Non-Alignment and the Power Balance," *Survival,* Vol. V (Nov.-Dec. 1963), p. 255.

may demonstrate the serenity of power. The United States, having chosen to intervene in Vietnam, has limited the use of its military force. Because no realignment of national power in Vietnam could in itself affect the balance of power between the United States and the Soviet Union—or even noticeably alter the imbalance of power between the United States and China—the United States need not have intervened at all. Whether or not it could have safely "passed" in Southeast Asia, the American government chose not to do so; nor have its costly, long-sustained efforts brought success. If military power can be equated with control, then the United States has indeed demonstrated its weakness. The case is instructive. The People's Republic of China has not moved militarily against any country of Southeast Asia. The United States could successfully counter such a move one would expect, by opposing military force with military force. What has worried some people and led others to sharpen their statements about the weakness of the powerful is that the United States, hard though it has tried, has been unable to put down insurrection and halt the possible spread of Communist ideology.

Here again old truths need to be brought into focus. As David Hume long ago noted, "force is always on the side of the governed."[15] The governors, being few in number, depend for the exercise of their rule upon the more or less willing assent of their subjects. If sullen disregard is the response to every command, no government can rule. And if a country, because of internal disorder and lack of coherence, is unable to rule itself, no body of foreigners, whatever the military force at its command, can reasonably hope to do so. If Communism is the threat to Southeast Asia then military forces are not the right means for countering it. If insurrection is the problem, then it can hardly be hoped that an alien army will be able to pacify a country that is unable to govern itself. Foreign troops, though not irrelevant to such problems, can only be of indirect help. Military force, used internationally is a means of establishing control over a territory, not of exercising control within it. The threat of a nation to use military force, whether nuclear or conventional, is

---

[15] "The soldan of Egypt or the emperor of Rome," he went on to say, "might drive his harmless subjects like brute beasts against their sentiments and inclination. But he must, at least, have led his *mamalukes* or *praetorian bands*, like men, by their opinion." "Of the First Principles of Government," in *Hume's Moral and Political Philosophy*, ed. by Henry D. Aiken (New York: Hafner, 1948), p. 307.

pre-eminently a means of affecting another state's external behavior, of dissuading a state from launching a career of aggression and of meeting the aggression if dissuasion should fail.

Dissuasion or deterrence is easier to accomplish than "compellence," to use an apt term invented by Thomas C. Schelling.[16] Compellence is more difficult to achieve than deterrence and its contrivance is a more intricate affair. In Vietnam, the United States faces not merely the task of compelling a particular action but of promoting an effective political order. Those who argue from such a case that force has depreciated in value fail in their analyses to apply their own historical and political knowledge. The master builders of imperial rule, such men as Bugeaud, Gallieni, and Lyautey, played both political and military roles. In like fashion, successful counter-revolutionary efforts have been directed by such men as Templer and Magsaysay, who combined military resources with political instruments.[17] Military forces, whether domestic or foreign, are insufficient for the task of pacification, the more so if a country is rent by faction and if its people are politically engaged and active. To say that militarily strong states are feeble because they cannot easily bring order to minor states is like saying that a pneumatic hammer is weak because it is not suitable for drilling decayed teeth. It is to confuse the purpose of instruments and to confound the means of external power with the agencies of internal governance. Inability to exercise *political* control over others does not indicate *military* weakness. Strong states cannot do everything with their military forces, as Napoleon acutely realized; but they are able to do things that militarily weak states cannot do. The People's Republic of China can no more solve the problems of governance in some Latin American country than the United States can in Southeast Asia. But the United States can intervene with great military force in far quarters of the world while wielding an effective deterrent against escalation. Such action exceeds the capabilities of all but the strongest of states.

Differences in strength do matter, though not for every conceivable purpose. To deduce the weakness of the powerful from this qualifying clause is a misleading use of words. One sees in such a case as Vietnam not the *weakness* of great military power in a nuclear

[16]Thomas C. Schelling, *Arms and Influence* (New Haven: Yale University Press, 1966), pp. 70-71.

[17]The point is well made by Samuel P. Huntington, "Patterns of Violence in World Politics," in *Changing Patterns of Military Politics*, ed. by Samuel P. Huntington (New York: The Free Press of Glencoe, 1962), p. 28.

world but instead a clear illustration of the *limits* of military force in the world of the present as always.

III

Only a sketch, intended to be suggestive, can here be offered of the connections between the present structure of the global balance of power, the relations of states, and the use of force internationally.

Unbalanced power is a danger to weak states. It may also be a danger to strong ones. An imbalance of power, by feeding the ambition of some states to extend their control, may tempt them to dangerously adventurous activity. Safety for all states, one may then conclude, depends upon the maintenance of a balance among them. Ideally, in this view, the rough equality of states gives each of them the ability to fend for itself. Equality may then also be viewed as a morally desirable condition. Each of the states within the arena of balance will have a modest ability to maintain its integrity. At the same time, inequality violates one's sense of justice and leads to national resentments that are in many ways troublesome. Because inequality is inherent in the state system, however, it cannot be removed. At the pinnacle of power, only a few states coexist as approximate equals; in relation to them, other states are of lesser moment. The bothersome qualities of this inevitable inequality of states should not cause one to overlook its virtues. In an economy, in a polity, or in the world at large, extreme equality is associated with instability. To draw another domestic analogy: where individualism is extreme, where society is atomistic, and where secondary organizations are lacking, government tends either to break down into anarchy or to become highly centralized and despotic. Under conditions of extreme equality, the prospect of oscillation between those two poles was well described by de Tocqueville; it was illustrated by Hobbes; and its avoidance was earnestly sought by the authors of the *Federalist Papers*. In a collection of equals, any impulse ripples through the whole society. Lack of secondary groups with some cohesion and continuity of commitment, for example, turns elections into auctions with each party in its promises tempted to bid up the others. The presence of social and economic groups, which inevitably will not all be equal, makes for less volatility in society.

Such durable propositions of political theory are lost sight of in the argument, frequently made, that the larger the number of consequential states the more stable the structure of world politics will be.[18] Carried to its logical conclusion, the argument must mean that perfect stability would prevail in a world in which many states exist, all of them approximate equals in power.

The analysis of the present essay leads to a different conclusion. The inequality of states, though not a guarantee of international stability, at least makes stability possible. Within the structure of world politics, the relations of states will be as variable and complex as the movements and patterns of bits of glass within a kaleidoscope. It is not very interesting to ask whether destabilizing events will occur and disruptive relations will form, because the answer must always be yes. More interesting are such questions as these: What is the likely durability of a given political structure, whether international or domestic? How does it affect the relations of states, or of groups and individuals? How do the relations of constituent units and changes within them in turn affect the political structure? Within a state, people use more violence than do governments. In the United States in 1965, 9,814 people were murdered, but only seven were executed.[19] Thus one says (with some exaggeration, since fathers still spank their children) that the state enjoys a monopoly of *legitimate* violence. Too much violence among individuals will jeopardize the political structure. In international relations it is difficult to say that any particular use of violence is illegitimate, but some states have the ability to wield more of it. Because they do, they are able both to moderate others' use of violence and to absorb possibly destabilizing changes that emanate from uses of violence that they do not or cannot control. In the spring of 1966, Secretary McNamara remarked that in the preceding eight years there had been "no less than 164 internationally significant outbreaks of violence. . . ."[20] Of course, not only violence is at issue. To put the point in more general terms, strong structures are able to moderate and absorb destabilizing changes; weak structures succumb to them.

No political structure, whether domestic or international, can guarantee stability. The question that one must ask is not whether a given distribution of power is stable but how stable different distributions of power are likely to be. For a number of reasons, the

[18] By "structure" I mean the pattern according to which power is distributed; by "stability," the perpetuation of that structure without the occurrence of grossly destructive violence.

[19] U.S. Bureau of the Census, *Statistical Abstract of the United States: 1966* (Washington, D.C.: Government Printing Office, 1966), p. 165.

[20] *The New York Times*, May 19, 1966, p. 11.

bipolar world of the past two decades has been highly stable.[21] The two leading states have a common interest in stability: they would at least like to maintain their positions. In one respect, bipolarity is expressed as the reciprocal control of the two strongest states by each other out of their mutual antagonism. What is unpredictable in such a two-party competition is whether one party will try to eliminate the other. Nuclear forces of second-strike capacity induce an added caution. Here again force is useful, and its usefulness is reinforced in proportion as its use is forestalled. Fear of major war induces caution all around; the Soviet Union and the United States wield the means of inducing that caution.

The constraints of duopolistic competition press in one direction: duopolists eye each other warily, and each is very sensitive to the gains of the other. Working in the opposite direction, however, is the existence of the immense difference in power between the two super-powers and the states of middle or lesser rank. This condition of inequality makes it unlikely that any shifts in the alignment of states would very much help or hurt either of the two leading powers. If few changes can damage the vital interests of either of them, then both can be moderate in their responses. Not being dependent upon allies, the United States and the Soviet Union are free to design strategies in accord with their interests. Since the power actually and potentially at the disposal of each of them far exceeds that of their closest competitors, they are able to control in some measure the possibly destabilizing acts of third parties or to absorb their effects. The Americans and Russians, for example, can acquire the means of defending themselves against the nuclear assaults that the Chinese and French may be able to launch by the mid-1970's. Anti-ballistic-missile systems, useful against missiles launched in small number, are themselves anti-proliferation devices. With considerable expectation of success, states with vast economic, scientific, and technological resources can hope to counter the armaments aand actions of others and to reduce their destabilizing effects.[22] The extent of the difference in national capabilities makes the bipolar structure

[21] For further examination of the proposition, see Kenneth N. Waltz, "The Stability of a Bipolar World," *Daedalus,* Vol. XCIII (Summer 1964), pp. 881-909. On the possibility of exercising control, see Waltz, "Contention and Management in International Relations," *World Politics,* Vol. XVII (July 1965), pp. 720-44.

[22] On the limitations of a small nuclear force, see Waltz, *Foreign Policy and Democratic Politics* (Boston: Little, Brown, 1967), pp. 145-48.

resilient. Defection of allies and national shifts of allegiance do not decisively alter the structure. Because they do not, recalcitrant allies may be treated with indifference; they may even be effectively disciplined. Pressure can be applied to moderate the behavior of third states or to check and contain their activities. The Suez venture of Britain and France was stopped by American financial pressure. Chiang Kai-shek has been kept on a leash by denying him the means of invasion. The prospective loss of foreign aid helped to halt warfare between Pakistan and India, as did the Soviet Union's persuasion. In such ways, the wielding of great power can be useful.

The above examples illustrate hierarchical control operating in a way that often goes unnoticed because the means by which control is exercised are not institutionalized. What management there now is in international relations must be provided, singly and occasionally together, by the duopolists at the top. In certain ways, some of them suggested above, the inequality of states in a bipolar world enables the two most powerful states to develop a rich variety of controls and to follow flexible strategies in using them.

A good many statements about the obsolescence of force, the instability of international politics, and the disappearance of the bipolar order are made because no distinction has been clearly and consistently drawn between international structure, on the one hand, and the relations of states on the other. For more than two decades, power has been narrowly concentrated; and force has been used, not orgiastically as in the world wars of this century, but in a controlled way and for conscious political purposes. Power may be present when force is not used, but force is also used openly. A catalogue of examples would be both complex and lengthy. It would contain such items, on the American side of the ledger, as the garrisoning of Berlin, its supply by airlift during the blockade, the stationing of troops in Europe, the establishment of bases in Japan and elsewhere, the waging of war in Korea and Vietnam, and the "quarantine" of Cuba. Seldom if ever has force been more variously, more persistently, and more widely applied; and seldom has it been more consciously used as an instrument of national policy. Since the war we have seen, not the cancellation of force by nuclear statemate, but instead the political organization and pervasion of power; not the end of balance of power owing to a reduction in the number of major states, but instead the formation and perpetuation of a balance à deux.

Bipolarity, Multipolarity, and the Future

R. N. Rosecrance

In April 1961 Dr. Stanley Hoffmann of Harvard University reminded us that it was no longer sufficient to design ideal schemes for the preservation of peace on earth (Hoffmann, 1961). World government might be completely desirable, but it was also unattainable. In future our projected utopias should also be "relevant." Various writers have since taken up Hoffmann's challenge, and we are now told that "bipolarity" on the one hand or "multipolarity" on the other are practical answers to major current difficulties (see Waltz, 1964; Deutsch and Singer, 1964). The purpose of the present essay is to examine these proposed "relevant utopias" and to offer an alternative view. In the end we will discover that neither bipolarity nor multipolarity provides general solutions to basic conflicts in the contemporary international system.

SOURCE: From *Journal of Conflict Resolution*, Vol. X, No. 3 (1966). Copyright © 1966 by the University of Michigan Press. Reprinted by permission of the author and the University of Michigan Press.

1. BIPOLARITY

The argument for bipolarity is dual: it is allegedly desirable, as opposed, say, to a multipolar international order; it is also a continuing state of affairs. Four reasons are given to persuade us that a bipolar order will reduce international violence. First, "with only two world powers there are no peripheries" (Waltz, 1964, p. 882). This juxtaposition entails a vital interest and involvement in all the outcomes of world politics. Both the Soviets and the Americans must be concerned with happenings in widely separated areas of the globe—Korea, Cuba, Vietnam, Eastern Europe, to name but a few. Far from leading to violence, however, the commitment on opposite sides has led to a solid and determinate balance. No expansion could be decisively successful; counterpressure is always applied. The very existence of serial confrontation renders the balance more stable. Each counterposition of power discourages the next. There are no realms open to aggrandizement.

Second, not only is the competition extensive, but its intensity has increased. The space race, economic growth, military preparedness, the propaganda struggle, and domestic issues of all sorts have assumed significance in international relations. "Policy proceeds by imitation, with occasional attempts to outflank" (Waltz, 1964, p. 883). Nothing escapes calculation in terms of the international balance. By asserting the interests of the two great powers in even minor equilibrations of the balance, the bipolar international system keeps on an even keel; nice adjustments do not pass unnoticed. A third stabilizing factor is the "nearly constant presence of pressure and the recurrence of crises" (Waltz, 1964, p. 883). Crises are natural and even desirable in a condition of conflict. If crises do not occur, it means that one side or the other is neglecting its own interests. Maintenance of the balance will then require small or large wars waged later on. As long as there are only two major protagonists, there can be no question of the impact caused by a favorable change in the position of one; there also, presumably, can be no uncertainty of an "equal and opposite reaction." "When possible enemies are several in number [however] unity of action among states is difficult to secure." Under bipolar conditions, moreover, "caution, moderation, and the management of crisis come to be of great . . . importance" (Waltz, 1964, p. 884). One pushes to the limit, but not beyond.

Fourth, and finally, the preponderant power of the two superstates means that minor shifts in the balance are not of decisive significance. The US "lost" China in 1949, the Soviet Union "lost" it in 1962, but neither change drastically altered the Russian-American equipoise. The two states were so strong they could accommodate change. While defection of a major Western European state would be significant, "a five percent growth rate sustained for three years would add to the American gross national product an amount greater than the entire gross national product of Britain or France or West Germany" (Waltz, 1964, p. 903). Rearmament, economic growth, scientific education—all these were means of internal compensation for international shifts in the balance. The US and the USSR confronted each other over each proximate issue, but few of the issues were of decisive importance.

Not only is bipolarity desirable—its proponents claim that it will continue indefinitely; it is a condition to which we must adjust. Patterns of economic growth indicate that the Soviet Union and the United States will have economic systems more than twice as large as any conceivable competitor until past the year 2000. Nor has the spread of nuclear weapons appreciably influenced the amount of power middle-ranking states can dispose. Britain's nuclear program, so it is argued, is dependent on the US, and while France may gain an independent capability, she is likely to find it vulnerable or useless in a crisis. If independent capabilities began to be significant militarily, the nuclear giants would merely increase their offensive or defensive postures (Waltz, 1964, pp. 894-95). As a result of modest exertions, the bipolar world would be restored.

2. BIPOLARITY: A CRITIQUE

There are, in rejoinder, three arguments against bipolarity as a desirable (or even as the best attainable) international system. The first is that bipolarity comprehends only one of the impulsions to expansion or aggression. While it may be true that international polarization helps to prevent successful expansion by either side, since it calls forth counterpressure by the opposing camp, it does not reduce motivations for expansion and may even increase them. Since the competition between poles is both intensive and extensive, each action by one will be viewed as a strategic gambit by the other. Even actions which may not be intended to have international reference will be seen in terms of the bipolar competition. This in turn must accentuate the political hostility between camps. The antagonism generated on one side by action of the other will be reciprocated, and the tempo of discord will increase. Since the competition is akin to that of a zero-sum game (see Waltz, 1964, p. 882), this is a quite natural outcome. Any advance in the position of one must take place at the expense of his adversary; hence the slightest improvement in the position of one must provoke the other to new exertions. The respective concern to advance or maintain one's position is realistic in the framework of a two-power competition. The psychological climate in which such a struggle takes place, moreover, is likely to be one of growing ill-will. At some point in this degenerative process one side may think not only of the risks consequent upon striking his opponent, but also of the risks he may suffer if he decides not to strike. Eventually reciprocal fears of surprise attack may grow to such a point that they cannot be endured. Preventive war may be seen to be preferable to war at the opponent's initiative.

A second disadvantage of the case for bipolarity is that two quite different notions of the term appear to be employed. According to one, the Soviet Union and the United States are engaged in a duel for world supremacy or, at minimum, in a struggle to maintain their relative positions. An action by one directly affects the position of the other; all international changes are of vital significance in that they affect the balance between the two. According to the other notion of bipolarity, however, substantial territorial and/or political changes can take place in international relations without impinging on the overarching stability. The US can "gain" or "lose" China without appreciable impact on the balance. If the latter is true, it is because international politics is not analogous to a two-person zero-sum game. The increment (or decrement) to the US is not a simultaneous loss (or gain) to the USSR. The "gain" is not at the expense of previously Soviet-held territory; the "loss" is not at the expense of previously American-held territory. China is an independent quantity in world politics, not merely a factor in Soviet or Western strength.[1] If this situation prevails, there can be important shifts in the international balance which do not upset the basic relation between the US and the USSR. That relation, however, is no longer bipolar. All changes are either vital in that they directly affect the bipolar balance, or they are not vital in that they fail to do so.[2]

[1] It should be noted that it is not pertinent to argue that the magnitude of bipolar power *vis-à-vis* Chinese power is so great that a change in Chinese allegiance is insignificant. If Chinese power is very slight compared with both bipolar powers, the balance between poles is narrow enough to make a switch in alliance of great importance.

[2] Waltz recognizes but does not assign due weight to this contradiction (see Waltz, 1964, p. 903).

Thirdly, the prescription "peace by crisis" is a dubious palliative. It seems equivalent to saying that the world's most peaceful place is on the brink of war. Pacific features may be present in one sense, in that nations presumably try harder to avoid war when they are faced with it as an immediate prospect. But if the will to avoid war is greater, the proximity of war is also greater. Cuban and Vietnamese crises may be stabilizing in that they teach techniques of "crisis management," but they are destabilizing in that there is always the possibility that the lessons will not be learned. When one decides to fight fire with fire, he engages in a policy of calculated risks. At minimum it is not unambiguously clear that serial crises are the best means to peace.

Bipolarity also seems to have been confused with *détente*. Under conditions of *détente* crises may be manageable, and peace may be preserved. But *détente* is directly contrary to one of the major formulations of bipolarity. *Détente* presumes that the interests of two parties can be advanced simultaneously. The zero-sum notion of bipolarity requires that the interests of one can be advanced only at the expense of those of the other. And if it is then maintained that the looser notion of bipolarity is to be accepted in consequence, one may rejoin that a loose bipolar system does not involve an absence of peripheries. The two poles may then remain partially indifferent and unaffected by even significant changes in the distribution of inter-national power. Immediate countervailing pressures, then, are not called forth by each change in the status quo. Imbalance may emerge. In the result one must choose between two different inter-national systems: a system in which change can be accommodated without drastic action by the two major camps and in which, as a result, disequilibrium can occur; or a system in which there is a taut balance maintained by vigilant employment of counterpressure and in which the antagonism between camps is likely to be very great. The first may permit *détente* but is not strictly bipolar; the second offers stringent bipolarity but rules out accommodation. The two notions are not compatible, and the argument for one undermines the contentions urged on behalf of the other.

3. MULTIPOLARITY

If bipolarity does not pass muster as a "relevant utopia" for inter-national relations, what of multipolarity? Does it have special advantages to offer? Again a dual argument may be given. Multi-polarity, it is maintained, not only meets the requirements of a reasonable utopia, but it can be approximated in future international politics.[3] Aside from the feasibility of multipolarity, however, three basic reasons commend it to our attention as a desirable international system. First, multipolarity affords a greater number of interaction opportunities (Deutsch and Singer, 1964, pp. 392-96). The number of possible dyadic relationships in a multipolar system is very great, and it rises in increasing proportion to the number of states (poles). This plenitude of interacting partners means that there is a greatly reduced danger of mutually reinforcing antagonism between two states. Individual states will have associations with a great variety of others; their cross-cutting loyalties will tend to reduce hostility expressed toward one particular state or against one particular cause. Multipolarity, it is claimed, avoids the major disadvantage of a bipolar international order. Since world politics would not be a zero-sum game, action by one nation would not require an offsetting response by its single opponent. Instead of the mutual reinforcement of hostility expressed in terms of "positive feedback" there may be the dissipation of hostility through "negative feedback" (Deutsch and Singer, 1964, p. 393). Multipolarity, then, provides the basis for a stable social system; bipolarity cannot do so. In addition, not only does the need for the expression of augmented hostility fail to appear, but the availability of alternative partners makes possible a response other than direct challenge or military threat. If a state finds itself the object of hostility, it may respond indirectly by firming its connections with other states. This in turn preserves the peaceful atmosphere.

A second argument offered on behalf of multipolarity is that it diminishes the attention paid to other states (Deutsch and Singer, 1964, pp. 396-400); ". . . as the number of independent actors in the system increases, the share of its attention that any nation can devote to any other must of necessity decrease" (p. 396). Since a nation can only actively attend to a certain maximum number of other states at any given time, a large multipolar international system will mean that a number of national actions will not reach the threshold of international significance. Conflicts may be limited in this manner. "It is perhaps not excessive to assume that the minimal attention ratio for an escalating conflict would have to be 1:9, since it does not seem likely that any country could be provoked very far

[3]Hedley Bull, for example, sees warrant for the view that in the next ten years "the system of polarization of power will cease to be recognizable; that other states will count for so much in world politics that the two present great powers will find it difficult, even when cooperating, to dominate them" (Bull, 1963, p. 21).

into an escalating conflict with less than 10 percent of the foreign policy attention of its government devoted to the matter" (Deutsch and Singer, 1964, p. 399). An eleven-state world (assuming relative equality of power) would, then, avoid serious conflict (p. 398).

Thirdly, it is contended that a multipolar system, in contrast to bipolarity, has a dampening effect upon arms races. If a state, A, is allocating half of its military strength against B and half against C and D together, and B begins to rearm, A's countervailing increment is only half of what it would be if A and B were the only powers in the system. The typical bipolar model, involving an escalating arms race between two opposed powers, then fails to predict the outcome. Multipolarity is responsible for limiting the arms competition.

The proponents of multipolarity admit that there are circumstances under which an international system of many equivalent powers could become unstable. In present-day international politics there are powers more reckless than the Soviet Union and the United States. If these powers obtained a nuclear weapons capability they might use it in a disruptive fashion (Deutsch and Singer, 1964, p. 404). But ". . . *if the spread of nuclear weapons could be slowed down or controlled,* a transition from the bipolar international system of the early 1950s to an increasingly multipolar system in the 1960s might buy mankind some valuable time to seek some more dependable bases for world order" (p. 406; authors' emphasis). It is also acknowledged that, while multipolarity is most likely in the near future, in the long run there seems to be a tendency for multipolar systems to break down. "If the probability of states' perishing is small, but larger than zero, and the probability of substantial new powers' arising is zero . . . then the model will predict a diminishing number of effective contenders, leading eventually to a two-power world or to the survival of a single power. . ." (p. 405). Assuming restraint on the dispersion of nuclear weapons and imminent multipolarity in the immediate future, however, one can look forward to a more peaceful international environment.

4. MULTIPOLARITY: A CRITIQUE

The case of multipolarity offers remedies for certain of the disadvantages of bipolarity mentioned above. There should be no cause under multipolarity for total international concentration on the reciprocally reinforcing hostility between two states. Alternative interests, antagonisms, and connections should distract attention from a focused bilateral struggle. If two-power arms races develop, they should be of much less consequence than under bipolarity. At the same time, multipolarity has its unique deficiencies. At least three points may be raised against it.

First, it seems highly probable that a multipolar world order will increase the number of international conflicts, though it may possibly reduce their significance. A bipolar system can have but one antagonism; multipolarity, on the other hand, may have virtually numberless frictions. While the attentions of international actors will be dispersed throughout the system, the variety of national interests expressed will multiply. Inevitably, national interests are a complex amalgam of popular attitudes, tradition, geographic situation, economic and military strength, ideological orientation, and governmental structure. Since in a multipolar order a great number of states will be significant actors in the system, a bewildering range of claims and interests must ensue. As other writers have contended, conflict is partly a function of the degree of particularity in the international system (see Waltz, 1959). The greater the gamut of demands, the harder it must be to accommodate them. Thus multipolarity, by increasing diversity, must also increase conflicts of interest.

This assessment may be countered by the argument that the results of multipolar conflict will be much less catastrophic for the international system than the potential results of bipolar conflict; that:

$$P_{bc} \times R_{bc} > P_{mc} \times R_{mc}$$

where P_{bc} and R_{bc} are the probability and results of bipolar conflict and P_{mc} and R_{mc} are similar quantities for multipolar conflict. The expectation of bipolar conflict (probability times results) would be greater than the expectation of multipolar conflict. This reformulation, however, is open to two difficulties. First, it shows that the advantages of the multipolar system depend on the variable magnitudes assumed. If a multipolar order limits the consequences of conflict, it can scarcely diminish their number. If a bipolar system involves a serious conflict between the two poles, it at least reduces or eliminates conflict elsewhere in the system. The choice between systems, then, depends upon the size of the respective quantities in a given case. Second, if nuclear weapons are widely disseminated in a multipolar environment, bipolarity must be seen to be the better alternative. In such circumstances the greater frequency of multipolar conflict would be accompanied by devastating or disastrous results, and the probability-times-results formula above would suggest that a bipolar system is preferable.

The second major criticism of the case for multipolarity flows directly from these considerations. If a multipolar international order is as harmonious as its proponents claim, even widespread distribution of nuclear weapons should not destabilize the system. As new states enter, the ensuing diminution of national attention should reduce friction. If states really fail to pay attention to their fellows, what differences should diffusion of nuclear weapons make? That the dissemination of weapons is viewed as crucial, however, indicates that multipolar exponents recognize the latent conflict in a multistate system. States are reckless only if they are, or conceive themselves to be, embroiled in conflict. Those features of multipolarity with which we are familiar (in the nationalist, underdeveloped world) are not characterized by lack of interest or attention. They are marked by a highly political awareness of the postures and attitudes of other states. And if some states do not attend to one another, as might be assumed to be the case in the relations of—say—Thailand and Bolivia, this is by no means a general feature of underdeveloped politics. The occasional discontinuities in communication in one part of the system are more than compensated by the range and depth of contacts, both friendly and hostile, which occur in others. Since these contacts link states of very different national interests, they are bound to produce antagonism. And atomic weapons superimposed on antagonism are a recipe for instability.

Thirdly, a multipolar international system, while reducing the significance of any single change of alignment or military posture, inevitably compounds uncertainty. In a bipolar world, an adjustment in relative position of the two poles is important for the entire system. Changes, however, are relatively simple to predict. In a multipower world a single alteration in alliance combination or military prowess may not be decisive for the system as a whole, but its consequences are far more difficult to calculate (see Burns, 1957). The number of tentative combinations is astronomic; military dispositions may take myriad forms. Multipolarity, then, raises the difficulty of policy-making. Results may be altogether unforeseen; choice becomes very complex. Since multipolarity raises incalculability, the system finds it more difficult to achieve stable results. War may occur, not through a failure of will, but through a failure of comprehension.[4]

---

[4]It is possible that the origins of World War I owe something to the inability to calculate policies of other states until it was too late to change them.

5. TOWARD AN ALTERNATIVE SYSTEM

The respective disadvantages of bipolarity and multipolarity as monolithic images of future international systems should not blind us to their attractive features. Bipolarity provides for well-nigh automatic equilibration of the international balance; in addition, while reinforcing conflict between the two poles, it at least has the merit of preventing conflict elsewhere in the system. Multipolarity reduces the significance of major-power conflict by spreading antagonism uniformly through the system. What we should wish for a future relevant utopia is to combine the desirable facets of each without their attendant disabilities. In practice, even the adherents of one or the other find merit in a wider view. The devotees of bipolarity seem implicitly to include the *détente* (which was a response of the United States and the Soviet Union to their position in a larger international system); the proponents of multipolarity draw back when it is proposed that nulcear weapons be part of the multipolar diffusion of power.

The objective can be accurately described, though it is difficult to give it an appropriate name. The relations between two major powers would be strongly conditioned by the presence and activity of other states. This means that international politics would not be a zero-sum competition between two superpowers. The resources of the international system would not be entirely divided up between the two major states with future outcomes dependent upon a bilateral competition between them. Rather, resources would remain to be appropriated, and the rivalry between the two major protagonists would occur in the external international environment as well as in the national preserves of each. Because external avenues of possible expansion would exist, neither major state need presume that only a direct conflict with its antagonist could decide the issue. The bilateral conflict might be adjusted or equilibrated through actions in the external realm; gains by one power could be made up by countervailing gains by the other. Nor should serial appropriation decide the ultimate fate of the external international world. If the two great powers merely proceeded to apportion slices of the remaining international pie, they would in time be brought back to a strict bipolar confrontation, with all the horrendous consequences which this might involve. The multipolar features of the external sphere should prevent substantial transfers of real estate and political allegiance. Neither hegemony would be acceptable to burgeoning power centers of the external area; changes of alignment or international disposition would not barter the fundamental independence of external states. The bipolar powers would continue to seek advantages in the multipolar realm, but they would fail to eliminate multipolar orientations.

This failure, in turn, might lead to disenchantment with equilibration via the external realm. The bipolar powers might then seek direct advantages in an intensified struggle over the national position of each. If the multipolar challenge were sufficiently great, however, the bipolar states might reduce their own competition for the purpose of making occasional common cause in opposition to external claims. Ultimately, the bipolar states might seek a *détente* based on mutual recognition of two rigidities: (1) the difficulty of achieving preponderance in direct internal competition; (2) the difficulty of making major gains in the external environment. Confronting external challenge, moreover, both might realize that the international status quo was preferable to possible foreshadowed deterioration. Since cooperation in international relations tends to be reinforced by conflict elsewhere in the system, resurgence of the multipolar region would produce a tendency toward bipolar agreement.

One of the uncertainties in such a situation would stem from reversals for either of the two major states in the multipolar realm. In order to recoup a lost position of strength, the bipolar states might be tempted to heighten the conflict between themselves to reinsure for a multipolar client the value of past association or alignment. And at present the United States has sought to reaffirm nuclear solidarity with its NATO allies by proposing a counterforce strategy directed against the Soviet Union. If the commitment to Europe is underscored in the one case, the *détente* with Russia is also affected. The multilateral nuclear force, designed to reassure several West European states, also generated Soviet opposition. On the other hand, Soviet attempts to reassure China and North Vietnam of the benefits of the Russian alliance are bound to impinge on US relations. Closer ties with China would inevitably weaken new-found bases of Western accord. In the short run, then, it seems likely that the US will have to accept some erosion of its past position in Europe, while the Soviets will have to adjust to a diminished role in both Eastern Europe and the Far East. If they fail to do so, it will be at the expense of cordiality at the bipolar level.

The maintenance of the *détente* is of fundamental international significance, both theoretical and practical. It is theoretically important because it avoids the antagonism of the zero-sum game in strict bipolar terms. It also obviates a general trend toward multi-polarity, with the loss of control and increase in the frequency of conflict that this would involve. A modicum of bipolar cooperation dampens hostility in the external sphere; interventions may be at least partially designed for the purpose of preventing multipolar conflict that could threaten central bipolar stability. In practical terms the *détente* is the means by which the spread of nuclear weapons may be channelled, controlled, or halted. It should be observed that nuclear weapons do not affect the theoretical questions of conflict and cooperation. A measure of bipolar agreement has been achieved despite opposing nuclear weapons systems. The dispersion of weapons is important not because of the new conflicts which it creates, but because it sanctions radical options in the waging of old conflicts. In so doing it threatens the balance attained at the bipolar level. Nuclear weapons may also, over a considerable period of time, give the appearance of transforming a bipolar-multipolar order into a system of general multipolarity. This fundamental alteration would be unlikely to occur in fact, but it is one of a range of possible future outcomes.

If the *détente* is desirable, it is possible to have too much of a good thing. A total bipolar *rapprochement,* an end to the Cold War, would be likely to create a new bilateral tension between major power and multipower spheres. In practical terms it would represent a conflict of rich countries and poor countries, industrial states and agricultural states, European and colored races, northern and southern nations. This emergent bipolarity would demand a rapid spread of nuclear weapons in previously multipolar areas. It would require a hasty amalgamation of economic systems and pooling of industrial resources: the multipolar area would transform itself through a new political coordination. The zero-sum game might be played once again.

A bipolar-multipolar system, on the other hand, would seek to avoid the extremes of either parent form. Enough bipolar control of multipolar realms would take place to prevent extremes of conflict, or, if conflict could be averted, to dissociate bipolar interests from outcomes in the area. At the same time bipolar competition would continue in multipolar as well as bipolar regions. The two major states would act as regulators for conflict in the external areas; but multipolar states would act as mediators and buffers for conflicts between the bipolar powers. In neither case would conflict be eliminated, but it might be held in check. Indeed, if hostilities were suddenly eliminated in one realm but not the other, the result would be adverse to general stability. If conflict cannot be eradicated both generally and simultaneously, its abolition in one part is deleterious to the whole.

6. BI-MULTIPOLARITY

It is now possible to list the characteristics of an intermediate international system, a system of bi-multipolarity.

A. Relationship of Interests

The significant feature of interests in such a system is that they would be partially opposed and partially harmonious. The relation between the bipolar nations would be cooperative in that it would reflect mutual interests in restraining conflict or challenge in the multipolar region. The relation between bipolar powers would be competitive in that each would seek to prevent the other from attaining predominance either militarily or in connections with the multipolar world. The multipolar states would have an equally ambivalent pattern of interests. In regard to one another there would be rivalries stemming from the variety of national perspectives and positions; there would also, however, be common interests in resisting the ambitions of the bipolar powers. In regard to the bipolar states there might be individual interests supporting military guarantees or economic assistance from one (or both) of the major powers. There would also be resistance to big-power encroachment. In no case, however, would the pattern of interests resemble that of a zero- or constant-sum game. Bipolar powers would not directly confront one another; multipolar powers would not develop irrevocable antagonisms among themselves; and the multipolar and bipolar worlds would not be completely opposed. Conflict within each sphere and between spheres would be restrained.

B. Equilibration

Equilibration, or the redressing of the international balance, will be a more difficult task in a bipolar-multipolar structure than in a strictly bipolar world. Since in the latter system interests are so clearly opposed, any advantage accruing to one evidently must be made up by the other. In a bi-multipolar system where interests are cooperative as well as conflictual, the consequences of a change in the position of one state will be harder to estimate. Since relationships will be more harmonious, on the other hand, the need for equilibration will be significantly reduced.

C. Predictability

Policy-making in a bi-multipolar system will be more difficult than in a system of bipolarity. A far greater range of separate national decisions must be considered. At the same time, since the bipolar states will exert an important influence on the trend of events in the multipolar fraction of the world, statesmen would not be confronted by the sheer indeterminacy of a strictly multipolar order. While shifts would be harder to predict than under general bipolarity, the momentousness of each shift would be appreciably less.

D. Probability of Overt Conflict

The probability of war, whether local or general, would be much smaller than in a multipolar system. Conflict would be mitigated on two scores: a multipolar buffer might help prevent the two nulcear giants from coming to blows; and the restraining influence of the bipolar states might in turn prevent extreme conflict among multipolar powers. While simple bipolarity would not exist, the influence of two superpowers would be crucial in limiting the outcomes of the system.

E. Results of Overt Conflict

The results of war, whether local or general, would be much more tolerable than in a bipolar system. Overt conflict would most generally take the form of wars among multipolar states, and while crises between bipolar states might not be ruled out, these would be tempered by recognition of significant mutual interests. As long as the *détente* continued, there would be few dangers of major nuclear war.

The probability and results of overt conflict in the three different international systems would be roughly as shown in Figure 1. The area of the dotted rectangle under the system-point in each instance indicates the amount of violence sustained by the international system. Bi-multipolarity does not eradicate violence, but it holds the prospect of limiting violence to far smaller proportions than does either bipolarity or multipolarity. If peace is the objective, a system combining bipolar and multipolar features may be a means of a reasonable approximation thereto.

7. DIFFUSION OF NUCLEAR WEAPONS

The situation depicted would change considerably if nuclear weapons began to be diffused among quite a number of states. The impact would be greatest on a strictly multipolar system, for the

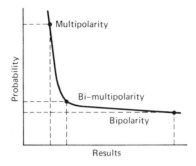

FIG. 1. *Probability and results of overt conflict in the three different international systems.*

incentives to acquisition would be substantial, and the disincentives involved in having to keep up with nuclear superpowers would be absent. Restraints on acquisition by the larger powers also would be lacking. In a bipolar world nuclear weapons would add least to the dangers already confronted. A cataclysm between two halves of the world would be dangerous enough, even without nuclear bombs, though they would clearly enhance the war's destructive power. In an intermediate international environment, the process of nuclear diffusion would also raise levels of violence, but bipolar influence within the system would either reduce the scope of diffusion or limit its disruptive impact.

The results would be roughly as shown in Figure 2. If PD charts the results of international conflict in a prediffusion era, line D

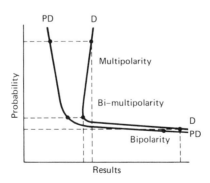

FIG. 2. *Probability and results of overt conflict before (line PD) and after (line D) nuclear weapons have become available to a large number of states.*

describes the outcomes after nuclear weapons have become available options for a large number of states. While bipolarity remains unattractive because of the dire consequences of conflict between the two protagonists, multipolarity has lost most of its previous advantages. Now the probability of conflict not only remains high, but the disastrous results of that conflict are clearly portrayed. Relative to the extremes of bipolarity on the one hand and multipolarity on the other, the intermediate system retains great appeal.

8. BI-MULTIPOLARITY AND THE PRESENT INTERNATIONAL SCENE

The system of bi-multipolarity should not be confused with the present international order. One of the major characteristics of the contemporary international scene resides in the difference in attitude and position of the allies of the great powers and neutral states. Two factors seem to account for this. On the one hand, nonaligned nations have received certain of the benefits of alliance protection and assistance without pledging political allegiance to either bipolar camp. This continuing phenomenon has occasioned some disaffection among the formal allies of the two major powers. It has, in a measure, devalued the currency of alliance. On the other hand, the partial attempts at *détente* have made alliances seem less necessary. If a continuing Cold War were not the order of the day, former client powers would have less reason to guard, via great power alliances, against a sudden unfavorable change.

At the moment we seem to be in a phase in which the two major powers are placing enhanced emphasis on their formal alliances. The Soviet Union has come back into Far Eastern international relations, apparently striving to improve its ties with China and to reassert its influence in North Vietnam. Until recently, at least, the United States seemed engaged in an effort to reestablish a strong position within NATO. In both cases it remains unclear whether maintenance of a strong alliance position or an enduring atmosphere of *détente* and/or peaceful coexistence is most important. The issue is a complicated one in practice because any disengagement of interests, justified on grounds of relaxation of tension, may be interpreted by a bipolar opponent as a sign of weakness and a signal for adventure.

In the longer run, however, there are potentialities for the bipolar-multipolar world we have been discussing. It will probably involve treating nonaligned states somewhat less favorably and aligned nations somewhat more favorably than has been the case up to the present. It seems uncertain, however, that the two aligned camps will

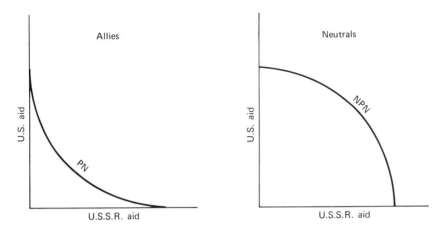

FIG. 3. *Differential treatment received by allies and neutrals in terms of economic aid from the US and the USSR. PN is a "penalize neutralism" curve, while NPN is a "not penalize neutralism" curve.*

continue as presently organized into the indefinite future. The reasons for this uncertainty can be seen in Figure 3.[5] The two diagrams show the differential treatment that allies and neutrals have received in the aid-giving behavior of the United States and the Soviet Union. Among neutrals, roughly speaking, the NPN (not penalize neutralism) curve has been followed, permitting a recipient country to receive sizable quantities of assistance from the opposing bipolar power. Among allies, on the other hand, the PN (penalize neutralism) curve has been followed, providing for substantial reductions of assistance as the ally in question gains additional aid from the opposing camp. If allies suffered in comparison to neutrals in terms of economic and other assistance, they had the compensation of participating in deterrence alliance systems, the protection of which was presumably denied to neutralist nations. As a result of the threatened spread of nuclear weapons today, however, it is no longer certain that allies alone may enjoy the benefits of deterrent protection. India, in particular, may be able to retain her nonalignment while participating in nuclear guarantees of the big powers. If this occurs generally in the neutralist world, an equivalent disproportion in the treatment of allies and neutrals might come to exist in the

---

[5] I am indebted to Professor Albert O. Hirschman of Columbia University for the basic notions of the figures which follow (Hirschman, 1964).

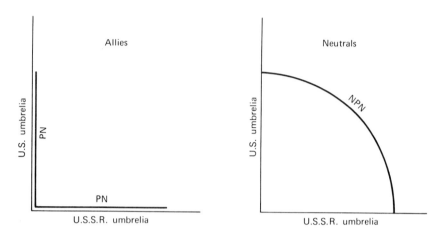

FIG. 4. *Differential treatment received by allies and neutrals in the nuclear "umbrella" guarantees of the US and the USSR. As in Fig. 3, PN and NPN indicate policies of penalizing and not penalizing neutralism.*

military sphere, as shown in Figure 4. Such outcomes would so disadvantage allies and reward neutrals that a considerable movement toward greater neutrality would have to be expected. A final equilibrium might be attained, covering both economic and military guarantees in roughly the form shown in Figure 5.

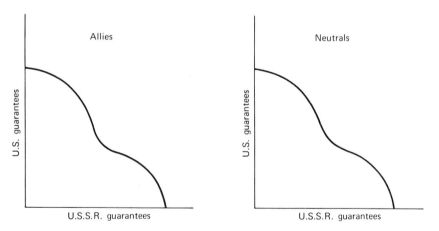

FIG. 5. *A possible final equilibrium position for allies and neutrals with respect to economic and military guarantees from the US and USSR.*

In such a case, of course, there would no longer be a difference between allies and neutrals. The growth of multipolar sentiment would presumably reinforce the *détente* between bipolar powers, and an important step in the direction of an intermediate international system would have been taken.

REFERENCES

Bull, Hedley. "Atlantic Military Problems: A Preliminary Essay," prepared for the Council on Foreign Relations meeting of November 20, 1963, p. 21.

Burns, Arthur. "From Balance to Deterrence: A Theoretical Analysis," *World Politics*, 10, 4 (July 1957).

Deutsch, Karl, and J. David Singer. "Multipolar Power Systems and International Stability," *World Politics*, 16, 3 (April 1964), 390-406.

Hirschman, A. O. "The Stability of Neutralism: A Geometric Note," *American Economic Review*, 54 (1964), 94-100.

Hoffmann, Stanley. "International Relations—The Long Road to Theory," *World Politics*, 13, 3 (April 1961).

Waltz, Kenneth N. "The Stability of a Bipolar World," *Daedalus* (Summer 1964).

_____. *Man, the State, and War.* New York: 1959.

The World Today: Multistate and Imperial Orders

George Liska

The pre-eminent position of the United States is responsible for what we have called the unifocal character of the contemporary international system, while the existence of competing imperial power imparts to international politics the special flavor of inter-empire relations. This does not mean that the present international system does not retain some and may not be regaining further features of a multipolar system. The interpenetration of features is reflected practically in the United States' being a globally primary power that is not—and should not try to be—paramount in each and every particular area or region of the world system. We shall deal with the definitional and general aspects of a mixed international order and then move into European questions by way of discussing Soviet-American relations as an example of interempire relations in the contemporary setting of an international system uncertainly evolving from a bipolar structure to a multipolar structure with a single focus.

An empire-centered (or imperial, or unifocal) international order differs in some key characteristics from order in a multistate system pure and simple, without an imperial focus or center, whether it be bipolar or multipolar. The differences in regard to "order" are comparable in nature to the differences previously outlined in regard to "system." Features that are basic to, and distinctive of, the pure multistate order have merely an ancillary, supporting role in the imperial order. Thus, the key structural guarantee of minimum order in a pure multistate system is the distribution of antagonistic power in a reciprocally countervailing pattern. In a system focused on one foremost imperial state (even if that system comprises more than one state that possesses or seeks to acquire the attributes of empire), the order rests in the last resort on the widely shared presumption of the ultimately controlling power of the imperial state; that is true even if the manifestation of the controlling power is only intermittent, because the countervailing dynamic continues to operate most of the time. Next in importance to the structure and dynamic of power in maintaining minimum order are certain norms of behavior. The principle of reciprocity in the multistate context is compounded in the empire-centered order with the principle of primary responsibility of the imperial state (however much such responsibility may be circumscribed by the duty of receptivity to the viewpoints of lesser states and their ultimate right of revolt against abuses). Finally, the difference lies in the character of typical or feasible individual or collective sanctions for disorderly or deviant behavior. In gross terms, deviancy will be defined in the pure multistate system as consisting of acts aimed directly or indirectly, forcibly or otherwise, at substantial unilateral changes in the status quo—"substantial changes" being construed as changes that more than routinely impair established interests and modify existing ratios of power and influence. In the imperial system, the critical deviant actions are those which, apart from aiming at substantial changes, are also calculated to abridge access by the responsible power to any particular area for purposes of police and protection against unilateral forcible changes, in such a way as to compel resort to a major display of force and authority if access is to be reopened. The present international quest for order displays a compound of multiactor and one-center situations and approaches, producing conflicts and maladjustments as well as a measure of reciprocal reinforcement.

The problem of countervailing and controlling power as the structural basis of order is of greatest significance. In Europe, the residual controlling power of the United States in Western Europe and of the Soviet Union in Eastern Europe continues to implement the checking and balancing policies of the superpowers. A parallelly emerging potential all-European order, however, is implicit in a Franco-Soviet entente with a countervailing intent vis-à-vis the United States as the globally primary power, whose European presence is to be reduced to the lowest level requisite for, and compatible with, the autonomy and equilibrium of a European state system. In Asia, the United States has been exercising a considerable measure of controlling influence while engaging—militarily in Vietnam and politico-diplomatically on a wider front—in a policy of countervailing the Communist Chinese attempt to supplant the United States as the controlling center of a Southeast Asian regional system. In Latin America, the United States has resisted, so far with success, the projection into the hemisphere of countervailing extraregional power in the interest of its paramount control in the region, regardless of whether such countervailing power were to take the form of a revolution in strategic relationships, such as was implicit in the installation of Soviet missiles in Cuba, or of Soviet or Communist Chinese efforts to export or exploit local social revolution. In regard to Africa, finally, the global picture has been that of a balancing of power and influence among several non-African greater powers, controlling pre-eminence of either being localized and fluctuating, while intraregional actors have been simultaneously engaged in attempts to set up co-operative agencies on the widest possible basis and to offset potentially controlling particular aggregations with countervailing ones.

The next problem is that of reciprocity vs. responsibility. Reciprocity can operate between both comparable and greatly unequal powers. As between the powers that are or can plausibly conduct themselves as "world powers," reciprocity has come to bear on access to political, economic, or cultural role and influence in regions where other powers exert or feel entitled to exert primary responsibility and more or less extensive control. This form of reciprocity is especially hard to work out; it is, however, increasingly the hard-core problem of contemporary world order. The issue of access has been raised between the United States and the Soviet Union, in regard to American access to Eastern Europe and Soviet access to either the Caribbean or Western Europe (or both); between the United States and Communist China with regard to Southeast Asia and Africa;

between the Soviet Union and Communist China with regard to South Asia and Eastern Europe; and between France and the United States with respect to Latin America and North Africa, largely as a counter in the competition over the distribution of influence in Western Europe herself. Between unequal powers, reciprocity does not mean reciprocal access but reciprocal performance; the *quid pro quo* of "mutual" assistance programs. It has arisen—and by its nature has never been stably settled—between, say, the United Arab Republic on one side and both the United States and the Soviet Union on the other, just as it has between the U.A.R. and the recipients of *its* assistance in Yemen. The issue of reciprocity in the international order has been pertinent more generally, of course, in regard to such matters as intensification or moderation in the nuclear arms race between the two superpowers, activation and deactivation of territorial and other demands in relations among the small new states, and admission of new members of the United Nations—all areas in which the two superpowers have claimed special and on occasion joint responsibility.

Reciprocal concession or denial of access presupposes the paramount responsibility by someone in a particular area. The American tradition of the Monroe Doctrine is that of persistent denial of access by either the reactionary Holy Alliance or an unholy alliance between indigenous sociorevolutionary movements and Soviet or Chinese communism in Guatemala, Cuba, the Dominican Republic, and everywhere else. One consequence of the American attitude has been to reduce the possibility of meaningful bargaining and barter aiming at a "new deal" between the United States and the Soviet Union with regard to Europe and other parts of the world which would go beyond generalized detente and beyond entente on selected nuclear issues only—an inhibition which is a key element favoring an ultimate "European" solution in and for Europe. By contrast, the French and the Soviets seem to be prepared to explore the possibility of combining primary role or responsibility within their respective regions with some reciprocity in sharing leadership and, especially, of shoring up each other's pre-eminence in the factors or areas in which either of them is or may become deficient. The conspicuous asymmetry in their respective power positions would be lessened by reciprocal attribution of individually most-needed assets: diplomatic standing (and technological know-how) for France and diplomatic respectability (and quality consumer goods) for the Soviet Union. Moreover, both powers would consolidate their position in Europe as a precondition to upholding in the longer run their primary responsibility in the extra-European geographic extensions of their immediate habitat: France's in North Africa, both affirmed and subtly undermined by such affairs as Bizerte and Ben Barka; Soviet Russia's in parts of Asia, more deliberately and dramatically threatened by the Chinese Communists than France's position in North Africa is either by the United States or the United Arab Republic and yet inconclusively affected by evolving Soviet attitudes toward conflicts between third powers over Kashmir or the seventeenth parallel.

The war in Vietnam, together with the partly derivative developments in Burma, Indonesia, and Thailand, has raised the issue of who has primary responsibility in Southeast Asia: the United States or Communist China. Aside from its ambiguity as either an anti-Communist crusade or a routine imperial war, the Vietnamese conflict has displayed also the complementary ambiguity about great power objectives. Have the United States and Communist China been asserting the claim to primary responsibility or only the right to access, even though the United States would not presently think of conceding to Communist China reciprocity in access to areas closer to the American homeland and more vital for American security than either Vietnam or Southeast Asia? It is probable that the issue of reciprocity will not arise between the United States and China, except concerning the conduct of the war, as long as Chinese policy continues to be Maoist and Maoism continues to reflect the present theses of Mao. However, the issue of reciprocity may well arise in some form, if only in regard to Southeast Asia, between the United States as the military victor in Vietnam and the Soviet Union or France as the interested powers with capacity either to mediate a negotiated settlement or else guarantee the North Vietnamese against wider implications of a *de facto* subsidence of the conflict in circumstances that would leave the United States in essential control of the military battlefield—even if not necessarily of the entire political battlefield.

Finally, the Vietnam issue illustrates the issue of the critical deviance from the basic norm in a pure multistate and an imperial order. For a multistate order, the critical issue is the attempt to effect unilaterally a forcible change pure and simple; such deviance calls for corresponding sanctions to be applied against the ostensibly and directly delinquent state. The agency currently entrusted with the task is the one that has so far in effect disclaimed competence in the Vietnamese crisis: the United Nations. From the viewpoint of a one-center, imperial order in present circumstances, the critical action is the attempt to abridge and even abolish the capacity of the United States to act decisively in Southeast Asia in the future without having to resort to an all-out (including nuclear) war or threat of war. The corresponding sanction is to retaliate in kind against the competing great power without meticulous regard for the precise degree of its complicity in the defiance and to bar its access to the area by way of action directed against either the ostensible, or the suspected real, culprit as a matter of expediency rather than principle. Similarly, Nasser's nationalization of Suez was from one viewpoint no more than a unilateral change with forcible implications, while from another viewpoint it was mainly an act to inhibit or deny access to the area by formerly dominant powers, notably insofar as it implied also abridgment or abrogation of the British treaty right to return to the Suez canal zone militarily in an emergency. The consequence of the two aspects of the case was conflict over the nature of even theoretically appropriate sanctions. Similarly, Indonesia's confrontation with Malaysia (and previously with the Netherlands over West New Guinea) was a bid not only for unilateral change but also for substituting local imperial control and responsibility for that of the extraregional center or centers, decreasingly Dutch and British and increasingly American. The nature of appropriate response and sanction would again have been different, depending on which aspect were to be selected as the dominant one, in part because the avowable one in this or that forum and context.

Not all possible threats to world order are ambiguous in the above sense. Somalia's territorial claims on Ethiopia and Kenya, for instance, raise the possibility of unilateral forcible change but not of regional imperial pre-eminence. Moreover, two boundary cases or classes of disorder are not necessarily covered by either case of deviance. One is acute chaos and low-level destruction, such as those occurring in the Congo and in Nigeria in the 1960s. The issue of unilateral change would arise only if the disturbance assumed external implications, for instance by way of the attempt by another state, such as Ghana in the case of the Congo, to exploit the situation for its direct aggrandizement. The issue of access did actually arise in the case of the Congo conjointly with its internationalization, in the form of the Soviet attempt to supplant the Western powers and the United States in particular, presumably as a preliminary to abridging Western access to the area. The attempt backfired in the framework of a United Nations action ostensibly concerned with other, more conspicuous aspects of the disorder. The success of the United States in asserting at once its global and local-regional primacy over the

Soviet Union was tarnished only when it tried, ill-advisedly, to have the Soviets share the costs of their own humiliation.

The other potential source of disorder and high-level destruction, which is in a class by itself, is nuclear diffusion. In principle, acquisition of nuclear weapons constitutes neither a unilateral change of a kind requiring or warranting multilateral sanction, nor does it provide in and by itself a warrant for action in defense of politico-economic access to a particular region. In practice, of course, the situation will be different. If nuclear weapons are acquired by countries with exceptional potential for internally disorderly and internationally deviant behavior, the latent sense of joint responsibility for order on the part of the superpowers is apt to be tested as to its being merely, or more than, declaratory and platonic—with momentous consequences for the nature and incumbency of ultimate authority in world affairs. If nuclear power passes into the hands of a major regional power, with potential for shaping a regional order in its image, the equation of countervailing power and the balance of controlling influences from within and outside the region will be changed in any event. But the specific attitude of the United States as the globally primary power in particular is apt to vary depending on the estimate of the point at which and the extent to which its conception of order will differ from that of the local power or powers. Nuclear weapons in the hands of the United Arab Republic is not the same as nuclear weapons in the hands of the United States from any viewpoint. Similarly, the United States—and the Soviet Union—is apt to view in quite a different light the dispersion of nuclear weapons to Japan or India and to Communist China in Asia, just as the Soviet Union—and the United States—is apt to be less upset by a French *force de frappe* than by a West German nuclear *streitmacht* in Europe. An abstractly formulated antiproliferation treaty that slurs over such differences may therefore well prove just as inappropriate and even counterproductive as did all comparable general instruments in the past which failed to differentiate realistically between cases of common disorder while providing guidelines for evasion and incentives for recrimination—often as a prelude to violation or denunciation of the basic treaty.

chapter seven

THE STRUCTURE OF REGIONAL AND OTHER SUBSYSTEMS

The International Relations of Regions*

Louis J. Cantori and Steven L. Spiegel

It is the purpose of this article to suggest a comparative approach for analyzing the role of the region in present-day international politics. We will consider regions to be areas of the world which contain geographically proximate states forming, in foreign affairs, mutually interrelated units. We will attempt here to provide a framework for studying the region in terms of the shared features of all regions. As a result of these shared features, comparisons become feasible and generalizations are facilitated.

Recently, there has been a good deal of concentration on the region as a subordinate system. This interest has developed simultaneously with studies of integration and international organization, both of which have also been largely region-centred. In this article we are concerned primarily with the subordinate system approach,

SOURCE: From *Polity, The Journal of the Northeastern Political Science Associations*, Volume II, No. 4, 1970. Copyright © 1970 by *Polity*. Reprinted and abridged by permission of the authors and *Polity*.

*Research for this study was provided by a grant from the Research Committee of the Academic Senate, University of California, Los Angeles.

which provides us with a unit of analysis that facilitates comparison and allows us to concentrate on the international politics of a region rather than on particular processes (for example, integration, organization). Since the dawn of the modern era, the present period is the first in which all regions of the world maintain a measure of independence. The present is also a time in which communications and technology permit scholars to become knowledgeable about events that occur simultaneously around the world. The gaining of independence and the increase of communications allow for an unprecedented capacity to compare regions to each other. But we are not interested in comparison for its own sake. Rather, we aim to develop a means of judging the causal factors which are responsible for the particular mixture of cooperation and conflict present among the nations within a particular region. We are interested in the relationship between such factors as culture and stability, power and order, communications and cohesion.

In this article we will attempt to explicate a framework for the delineation of subordinate systems in order to establish a basis for the study of regional international politics.[1] We will begin with a discussion of some of the problems inherent in the identification of subordinate systems and then proceed to propose a method for subdividing them into analytic sectors. We will then provide four categories in the form of pattern variables which are helpful in delineating subordinate systems and in explaining regional politics within them. We will attempt to show the relationships between the pattern variables and sectors, and conclude with a brief discussion of intersubordinate system relations.

I. THE IDENTIFICATION OF
SUBORDINATE SYSTEMS

Nation-states are delineated by events, political practice, and (at least in part) membership in the United Nations. The dominant system, composed of the most powerful of states in any period of history, is more difficult to discern and its precise membership is a matter of constant conjecture, but there are at least a minimum of contenders for predominant status and therefore a minimum of

---

[1] For further elaboration see Louis J. Cantori and Steven L. Spiegel, *The International Politics of Regions: A Comparative Approach* (Englewood Cliffs, N.J.: Prentice-Hall, 1970), and "Regional International Politics: The Comparison of Five Subordinate Systems," *International Studies Quarterly* (December, 1969).

potential configurations. There is also a degree of consensus among most observers: some form of bipolarity is present. Regional or subordinate systems, on the other hand, do not easily lend themselves to clear-cut identification: there are many alternatives, potential definitions, and groupings. Consequently, the determination of subordinate systems is difficult and complex.

Given the complications of identifying subordinate systems, the authors have attempted nonetheless to identify fifteen subordinate systems. . . . They have done so on the following bases:

Every nation-state (no matter how strong or how weak) is a member of one subordinate system. There are two exceptions to this generalization: the most powerful states are also active in other subordinate systems besides their own, and there are a few states which exist on the borderline between two subordinate systems and may be considered to coexist in some degree in both (for example, Finland, Turkey, Afghanistan, and Burma).

All subordinate systems are delineated—at least in part—by reference to geographical considerations, but social, economic, political, and organizational factors are also relevant. Consequently, members of subordinate systems are proximate, but they need not be contiguous.

Size does not necessarily determine the existence of a subordinate system. It may consist of one nation and be relatively large (the USSR),[2] or may consist of several nations and be relatively compact in area (the Middle East). Where only one nation is a member of a region we can say that the internal (or domestic) and subordinate systems are identical.

Within the boundaries of a subordinate system, there is a complex interaction between political, social, and geographic factors. It is this interaction which is most important in defining the limits of a subordinate system. For example, primarily political boundaries divide East and West Europe; social and political boundaries divide Latin America and North America; geographic boundaries help to identify the Middle East and divide North Africa from the rest of Africa.

Indigenous political relationships (antagonistic and cooperative), geographic factors, and social and historical backgrounds help to

[2]The Soviet Union has been considered a region in and of itself because with reference to social, political, and geographic factors it resembles many of the other subordinate systems. While many of the states on the Soviet Union's borders might have been considered as part of its periphery, Soviet relations with these states resemble more closely intrusive relations elsewhere rather than core-periphery relations.

define a subordinate system. Thus, the authors believe that, despite the Organization of African Unity (OAU), the African continent is fragmented by a variety of local interactions, while in Latin America, despite great differences, the area has shown more frequent inter-related characteristics.

Outside powers play a role in defining a subordinate system. This is particularly the case in East Europe, Southeast Asia, and Latin America.

Although geographic boundaries do not easily change and social factors rarely do, political and ideological factors are fluid. Consequently, the identity of a subordinate system is both tenuous and dynamic. For example, the nineteenth-century writer would probably have suggested the significance of the Central European subordinate system, but he would not have found most of the nation-states which are presently located in the Middle East.

We can thus conclude that a subordinate system consists of one state, or of two or more proximate and interacting states which have some common ethnic, linguistic, cultural, social, and historical bonds, and whose sense of identity is sometimes increased by the actions and attitudes of states external to the system. The seven foregoing basic generalizations, plus this definition, should be sufficient to enable us, at least tentatively, to identify a subordinate system. It will become clear as we proceed to elaborate the components of our approach that we are at the same time elaborating our definition.

. . .

II. FOUR PATTERN VARIABLES

Granted the identification of a subordinate system in which the preceding generalizations are operative, it is possible to differentiate it further into three subdivisions: the core sector, the peripheral sector and the intrusive system. Before turning to a discussion of these three subdivisions of the subordinate system, we shall first proceed to a discussion of four pattern variables which we believe to be crucial to the demarcation of these subdivisions. These are: (1) nature and level of cohesion, (2) nature of communications, (3) level of power, and (4) structure of relations. These variables are crucial to the comparison of subordinate systems with diverse qualities.

Nature and Level of Cohesion

By cohesion we mean the degree of similarity or complementarity in the properties of the political entities being considered and the degree of interaction between these units. The concept of cohesion plays a similar role in the consideration of regions to that which the concept of integration has played in the analysis of nation-states. In the study of comparative national politics, integration has been used to mean, "The problem of creating a sense of territorial nationality which overshadows—or eliminates—subordinate parochial loyalties."[3] When applied to the study of international relations the concept of integration can thus represent an assumption that the states being compared will lose their independence as they become more inter-locked. Cohesion involves no such assumption. As states become more similar and more interactive, there is no guarantee that they will unite or federate; on the contrary, cohesiveness may as likely lead to disunity as to unity. When the term "integration" is applied to regions it is usually assumed at a minimum that warfare does not exist among the members or that a more encompassing political institution results from the process. "Integration and security community. . . imply stable expectations of peace among the par-ticipating units or groups, whether or not there has been a merger of their political institutions," or "Political integration is the process whereby political actors in several distinct national settings are persuaded to shift their loyalties, expectations and political activities toward a new center, whose institutions possess or demand juris-diction over the preexisting national state."[4] There is, on the other hand, no direct correlation between cohesion and absence of warfare or between cohesion and a shift of political loyalty.

The concept of cohesion as discussed here can be further differ-entiated into its social, economic, political, and organizational elements. Under the rubric of social cohesiveness, attention is focused upon the contributive factors of ethnicity, race, language, religion, culture, history, and consciousness of a common heritage. The contrasts that these factors may present can be seen in the extremes of the Middle East subordinate system's high degree of social cohesion and Southeast Asia's extremely low degree of social cohesion. Under the rubric of economic cohesiveness, the focus is upon the distribution and complementarity of economic resources as

[3]Myron Weiner, "Political Integration and Political Development," in *Political Modernization*, ed., C. Welch (Belmont, Calif.: Wadsworth, 1967), 150-51. Reprinted from *The Annals*, CCCLVIII (March, 1965), 52-64.

[4]The first quotation is from Karl Deutsch, "Security Communities," in *International Politics and Foreign Policy*, ed., J. Rosenau (New York: The Free Press, 1961), 98. The second is from Ernst Haas, *The Uniting of Europe* (Stanford, California: Stanford University Press, 1958), 16.

well as on the character of trade patterns. The extremes of this factor can be seen in the West European system's high degree of economic cohesiveness and the West African and Middle Eastern systems' low degree. Under the rubric of political cohesiveness we are concerned with the manner in which the pattern and degree of complementarity of types of regime contribute or detract from the cohesion of a subordinate system. In this respect one could compare West Europe, with its multitude of reconciliation or parliamentary-type regimes, and the Middle East, with its contrasting mobilizational and modernizing autocracies.[5]

Finally, under the rubric of organizational cohesion we should note the possible effects upon cohesion of membership in the United Nations and in regional organizations. The analysis of voting behavior in the United Nations has revealed the existence of groupings of states identifiable as Afro-Asian, Latin American, and so forth, all of which contribute in some degree to regional consciousness.[6] As for regional organization, we should note to what extent a regional organization is coterminus with the region's boundaries, contrasting, for example, the European Common Market and the Arab League. If all members of a subordinate system or a sector of a subordinate system belong to a regional international organization, this tends to reinforce cohesion, particularly if the boundaries of the membership coincide with the system's or sector's boundaries.

Nature of Communications

The second pattern variable, the nature of communications, is divisible into four aspects: personal communications (mail, telephone, telegraph); mass media (newspapers, radio, television); exchange among the elite (intraregional education, tourism, diplomatic visits within the region); and transportation (road, water, rail, air). It is evident that literacy rates and differences in language will affect the first three and that geography and technological development will affect all four. Regions will differ from each other with the degree to which these four factors are present and applicable. Southeast Asia is weak in all four, for example, as is West Africa, while West Europe has been able to outweigh linguistic differences by the sheer profusion of channels of communications and other pattern variables.

[5] For this classification of political systems, see David Apter, *The Politics of Modernization* (Chicago: University of Chicago Press, 1965), 28-38, Chapters 9, 11.

[6] For an analysis along these lines, see Bruce Russett, *International Regions and the International System* (Chicago: Rand McNally & Co., 1967), Chapters 4, 5.

Level of Power

"Power," the third pattern variable, is defined here as the present and potential ability and the willingness of one nation to alter the internal decision-making processes of other countries in accordance with its own policies. We can isolate three broad aspects of a nation's power: material, military, and motivational. The material elements of power comprise the basis of a nation's capacity: these include its location and resources; the size, quality, and structure of its population; its economy and industrial capacity (particularly to be measured by gross national product (GNP), per capita GNP, and production and consumption of energy) and the relative efficiency of its administration and government. The military elements of power comprise a nation's ability to wage war: its military techniques, weaponry, manpower, and efficiency. They also include the effect which scientific and technological developments have on the ability of stronger nations to increase their margin of superiority over weaker nations or of weaker countries to overtake the leaders. Finally, the motivational elements of power center on a nation's will to seek prestige and status in international affairs, and on its readiness to sacrifice consumer satisfaction to build its material and military power. Motivation is influenced by such elements as ideology, national character and morale, nationalism, history, the personalities and abilities of particular statesmen, and diplomatic skill.

Because existing and potential[7] national strengths and weaknesses are frequently contradictory, it is difficult to produce a "power calculation" in order to compare states. Given the complexity of the process, the attempt to estimate the power of nations nevertheless produces valuable information about the distribution or balance of power among nations in a subordinate system. This analytical process also facilitates the comparison of the character of various subordinate systems.

It is possible to detect seven types of nation-states in the current period: primary powers, secondary powers, middle powers, minor powers, regional states, micro-states, and colonies. Which category a nation-state belongs in depends on its degree of power, as suggested

---

[7] "Potential" applies to each factor of power (material, military, and motivational). An advanced state may be capable of growing further or may change in motivation as a result of altered international conditions or a new domestic regime. A developing state's potentiality may be long or short-term, depending upon its possible development and rate of growth.

by the three factors discussed above and its range of influence, as indicated by the number or location of states with which a particular nation is able to exercise its power.

Primary Powers. The primary powers (the US and USSR), together with the secondary powers constitute the great powers, that is nations which influence domestic politics and foreign policies of other countries in several areas of the world and are individually superior to other nations materially, militarily, and in motivation. Primary powers are superior to secondary powers on the basis of these three factors, but both types compose the dominant system in international politics.

Secondary Powers. Compared to primary powers, secondary powers (the United Kingdom, France, West Germany, Japan, and China) have a limited capacity to participate in selected subordinate systems of the world.

Middle Powers. Middle powers (for example, Italy, Canada, Australia, East Germany) are those states whose level of power permits them to play only decidedly limited and selected roles in subordinate systems other than their own.

Minor Powers. Minor powers (for example, Cuba, Algeria, United Arab Republic) are those states which play leading roles in the international relations of their own systems.

Regional States. Regional states (for example, Greece, Hungary, Syria) are those states which are able on occasion to play a limited but not leading role in their own subordinate systems. They also tend to have greater flexibility with reference to stronger powers than do micro-states and colonies.

Micro-States. Micro-states (for example, Jamaica, Togo, Laos) are states which have little or no influence in regional international relations because their power calculation leaves them almost totally within the orbit of one or more large powers.

Colonies. Colonies (for example, Spanish Sahara, Angola, Hong Kong) are the few remaining political entities which have little or no independent motivational power.

This categorization allows us to make an estimate of both the distribution and hierarchy of power within a subordinate system. West Europe is distinctive for its prevalence of secondary and middle powers. In Latin America there are only one middle power (Brazil), a few minor powers and a few regional powers, and many micro-states. In the Arab sector of the Middle East congeries of regional and micro-states are all minor powers. The categories also facilitate the comparison of subordinate systems: the predominance of secondary and middle powers in West Europe indicates that its level of power is greater than that of either Latin America or the Middle East.

Structure of Relations

The fourth pattern variable, the structure of relations, refers to the character of the relationships which exist among the nation-states that compose a subordinate system. It is important here to determine: (1) which states are cooperating and which are in conflict (the spectrum of relations); (2) the bases for their amity or antagonism (the causes of relations); and (3) the instruments which they use to effect their relations—for example, types of weapons, ways of ameliorating conflict, methods of cooperation (the means of relations).

The Spectrum of Relations.[8] The structure of a system's interrelations can be described by reference to the conditions depicted in Table 1 which shows a spectrum extending from the close cooperation of a bloc to the exacerbated conflict of direct military confrontation.

TABLE 1   Spectrum of Relations

bloc
alliance
    limited
    cooperation
                    equilibrium
          stalemate
    sustained
    crisis
direct
military
conflict

Conditions of amity include: a bloc, in which two or more nations act in international politics as if they were one political entity; an alliance, in which they agree to aid each other in specified ways—usually including military means; and tentative cooperation, in which they coordinate their actions for specific purposes and over a very short period of time (days rather than weeks, weeks rather than

[8]The concept of power, the seven types of nations, and the spectrum of relations are discussed in greater detail in a forthcoming book by Steven L. Spiegel to be published by Little, Brown and Company.

months). From the opposite direction, conditions of antagonism include: direct military conflict, in which combat occurs between the troops of two opposing sides; sustained crisis, in which contending parties make persistent attempts, short of direct military conflict, to alter the balance of power between them; and stalemate, in which contention continues while neither side is prepared or able to alter the existing relationship. In direct conflict, the means used to change the status quo are forceful and deliberate, but in sustained crisis the primary means of contention are more subtle: they include political maneuvering among neutral and independent states, arms races, limited local warfare between parties aligned on either side, vituperative exchanges, crises, and in gereral a chaotic atmosphere filled with tension. In stalemates, contention is at a lower level because both sides decide that, given existing conditions, they would prefer to live with the situation than face the consequences of attempting to upset the prevailing balance of forces.

Only when we arrive at equilibrium do we find a standoff in competitive power between two sides that is mutually acceptable. Whether or not an equality of power exists, the effect is the same: the statesmen of both sides not only accept the situation but prefer it to any foreseeable alternative. The status quo becomes a standard of the acceptable balance of power, and so long as neither side moves to alter it or perceives that it is being altered the equilibrium will continue. The difference between stalemate and equilibrium is that in a stalemate one or both sides would change conditions if they could and are seeking means of doing so; in equilibirum neither side believes that it would alter the balance of power even if it had the means to do so. Equilibrium is a prerequisite to most stages of amity—except the lowest forms of limited cooperation.[9]

The Causes of Relations. States are, of course, not always consistent in their relations. In any relationship between two or more states there may be elements of conflict on one level and of cooperation on others. Many Latin American states (for example, Peru, Chile, Bolivia) arc in a stalemate with reference to border issues while they are allied in economic and diplomatic international organization. Saudi Arabia and the UAR have been in a sustained crisis in regard to Yemen but in an alliance in regard to

[9]The spectrum we have presented does not include nations which are "neutral" toward each other in the sense of noninvolvement in hostile relations. In current subordinate sytems, equilibrium or stalemate in respect to two conflicting sides is frequently either the cause or the effect of neutral policies of individual states.

Israel. It is therefore necessary to consider the relative significance of major issues which cause conflict or cooperation between particular states in a subordinate system. In Latin America, the effect of American influence has been to subordinate local issues to regional pursuits. Similarly, in the Middle East, intra-Arab disputes are muted by the confrontation with Israel.

When there is conflict, the nature of the disputed issues reveals the intensity of the contention. For example, border and economic disputes are usually less damaging to peaceful international relations in the region than racial, religious, ideological, and historical rivalries. Similarly, when there is cooperation the reasons for collaboration indicate the strength of the cross-national ties. A common enemy is likely to be a stronger tie than mutual economic interest; under present conditions, economics is likely to be a stronger incentive to cooperation than are religious ties.

The Means of Relations. The spectrum of relations within a subordinate system is further elucidated by reference to the means which are used in such relations. The type of warfare (for example, guerrilla versus conventional) being carried on helps to explain the relations which exist. Moreover, the manner in which conflicts are ameliorated and terminated indicates the strength of particular conditions in the spectrum of relations. For example, conditions in Latin America, where an elaborate set of diplomatic devices exists for the settlement of many types of conflict, are very different from conditions in the Middle East, where cease-fires are arranged by intermediaries and there is little or no contact between the Arabs and Israelis. West Europe, where states are also likely in the current period to resort to established means of amelioration, is different from Southeast Asia, where guerrillas either emerge victorious or fade into the interior and where rare agreements are broken freely. Finally, the extent of established consultative devices and the range of ties between cooperating governments not only help to indicate whether a bloc, alliance, or limited cooperation is in progress; they also hint at the durability of these relationships.

These three elements, then, provide a frame of reference for examining the prevailing nature of relationships within a subordinate system. They enable us to make comparisons with other subordinate systems, both with respect to the influence of what we shall call the "intrusive system" and the effect of levels of cohesion, power, and communication. As we shall see, these four pattern variables, when applied to a given subordinate system, unveil the existence of what we term "core" and "peripheral" sectors.

III. THE CORE AND THE PERIPHERY

The Core Sector

The core sector consists of a state or group of states which form a central focus of the international politics within a given region. It usually consists of more than one state, and when it does the constituent units possess a shared social, political, and/or organizational background or activity. There may be more than one core sector within a given subordinate system.

We can make our definition more specific and useful by examining a hypothetical core sector in terms of our four pattern variables: the level of cohesion, the nature of communications, the level of power, and the structure of relations.

. . .

It can thus be seen that while the initial delineation of the subordinate system may itself be considered somewhat subjective, the application of the four pattern variables soon reveals the identity of the subordinate system and of the more well-defined core sector as well. In fact, our ability to delineate the core sector so sharply in turn assists us to define the subordinate system itself.

The Peripheral Sector

The peripheral sector includes all those states within a given subordinate system which are alienated from the core sector in some degree by social, political, economic, or organizational factors, but which nevertheless play a role in the politics of the subordinate system. While the core sector tends towards cultural, social, and political homogeneity, the peripheral sector is characteristically heterogeneous, and there is usually little interaction among periphery members. The minimal factor accounting for the inclusion of the member states of the peripheral sector in the subordinate system appears to be primarily geographical, although additional social, cultural, political, and historical factors exist. It follows, then, that the peripheral sector, as compared with the core sector, is characterized by less cohesion, less communication, relatively unrelated levels of power, and much more fluid relations.

. . .

IV. THE INTRUSIVE SYSTEM

An intrusive system consists of the politically significant participation of external powers in the international relations of the subordinate system. While the core and peripheral sectors both involve the states located within the region, an analysis of almost every region reveals that these states are not the only ones which play a role in the activities of the subordinate system. As one would expect in an international system with a hierarchy consisting of seven types of nations, external countries involve themselves in the international politics of subordinate systems other than their own. This pattern is only absent in the North American core and in the Soviet Union, where the level of power is extremely high. Additionally, in the core of North America, the level of cooperation between the two members, the United States and Canada, is extremely high.[10]

There are two types of externally based regional participation: politically significant involvement and politically insignificant involvement. Politically insignificant involvement comprises material aid, trade, economic investment, and cultural and educational efforts which do not usually produce participation in the balance of power of the region. Middle powers, and to some degree secondary powers, are most likely to undertake this type of involvement. Spanish involvement in the Middle East and Canadian aid to India are examples. Much of Japanese and West German aid (except West Germany's activity in East European politics and its Hallstein Doctrine) has not been politically motivated or accompanied by a desire to participate in local international relations. These conditions may change, however.

Politically significant involvement, on the other hand, produces participation in the balance of power of the subordinate system and may affect the dominant system's balance as well. This participation is expressed by the possession of a colony; economic or military aid producing an alteration in the balance of power in the region; formal alliance, troop commitment, or any agreement which causes the external power to act in ways which resemble the types of actions that would ordinarily be taken by a country indigenous to the region. This type of involvement is also determined by reference to the objectives, power, motivation, location, and international position of the intruding nation. Since only politically significant members can be defined as being members of the intrusive system, we will primarily be concerned here with these types of external powers. Even politically significant involvement by one state, once

[10]It might be suggested that French and British involvement in Canada is in form similar to intrusive action in other subordinate systems. The authors rejected this interpretation, however, because of both the indigenous power of Canada and its close relationship with the U.S.

identified as such, has to be judged further in relation to other intrusive powers. Thus, for example, Australia and Portugal meet the minimum requirements for politically significant involvement in Southeast Asia, but their participation is nowhere near as significant as that of the United States, China, or the Soviet Union.

We can isolate nine characteristic ways in which external powers participate in the politics of a given region. These are: multilateral arrangements; bilateral arrangements; trade and economic investment; possession of a colony; military intervention, subversion; use of the United Nations; cultural and educational activities; and propaganda. All of these are employed in one situation or another by politically significant external powers, while a few—particularly the economic and cultural avenues—are used occasionally by those which are politically insignificant.

These characteristic ways of participation in the intrusive system have both positive and negative effects upon the four pattern variables of the subordinate system: cohesion, communications, power, and the structure of relations.

Cohesion

The social, economic, political, and organizational aspects of the cohesion of a subordinate system are affected in a number of ways by the participation of an external power. Social cohesion can be enhanced by the educational efforts of an external power, if these efforts reinforce the pre-existing educational and linguistic patterns within the system. An example of this type of activity is the continued educational efforts of the French in their former colonies in North Africa and sub-Saharan Africa. Another way an intrusive power may affect social cohesion is to assist in the transfer of populations (for example, the Russians, in moving the German and Polish populations westward after World War II). In general, however, external powers are less able to affect social cohesion as such. Economic cohesion can be increased if economic assistance programs have as their aim the enhancement of economic complementarity through the encouragement of industrialization, improved methods of agriculture, or economic integration. Examples of external attempts to influence economic cohesion include American efforts in Latin America and West Europe, Russian efforts in East Europe, and British efforts in East Africa. In each case the purpose of external pressure and effort has been at least in part the encouragement of a division of labor within the region. The effect of external participation upon political cohesion may be seen when the support of a given power serves to perpetuate a conservative, radical, or moderate regime in power, or to prevent a particular type of regime from coming to power, thereby reinforcing or reducing cleavages within the system. In addition, there are instances where the concern of an external power with regional security arrangements or economic arrangements has either contributed to or hindered the organizational cohesion of a subordinate system. Intrusive powers have been able to act whether or not they have actually been members of these international organizations (for example, NATO, CENTO, COMECON).

Communications

External powers influence communications within subordinate systems in a variety of ways. Economic assistance programs have aided in mail delivery and telephone and telegraph facilities. In a variety of circumstances they have also led to improvements in transportation systems and have expedited the introduction of radio and television. The activities of an external power in a region can also encourage interchange of elite groups. Diplomatic visits and education within the region have been promoted by intrusive powers. Moreover, students and diplomats have found themselves in contact with members of other elite groups of their own region, on the territory of an intrusive power, at its universities, and at conferences sponsored by it.

Level of Power

It is upon the pattern variable of level of power that external powers have perhaps their greatest effect. External powers can promote the material power of members of subordinate systems by providing economic aid, food, technical assistance, favorable trade terms, birth control assistance, teachers, and administrative advice. Of more direct effect on the balance of power of a subordinate system is a change in military power. In ascending order of importance, the types of this kind of aid external powers can give members of the subordinate system are: economic aid which frees funds for arms purchases; grants or sales of arms and the training necessary for the use of these arms; transfer of the technology, know-how, and material necessary to permit indigenous manufacture of weaponry; and finally, the commitment of troops.

Of the three factors of power, the motivational factor is here the most significant. Through their participation in the region, external powers may affect the political, social, and ideological direction wich particular nations in the subordinate system follow. Exterior powers will decide whether to support existing governments or whether to support opposition or rebellious groups, and they may either moderate or encourage the desire of indigenous countries for increased influence of their own. External powers may then play an essential role in determining which elite comes to power in a large number of states of the region and which kinds of political institutions will prevail. In extreme cases, they may even affect the number of states which exist in the subordinate system.

Structure of Relations

As this analysis of the risks attendant upon the involvement of intrusive powers suggests, external powers affect and indeed at times determine the structure of relations within a subordinate system. The high degree of cooperation in both East Europe and Latin America is affected by the primacy of the Soviet Union and the United States, respectively, in these intrusive systems. It is interesting to note that when either the United States or the Soviet Union loses power in either of these regions, regional conflict tends to be aggravated. On the other hand, the competition of intrusive powers exacerbates conflict in the Middle East, Southeast Asia, East Asia, North Africa, and West Africa. In the Middle East and Southeast Asia particularly, sustained crisis and direct military conflict have become prevalent as the conflicts of the dominant and subordinate systems have fused.

The type of military aid and involvement of intrusive powers affects the means of relations. Consultation and amelioration are facilitated by one or more of the intrusive powers in West Europe, Latin America, East Europe, North Africa, and South Asia. In Southeast Asia and the Middle East, on the other hand, massive military aid has raised the level of conflict and made it far more dangerous. In addition, China has contributed to the turmoil in Southeast Asia through its conceptual and practical assistance in guerrilla warfare. The great influence of the intrusive powers upon the means of relations in Southeast Asia is attested to by the fact that regional wars are frequently accompanied by peace conferences attended by several great powers.

Intrusive powers usually have less influence on the causes of relations than on the other elements of the structure of relations. They may not be responsible for local religious and racial rivalries, but as we have already suggested they are capable of fanning the flames of contention by introducing ideological rivalries, by imposing their own political competitions on the area, and by encouraging local adventurism. The division of Korea and of Vietnam may be cited as examples of external powers influencing local conflict. In like manner, although to a lesser extent, they can organize local blocs and alliances to support their policies (for example, NATO, Warsaw Pact) and thereby enforce cooperation among local parties. In general, the experience of intrusive powers has been that it is easier to impose conflict than cooperation upon the members of a subordinate system.

External powers can thus serve to intensify or reduce the level of conflict of subordinate systems. Their presence may encourage division or integration among the nation-states of these areas. Intrusive powers may promote regional associations as a means of extending their control or of aiding the economic development of the indigenous states. On the other hand, their presence may limit regional cohesiveness and produce fissiparous tendencies. Whatever their effect, the external powers must be viewed as an integral part of the international politics of almost every region without which the form of each subordinate system would be considerably dissimilar.

V. RELATIONS BETWEEN SUBORDINATE SYSTEMS

The final subject to be considered here is the relationship between subordinate systems. We can distinguish two fundamental types of such relationships, that oriented toward cohesion and that oriented toward power. Relations which are oriented toward cohesion are based primarily (although not solely) on the effect of the first two pattern variables: cohesion and communications. They tend to occur among subordinate systems which are geographically proximate, have similar political and social backgrounds, and have a high degree of interaction. Examples of such relations between systems are the Middle East and North Africa, and Central Africa and West Africa. Power-oriented relations are influenced primarily by the pattern variables of level of power and the structure of relations, and are characterized by the presence of intrusive systems. The most powerful subordinate systems are the most highly interactive. In general, relations oriented toward cohesion exist between regions which are similar in power, and power-oriented relations exist between subordinate systems unequal in power. Of course, subordinate systems do not always relate to each other as a whole; in particular cases, one sector or even one country may be more important than others in determining the pattern of relations with another region. In individual cases, then, we must investigate the countries or group of countries which relate to another system, as well as the role of the periphery and the core in these relations.

Let us select a single subordinate system by way of illustration. In the Middle East, relations with North America, the Soviet Union West Europe, East Europe, and, to a minor degree, East Asia are power-oriented. They are determined largely by the level of power and the spectrum of relations with geographic proximity also playing an important role in some cases. On the other hand, the factors of cohesion and communications are particularly—although not solely—significant in the cohesive relations of most Middle Eastern states with North Africa and, to a much lesser degree, with West, East, and Central Africa. Factors of cohesion and geographic proximity are most important in the region's cohesive relations with South Asia and, to a lesser extent, in its cohesive relations with Southeast Asia, where the Islamic solidarity between most of the Middle East and Malaysia and Indonesia is the most significant influence. Israel, unlike the other states in the Middle East, conducts power-oriented relations with many countries in sub-Saharan Africa, Southeast Asia, and parts of Latin America.

Besides identifying the factors which contribute to relations between two or more systems, it is necessary to form some estimate of the intensity of these relations between subordinate systems. In this regard, one of the most significant indices is the degree of shared participation in international organizations, which may operate either toward cohesion or power. For example, OECD and NATO represent the cohesive interconnectedness of West Europe and North America, but they also are significantly power-oriented. The Arab League is an indicator of the cohesive ties between the Middle East and North Africa, and the OAU links the various regions of Africa in a broader manner. To a lesser extent, power-oriented organizations encourage more cohesive relations between subordinate systems: the Colombo Plan has encouraged greater cohesive contacts between South and Southeast Asia; OCAM links Francophonic Africa; the British Commonwealth, in a much broader way, has served to increase incipient cohesive links between a variety of subordinate systems. In this way, international organizations like OECD, NATO, the OAU, OCAM, the Arab League, and the British Commonwealth can be viewed as supraregional in character; that is to say, they tend to function as aggregators of regions. By providing forums for greater interchange they enable particular subordinate systems to intensify their interactions toward either cohesion or power.

Thus, relations between subordinate systems, while largely unstructured and uneven, can have a significant effect upon the international politics of particular areas of the world. The relationships between diverse subordinate systems, between individual countries in different regions, and between cores or peripheries of different regions, can affect local balances, local intrusive systems, and the dominant system. Consequently, in any complete analysis of the international system it is insufficient to consider each subordinate system in isolation. Its relationship to other systems must also be explored.

VI. CONCLUSION

We have been engaged in the exploratory venture of attempting to characterize the nature of the international relations of a region. As our point of departure, we have endeavored to treat the region as a unit of analysis unto itself, a unit which possesses its own internal dynamic processes. We have attempted to do this by means of an inductively arrived at classificatory system which can be used to specify how the subordinate system can be identified and what its component elements can be said to be: core sector, peripheral sector, and intrusive system. Our introduction of the four pattern variables—level of cohesion, nature of communications, level of power, and the structure of relations—was intended to establish that these matrical elements are of intrinsic importance to the delineation and understanding of the core and peripheral sectors and the intrusive system.

As part of the four pattern variables, we included a seven step ranking system to estimate the level of power of each member state of the international system, as well as a spectrum of international relations which encompasses conditions of cooperation and antagonism. We attempted to show, by means of these categories, that both antagonistic and cooperative relationships contribute to the delineation of a subordinate system and its sectors. Both antagonistic and cooperative relationships exist within the core and the peripheral sector and between the core and peripheral sectors, and these assist us in identifying a particular subordinate system.

We cannot fully understand the inner dynamics of a subordinate system, however, until the effects of politically significant participation by external powers in what we have called the "intrusive" system have been added. Only a consideration of the antagonism and cooperation inculcated within the subordinate system by external powers can provide a complete panorama of the full network of relations at work within any particular subordinate system. As we have seen, the support or withdrawal of support of an external power can radically alter the internal balance of a subordinate system.

Thus, our attempt here has been to provide a schema for the comparison of the international relations of regions. We have sought to produce a basis for analyzing units of international relations of diverse social and political backgrounds. Any such effort runs the risk of ignoring crucial factors or magnifying minor elements. We have entertained such a risk, being convinced of the significance of beginning to categorize and illustrate the patterns and processes at work in the intermediate arena of the international system—the subordinate system. For in this era of the collapse of European influence in international affairs and of the decolonization of formerly dependent peoples, the region has become one of the crucial units of international politics.

part three
Processes in the International Political System

Introductory Note

Political decisions or outcomes, whether at the national or international level, result from the collective interactions of the members of a particular political system. A political action is one that attempts—regardless of the means chosen—to either maintain or change a given distribution of coveted values. As suggested in the Introduction, income, security, and deference are useful categories in designating those things that stand at the center of the political maelstrom. This implies that not all of the activities of international actors are necessarily political, only those designed to change or maintain a certain distribution of values. But within those parameters, men and nations have been extremely inventive. The object of Part Three is to examine the general types of political behavior that appear to be most characteristic of the present international system.

Aside from the use of force (and sometimes in conjunction with it), diplomatic negotiations are the most venerable means by which international actors have sought to alter their political situation. The selections of Chapter Eight are designed to shed light on this important process; but in doing so, they go well beyond simple description. Professor Fred Iklé's short piece is meant only to define and introduce the idea of negotiation. In the second selection, however, Professors Jack Sawyer and Harold Guetzkow attempt to develop a model of negotiation in international politics. The theoretical heart of their model is non zero-sum game theory which, they argue, reveals the quintessential nature of the bargaining process.

Military force, overt or covert, implied or explicit, represents the ultimate means for effecting changes in the international arena. The four articles of Chapter Nine do not pretend to be more than an introduction to a vast and complex field of inquiry. Professors Robert Osgood and Robert Tucker address themselves to the fundamental question of why it is that force has always loomed so large in men's political affairs, especially at the international level. Professor Morton Halperin concentrates on the types of war possible under contemporary, that is, nuclear, conditions, and the circumstances under which they might occur. Guerrilla warfare is examined by Professor Samuel Huntington. He tries to differentiate it from more traditional forms and to assess its effectiveness. In a more extensive article, the same author analyzes arms races—a phenomenon that has gained in importance as the possibility of actually using weapons has decreased. In a very real sense, arms races have and can function as surrogates for actual combat.

The concern of Chapter Ten is economic processes, especially foreign aid. To many people, foreign aid is the political process most characteristic of the nuclear era. Professor David Baldwin investigates the uses to which economic and military assistance programs have been put. Also closely associated with the contemporary international system is propaganda and psychological warfare, the topic of Chapter Eleven. The genesis and significance of this process is examined by Professor Terence Qualter.

chapter eight
BARGAINING AND NEGOTIATION AS PROCESSES

What Is Negotiation?

Fred Charles Iklé

Certain subjects seem quite clear as long as we leave them alone. The answers look obvious until we ask questions, the concepts appear to be well understood until we wish to define them, causes and effects are easily recognized until we seek to explain them, and all the rules pass for valid until we try to prove them. The social scientist, alas, shares the honor with the philosopher of often moving in his inquiries from the obvious to the obscure. Of course, he hopes to go beyond and to emerge with a clearer view of the whole and a better knowledge of the details than he first had on the basis of folklore and common sense. But to begin with, he must challenge the old answers with new questions.

Negotiation is a subject on which much has been said and written that seems self-evident until examined more closely. To resolve conflict and avoid the use of force, it is said, one must negotiate (Is this always the best way to settle conflict?). Negotiation requires a

SOURCE: From Fred Charles Iklé, *How Nations Negotiate.* Copyright © 1964 by Fred Charles Iklé. Reprinted by permission of the author and Harper and Row Publishers, Inc.

willingness to compromise (Why?), and both sides must make concessions (According to which law?). Neither side can expect to win all it wants (Not even if its objectives are modest?). If both sides negotiate in good faith (Who judges "good faith"?), they can always find a fair solution (And what is "fair"?). If there is a conflict about many issues, the less controversial ones should be solved first because agreement will lead to further agreement (Or will the postponed issues become harder to solve?). A negotiator should never make a threat he is not prepared to carry out (What is wrong with successful bluffing?). Each side has its minimum beyond which it cannot be moved (But how about moving the opponent's minimum?).

This book is concerned with the process and effects of negotiation between governments; in particular, it seeks to relate the *process* of negotiation to the *outcome*. To begin with, two elements must normally be present for negotiation to take place: there must be both common interests and issues of conflict. Without common interest there is nothing to negotiate for, without conflict nothing to negotiate about.

There are many ways in which governments—always subject to change, idiosyncrasy, and pressure from within—relate their common interests to their conflicting interests. They may be isolationist and try to stay apart to avoid all conflict, while sacrificing the pursuit of possible common interests. Or they may simply follow habits and rules that regulate their interests and conflicts automatically without bargaining. The observance of some diplomatic practices is of this character. (So is routine buying and selling at fixed prices.) But usually a government takes account of the fact that its interests and its ability to pursue national objectives are influenced by decisions of other nations. Likewise it realizes that these other nations will be affected by its own decisions. It may try to coordinate this interaction without explicitly saying so—a process of "tacit bargaining." Or it may communicate with other governments for the explicit purpose of working out a particular combination of conflicting and common interests; that is, to reach an agreement.

One should perhaps distinguish between two kinds of common interests: an *identical common interest* in a single arrangement or object, and a *complementary interest* in an exchange of different objects. In the identical common interest, the parties want to share the *same* object or benefit from the same arrangement, which, however, they can bring about only by joining together. Hence they have to agree on the object's characteristics (concerning which they may have different preferences) and on the division of the costs and gains (where their interests are likely to conflict). Examples of agreements on such identical common interests are the U.S.-Canadian treaty on the St. Lawrence Seaway, international fishery agreements to protect the supply of fish, and, in a sense, cease-fire agreements.

When parties are interested in an exchange, they want *different* things. These they cannot obtain by themselves but can only grant to each other. The clearest examples are barters and sales. Similarly, commercial aviation agreements, where each country wants to have its planes fly to the other country, have the purpose of settling an exchange. So do agreements for mutual tariff concessions.

In reality, however, most negotiations embrace a combination of identical common interests and complementary interests. When the six European countries set up the European Economic Community, they had complementary interests in the exchange of tariff concessions and common interests in a large, unified European market. The nuclear test-ban treaty between the United States and the Soviet Union can satisfy the complementary interest in slowing down the opponent's development of new weapons and the common interest in preventing an increase in radioactive fallout or in discouraging the proliferation of nuclear weapons. Whether the identical common interests or the complementary interests dominate depends on how the purposes of the agreement are defined.

The process by which two or more parties relate conflicting to common interests is the warp and woof not only of international relations but of human society; individuals, groups, and governments engage in it all the time. We become aware of it only when we call it something special—like Molière's Monsieur Jourdain when he discovered that for forty years he had been speaking "prose." There seems to be no established term for all the ways in which parties with conflicting and common interests interact—whether explicitly or tacitly—though "bargaining" is sometimes used that broadly.

"Negotiation" in a narrower sense denotes a process that is different from tacit bargaining or other behavior that regulates conflict. As used here, *negotiation is a process in which explicit proposals are put forward ostensibly for the purpose of reaching agreement on an exchange or on the realization of a common interest where conflicting interests are present.* Frequently, these proposals deal not only with the terms of agreement but also with the topics to be discussed (the agenda), with the ground rules that ought to apply, and with underlying technical and legal issues. It is the confrontation of explicit proposals that distinguishes negotiation (as here defined) from tacit bargaining and other types of conflict behavior. Beyond this confrontation appear other moves that the negotiating parties make to strengthen their own position, to weaken that of the opponent, or to influence the outcome in other ways. The subject matter of this book includes all these moves and the ways in which they relate to the outcome. That is, bargaining moves are included in the broader sense, to the extent that they serve pending or ongoing negotiations where explicit proposals are being put forward.

Only part of the frequent changes in relations between countries are the result of negotiation. Governments often revise their expectations and attitudes toward other countries as a result of unilateral actions or tacit bargains. Military and technological developments, growth or decline in economic strength, and internal political changes continually cause the rearrangement of conflicting and common interests between nations, and this happens whether or not diplomats negotiate.

There is no simple rule as to when negotiation is needed, and when tacit bargaining or even less conscious confrontations are more effective to restructure international relations. For certain arrangements negotiation clearly cannot be dispensed with; for others it is optional; and there are some issues which are better settled without it.

Negotiation is necessary for any arrangement that establishes complicated forms of collaboration, such as a joint war effort or Britain's attempted entry into the Common Market. (In contrast, the entry of, say, the Ivory Coast into the United Nations did not require significant negotiations.) Negotiation is needed for most exchanges, such as exchanges of prisoners or the granting of mutual consular facilities, and for all transactions involving monetary compensation, as in the payment of oil royalties or the leasing of air bases. Negotiation is, of course, necessary for the setting up of formal international institutions and for any arrangement where an *explicit* agreement is essential, such as a peace treaty or an alliance system.

On the other hand, certain undertakings are arrived at in such a delicate way that explicit proposals might interfere with the process. The mutually observed restrictions in the Korean War (for instance, no attacks on the supply lines leading into North and South Korea) is an example of arrangements that would not have been facilitated or might even have been upset by negotiation. The very uncertainties of a tacit understanding may have made these restrictions more stable, because both sides were unwilling to probe and push toward the limits of the "bargain," lest it all be upset. The negotiation of an explicit *quid pro quo* might have given rise to new demands and invited more haggling and tugging than the arrangement which the parties never discussed and never explicitly settled. Furthermore, while soldiers were being killed fighting the enemy, negotiations to establish rules and restraints for the battle or on the interdiction of supplies would have clashed with domestic opinion and perhaps adversely affected the morale of the troops.[1]

Likewise, if there is a deep-seated hostility between the populations of two countries, governments may be unable to negotiate because of public opposition but may work out some arrangements of mutual interest through tacit bargaining. The relationship between Jordan and Israel is an example.

In the field of arms control and disarmament, where we have become so accustomed to large and formal conferences, important understandings can at times be arrived at without negotiation. Formal talks might, in fact, make it more difficult to harmonize some arms policies insofar as they inevitably introduce political issues or questions of prestige and legal precedents.[2]

Negotiation plays an important role in formalizing turning points in international relations, in catalyzing or at least clarifying changes that were caused by tacit bargaining or other processes, and in working out those finer shades in new arrangements between nations that the brute interplay of latent strength cannot define.

Although negotiation is necessary for any new relationship that is based on explicit agreement, an explicit agreement is usually only part of the outcome of negotiation. Negotiation may change the positions of the parties and their mutual relations in many other ways. The outcome may include, for example, tacit understandings between the parties, a clarification of the points of disagreement, a reorientation of national objectives, new commitments to third parties (allies, domestic groups, or world opinion), and propaganda effects. Many of these results may outweigh in importance whatever explicit agreement is arrived at. And even agreements themselves vary widely in their degree of specificity and the amount of disagreement that they leave unsettled.

[1] A pioneering analysis of the role of tacit bargaining in limited war is given by Thomas C. Schelling, *The Strategy of Conflict* (Cambridge, Mass.: Harvard University Press, 1960), chap. iii and appendix A. The delicate interaction of tacit limitations on air-attacks in the Korean War is discussed by Morton H. Halperin, *Limited War in the Nuclear Age* (New York: John Wiley, 1963), pp. 53-55.

[2] On the importance of tacit bargaining for arms control, see Thomas C. Schelling and Morton H. Halperin, *Strategy and Arms Control* (New York: Twentieth Century Fund, 1961), pp. 77-82.

Bargaining and Negotiation in International Relations*

Jack Sawyer and Harold Guetzkow

"Let us not be blind to our differences—but let us also direct attention to our common interests and to the means by which those differences can be resolved. And if we cannot now end our differences, at least we can help make the world safe for diversity"—John F. Kennedy, American University, June 10, 1963.

Morgenthau (1956) points out that nations, in resolving their differences, ". . . have always had a choice among three alternatives: diplomacy, war, and renunciation . . . [but] modern technol-

SOURCE: From Herbert C. Kelman (ed.), *International Behavior: A Socio-Psychological Analysis.* Copyright © 1965 by Holt, Rinehart and Winston, Inc. Reprinted and abridged by permission of the authors and Holt, Rinehart and Winston, Inc.

*The authors are grateful to Peter Allen for his insightful comments and suggestions on the manuscript, to Lawrence A. Eberhardt and Ellen Kay Trimberger for their diligent and highly informed search of the international relations and social-psychological literature, respectively, and to Herbert Kelman for his continued intellectual contributions and personal stimulation throughout the production of the present analysis.

ogy . . . has destroyed this rational equality . . . there is no longer safety in renunciation or victory in war" (pp. 410-411). To the remaining possibility of diplomatic negotiation, this chapter is devoted.

Negotiation is a process through which two or more parties—be they individuals, groups, or larger social units—interact in developing potential agreements to provide guidance and regulation of their future behavior. Such negotiation is conducted not only between nations, but also between government departments, political factions, labor and management, gangs, neighbors, and spouses.

At the international level, negotiation may be regarded as one of the major functions of diplomacy that together constitute "the conduct of business between states by peaceful means" (Satow, 1957, p. 1). Other major functions include the interchange of political, economic, and military information, including "technical discussions" that do not seek agreement; and the execution of procedures (such as routine consular arrangements for commercial and tourist traffic) reflecting in some cases traditional practice or previous negotiation, and in others trivial or noncontroversial problems that do not require formal negotiation.

The present analysis is not directly concerned with the whole of diplomacy, let alone of the larger sphere of international relations, though these are both crucial in providing its context. Further, *within* the area of international negotiation, the focus of the present analysis is upon social-psychological aspects.* This is not to assert that international conflict arises simply from misperception and misunderstanding; on the contrary, conflict appears to result in large part from objective incompatibility of goals among states. It is the thesis of this analysis, however, that even such genuine conflict of interests may be heightened or mitigated by psychological factors, and that these may influence its eventual outcome.

. . .

For social-psychological analysis, negotiation may be regarded as composed of five aspects: (a) *goals,* motivating the parties to enter and sustain (b) the *process* of negotiation itself, which involves communications and actions leading to (c) certain *outcomes* for each—all occurring within and influenced by (d) preexisting *background* factors of cultural traditions and relations between and within parties, and (e) specific situational *conditions* under which the

Editor's Note: Most of Professor Sawyer and Guetzkow's social-psychological research has been deleted to shorten the article. The reader is urged to consult the original essay for this aspect of the authors' work.

negotiation is conducted. These five aspects and their relations constitute a preliminary social-psychological model of negotiation, portrayed in Figure 1.

This model provides a framework for the present analysis, which devotes a major section to each of the five aspects. Within each, a number of more specific elements are treated, as indicated in Figure 1. Attention is thus directed not only to the narrower problem of bargaining over given alternatives, but also to such processes as establishing the domain of initial concern, searching for new alternatives, or arranging for the execution of negotiated agreements. Figure 1 also shows the approximate temporal flow of negotiation: *Goals* and *background* factors exist initially, and both influence the on-going *process,* as do the contemporary *conditions;* the resulting *outcome* may at any given time also produce feedback that alters the goals or process.

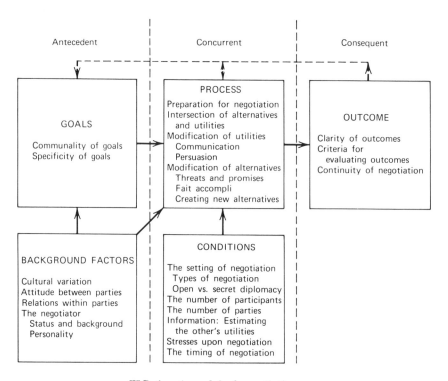

FIG. 1. *A model of negotiation.*

GOALS OF NEGOTIATION

As Haas and Whiting (1956) point out, the underlying purpose of negotiation may not be agreement at all, but rather delay or propaganda. Delay forestalls action while one awaits more favorable circumstances; propaganda seeks to embarrass the other party, to promote positions world opinion will favor, or simply to avoid the onus of failing to negotiate. Other side effects, Iklé (1964) suggests, include maintaining contact, substituting for violent action, intelligence, and deception. These important functions of negotiation are not treated in the present analysis since they minimize the relevance of the process of direct exchange which forms the present focus. Rather, this analysis examines those situations in which potential outcomes are sufficiently promising to encourage serious efforts toward agreement.

In such bargaining in good faith, the goal of each party may be taken as the end-state it desires to achieve. Many outcomes (including lack of agreement) are possible, and each party may establish an order of preference among them. Then the goal of each party may be stated more broadly, and more realistically: to obtain the most favored outcome to which the other party will agree. Favorability of the outcomes the parties are likely to obtain depends in considerable part on the way their interests are related. Considering international relations, Friedrich (1963, p. 486) distinguishes four cases: common interest, complementary interests, conflicting interests, and completely contradictory interests. While little if any social-psychological research deals with the effect of national goals, there is evidence, presented in the following section, on effects associated with perceived or actual communality or conflict of goals.

Communality of Goals

Probably the factor most promotive of the mutual satisfaction of both parties to a negotiation is the extent to which their goals are, or can be made to be, in agreement. As Thucydides observed in ancient Greece, "identity of interests is the surest of bonds, whether between states or individuals."

. . .

One common goal at the international level is suggested by Riker (1962), who characterizes contemporary international relations as the "age of maneuver," in which the main though perhaps implicit goal for both major powers is simply ". . . the prolongation of the age for the greatest possible duration . . . since the end of the age is likely also to be the end of the leadership of both powers . . ." (p. 238). Thus they illustrate a supranational communality of goals, in their joint desire to avoid nuclear war and to control the price paid in the continuing negotiation for allies.

Another type of objective communality occurs when two parties have complementary goals. Through certain activities, such as international trade, reciprocal benefits may accrue from a meshing of the varying needs and capabilities of different nations. This phenomenon of reciprocal advantage operates at many levels.

. . .

Communality of goals . . . is influential in negotiation not only as an actuality, but also in the way it is perceived. Yet perceived and actual communality of goals may differ widely. Parties to a conflict may subjectively define their interests in such a way as to be mutually incompatible. Each party may desire not merely to be strong, but strong*er* than the other, not just rich, but rich*er;* such relative goals are necessarily antagonistic, since they cannot simultaneously be achieved by both parties.

. . .

Specificity of Goals

It seems reasonable that negotiation involving broad, loosely defined goals would differ from that involving more specific goals. As then Foreign Minister Pearson of Canada noted, if you are unclear in the definition of your goals, ". . . you are not likely to be clear in their expression" (1959, p. 49).

Generality and long-time perspective appear to contribute to vagueness of goals; it is easier to be precise concerning given situations and times. Yet among a number of reasonably well defined, short-run goals particular to different given situations there may be considerable inconsistencies; this is the situation confronting a major power with global interests. To rationalize such a range of goals requires a highly general statement, such as that of the United States President's Commission on National Goals (1960, pp. 15-20).

. . .

Vagueness and generality of goals is sometimes associated with the presence of an all-encompassing ideology. Disagreement may thus be extended from a conflict of interest to a conflict of values, arising not from scarcity but from ". . . dissensus concerning the normative value of a social object" (Aubert, 1963, p. 29). Such is the case in a "struggle for men's minds" in which competing systems each aspire to impose their moral codes universally.

. . .

THE PROCESS OF NEGOTIATION

The prospect of achieving their interdependent goals through negotiation leads nations to the process itself. The process of negotiation includes all actions or communications, by any party to the negotiation, either made within the negotiating situation or intended to influence its outcome. Steps in this process, as treated in the following sections, include (a) preliminary negotiation concerning procedure and agenda, (b) formulation of alternatives and preferences of each party into a joint decision matrix, (c) communication and persuasion intended to alter the other party's perception of the situation, and (d) threats and promises, *faits accomplis,* and creative problem-solving activity intended to narrow or widen the range of available outcomes and alternatives.

Preparation for Negotiation

Specific motivations to seek negotiation include impending expiration of a previous agreement (such as a lease of a foreign location for a defense base), the development (often through technological advance) of a previously inconsequential or nonexistent area (such as production of fissionable materials), and specific political acts of another nation (such as violation of an existing agreement). Changing circumstances such as these may initiate a sequence of procedural negotiation, agenda development, and finally, a decision to enter upon substantive negotiation.

. . .

Procedural Negotiation. Questions of procedure include the number and rank of participants to represent a party, the length and frequency of sessions, the languages to be employed (treated separately later), and the rules by which discussion is to proceed. Any of these arrangements may have an influence upon later negotiation, and consequently, particularly if the stakes in the eventual substantive negotiation are large, much time may be consumed in this stage. When problems of *how* negotiation is to be conducted are settled, however, attention may be concentrated upon the question of specifically *what* is to be negotiated.

Agenda Development. Starting with proposals from each party for issues to be negotiated, the parties must jointly decide which issues shall constitute the agenda. The choice is critical, as it influences the outcome of negotiation itself; Schattschneider (1957), referring to domestic politics, asserts that, "The definition of alternatives is the supreme instrument of power . . . [it] is the choice of conflicts, and the choice of conflict allocates power" (p. 937). For this reason, many higher-level officials will enter negotiation only after the agenda has been specified.

Agenda vary markedly in the number of issues they contain, and advantages can be cited for both the long and the short. Narrow agenda may confine negotiation to that area that has best promise of resolution and prevent jeopardizing it by unduly contentious items. However, upon any single issue, parties are likely to reach alternatives in which their interests are strictly opposed, and relative gain by one implies relative loss by the other. As Rusk (1955, p. 129) observed of debate in the United Nations, the tendency to isolate issues makes them more difficult to adjust. Through widening the agenda to include unrelated items, it may be possible to effect trading, in which, for each party, losses in one area are balanced by gains in another.

. . .

The Decision to Enter Negotiation. Given the prospective agenda, the parties make a decision (perhaps implicit) to go ahead with substantive negotiation at that time, to postpone negotiation, or to call it off altogether. To enter negotiation implies expectation of a better result from participating than from refraining, whether based upon the motivations for delay or propaganda characterized earlier or upon the expected outcome of the negotiation itself.

. . .

Intersection of Alternatives and Utilities

At the onset of negotiation, the situation may be conceptualized in terms of four main elements: (a) the negotiating parties, (b) the alternative actions that might be taken by each party, (c) the various outcomes expected to result from their combined actions, and (d) the utility each party ascribes to each of the various outcomes. Such a formulation, derived from the theory of games, has proven highly stimulating of both theory and empirical research dealing with interaction situations, not only in the field of economics (Shubik, 1959), which originally motivated game theory (Von Neumann & Morgenstern, 1944), but in other social sciences as well, including both social psychology (Rapoport, 1960; Thibaut & Kelley, 1959) and international relations (Kaplan, 1957; Schelling, 1960). . . .

The Decision Matrix. The four elements of parties, alternatives, outcomes, and utilities may profitably be placed in matrix form, of which Figure 2 provides a highly simplified example. Consider two nations, A and B, negotiating over possible reduction in tariffs. For

Alternatives for Nation· B / Alternatives for Nation A	HOLD OUT for present high tariff	Lower tariff to a COMPROMISE level
HOLD OUT for present high tariff	Outcome Status quo: both tariffs remain high Utility 0 for A 0 for B	Outcome A's tariff remains high B's tariff lowered Utility +10 for A −5 for B
Lower tariff to a COMPROMISE level	Outcome A's tariff lowered B's tariff remains high Utility −5 for A +10 for B	Outcome Both tariffs are lowered Utility +5 for A +5 for B

FIG. 2. *Illustrative matrix of outcomes and utilities when each of two nations may alternatively lower its tariff to a "compromise" level or "hold out" at the present high level.*

purposes of illustration, let Nation A have but two alternative actions that it might eventually take (though game theory can accommodate any number of alternatives): to reduce its tariff on the commodity in question to a lower "compromise" level, or to "hold out" at the present higher level. These two alternatives are represented by the first and second rows of the matrix. Nation B has two corresponding alternatives, represented by the two columns.

Designation of the alternatives as "compromise" and "hold out" is intended to suggest that such a matrix formulation as here illustrated with tariffs may also be applied to a much wider range of interaction situations. The alternatives at stake could just as well involve the number of inspections of suspected nuclear explosions, the terms of a development loan, or the size and extent of cultural exchange.

In the illustration involving tariffs, if each nation can take either action, independently of the other, there are four possible outcomes, as indicated in the four cells of the matrix: both tariffs may be lowered, only A's may be lowered, only B's may be lowered, or both may remain high. Let each of these four outcomes have a certain utility for each party, as shown by the numbers in Figure 2. The status quo of the existing higher tariffs is taken as a reference point, so that this outcome has zero utility for each party. The utilities of the other outcomes are shown as incremental amounts over the utility of the status quo; the negative utility for a nation when it alone lowers its tariff represents a worsening over the status quo for that nation.

It is important to note that the sum of the utilities to the two parties is higher for some outcomes than for others; in other words, this matrix belongs to the class referred to as nonconstant-sum (or non-zero-sum). These are to be distinguished from zero-sum situations, in which one party gains only at the direct expense of the other; in such situations, negotiation is pointless. When some outcomes are better for both parties, however, and some worse, negotiation offers promise; it is these situations with which the present analysis is concerned.

The utilities in a decision matrix represent the over-all value placed upon the particular outcomes. In some cases, it is possible to translate this directly into monetary terms; for example, the values given in Figure 2 might represent millions of dollars. More commonly, political and other values for which, unlike money, there is no standard metric, do not permit such ready translation between objective and subjective utility measures. In practice, then, utility of outcomes is generally assessed by the judgmental evaluation of policy officials, as described earlier. In any event, utility is taken, both operationally and conceptually, to correspond directly to preference; outcomes of higher utility are those that are more highly preferred, and vice versa. The correspondence, though, is strictly definitional: Higher utilities do not "cause" higher preferences.

It is the resulting matrix of utility values that makes explicit the "intersecting alternatives and utilities" with which the present section is concerned. This matrix specifies the way in which the utility experienced by each party depends upon the choices of both, thus promoting the ability of a party to understand how it may achieve as good an outcome as possible, given that the other party is trying to do the same.

In the present example, the best outcome for either nation occurs when it retains high tariffs while the other nation reduces its tariffs. Regardless of whether the other nation retains or lowers its tariffs, however, it is better for a nation to retain its own at the high level. (For example, if B retains its tariffs, A prefers 0 to −5; if B has lowered its tariffs, A prefers 10 to 5.) Yet if each nation adopts this orientation and independently chooses to retain its current high tariffs, the result is the status quo, which both prefer less than a mutual reduction. Thus, such a choice situation presents a dilemma, in that two parties, each choosing independently to its own advantage, together produce an outcome neither prefers.[1] The way out of such a dilemma, of course, is for the choices to be not independent, but rather the result of mutual agreement.

. . .

Dynamic Alternatives and Utilities. In most analyses of interacting alternatives and utilities . . . both alternatives and utilities for outcomes have been assumed, explicitly or implicitly, to be completely static. In an experiment, for example, this assumption may be reflected by a fixed matrix in which there is no opportunity over the course of interaction for change either in the utilities in the cells of

---

[1]Some economists argue that unilateral tariff reduction benefits a nation, regardless of the actions of other nations—which says that the utilities in the illustrative matrix misrepresent the actual value that would be derived. Nonetheless, the reluctance of nations to reduce tariffs implies they do not perceive such unconditional gain—and it is their *perception*, right or wrong, that determines their decisions.

When perceived utilities *are* as in Figure 2, the situation, given another context, is the "Prisoner's Dilemma" (Luce & Raiffa, 1957), whose peculiarly self-defeating characteristics have stimulated much theoretical and empirical investigation, some of which is later analyzed. The context of the original formulation involves two prisoners, whom the district attorney knows to be guilty, though he lacks the evidence to convict. He holds the two prisoners separately and tells each that if he confesses and the other does not, he will be given but a very light sentence for turning state's evidence whereas the other will receive a maximum sentence. If both confess, each will receive heavy sentences, though less than maximum. If neither confesses, the district attorney will press other minor but provable charges which would result in moderately light sentences for each. Thus, choosing independently, each prisoner finds it better to confess, regardless of whether he expects the other to confess or not.

the matrix or in the alternatives represented by the rows and columns. Yet such a static situation, while providing a basic formulation for negotiation, is rare in practice.

Two modifications of the basic situation, more common in practice, are (a) those in which utilities for outcomes may change during the course of negotiation, though alternatives remain fixed, and (b) those in which alternatives themselves may also be added, modified, or eliminated. Thus change results either in the utility entries in the matrix, or in the defining rows and columns themselves, producing in either case a new matrix. These two important cases provide the foci for the remaining two sections dealing with process; they are, indeed, the core of what is generally taken as the central process of negotiation—reciprocal argument and counterargument, proposal and counterproposal, in an attempt to agree upon actions and outcomes mutually perceived as beneficial. . . .

Modification of Utilities: Communication and Persuasion

To change the utilities certain outcomes hold for the other party is frequently a major interim goal for a negotiator, for if the other party can be made to value more highly the outcomes one prefers himself, the probability of obtaining these is increased. Communication and persuasion, major agents in the process of modifying utilities, concern the way in which the arguments and proposals of each party are understood by the other.

Communication. Communication between parties to an international negotiation is complicated first of all by language. Shades of connotative differences and culturally specific meanings hinder effective translation. . . . If the Russian phrase whose literal translation is "We will bury you" and which connotes "We will outlive you" is instead interpreted "We will destroy you," quite different implications are perceived (Klineberg, 1964, p. 153).

The history of diplomatic practice suggests that as the fullness of communication increases, negotiation becomes easier.

. . .

But the very conflict that negotiation might resolve may itself make communication more difficult to commence. As the result of another experiment, Deutsch and Krauss (1962) suggest that, "Where barriers to communication exist, a situation in which the parties are compelled to communicate will be more effective than one in which the choice to talk or not is put on a voluntary basis" (p. 75). The increasing activity of international organizations, such as the United Nations, provides considerable opportunity for communication, much of it of an informal nature where specific issues are not at stake or in public view and hence wider exploration of alternatives may be conducted. . . .

Persuasion. The aim of much communication in negotiation is to persuade the other party that his self-interest is not what he thought, by providing information, interpretation, or implications that cause him to reassess the utility of various outcomes. This purported mis-evaluation may stem from three sources—the effect of the act itself upon its maker, the effect of consequent behavior by the other, and the effect of consequent behavior by third parties—thus furnishing a persuader three somewhat distinct appeals:

1. Intrinsic interest: You should want to do this for its direct benefit, which possibly you do not fully perceive. "Lower tariffs will permit your people to buy imported goods more cheaply."
2. Second party effects (for example, threat of force): If you don't do it, I may do something you won't like. "If you do not lower your tariffs, we may raise ours."
3. Third party effects (for example norms): Others want you to do so, and will give their approval. "Other countries will approve if you lower your tariffs.". . .

Each of these appeals, if successful, would result in the reappraisal of the values of certain outcomes, so that a party's self-interest might dictate different choices than before.

· · ·

The modification of utilities by the most skillful diplomatic persuasion, however, will seldom result in situations in which the most favored outcome of one party is also the most favored outcome of the other. . . . At this point, bargaining often becomes a matter of trying to establish what is the least the other will take and convincing him that that is the most one will give.

· · ·

Modification of Alternatives

If modifications are considered to be of two kinds—those that only subtract from the available set of alternatives, and those that add as well as possibly subtract—successful threats, promises, and *faits accomplis* are of the first kind, and creative problem-solving approaches are of the second kind. Which may be called for depends, as we shall see, on the initial state of the decision matrix of alternatives and preferences.

Threats and Promises. A threat is a representation that if another party acts in a way one disfavors, one will take an action detrimental to the other. It is important, however, that the other party be convinced that the detrimental action will not also be taken even if he complies. For this reason, as pointed out by Schelling (1960), a threatened action must be detrimental not only to the recipient, but to the initiator as well. The threat of massive retaliation furnishes an example: Its purpose (as that of threats generally) is to deter; but whether it succeeds or fails in deterring the initiator has no immediate motivation to carry out the threat, since it harms him as well as the other.

The logical structure of promises is essentially similar to that of threats. Promises are representations that if the other behaves in a way one favors, one will then take an action beneficial to the other, even though one would then prefer not to do so. . . .

Thus, in either threats or promises, one represents that given certain action by the other, meant to be deterred or induced, he will choose against his own immediate welfare. For such a representation to be credible, a party must have a way of demonstrating to the other that he would in fact be bound (by honor public opinion, or other restraints) to carry out the otherwise undesired action; it will be most convincing, indeed, if he can show the other how the carrying out is an automatic consequence of the other's action, in which no intervention is possible.

. . .

If a threat or promise is sufficiently credible for the party who is its target to believe that it would actually be carried out, then it should have the primary effect intended: effectively to reduce the possibilities with which the party is confronted. (The reduction actually occurs directly in outcomes: The target party knows that if he chooses a certain alternative, only an undesired outcome is possible; then effectively that entire alternative is eliminated.) Thus the result is a reduced matrix of alternatives and preferences defining a different interaction situation.

. . .

Fait Accompli. Like a successful threat or promise, a *fait accompli* reduces the decision matrix by eliminating as possibilities certain outcomes and alternatives. The result is likewise similar: The party who is the target is left with a situation in which his best outcomes are eliminated and the least undesirable of the remainder are just the ones preferred by the initiating party. If the target party then chooses to his advantage, the initiator benefits. The preemptory nature of the *fait accompli* may to such an extent antagonize its target, however, that punishing the other (even at one's own loss) becomes attractive—if only to discourage repetition.

As an illustration of the *fait accompli*, Lerche (1956) indicates how unilateral action by the United States in establishing SEATO minimized the extent of its compromise in reaching final agreement with Great Britain on the nature of the alliance.

. . .

Creating New Alternatives. Frequently, two parties to negotiation will be confronted by a decision matrix in which there is no single outcome that both prefer to lack of agreement. Negotiation will then necessarily fail unless higher utilities emerge either through reassessment of existing outcomes or through development of new outcomes. The first possibility has been considered in connection with communication and persuasion. Often, however, the initial evaluations of outcomes have been made after extensive and public review, and consequently these may be little subject to modification, if only for the reason that otherwise the negotiators might be charged with abandoning their constituency.

Through the modification and addition of alternatives, though, it may be possible to create new outcomes on which agreement can be achieved, as did Churchill, Truman, and Stalin when they solved their problem of precedence in entering the Potsdam negotiating chamber by emerging simultaneously through three doors. New outcomes should, then, in comparison with prior outcomes, increase the utility for one party while, at the least, not decreasing that of the other. . . .

The process of devising more favorable alternatives and outcomes may be characterized as one of "creative problem-solving" since it involves innovation rather than mere selection among given possibilities. As with creative processes more generally, however, relatively little is understood of its operation.

. . .

THE OUTCOME OF NEGOTIATION

Out of the matrix of modified alternatives and utilities resulting from the process of negotiation may eventually come resolution upon a specified outcome. In international negotiation, the form of these outcomes varies widely, from formal and highly explicit treaties to informal and often vague understandings, with the result sometimes being a virtual lack of any agreement at all. The degree of explicitness is one of the most crucial dimensions on which agreements vary, since it affects the influence they have on future conduct. Another important aspect is how "good" an outcome results, and in what senses this may be evaluated. Finally, it is important to note the continuing nature of negotiation. An outcome itself may provide stimulus for future negotiation and in any event has influence upon the larger continuing process of international relations. The following three sections treat these aspects of clarity of outcomes, criteria for outcomes and their implications for continuity of negotiation.

Clarity of Outcomes

The extent to which outcomes may vary in explicitness is illustrated in the five forms Schelling and Halperin (1961) outline for arms control agreements, which include formal treaties with detailed specifications, executive agreements, explicit but informal understandings, tacit understandings, and mere self-restraint consciously contingent upon the other's behavior. Though these vary widely, even the most formal agreement cannot provide for all contingencies, or necessarily provide exact interpretation in each case. Yet specificity is often crucial; as Davison (1958) notes, the vagueness of the Potsdam agreement in 1945 permitted continuing disagreement among the great powers in interpreting the status of Berlin.

Imperfect clarity of outcomes may stem not from the difficulty of exhaustiveness but from the difficulty of agreement itself. Sometimes an ambiguously worded clause is purposely inserted to permit agreement where otherwise an entire negotiation would fail. The Convocation of Bishops in 1531 acquiesced in acknowledging Henry VIII "the protector and only supreme head of the Church and clergy of England" only after devising the phrase, ". . . so far as the law of Christ allows," thus satisfying themselves in principle and Henry in practice (Durant, 1957, p. 545). . . .

When there is sufficient consensus to arrive at a fairly definitive agreement, and clarity is desired, it is then important to concert upon an alternative that is eminently clear to all parties. Schelling (1960), in considering the effect of the prominence of an alternative, points out that the largely tacit agreement in World War II upon "*no poision gas*" was, among the many alternatives (limit its use to military personnel, or only with warning, and so on), the only completely unambiguous one.

Even in explicit negotiation, prominence furnishes a strong guide, as illustrated by the prevalence of rivers as territorial boundaries and of round numbers in the settlement of damage suits. In the negotiation of tariffs, an across-the-board reduction of constant percentages on all commodities is a highly prominent alternative; once this principle (often defended as that) is abandoned, it is difficult to justify any particular set of differential percentages.

. . .

Criteria for Evaluating Outcomes

Whatever the clarity of the outcome, each party may place upon it at least an approximate value, if not a completely determinate one. Then the question may be asked, given the alternatives among which each party had to choose, and the values of their associated outcomes, "Is this a "good" solution?"

. . .

In one sense, having formal principles providing generally agreed upon solutions may seem impossible or irrelevant, since, as suggested in considering modes of persuasion, each party may simply desire to convince the other that it will absolutely take no less than the maximum the other can give, and otherwise prefers nonagreement. Yet in the long run, the best solution may not be the one whose outcome provides most immediate utility, for as pointed out by Callieres in 1716 and frequently before and since, ". . . there is no durable treaty which is not founded on reciprocal advantage" (1919, p. 110). A nation should, in its own interest, be concerned that the other's outcome is sufficiently high to motivate him to keep the agreement. If one nation, by hard bargaining succeeds in getting the other to accept an agreement providing an outcome only slightly above its minimum disposition, a small shift in the relative power of the two nations may cause the agreement to be unacceptable. Many labor economists (for example, Hicks, 1948) and negotiators have stressed that the goal of arbitrators and mediators should not be to promote "fair" solutions (exceedingly difficult in any event, because of varying standards of what is "fair") but rather to achieve acceptable solutions that adequately reflect the respective power of each party, and hence are likely to be kept.

. . .

Continuity of Negotiation

When negotiation results in agreement, provision must be made for its execution, the conduct of which frequently though not invariably falls into the classification of nonnegotiative diplomacy distinguished at the very outset of this chapter. But the impossibility of complete explicitness may necessitate later interpretation of unforeseen cases. Many agreements provide procedures for their interpretation, which may take the form of minor negotiation themselves. Agreements may also provide for their extension to related, though as yet un-agreed-upon areas, and thus preface further negotiation.

To provide routinely for handling minor adjustments subsequent to a negotiaton may imply some institutionalization of the negotiating relation. In labor-management relations, grievance procedures treating specific cases within the framework of a larger agreement function to prevent such cases from precipitating major conflict. At the internatinal level, Schelling and Halperin (1961) suggest that inspection of arms control agreements may facilitate continuing negotiation, by providing opportunity for informal consultation and discussion.

In other ways, too, negotiation perpetuates itself. Agreement, even in a minor area, may provide future expectation of successful negotiation. Further, the act of negotiation itself may, through the necessity of coordination of procedure and related matters, broaden areas of common values. Finally, particular negotiations and their outcomes influence concurrent and subsequent negotiation not only in that area but more generally, providing a constant feedback that modifies the goals, process, and outcome of the larger continuing negotiation among nations.

CONDITIONS INFLUENCING
THE PROCESS OF NEGOTIATION

The first three parts of this chapter have followed the natural sequence of goals, process, and outcome as they develop over the course of negotiation. They have treated the essence of what actually occurs during negotiation. Influencing what occurs, however, are two other major aspects: the conditions under which the process of negotiation transpires, and background factors existing at the onset of negotiation. The distinction between background and conditions is temporal, as indicated in Figure 1; though some characteristics cannot be unambiguously ordered, in general this distinction is maintained. Thus, the present portion treats concurrent conditions whose values are specific to particular negotiating situations. The next following portion treats more general factors of background, that can usually be assessed prior to the onset of negotiation.

The concurrent conditions influencing the process of negotiation are considered in five general classes: (a) the setting, whether summit, embassy, or other levels, with open or closed proceedings; (b) the number of individual participants; (c) the number of negotiating parties; (d) the amount of information each party possesses about the utilities of the other; and (e) the amount of stress impinging upon the negotiation (because of its importance, difficulty, etc.). . . .

The Setting of Negotiation

One of the most crucial factors in a negotiation is the diplomatic level at which it is conducted. This factor, together with the distinction between negotiations arranged for more general or more special purposes, permits distinguishing four situations that constitute principal types of negotiation.

Types of Negotiation. Most common is traditional bilateral diplomacy conducted routinely between the embassy in a foreign country and the corresponding part of that country's foreign office. More recent, embodied in the League of Nations but represented much more extensively by the United Nations, is parliamentary diplomacy, with a permanent body, regular meetings, general interests, and broad membership. . . . Conference diplomacy consists of *ad hoc* meetings for particular purposes, though these may be of a long-continuing nature, as in the post-World War II disarmament negotiations. Summit meetings may be considered as a special type of conference diplomacy, in which the negotiators are heads of state. Like all conference diplomacy, these meetings may be bilateral or multilateral. Another important, though somewhat less prominent, type of negotiation, involves the "consultative diplomacy" that transpires within such international organizations as NATO and the Organization of American States.

. . .

Open vs. Secret Diplomacy. The call, around the end of World War I, for "open covenants, openly arrived at," by figures as diverse as Wilson and Trotsky, signaled the beginning of an era in which not only the outcome, but also the day-by-day process of international negotiation is frequently known far beyond the small circle of principal negotiators. Increasing ease of transportation and communication have promoted both the desire and the means for making public, as it occurs, the continuing process of negotiation. Widespread publicity for negotiation necessarily makes it more likely that a party, in selecting strategies, will consider not only their likelihood of promoting a beneficial agreement, but also their effect upon interested onlookers. Information officers for each nation typically brief members of the press, before the conference, on their delegation's position; and following each closed session, they report their view of the proceedings. Rusk (1955) decries this "football stadium psychology" in the United Nations, which emphasizes scoring points in a debate, and tends to freeze positions as soon as they are put forward hindering subsequent accommodation.

Aside from the effects of playing to the audience outside the conference room, the more open the negotiation, the greatrer the restrictions placed upon the principal negotiator by the presence of numerous experts with interests in various parts of his proposals. A negotiator may be deterred from reaching an agreement, which his government as a whole would accept, by various special pleadings from those who feel that, in their particular area, too much is being bargained away.

. . .

The Number of Individual Participants

Quite apart from the number of parties represented (to be treated in the following section), the sheer number of individual participants has many consequences for the negotiating process; secrecy, for example, becomes most unlikely when scores, or even hundreds occupy the conference room.

Several concomitants of size have been studied among small groups. Bales and Borgatta (1955), in observing differences in the type of interaction in twenty-four groups of sizes two through seven, conclude that "Most of the trends observed appear to be results of two gross factors. The first is that the relative talking time available per member decreases as size increases. The second is that each person is confronted with an absolutely larger number of persons as size increases. Each is under pressure to maintain a more or less adequate relationship with each other. Thus as size increases, each member has more relationships to maintain, and less time to do so" (p. 401).

. . .

Although felt tension or antagonism toward others is difficult to assess, its overt expression has been observed to increase with group size; Thomas and Fink (1963), surveying thirty-one studies involving group size, conclude that, "Tentatively it would appear that smaller groups inhibit expression of disagreements and dissatisfactions more than larger groups . . ." (p. 375). The authors also find effects on group organization: ". . . as size increases there will be decreasing group cohesiveness and increasing organization and division of labor in the group . . ." (p. 375).

. . .

The Number of Negotiating Parties

Added parties to a negotiation contribute not only to group size but also to the strategic complexity of the situation. In multilateral diplomacy, the existence of interacting alternatives and utilities of several nations, rather than only two, means that many more outcomes are possible, each of them more complex. Yet it is still possible to represent these multiparty situations within a game theoretic formulation analogous to that employed for two parties in Figure 2 ... simply by extending the dimensionality. Analysis becomes more difficult, though, and "solutions" progressively less definitive.

. . .

Added parties to a negotiation may function not in a symmetrical role, but rather as mediators, arbitrators, or others whose actions are not the object of agreement. Such third parties may perform or aid in any of the previously described processes of negotiation. . . . Sometimes the only unacceptable feature of a proposal lies not in its terms but merely in its being forwarded by the other party, making its acceptance appear as a loss of face. The impasse resulting when both parties feel this way may be resolved, Schelling and Halperin (1961) suggest, by a mediator acting as a neutral source for the basically acceptable proposal. Another way in which a mediator may function is in providing information to each party about the strength with which the other holds his position—information shown in the following section to be both crucial and difficult to obtain.

Information: Estimating the Other's
Utilities for Various Outcomes

In all of the processes of negotiation that have been considered, information concerning the utilities the other places upon the various possible outcomes has been crucial. Imperfect information about the other's utilities complicates not only the original decision matrix but also the processes of communication and persuasion and of creating new alternatives. Consequently, it is important to examine the sources of such obscurity.

The Difficulty of Knowing Another's Values. To know what is the best outcome one may expect to achieve one must know the expectations of the other, but these, in turn, depend upon one's own. Lack of such information lends importance to the previously described process of persuasion, in which each party tries to alter the other's utilities for certain outcomes while leaving unchanged or strengthening his own utilities, as the other sees them. Frequently, a principal aspect of the negotiation may be this attempt to establish to the other party the strength of one's values, for if it is known just how much each party desires certain outcomes—exactly how far it would go to achieve them and precisely what it would do if frustrated—the solution is often readily apparent to all.

Morgenthau (1960) suggests that, "To demonstrate to the rest of the world the power one's own nation possesses, revealing neither too much nor too little, is the task of a wisely conceived policy of prestige" (p. 85). A nation whose power is underestimated, such as that of the Soviet Union or the United States in 1940, may suffer attacks that would otherwise be deterred. While there may be at least temporary advantage in having one's power overestimated (as Britain's was by Hitler in 1940), there seems to be, as these examples suggest, little gained in having it underestimated, and a nation needs to be able to demonstrate its true strength.

. . .

Stresses upon Negotiation

"Stress" is taken to incorporate the possible effects upon negotiation of such generally complicating factors as a constraint to reach agreement by a certain time, a high level of antagonism between parties, threatened detrimental unilateral actions in the event of non-agreement, gross incompatibility of bargaining positions, importance of the negotiation, and other conditions usually impeding agreement. To qualify as stressful, however, these conditions must be perceived as such by the participants; a time constraint, for example, may sometimes be found stressful and at other times not. "Stress" here refers also to what is often characterized as "tension" or as "threat" (in a psychological sense, not in the sense of threats and promises as strategies).

. . .

The relation of stress to performance is generally thought to be curvilinear: Mild stress tends to improve performance, but beyond a certain intensity, added stress is detrimental. One of the ways in which higher levels of stress may operate to decrease performance is through restriction in perception of alternatives, so that in time of stress the ability to add or modify alternatives may be curtailed. . . . A closely related phenomenon is decreasing complexity of the perceptual space in which objects and persons are located; there may occur an increasing tendency under stress to locate all stimuli on a single dimension ranging from good to bad, and this single dimension may even collapse to two points—simply "which side are you on?"

. . .

BACKGROUND FACTORS
INFLUENCING NEGOTIATION

The conditions discussed in the foregoing sections form a part of the specific negotiating situation itself; in addition, however, there are certain factors providing a more or less set background against which the negotiation occurs. These background factors also influence the course of negotiation, though in general less immediately and directly. In the following sections, they are treated in an order of roughly decreasing scope and increasing specificity. We shall consider the effect upon negotiation, first, of broad cultural traditions of the negotiating nations, next of the particular existing relations between the nations, then of the relations between different units within a single nation (as those of the negotiating team to other parts of its government), and finally, of the characteristics of individual negotiators.

Cultural Variation

As a result of their distinct historical development, nations come to acquire what may be regarded as "national character . . . *relatively enduring personality characteristics and patterns that are modal among the adult members of the society"* (Inkeles & Levinson, 1954, p. 983). National character is related to many other aspects of a society's general socio-cultural system, from child-rearing practices to the type of political system it supports, and consequently influences the types of goals and processes the society pursues in negotiation. . . . More and more, such differences in national character may affect interaction among the elites who conduct international relations, because both the democratization of diplomacy over recent centuries and technological advances in communication and transportation have tied diplomats more closely to the rest of their nation. No longer is it so likely, as in seventeenth- and eighteenth-century Europe, when diplomats were often part of a common aristocracy, that they may have more in common with their counterparts from other nations than with the nation they represent.

. . .

Attitude between Negotiating Parties

As a result of all the prior relations between a given pair of nations, each may be considered to hold a certain "attitude" or "image" of the other. These attitudes or images are crucial to the process and outcome of international negotiation because—distorted or not—they influence substantially both (a) the actions one party takes toward the other, and (b) the interpretations he places upon the acts of the other.

In contrast with broad cultural characteristics, which presumably influence a nation's relations with all others, these attitudes derive from and in turn influence the history of relations between two particular nations. In integrating the previous history into an attitude at a given moment, varying weights may be given to specific incidents; presumably more weight is given to those crucial to the "national interest," though matters more relevant to pride than power may also be weighted heavily. Past animosities (and friendships, too) are frequently heavily discounted, as in Anglo-American relations, or even in relations involving much more recent colonies, such as the six former French-African colonies that opted for full membership in the French Community.

. . .

It seems likely that assumptions about foreigners—like stereotypes in general—are usually partly but not wholly true (Klineberg, 1950). But true or false, if acted upon, they may influence international negotiation, not only through beliefs of negotiators and policymakers themselves, but also through constraints placed upon them by the beliefs of their publics. Strong American distaste for revolutionary Bolsheviks may have contributed to the delay from 1917 to 1933 in official United States recognition of the government of the Soviet Union. Stereotypes may even have an effect upon those stereotyped, by justifying or otherwise making more likely the imputed characteristic, as Bronfenbrenner (1961) suggests in his discussion of the Soviet-American "mirror-image phenomenon."

. . .

The importance to negotiation of . . . stereotypy, like that of attitude in general, lies in its influence upon the way in which the actions of the other party are perceived and responded to.

. . .

Relations within a Negotiating Party

For negotiating parties as complex as nations, the goals, process, and outcome of negotiation are influenced not only by attitudes reflecting previous relations *between* the parties, but also by the relations *within* each party. Many influences from within the nation impinge upon the negotiator, ranging from broad and diffuse factors of public opinion, through more specific pressures from various offices within his government, even to the highly particular concerns of other members of his negotiating team sitting in the same room.

Though these forces may conflict, with each other and with what the negotiator himself might feel is intrinsically the best course, they nonetheless are part of the background that influences his actions. These conflicts arise, according to the present analysis, because of different experiences and interests on the part of the various groups and individuals. In examining the characteristics of these influences, we shall begin with the more general and then proceed to the more specific.

Most general of all is public opinion, whose support is often crucial for given negotiations. Yet as Dahl (1950) points out, the influences of public opinion pose a dilemma: "Only if public opinion is fluid and undecided will the full range of theoretical alternatives be open; to the extent that public opinion hardens, alternatives are foreclosed. But because effectiveness in foreign policy depends finally upon the willingness of a nation to indulge in collective sacrifices, to rely on a fluid and indefinite public opinion is to substitute a reed for a sword" (p. 247). Thus if the effect of public opinion upon negotiation is to limit its freedom while increasing its power, it is important to examine the nature of these limitations. Three basic limitations are that public opinion (a) inclines toward simple alternatives, (b) is frequently hard to change, and (c) may well be inconsistent in its various positions. . . .

The force toward simple solutions is associated with the intrinsic difficulties of a large and amorphous entity such as public opinion in exchanging and processing complex information. It is difficult for public opinion to formulate new alternatives; rather its expression generally consists in favoring or disfavoring certain simply formulated existing alternatives. . . .

In favoring and disfavoring existing alternatives, the effect of public opinion is to narrow the range of alternatives, and thus to reduce the flexibility of the negotiator to propose new alternatives he sees as beneficial. Yet such limitations may sometimes result in strategic advantage, by serving as evidence of commitment to a certain position; leaders may convincingly claim they are not free to accept the proposals of the other party because their constituency would not support such an agreement. Thus, like *faits accomplis* and successful threats and promises, such narrowing of alternatives through the action of public opinion may serve to reduce the choice of the other in a way advantageous to oneself.

Yet because a position strongly held by public opinion is often not easily modified, such a strategy may create difficulties if the demanded alternative is not obtained.
. . .

The Negotiator

According to Harold Nicolson, British career diplomat, "Nobody who has not actually watched statesmen dealing with each other can have any real idea of the immense part played in human affairs by such unavowable and often unrecognizable causes as lassitude, affability, personal affection or dislike, misunderstanding, deafness or incomplete command of a foreign language, vanity, social engagements, interruptions and momentary health" (1946, p. 19). Characteristics associated with the negotiator are considered in two classes: (a) those involving the role of negotiator, especially the effect of his status level and background, and (b) personality attributes of the individual.

Status and Background of Negotiators. The level of the senior representatives in any particular negotiation varies widely, including heads of state, foreign ministers, professional diplomats, military, and other special representatives. Each of these levels has certain advantages and disadvantages that make it more appropriate to one situation than another (Haas and Whiting, 1956). Heads of state have the unique advantage of being best able to commit their nations, but often suffer from lack of time, lack of specific experience, and undue pressures to produce results. . . .

The frequently extreme visibility and consequent pressure when heads of state negotiate may make the desire to avoid loss of face a principal motivation; this may also be used as a bargaining tactic, but if employed by both chiefs, it appears likely to result in stalemate. Foreign ministers usually have more experience with the particular issues, may be less able to commit their nation, and otherwise suffer most of the same disadvantages, to a somewhat lesser degree, as do heads of state.

Typically, the bulk of bilateral negotiation is carried out through diplomats stationed at an embassy in the foreign capital. These include both career diplomats and political appointees. Special representatives are frequently experts whose background is particularly suited for specific negotiations.

. . .

Personality of Negotiators. In the eighteenth century, Callieres observed that ". . . the passions of princes and of their ministers often overrule their interests . . . men do not act upon firm and stable maxims of conduct . . . as a rule they are governed by passions and temperament more than by reason" (1919, p. 47-48).

. . .

One personality characteristic, authoritarianism, has been shown in a number of studies to be related to international attitudes and to cooperative interpersonal behavior. Lane (1955) found those higher on authoritarianism, as measured by four items from the F Scale (Adorno, Frenkel-Brunswik, Levinson, & Sanford, 1950), to be less willing to compromise: They tended to reject, in 1952, the alternative "Keep on trying to get a peaceful settlement" in favor of one extreme—"Pull out of Korea entirely"—or the other—"Take a stronger stand and bomb Manchuria and China." More authoritarian persons are also thought to change their attitudes less readily; for example, Mischel and Schopler (1959) found those who, after the second Soviet Sputnik, still thought the United States would reach the moon first to be more authoritarian. The point is not that nonauthoritarians are better predictors of the eventual landing, but rather that they seem to account for new information more reasonably; nonauthoritarians might presumably also change back to their original attitude more easily, if additional information appeared.

. . .

Thus a number of studies consistently find authoritarian individuals to be less willing to compromise and generally less likely to change their position. Paired together in negotiating situations similar to the Prisoner's Dilemma, such individuals seem likely to fare poorly. Paired against a nonauthoritarian, an authoritarian individual might do rather well, at least temporarily, though continued noncooperative choices by another person tend to result eventually in noncooperation on the part of even an originally cooperative person. Whether authoritarianism is generally functional or dysfunctional for the process of negotiation would seem to depend also upon whether the particular negotiating situation calls for rigidity or flexibility; if this is known prior to negotiation, it appears reasonable to select as negotiator a person whose natural disposition fits the role requirement.

. . .

REFERENCES

Adorno, T. W., Frenkel-Brunswik, Else, Levinson, D. J., & Sanford, R. N. *The authoritarian personality.* New York: Harper, 1950.

Aubert, V. Competition and dissensus: Two types of conflict and of conflict resolution. *J. Confl. Resol.,* 1963, 7, 26-42.

Bales, R. F., & Borgatta, E. F. Size of group as a factor in the interaction profile. In A. P. Hare, E. F. Borgatta, & R. F. Bales (Eds.), *Small groups: Studies in social interaction.* New York: Knopf, 1955, Pp. 396-413.

Bronfenbrenner, U. The mirror image in Soviet-American relations. *J. soc. Issues,* 1961, 17(3), 45-56.

Callieres, F. C. de *On the manner of negotiating with princes; on the uses of diplomacy; the choice of ministers and envoys; and the personal qualities necessary for success in missions abroad.* Paris: Michel Brunet, 1716. (Translated by A. F. Whyte. New York: Houghton Mifflin, 1919. Reissued, South Bend, Ind.: Univer. Notre Dame Press, 1963.)

Dahl, R. A. *Congress and foreign policy.* New York: Harcourt, 1950.

Davison, W. P. *The Berlin blockade: A study in Cold War politics*, Princeton: Princeton Univer. Press, 1958.

Deutsch, M., & Krauss, R. M. The effect of threat upon interpersonal bargaining. *J. abnorm. soc. Psychol.*, 1960, *61* 181-189.

Durant, W. *The story of civilization: Part VI. The Reformation.* New York: Simon & Schuster, 1957.

Erikson, E. *Childhood and society* (ed. 2). New York: Norton, 1963.

Friedrich, C. J. *Man and his government: An empirical theory of politics.* New York: McGraw-Hill, 1963.

Haas, E. B., & Whiting, A. S. *Dynamics of international relations.* New York: McGraw-Hill, 1956.

Hicks, J. R. *The theory of wages.* New York: Peter Smith, 1948.

Iklé, F. C. *How nations negotiate.* New York: Harper, 1964.

Inkeles, A., & Levinson, D. J. National character: The study of modal personality and sociocultural systems. In G. Lindzey (Ed.), *Handbook of social psychology*, Vol. II. Reading, Mass.: Addison-Wesley, 1954, Pp. 977-1020.

Kaplan, M. A. *System and process in international politics.* New York: Wiley, 1957.

Klineberg, O. *Tensions affecting international understanding.* New York: Social Science Research Council, 1950.

Klineberg, O. *The human dimension in international relations.* New York: Holt, Rinehart and Winston, 1964.

Lane, R. E. Political personality and electoral choice. *Amer. polit. Sci. Rev.*, 1955, *49*, 173-190.

Lerche, C. O. The United States, Great Britain, and SEATO: A case study in *fait accompli. J. Polit.*, 1956, *18*, 459-478.

Luce, R. D., & Raiffa, H. *Games and decisions.* New York: Wiley, 1957.

Mischel, W., & Schopler, J. Authoritarianism and reactions to "Sputniks." *J. abnorm. soc. Psychol.*, 1959, *59*, 142-145.

Morgenthau, H. J. The art of diplomatic negotiation. In L. White (Ed.), *The state of the social sciences.* Chicago: Univer. Chicago Press, 1956. Pp. 404-414.

Morgenthau, H. J. *Politics among nations: The struggle for power and peace* (ed. 3). New York: Knopf, 1960.

Nicolson, H. *The Congress of Vienna.* New York: Harcourt, 1946.

Pearson, L. B. *Diplomacy in the nuclear age.* Cambridge, Mass.: Harvard Univer. Press, 1959.

Rapoport, A. *Fights, games, and debates.* Ann Arbor: Univer. Michigan Press, 1960.

Riker, W. *Theory of political coalition.* New Haven: Yale Univer. Press, 1962.

Rusk, D. Parliamentary diplomacy—debate versus negotiation. *World Affairs Interpreter*, 1955, *26*, 121-138.

Satow, E. M. *A guide to diplomatic practice* (ed. 4). New York: McKay, 1957.

Schattschneider, E. E. Intensity, visibility, direction, and scope. *Amer. polit. Sci. Rev.*, 1957, *51*, 933-942.

Schelling, T. C. *The strategy of conflict.* Cambridge, Mass: Harvard Univer. Press, 1960.

Schelling, T. C., & Halperin, M. H. *Strategy and arms control.* New York: Twentieth Century Fund, 1961.

Shubik, M. *Strategy and market structure: Competition, oligopoly, and the theory of games.* New York: Wiley, 1959.

Thibaut, J. W., & Kelley, H. H. *The social psychology of groups.* New York: Wiley, 1959.

Thomas, E. J., & Fink, C. F. Effects of group size. *Psychol. Bull.*, 1963, *60*, 371-384.

Tocqueville, A. de. *Democracy in America,* Vol. I. New York: Knopf, 1959.

U.S. President's Commission on National Goals. *Goals for Americans: Programs for action in the sixties.* Englewood Cliffs, N.J.: Prenctice-Hall, 1960.

Von Neumann, J., & Morgenstern, O. *Theory of games and economic behavior.* Princeton: Princeton Univer. Press, 1944.

chapter nine

MILITARY AND PARAMILITARY PROCESSES

The Persistence
of Force

Robert E. Osgood and Robert W. Tucker

1. THE FUNDAMENTAL QUESTION

Is military power in the nuclear age obsolete, or does it remain an indispensable instrument of conflict and order among autonomous states? This is a fundamental question of our time. It is a recurrent question, which deserves to be taken more seriously than ever before because the destruction that could be swiftly inflicted—by at least two states now and probably by several more in the future—would nullify any rational purpose of war for either belligerent and inflict unconscionable damage on many other nations as well.

The question of military power includes more than the obsolescence or utility of war. By "military power" we mean the ability of states to affect the will and behavior of other states by armed coercion or the threat of armed coercion. It is equivalent to "force," broadly defined. Moreover, the threats of war with which we are

SOURCE: From Robert E. Osgood and Robert W. Tucker, *Force, Order and Justice.* Copyright © 1967 by the Johns Hopkins Press. Reprinted and abridged by permission of the authors and Johns Hopkins Press.

concerned may be explicit or implicit, and may range from un-
qualified ultimatums, in which one state tries to compel another to
comply with specific demands by open threats of war, to implied and
ambiguous prospects of war, conveyed simply by the determined
opposition of one state to another's policies.

By "obsolete" we mean more than "out of date." As generally
used in reference to war or force, "obsolete" implies "dysfunctional." Therefore, to ask whether military power is obsolete is
not necessarily to question its existence or the possibility of war but
rather to pose the broader question of whether force can serve the
functions of security, domination, status, and influence which it has
served in the past.

The answer to this question has crucial implications for national
policy and, more fundamentally, for the very nature of international
politics. If nuclear weapons jeopardize civilization, our only salvation
may be to get rid of them or perhaps to put all weapons under the
control of a supranational government. A number of observers of
international politics who are by no means pacifists or utopians have
reached conclusions as drastic as this.[1] Yet conventional wisdom and
historical evidence suggest that in our time the prevailing system of
autonomous states is quite unlikely to be transformed so as to
eliminate war and the threat of war. And there are no examples of
weapons being abolished, once developed. If there is no practical
point in speculating about a visionary world, even if the familiar one
is doomed, the best we can do is to try to ameliorate the hazards of
the existing military and political realities and hope that the very
prospect of catastrophe may foster the orderly control of force. Yet
an international order based on the perpetual fear of sudden catastrophe leads to the possibility that either continual peace will undermine the credibility of a nuclear strike or continuing tension will
sooner or later lead to nuclear war. In either case the basis of order
would be destroyed.

[1] For example, Hans J. Morgenthau reaches this general conclusion without
specifying the exact nature of the transformation that is required: "Instead of
trying in vain to assimilate nuclear power to the purposes and instrumentalities
of the nation-state, we ought to have tried to adapt these purposes and instrumentalities to the potentialities of nuclear power. We have refrained from doing
so in earnest, because to do so successfully requires a radical transformation—psychologically painful and politically risky—of traditional moral values,
modes of thought, and habits of action. But short of such a transformation,
there will be no escape from the paradoxes of nuclear strategy and the dangers
attending them." "The Four Paradoxes of Nuclear Strategy," *American Political
Science Review*, LVIII (March, 1964), 35.

Theoretically, there is a third possibility for avoiding catastrophe, one that involves no radical transformation of the international system. The incentives for avoiding war may be so overwhelming in the nuclear age that independent states could learn to wage their conflicts without reference to military power. International politics would continue, but regular war and the threat of war would wither away. This proposition strains the conventional imagination no less than the prospect of centralizing international force. Yet the seriousness of the problem it is intended to cope with should compel us to re-examine the basic premises about the relationship of force to politics upon which it rests. For if force is not a fundamental and inseparable aspect of international politics, the excesses of nuclear power may simply provide us with the necessary incentive to do something that has always been possible: to expunge it from international politics. But if force is essential to international politics, if it is as persistent as the international system itself, we cannot avoid the problems of coping with it, whatever we may think about the incompatibility of modern weapons with the system.

2. THE BASIC MOTIVES OF FORCE

The history of international politics gives us no reason to suppose that all major states with conflicting interests can pursue their interests without exploiting force and, occasionally, resorting to war. There is too much evidence of the pervasiveness of force and of the multifarious functions it has served in international—and, for that matter, intertribal and interprincipality—relations. One simply cannot comprehend the rise, spread, and decline of ancient civilizations and peoples, or the creation, unification, expansion, and protection of modern nation-states, except in relation to force. The boundaries of states, their external holdings and rights, their internal strength or weakness, their influence and status, the harmony or discord of their relations—in short, the very identity of states—have been decisively shaped by competition for military power and by the fortunes of war. Indeed, the whole astonishing explosion of modern Western civilization is linked with a distinctive bellicosity in its organized political life.[2]

Nevertheless, the central role of force in the past is not a conclusive forecast of the future if nuclear weapons constitute a radical qualitative change in the nature of military power. Furthermore, the

[2]William H. McNeill expounds this proposition throughout *The Rise of the West* (Chicago: University of Chicago Press, 1963). See, for example, pp. 569ff.

fact that some states some of the time—indeed, most states most of the time in many periods of history—have contested their conflicts without war or even the threat of war makes it at least conceivable that all states could dispense with force all of the time. To determine whether force is a necessary element of international politics we must examine the basic reasons for its pervasiveness in the past and ask whether these reasons persist.

Some find these basic reasons in man's innate aggressiveness and pugnacity.[3] But these propensities, whether innate or socially conditioned, are no more conclusive than the historical record as a reason for thinking that war or even the threat of war must persist. Aggressiveness and pugnacity can be indulged in many ways other than armed coercion. Even those who regard war as a manifestation of biological instincts generally maintain that such instincts can be diverted into harmless or even constructive channels.[4] Regardless of whether these instincts are basic sources of violence among

---

[3] For analyses of the roots of war in pugnacity and aggressiveness, through the process of displacement and projection, see Sigmund Freud, *Civilization, War and Death* (London: Hogarth Press, 1953); E. F. M. Durbin and John Bowlby, *Personal Aggressiveness and War* (New York: Columbia University Press, 1939); William McDougall, *An Introduction to Social Psychology* (London: John W. Luce, 1915); and John Dollard et al., *Frustration and Aggression* (New Haven: Yale University Press, 1939). For a short review of this approach, see Quincy Wright, *A Study of War* (Chicago: University of Chicago Press, 1942), 1, 131-43. Analyses that emphasize the instinctual basis of war generally share with analyses that view war as a product of social conditioning the confidence that men are basically similar and good, that they can be masters of their social and political as well as their material environment, and that, having rationally ordered the conditions of their education and living, they can live harmoniously without resort to violence. For representatives of this school of behaviorism, see Mark A. May, *A Social Psychology of War and Peace* (New Haven: Yale University Press, 1943), and Edward C. Tolman, *Drives Toward War* (New York: D. Appleton-Century-Crofts, Inc., 1942). For a critical analysis of the psychological and sociological interpretations of the basic causes of war, see Kenneth N. Waltz's examination of the literature of modern behavioral science in *Man, The State, and War* (New York: Columbia University Press, 1954), chap. iii.

[4] Konrad Lorenz, the noted Austrian student of ethology, takes a comparable position when he contends, in opposition to those who attribute aggression to environmental conditions and frustrations, that human beings, like animals, must act out the drama of their innate impulse for aggression without the benefit of their animal antecedents' instinctive or habitual restraints upon intraspecies fighting, yet concludes that men can channel their aggressiveness away from war by cultivating international competition in sports. *On Aggression*, trans. M. K. Wilson (New York: Harcourt, Brace & World, Inc., 1966).

individuals, they need not lead to violence among states, since the functions of fighting within a community and among individuals are not the same as the functions of war between political units.[5]

But if the psychosocial roots of man's behavior do not conclusively establish that force is an integral part of international politics, the evidence of man's basic *political* behavior is more difficult to dismiss. Psychosocial analysts, like philosophers, properly probe beneath the historians' data to examine the roots of organized violence that lie in human nature. What most of them fail to appreciate, however, is that the persistence of force among states springs not only from individual psychic drives and social needs but from basic political imperatives that operate among all autonomous and interacting political units.

Like faithful children of the Enlightenment, they reject the state's concern with power and status as though it were a remnant of feudal society or aristocratic privilege which is now a needless obstacle to the common interests of all peoples in advancing their material and social welfare. Moreover, they may be so convinced of the primacy of the common interest of humanity over the conflicting interests of states that even the security of the state does not warrant, in their minds, the resort to force. Why, they ask, should men wage and threaten war if they are not somehow compelled to do so by instinct or cultural conditioning? Why, indeed, unless men entertain ends or values that can be secured only through the exercise of force? If, however, these ends are rejected, war or the threat of war must appear a useless atavism, an entirely dysfunctional institution that has somehow managed to survive an advanced stage in man's social and cultural progress.

On the basis of these assumptions it is understandable that behavioral scientists should view war as the result of abnormal international tensions caused by avoidable or remediable personal or social frustrations, maladjustments, biases, and stereotypes.[6] It is understandable that one analyst anticipates the eradication of war

[5] Among others, the noted anthropologist Bronislaw Malinowski makes this point in "An Anthropological Analysis of War," *American Journal of Sociology*, XLVI (January, 1941), 521-50, reprinted in *War: Studies From Psychology, Sociology, and Anthropology*, eds. Leon Bramson and George W. Goethals (New York: Basic Books, 1964), pp. 245-68.

[6] This view is fully represented in the psychosocial analyses of international tension after World War II. See, particularly, Otto Klineberg, *Psychological Factors of Peace and War* (New York: Columbia University Press, 1950), and Hadley Cantril (ed.), *Tensions That Cause Wars* (Urbana, Ill.: University of Illinois Press, 1950).

through the replacement of man's pugnacity by his instinct for "emulation," as manifested, particularly, in commercial competition, and that another concludes that since war has been learned, it can be replaced simply by learning "a new technique or way of life."[7]

A realistic view of political behavior, however, must reject the assumption that individuals have common interests so compelling as to obviate serious conflicts of interest among states or the need of states to support their interests through force. Given the reality of man's primary loyalty to autonomous states, the need for force springs from compelling functional needs—most fundamentally, from the need of states to rely primarily on self-help in order to secure the conditions of their survival and welfare. This functional need is not ephemeral or atavistic. The modern nation-state is, after all, the most inclusive, deep-seated popular institution of our time. It is the chief repository and guarantor of the very values that the deprecators of force exalt. Its overwhelming appeal, whether among the old and industrially advanced or the new and poor states, is, if anything, increasing. The social scientists who recognize that force has a deep-seated functional relationship to particular forms of social and political relations come closer to describing reality than those who stress psychological aberration. But when they compare the role of force among nations to the once-pervasive but now generally obsolete institution of duelling, let alone slavery and trial by ordeal, they mistakenly equate the mores of men in secondary social relationships with the imperatives confronting men acting in behalf of political communities engaged in the competition for power.[8]

[7] The first view is presented by William McDougall, the second by Mark A. May, in their works previously cited.

[8] Margaret Mead, for example, makes these comparisons in defining war as a social invention and concludes that just as duelling and trial by ordeal went out of fashion when methods more congruent with the institutions and feelings of the period were invented, so the ingrained habit of war can be replaced by a better invention, provided only that "the people must recognize the defects of the old invention, and someone must make a new one." Margaret Mead, "Warfare Is Only an Invention—Not a Biological Necessity," *Asia*, XL (August, 1940), 402-5, reprinted in Bramson and Goethals, *op. cit.*, p. 274. Duelling is analogous to force among states since it was a method of settling conflicts of interest and honor by violence. But it became obsolete and disappeared largely because the state assumed this function, whereas there is no foreseeable institution to replace the state in this respect. Moreover, individuals could protect their security and their interests without duelling, whereas eschewing force leaves a state defenseless. John G. Millingen, *The History of Duelling* (2 vols.; London: R. Bentley, 1841). See also Quincy Wright's discussion of war and duelling in Wright, *op. cit.*, Vol. II.

We can find clues to the *political* motives of organized violence in the elemental drives that appear to move men who act not merely from individual or social motives but from group-oriented motives— that is, in the purposes of men who exercise force in behalf of all sorts of political organizations that are outside the authority of central government.[9]

Among primitive tribes, survival and subsistence, material gain (land, food, cattle, slaves, and booty), sport and glory, the acquisition of women, and religious ritual are the primary motives.[10] Among some clans, as among medieval kingdoms, honor, adventure, and plunder have been the predominant drives behind war. Modern states, however, pursue more impersonal and explicitly rationalized ends: security, material and commercial gain, influence and dominion, status or prestige, and religious or ideological supremacy.

These motives, of course, do not in themselves compel the resort to war. They are values for which tribes, clans, kingdoms, and states may or may not fight. All of them—except sport, adventure, and glory—can be and often are pursued by persuasion and propaganda, purchase and barter, or institutional and legal arbitrament. Why is it, then, that they so frequently lead to violent conflict and repeatedly evoke the prospect of violence?

Undoubtedly, as the psychosocial interpretations perceive, the answer does lie partly in innate pugnacity and the gratifications of

[9]The distinction between motives sanctioned by a political group in external conflict with another such group and the motives behind sanctioned forms of privately initiated violence among individuals or lesser groups (as in the case of some feuds) is often unclear in the case of primitive groups with less highly organized central institutions and more individually oriented standards of political behavior than in modern states. In states, as in lesser political units, there are, of course, all sorts of personal motives for going to war, which may or may not correspond to the group-oriented motives; but to assume that these are preponderant is to ignore the determining reality of highly developed group allegiance.

[10]On primitive warfare, see Wright, *op. cit.*, Vol. 1, chap. vi; Maurice R. Davie, *The Evolution of War* (New Haven: Yale University Press, 1929); Leonard T. Hobhouse, Gerald C. Wheeler, and Morris Ginsberg, *The Material Culture and Social Institutions of Simpler Peoples: An Essay in Correlation* (London: Chapman & Hall, 1930); Harry Holbert Turney-High, *Primitive War: Its Practices and Concepts* (Columbia. S. C.: University of South Carolina Press, 1949); Max Gluckman, *Custom and Conflict in Africa* (Oxford: Basic, Blackwell, & Mott, 1959); Lucy Mair, *Primitive Government* (Baltimore: Pelican Books, 1962). Roger D. Masters examines the relevance of the literature on primitive war and politics to international relations in "World Politics as a Primitive Political System," *World Politics*, XVI (July, 1964), 595-619.

308 The International Political System

organized violence. Clearly, like primitive tribes, the governments and citizens of the most civilized nations manifest these proclivities, however rationalized or sublimated they may be. Indeed, once aroused, the martial spirit of the organized mass, especially in a democratic country, is the most intense and unrestrained form of bellicosity. Yet the notable difference between modern states and tribes—or, for that matter, medieval kingdoms—is the much greater extent to which states consciously regard force, and especially the uses of force short of war, from a utilitarian standpoint, that is, as power to be used, if necessary, for an explicit collective purpose after calculating costs, gains, and risks, rather than as merely a customary way of doing things, needing no specific justification.[11] This remains true even though the general stakes of international politics and war have become less tangible and more ideological since the French Revolution.

In modern states, sport, adventure, and glory may still be powerful *personal* motives for going to war.[12] Similarly, the desire of social and economic groups within the nation to improve their status has sometimes enhanced the militancy or bellicosity of states.[13] But, unlike the motives of men waging war in behalf of primitive tribes and medieval kingdoms, these personal and socioeconomic motives are readily distinguished from the determining, highly rationalized,

[11]Turney-High, *op. cit.*, p. 169.

[12]The classic discussion—and exaggeration—of the "play" element of warfare is Johan Huizinga, *Homo Ludens* (Boston: Beacon Press, 1962). Hans Speier draws a useful distinction between "agonistic" war, which has the quality of play, and "instrumental" war. *Social Order and the Risks of War* (Cornwall, N.Y.: George W. Stewart, Inc., 1952), chap. xviii. Clearly, the agonistic element in modern state wars is subordinate to instrumental motives so far as those acting in behalf of governments are concerned.

[13]On the nature, sources, and history of modern militarism, see Alfred Vagts, *A History of Militarism* (rev. ed.; Cleveland: Meridian Books, 1959). There is a huge body of literature ascribing military preparations and war to various class and economic motives. Since World War II, the popular version of this interpretation is represented in the U.S. most ably in C. Wright Mills, *The Power Elite* (New York: Oxford University Press, 1956), which contends that the growing emphasis on military policies in the U.S. reflects the preponderance among ruling groups of an alliance between business, military, and political elites. For a critical analysis of this tenuous thesis, see Talcott Parsons, "The Distribution of Power in American Society," *World Politics*, X (October, 1957), 123-43.

officially sanctioned motives of nations and governments. Moreover, governments have grown notably more cautious, deliberate, and impersonal in contemplating war as the state has become dissociated from the rule of the monarch, as the prospect of war has confronted citizens emotionally involved in the affairs of state with a fearful sacrifice, as warfare has become more impersonal, and as the state's management of military power has become more complicated and systematic. It is principally *after* nations have reluctantly become engaged in war that honor, glory, and revenge, which were typically elements of a code restraining conflict in primitive and medieval societies, have acted as mass catalysts of unrestrained bellicosity. And now the memory of two world wars, not to mention the prospect of nuclear catastrophe, may finally have deprived modern war of these emotional indulgences.

3. THE INTEGRAL ROLE OF FORCE IN INTERNATIONAL POLITICS

Pugnacity and the emotional satisfactions of war may help to explain why states are sometimes bellicose, but they do not explain why states that would obviously prefer to secure their ends, whether offensive or defensive, without war habitually find it necessary to resort to war or the threat of war. They do not explain why war is endemic in international politics. The chief explanation for this phenomenon lies in the nature of the international system. More specifically, it lies in the conflicts among autonomous but interdependent political units that are organized for their own protection and advancement but that are not subordinate to a central political authority and police force. In this anarchical system, as in others where the sovereign authority and capacity to use force reside in independent political entities, armed coercion necessarily has a distinct utility that persuasion, negotiation, adjudication, and even nonviolent forms of coercion lack.

As in serious conflicts of interest within a community, force is the final argument after appeals to reason, sympathy, or tradition have failed, since it promises to gain an objective by direct means—by compelling one will to comply with another rather than by inducing one mind to consent to another. If men had an unlimited capacity to accommodate each other by appeals to reason and sympathy or custom, there would be no need for force. In fact, however, without organized force to prod reason, sympathy, and custom—or to compensate for their absence—all but the most static and isolated societies would be in chaos.

Within a well-ordered political community the preponderant power of compulsion lies in the hands of a government commanding the consent of the governed. In such a government force provides the ultimate sanction for a system of orderly relations in which conflicts are normally resolved peacefully. In the relations of competing political groups independent of a central government, however, the power of compulsion must reside in each group. In this sense, therefore, wars occur between political groups simply because there is nothing to stop them.[14] In international politics, moreover, the role of force, though not necessarily the propensity to war, is accentuated by the ability of popular states to mobilize mass loyalties, by the diversity of their interests and circumstances in a rapidly changing civilization, by their growing psychological, if not economic, interdependence, and by the great magnitude of the force they can marshal. Under these conditions the diffusion of force among a number of states in close communication with each other accentuates mutual suspicions and animosities and reinforces the need of every major state for its own armed force.

It is true that most wars are perpetrated by states who want something they do not have rather than by states that are content to defend what they already have. Hence the imprudence of defensive states neglecting their military power. On the other hand, even if all states were purely defense-minded—a utopian supposition—there would still be need for force. The very search for security in a system of politics without government compels reliance upon military self-help, which, in turn, fosters conflict and a competition for military power.[15] The expansion of the meaning and conditions of national security to embrace tangible and intangible assets beyond the territorial boundaries of states makes this especially true. Only if all nations sought no more than the protection of their boundaries and, if at the same time, there were no conflicting requirements of such protection, could the competition for military power be

---

[14]This is the general conclusion that Waltz reaches in following Rousseau's views. *Op. cit.*, especially chap. viii.

[15]See John Herz's exposition of the "security dilemma" in *Political Realism and Political Idealism* (Chicago: University of Chicago Press, 1951), chap. ii. Cf. n. 11, p. 256.

avoided.[16] But this prescription is a fantasy, if only because security has become so much broader a concept.

Increasingly, major powers feel compelled to protect their territory at places beyond their boundaries. Quite apart from the expanding range of their interests, they realize that the growing material and psychological interdependence of states—in conventional metaphor, the "shrinking" of the world—requires them to extend their defenses farther and farther into the surrounding international environment.[17] To feel secure, they must guard against a variety of external developments that are far down the chain of threatening circumstances: developments affecting commercial and military lines of communication, the strength of friendly nations, the distribution of power, and the credibility of their will to use force.

Furthermore, the national entity that the governments of major powers are bound to secure transcends territory to include the protection of national rights and privileges, the maintenance of national prestige and honor, and even the vindication of political values in the world. The intangible quality of the ends encompassed in the concept of security is implicit in the identification of individual citizens with an abstract national personality for which they seek the gratifications once enjoyed only by monarchs. As the ends of monarchical states were broader and less tangible than the struggles for food, slaves, cattle, and women among primitive societies, so the ends of popular nation-states are broader and less tangible than those of kingdoms.

The broad nature of the ends of states generalizes the function of force in supporting those ends. But this is a mark of the integral role

[16]Thus Rousseau believed that the ideal but probably unachievable solution to the problem of war lay in a world of states effectively insulated from each other: small, self-sufficient republics that would use military power only to defend their territories from attack. For an acute analysis of this and other aspects of Rousseau's thoughts on international politics and war, see Stanley Hoffmann, *The State of War* (New York: Frederick A. Praeger, 1965), chap. iii.

[17]On this point, see Arnold Wolfers' explanation of the protean scope of security and the distinction between territorial and environmental goals (which he calls "possession" and "milieu" goals) in his essay "National Security as an Ambiguous Symbol" and on pp. 73ff. in *Discord and Collaboration* (Baltimore: The Johns Hopkins Press, 1962). Also relevant to this point is Charles de Visscher's view that the notion of security is strongly connected with the distribution of power and, hence leads to "balanced tensions" and "hegemonial tensions." *Theory and Reality in Public International Law* (Princeton: Princeton University Press, 1957), pp. 78-87.

of force in international politics, not of its unreality or dispens-
ability. In its most general function force is an asset that is desirable
in itself: desirable not from infatuation with power but from a
purely utilitarian standpoint. For, like money, military power is an
indispensable means for meeting future, unspecified, and largely unpredictable contingencies.[18] It is common currency in international
intercourse. A nation's reputation for using force to support its vital
interests is much more important to it than is an individual's reputation for solvency or wealth to him. Especially when security
depends so much on deterrence, the importance of preserving this
reputation against a challenge will usually exceed by far the intrinsic
importance of the immediate and tangible point of contention.

On the other hand, military power and, even more, the will to use
it are much more difficult than money to measure or to relate to the
values they can acquire. Therefore the tests of sufficiency are far
more subjective and varied. Moreover, since military power exerts its
effects chiefly through compulsion instead of reward, the power that
one state acquires tends to incite, through fear and distrust, the
counter-acquisition of power by other states. Thus the practical
utility of military power in international politics justifies coveting it
with an intensity which, if applied to the private pursuit of money,
could spring only from avarice or vanity.

For these reasons war and the threat of war are endemic in international relations. The fact that most states are at peace most of the
time and some are at peace all of the time, the fact that many states
with conflicts of interest do not arm against each other or raise the
prospect of war, does not argue against the integral relationship of
force to international politics.[19] Since there is no other way for
states to pursue what they regard as vital interests when other states
are determined to oppose them, force must be as essential to inter-

[18]Many political theorists have dealt with the analogy of military power to
money or credit. See, for example, Rousseau's exceptions to the analogy in
Jugement sur la Paix Perpetuelle de l'Abbé de Saint Pierre; C. E. Vaughan, *The
Political Writings of J. J. Rousseau* (Cambridge: Cambridge University Press,
1915), I, 391. For a contemporary exposition of the analogy between power and
monetary credit, see Talcott Parsons' suggestive essay, "Some Reflections on the
Place of Force in Social Progress," *Internal War,* ed. Harry Eckstein (Glencoe,
Ill.: Free Press, 1964).

[19]"War consisteth not in battle only, or the act of fighting, but in a tract of
time, wherein the will to contend by battle is sufficiently known; and therefore
the notion of *time* is to be considered in the nature of war, as it is in the nature
of weather. For as the nature of foul weather lieth not in a shower or two of rain

national politics in an anarchy as elections are to domestic politics in an organized democracy.

. . .

4. THE CONTEMPORARY RELEVANCE OF FORCE

Nevertheless, the thesis that military power is obsolete does point up some crucial aspects of reality. Unrestricted war between the nuclear superpowers could indeed be useless, because self-defeating. The general appreciation of this fact has affected the role of military power and the modes of international politics in significant ways.... On the other hand, even a cursory survey of the contemporary scene indicates that the effects of nuclear weapons have been neither so radical, so simple, nor so novel as the proponents of military obsolescence believe.

If military power is obsolete, why are the states with supposedly the most obsolete kind of power—nuclear weapons—so concerned with maintaining and managing it? Never before have such vast economic, material, and scientific resources been so systematically directed toward the continual pursuit in peacetime of an advantageous balance of military power. The organization of military planning, research, development, and production in the United States and the Soviet Union is now as comprehensive during peace as it has ever been in total war. To suppose that this vast mobilization of national energies springs from an illusion or from purely internal forces is naive.

Even where the thesis of military obsolescence seems most convincing—namely, in denying the utility of war between the superpowers—it must be qualified. The utility of war between the superpowers is very doubtful, chiefly because it is doubtful whether such wars could be limited and controlled for a useful political purpose. Yet the practical question, aside from the problem of deterrence, is whether such wars are so unlikely to occur or so unlikely to be kept within rational limits if they do occur as to warrant not preparing to fight them as rationally as possible. Suffice it to state here that this

but in an inclination thereto of many days together, so the nature of war consisteth not in actual fighting but in the known disposition thereto during all the time there is no assurance to the contrary." Thomas Hobbes, *Leviathan*, chap. xiii.

question cannot be responsibly answered categorically, because one of the dominant characteristics of military power in the nuclear age is the conjunction of war's terrible potentialities with its immense uncertainties.

If one looks at the lower instead of the upper end of the spectrum of violence, however, there can be no reasonable doubt that war is far from obsolete. Since World War II local wars—civil, revolutionary, and between the organized armies of states—have been as pervasive and decisive an instrument of international politics as in any modern period.

Yet the principal deficiency of the thesis of military obsolescence lies less in its depreciation of the utility of war than in its failure to appreciate the subtle and varied role of military power short of war. Whatever the utility or uselessness of actual war among the advanced industrial-technological states may be, every day demonstrates that the fearful prospect of war and the policies for using, deterring, controlling, and disarming armed forces in the shadow of this prospect play a decisive role in international politics. In many ways that role is more pervasive than in previous periods of history when war was less dangerous.

This is not surprising, for when states dare not resort to war, yet dare not renounce the resort to war, international politics is bound to depend heavily upon the threat or prospect of war. The prospect that any war involving nuclear powers might become an uncontrollable cataclysm engenders great uncertainty about the circumstances in which states might actually fight, but it does not exclude that possibility as long as states must depend upon self-help to support vital interests. Just because governments wish to avoid war, they must act *as if* they might use their armed forces; and this necessity gives a certain reality to a resolve that neither they nor their adversaries can afford to assume is pure bluff.

The unprecedented magnitude, decisiveness, and psychological impact of forces-in-being and forces-in-development have greatly enhanced the uses of military power short of war. Thus confrontations and crises, testing national will and nerve under the shadow of war, have become major modes of international politics. The art of coercion short of war and on the brink has never been as finely developed or as deliberately applied. Deterrence, now the first prerequisite of military security, has become a highly sophisticated calculus. But deterrence is only the most explicit form of nonviolent military pressure in a copious arsenal of dissuasion, persuasion, compulsion, and intimidation.

Military strategy now embraces not only the waging of war but all the uses of force as an instrument of policy short of war. In fact, it is itself a major instrument of policy in peacetime. Thus strategic pronouncements can have the impact of major diplomatic statements, and the strategic "dialogue" with one's allies can be as politically significant as the communication of strategic intentions to one's adversaries.

Novel inhibitions against using modern weapons have blurred the distinction between technical military and political issues. The political repercussions of the command and control of nuclear weapons in NATO illustrate the point. As in the case of strategy, highly technical matters that used to be the exclusive concern of military officers are now the subject of national and international controversy because they are suffused with political import.

Even the continual attention commanded by arms control and disarmament, far from indicating the obsolescence of military power, testifies to the preoccupation of statecraft with military concerns. The widespread belief that the spread of nuclear ownership will have major consequences for international politics belies the assertion by some of the most vigorous opponents of nuclear proliferation that military power—even when based on the most "useless" weapons—is obsolete.

The prophets of military obsolescence not only ignore the uses of force short of war, but with the same overly materialistic view of the military function, they underestimate its continuing relevance to the broad, intangible issues of politics. They contend that because international politics is now more concerned with ideology, status, and political influence and less concerned with territory—a proposition, incidentally, that requires considerable qualification—military power tends to be increasingly irrelevant.[20] Yet military power is in many ways inseparable from these issues.

Is the prestige of a great power at stake? Few things can affect its prestige more than its reputation for using armed force prudently

---

[20]Clearly, the function of territory for advanced states has changed since the eighteenth century, when it was more directly related to tangible military and economic assets; and the forceful acquisition of territory has generally become more costly, materially, politically, and morally. But the defense of foreign territories and the contest for political or ideological primacy in them are, in many ways, at least as important features of international politics as ever. Klaus Knorr examines the declining value of territorial conquest with pertinent qualifications in *On the Uses of Military Power in the Nuclear Age* (Princeton: Princeton University Press, 1966), chaps. ii and iii.

and effectively or rashly and ineffectively, resolutely and flexibly or hesitantly and without restraint.

Is the political independence or the domestic political system of a nation the issue? Scarcely any of the important changes in these two matters in the last twenty years can be explained without reference to military power. Most of them were achieved through war or military occupation.

Is the issue winning the "hearts and minds of men"? The outcome of the Korean War, the Cuban or Berlin crises, or the war in Vietnam will have been every bit as fateful as economic aid, political competition, or the power of example in determining the orientation of hearts and minds. If one side abandoned the military contest, no one would doubt this point.

As always, the issues of power, status, and influence have an abstract quality. Their abstractness, however, does not divorce the contention surrounding them from tangible evidence of military strength and the will to use it. Most of these issues come to a head in specific conflicts of interest in which armed force plays a determining role. They are mightily affected by the capacity of states to convey an impression of power through exploitation of the enhanced psychological and political impact of awesome but unused military technology. Space exploits exert something of the same impact of advanced technology upon impressionable contemporary minds; but although their efficacy as propaganda gains much from their implication of military prowess, their psychological and political impact is no substitute for the almost morbid awe inspired by weapons of sudden obliteration. In comparison, the majesty of battleships in an earlier period seems almost quaint.

Military power, then, is not losing its relevance to international politics. Indeed, in some respects, its role has expanded. It has expanded, however, not in opposition to politics but *through* politics. Political and military factors have come to suffuse each other in a way that makes the conventional distinctions of previous eras irrelevant. International politics have, in a sense, become militarized; but, at the same time, military power has become politicized.

5. THE IMPACT OF NUCLEAR WEAPONS UPON INTERNATIONAL POLITICS

The continuing and pervasive role of military power in international politics leaves open the possibility that it may have changed so radically as to require or produce a transformation of international politics. The obsolescence of the prevailing system of international politics would be no less momentous than the obsolescence of war and the threat of war.

The view that nuclear weapons must transform international politics is common. Yet its proponents furnish scant supporting evidence. They base their view, first, on the novel capacity of nulcear weapons to inflict catastrophic civilian damage suddenly and at great distances. In interpreting the significance of this capacity they stress a number of its outstanding characteristics: the ability to destroy a nation without defeating its armed forces, the inability of states to protect their territory and its inhabitants from devastation, the "overkill" or superfluous destructive power available to the nuclear superpowers, the parity or mutually nullifying effect of their military power, or the disproportion between the relative military strength of the superpowers and their capacity to use or threaten to use it against weaker powers. To these special characteristics of nuclear power they attribute various fundamental changes in the nature of international politics: the obsolescence of the classical system of power politics, the "political obsolescence" of military alliances, or the equalization of the power of small and giant states.[21]

Significantly, however, the analyses of these changes generally note a disparity between the expected effects of nuclear weapons upon international politics and the actual state of affairs. They then attribute the disparity between logic and fact to an intellectual, political, or institutional lag, which, purportedly, will lead to disaster

---

[21]On the drastic implications of territorial vulnerability for international politics, see John Herz, *International Politics in the Atomic Age* (New York: Columbia University Press, 1959); his "International Politics and the Nuclear Dilemma," *Nuclear Weapons and the Conflict of Conscience*, ed. John C. Bennett (New York: Charles Scribner's Sons, 1962); and Kenneth E. Boulding, *Conflict and Defense* (New York: Harper & Row, 1962), chap. xvi. On the obsolescence of the classical system of power politics because of "overkill" see Max Lerner, *The Age of Overkill* (New York: Simon & Schuster, 1962), chap. i. On the political obsolescence of alliances, stemming from the alleged equalizing effect of nuclear weapons and the purported unwillingness of one nation to protect another at the cost of nuclear retaliation, see Hans J. Morgenthau, "The Four Paradoxes of Nuclear Strategy," *op. cit.*, pp. 23-25. A military rationale of this argument lies in the theory of proportionate deterrence, as expounded by Pierre Gallois in *Stratégie de l'Âge Nucléaire* (1960), considerably revised in *The Balance of Terror* (Boston: Houghton Mifflin, 1961) and in earlier articles in *Politique Etrangère*.

unless eliminated by some transformation of the international system. Since this kind of analysis depends more on logical speculation than on empirical observation, it is difficult to tell whether it is clairvoyant or merely a mode of exhortation. But even if its conclusions are correct, they are of little practical help when they demand transformations of international politics that are almost certainly unattainable in time to save us. Therefore, rather than jump to conclusions about the political consequences of contemporary military technology, it is incumbent upon us to seek instruction, if not solace, from history.

In order to judge the validity of the proposition that radically new weapons must lead to radically new politics, it seems reasonable to look first at the nature of the relationship between new weapons and international politics in the past. The historic interaction between military power and international politics provides some basis for judging more precisely what aspects of nuclear power are so radically new as to make prenuclear modes of international politics obsolete and what aspects are extensions of older trends in military power, which may continue to be assimilated to traditional modes of international politics.

Many of the changes in the relationship of military power to international politics—which the proponents of international political transformation attribute to the invention of nuclear weapons—are continuations of trends that have been particularly significant since the latter part of the nineteenth century. Others seem less the product of nuclear weapons than of gradual changes in the stakes of international politics, the climate of opinion, and the diffusion or concentration of power among states.

There are, indeed, some characteristics of nuclear weapons that are radically new and that cannot readily be assimilated to traditional modes of power politics. Yet, for about three centuries these modes have shown a notable flexibility in adapting to military innovations within the modern international system. In this respect man's political ingenuity is as remarkable as his technological inventiveness. We simply cannot know whether his ingenuity will measure up to the task of assimilating nuclear weapons without touching off a catastrophic war, but there seems to be no practical alternative to his trying. In fact, the effort has begun.

Arms Races: Prerequisites and Results

Samuel P. Huntington

INTRODUCTION

Si vis pacem, para bellum, is an ancient and authoritative adage of military policy. Of no less acceptance, however is the other, more modern, proposition: "Armaments races inevitably lead to war." Juxtaposed, these two advices suggest that the maxims of social science, like the proverbs of folklore, reflect a many-sided truth. The social scientist, however, cannot escape with so easy an observation. He has the scholar's responsibility to determine as fully as possible to what extent and under what conditions his conflicting truths are true. The principal aim of this essay is to attempt some resolution of the issue: When are arms races a prelude to war and when are they a substitute for war?

SOURCE: From Carl J. Friedrich and Seymour E. Harris (eds.), *Public Policy*. Copyright © 1958 by the Harvard Graduate School of Public Administration. Reprinted and abridged by permission of the author and the Harvard Graduate School of Public Administration.

Throughout history states have sought to maintain their peace and security by means of military strength. The arms race in which the military preparations of two states are intimately and directly inter-related is, however, a relatively modern phenomenon. The conflict between the apparent feasibility of preserving peace by arming for war and the apparent inevitability of competitive arms increases resulting in war is, therefore, a comparatively new one. The second purpose of this essay is to explore some of the circumstances which have brought about this uncertainty as to the relationship between war, peace, and arms increases. The problem here is: What were the prerequisites to the emergence of the arms race as a significant form of international rivalry in the nineteenth and twentieth centuries?

For the purposes of this essay, an arms race is defined as a pro-gressive, competitive peacetime increase in armaments by two states or coalition of states resulting from conflicting purposes or mutual fears. An arms race is thus a form of reciprocal interaction between two states or coalitions. A race cannot exist without an increase in arms, quantitatively or qualitatively, but every peacetime increase in arms is not necessarily the result of an arms race. A nation may expand its armaments for the domestic purposes of aiding industry or curbing unemployment, or because it believes an absolute need exists for such an increase regardless of the actions of other states. In the 1880s and 1890s, for instance, the expansion of the United States Navy was apparently unrelated to the actions of any other power,[1] and hence not part of an arms race. An arms race reflects disagreement between two states as to the proper balance of power between them. The concept of a "general" arms race[2] in which a number of powers increase their armaments simultaneously is, conse-quently, a fallacious one. Such general increases either are not the result of self-conscious reciprocal interaction or are simply the sum of a number of two-state antagonisms. In so far as the arms policy of any one state is related to the armaments of other states, it is a function of concrete, specific goals, needs, or threats arising out of the political relations among the states. Even Britain's vaunted two-power naval standard will be found, on close analysis, to be rooted in specific threats rather than in abstract considerations of general policy.

[1] See George T. Davis, *A Navy Second to None* (New York, 1940), pp. 48, 96-97. For elaboration of the distinction between absolute and relative arms goals, see below, pp. 15ff.

[2] See Quincy Wright, *A Study of War* (Chicago, 2 vols., 1942), II, 690.

PREREQUISITES FOR AN ARMS RACE

Prior to 1789 certain antagonistic relationships among states did at times have some characteristics of the modern arms race. Such relationships, however, were exceptional, and they usually lacked many essential features of the modern type of race. Certain conditions peculiarly present in the nineteenth and twentieth centuries would appear to be responsible for the emergence of the arms race as a frequent and distinct form of international rivalry. Among the more significant of these conditions are: a state system which facilitates the balancing of power by internal rather than external means; the preëminence of military force-in-being over territory or other factors as an element of national power; the capacity within each state to increase its military strength through quantitative or qualitative means; and the conscious awareness by each state of the dependence of its own arms policy upon that of another state.[3]

Balancing Power: External and Internal Means. Arms races are an integral part of the international balance of power.[4] From the view-

[3]Since an arms race is necessarily a matter of degree, differences of opinion will exist as to whether any given relationship constitutes an arms race and as to what are the precise opening and closing dates of any given arms race. At the risk of seeming arbitrary, the following relationships are assumed to be arms races for the purposes of this essay:

1. France v. England	naval	1840-1866
2. France v. Germany	land	1874-1894
3. England v. France & Russia	naval	1884-1904
4. Argentina v. Chile	naval	1890-1902
5. England v. Germany	naval	1898-1912
6. France v. Germany	land	1911-1914
7. England v. United States	naval	1916-1930
8. Japan v. United States	naval	1916-1922
9. France v. Germany	land	1934-1939
10. Soviet Union v. Germany	land	1934-1941
11. Germany v. England	air	1934-1939
12. United States v. Japan	naval	1934-1941
13. Soviet Union v. United States	nuclear	1946-

Editor's Note: The bulk of Professor Huntington's supporting historical evidence has been deleted to shorten the article. The reader is urged to consult the original essay for a fuller understanding of arms races.

[4]On the balance of power, see Carl J. Friedrich, *Foreign Policy in the Making* (New York, 1938), ch. 5; Hans J. Morgenthau, *Politics Among Nations* (New York, 2nd ed., 1954), pp. 155-203; Wright, *Study of War*, II, ch. 20; Ernst B. Haas, "Balance of Power: Prescription, Concept, or Progpaanda, *World Politics*, V (July, 1953), pp. 442-77.

point of a participant, an arms race is an effort to achieve a favorable international distribution of power. Viewed as a whole, a sustained arms race is a means of achieving a dynamic equilibrium of power between two states or coalitions of states. Arms races only take place between states in the same balance of power system. The more isolated a nation is from any balance of power system the less likely it is to become involved in an arms race. Within any such system, power may in general be balanced in two ways: externally through a realignment of the units participating in the system (diplomacy), or internally by changes in the inherent power of the units. The extent to which the balancing process operates through external or internal means usually depends upon the number of states participating in the system, the opportunity for new states to join the system, and the relative distribution of power among the participating states.

The relations among the states in a balance of power system may tend toward any one of three patterns, each of which assigns somewhat different roles to the external and internal means of balancing power. A situation of *bellum omnium contra omnes* exists when there are a large number of states approximately equal in power and when there is an approximately equal distribution of grievances and antagonisms among the states. In such a system, which was perhaps most closely approximated by the city-states of the Italian Renaissance, primary reliance is placed upon wily diplomacy, treachery, and surprise attack. Since no bilateral antagonisms continue for any length of time, a sustained arms race is very unlikely. A second balance of power pattern involves an all-against-one relationship: the coalition of a number of weaker states against a single *grande nation*. The fears and grievances of the weaker states are concentrated against the stronger, and here again primary reliance is placed upon diplomatic means of maintaining or restoring the balance. European politics assumed this pattern in the successive coalitions to restrain the Hapsburgs, Louis XIV, Frederick II, Napoleon, and Hitler. At times, efforts may be made to bring in other states normally outside the system to aid in restoring the balance.

A third pattern of balance of power politics involves bilateral antagonisms between states or coalitions of states roughly equal in strength. Such bilateral antagonisms have been a continuing phenomenon in the western balance of power system: France *vs.* England, Austria *vs.* France and then Prussia (Germany) *vs.* France, Austria-Hungary *vs.* Russia, the Triple Alliance *vs.* the Triple Entente, and, now, the United States *vs.* the Soviet Union. In these relationships the principal grievances and antagonisms of any two states become concentrated upon each other, and, as a result, this antagonism becomes the primary focus of their respective foreign policies. In this situation, diplomacy and alliances may play a significant role if a "balancer" exists who can shift his weight to whichever side appears to be weaker. But no balancing state can exist if all the major powers are involved in bilateral antagonisms or if a single overriding antagonism forces virtually all the states in the system to choose one side or the other (bipolarization). In these circumstances, the balancing of power by rearranging the units of power becomes difficult. Diplomatic maneuvering gives way to the massing of military force. Each state relies more on armaments and less on alliances. Other factors being equal, the pressures toward an arms race are greatest when international relations assume this form.

In the past century the relative importance of the internal means of balancing power has tended to increase. A single world-wide balance of power system has tended to develop, thereby eliminating the possibility of bringing in outside powers to restore the balance. At the same time, however, the number of great powers has fairly constantly decreased, and bilateral antagonisms have consequently become of greater importance. Small powers have tended to seek security either through neutrality (Switzerland, Sweden) or through reliance upon broadly organized efforts at collective security. ... Alliances were perhaps the primary means of balancing power in Europe before 1870. Between 1870 and 1914, both alliances and armaments played important roles. Since 1918 the relative importance of armaments has probably increased. The primary purpose of the military pacts of the post-World War II period, with the possible exception of NATO, generally has been the extension of the protection of a great power to a series of minor powers, rather than the uniting of a number of more or less equal powers in pursuit of a common objective. In addition, the development of democratic control over foreign policy has made alliances more difficult. Alignments dictated by balance of power considerations may be impossible to carry out due to public opinion. Rapid shifts in alliances from friends to enemies also are difficult to execute in a democratic society. Perhaps, too, a decline in the arts of diplomacy has contributed to the desire to rest one's security upon resources which are "owned" rather than "pledged."

Elements of Power: Money, Territory, Armaments. Arms races only take place when military forces-in-being are of direct and prime importance to the power of a state. During the age of mercantilism, for instance, monetary resources were highly valued as an index of power, and, consequently, governmental policy was directed toward the accumulation of economic wealth which could then be transformed into military and political power. These actions, which might take a variety of forms, were in some respects the seventeenth century equivalents of the nineteenth and twentieth century arms races.[5] In the eighteenth century, territory was of key importance as a measure of power.[6] The size of the armies which a state could maintain was roughly proportional to its population, and, in an agrarian age, its population was roughly proportional to its territory. Consequently, an increase in military power required an increase in territory. Within Europe, territory could be acquired either by conquest, in which case a surprise attack was probably desirable in order to forestall intervention by other states, or by agreement among the great powers to partition a smaller power. Outside of Europe, colonial territories might contribute wealth if not manpower to the mother country, and these could be acquired either by discovery and settlement or by conquest. Consequently, territorial compensations were a primary means of balancing power, and through the acquisition of colonies, states jealous of their relative power could strive to improve their position without directly challenging another major state and thereby provoking a war.

During the nineteenth century territory became less important as an index of power, and industry and armaments more important. By the end of the century all the available colonial lands had been occupied by the major powers. In addition, the rise of nationalism and of self-determination made it increasingly difficult to settle differences by the division and bartering of provinces, small powers, and colonies. By expanding its armaments, however, a state could still increase its relative power without decreasing the absolute power of another state. Reciprocal increases in armaments made possible an unstable and dynamic, but none the less real equilibrium among the major powers. The race for armaments tended to replace the race for colonies as the "escape hatch" through which major states could enhance their power without directly challenging each other.

The increased importance of armaments as a measure of national power was reflected in the new emphasis upon disarmament in the efforts to resolve antagonisms among nations. . . .

Capacity for Qualitative and Quantitative Increases in Military Power. An arms race requires the progressive increase from domestic sources of the absolute military power of a state. This may be done

[5] See Eli F. Heckscher, *Mercantilism* (London, 2 vols., 1931), II, pp. 31 ff.

[6] See Wright, *Study of War*, II, p. 743, pp. 768-69; H. A. Smith, "The Problem of Disarmament in the Light of History," *International Affairs*, X (Sept., 1931), pp. 611-12.

quantitatively, by expanding the numerical strength of its existing forms of military force, or qualitatively, by replacing its existing forms of military force (usually weapons systems) with new and more effective forms of force. The latter requires a dynamic technology, and the former the social, political and economic capacity to reallocate resources from civilian to military purposes. . . . Beginning with the Industrial Revolution, however, the pace of innovation in military technology constantly quickened, and the new weapons systems inevitably stimulated arms races. The introduction, first, of the steam warship and then of the ironclad, for instance, directly intensified the naval competition between England and France in the 1850s and 1860s. Throughout the nineteenth century, the importance of the weapons technician constantly increased relative to the importance of the strategist.

Broad changes in economic and political structure were at the same time making quantitative arms races feasible. The social system of the *ancien regime* did not permit a full mobilization of the economic and manpower resources of a nation. So long as participation in war was limited to a small class, competitive increases in the size of armies could not proceed very far. The destruction of the old system, the spread of democracy and liberalism, the increasing popularity among all groups of the "nation in arms" concept, all permitted a much more complete mobilization of resources for military purposes than had been possible previously. In particular, the introduction of universal military service raised the ceiling on the size of the army to the point where the limiting factor was the civilian manpower necessary to support the army. In addition, the development of industry permitted the mass production and mass accumulation of the new weapons which the new technology had invented. The countries which lagged behind in the twin processes of democratization and industrialization were severely handicapped in the race for armaments.

In the age of limited wars little difference existed between a nation's military strength in peace and its military strength in war. During the nineteenth century, however, the impact of democracy and industrialism made wars more total, victory or defeat in them became more significant (and final), military superiority became more critically important, and consequently a government had to be more fully assured of the prospect of victory before embarking upon war. In addition, the professional officer corps which developed during the nineteenth century felt a direct responsibility for the military security of the state and emphasized the desirability of obtaining a safe superiority in armaments. As a result, unless one of the participants possessed extensive staying power due to geography or resources, the outcome of a war depended almost as much upon what happened before the declarations of war as after. By achieving superiority in armaments it might be possible for a state to achieve the fruits of war without suffering the risks and liabilities of war. Governments piled up armaments in peacetime with the hope either of averting war or of insuring success in it should it come.

Absolute and Relative Armaments Goals. A state may define its armaments goals in one of two ways. It can specify a certain *absolute* level or type of armaments which it believes necessary for it to possess irrespective of the level or type possessed by other states. Or, it can define its goal in *relative* terms as a function of the armaments of other states. Undoubtedly, in any specific case, a state's armaments reflect a combination of both absolute and relative considerations. Normally, however, one or the other will be dominant and embodied in official statements of the state's armaments goals in the form of an "absolute need" or a ratio-goal. Thus, historically Great Britain followed a relative policy with respect to the capital ships in its navy but an absolute policy with respect to its cruisers, the need for which, it was held, stemmed from the unique nature of the British Empire.

If every state had absolute goals, arms races would be impossible: each state would go its separate way uninfluenced by the actions of its neighbors. Nor would a full scale arms race develop if an absolute goal were pursued consistently by only one power in an antagonistic relationship: whatever relative advantage the second power demanded would be simply a function of the constant absolute figure demanded by the first power. An arms race only arises when two or more powers consciously determine the quantitative or qualitative aspects of their armaments as functions of the armaments of the other power. Absolute goals, however, are only really feasible when a state is not a member of or only on the periphery of a balance of power system.

. . .

The armaments of two states can be functionally interrelated only if they are also similar or complementary. An arms race is impossible between a power which possesses only a navy and one which possesses only an army: no one can match divisions against battleships. A functional relationship between armaments is complementary when two military forces possessing different weapons systems are designed for combat with each other. In this sense, an air defense fighter command complements an opposing strategic bombing force or one side's submarine force complements the other's antisubmarine destroyers and hunter-killer groups. A functional relationship is similar when two military forces are not only designed for combat with each other but also possess similar weapons systems, as has been very largely the case with land armies and with battle fleets of capital ships. In most instances in history, arms races have involved similar forces rather than complementary forces, but no reason exists why there should not be an arms race in the latter. The only special problem posed by a complementary arms race is that of measuring the relative strengths of the opposing forces. In a race involving similar forces, a purely quantitative measurement usually suffices; in one of complementary forces, qualitative judgments are necessary as to the effectiveness of one type of weapons system against another.

. . .

Two governments can consciously follow relative arms policies only if they are well informed of their respective military capabilities. The general availability of information concerning armaments is thus a precondition for an arms race. Prior to the nineteenth century when communication and transportation were slow and haphazard, a state would frequently have only the vaguest notions of the military programs of its potential rivals. Often it was possible for one state to make extensive secret preparations for war. In the modern world, information with respect to military capabilities has become much more widespread and has been one of the factors increasing the likelihood of arms races. Even now, however, many difficulties exist in getting information concerning the arms of a rival which is sufficiently accurate to serve as the basis for one's own policy. At times misconceptions as to the military strengths and policies of other states become deeply ingrained, and at other times governments simply choose to be blind to significant changes in armaments.... Nonetheless, fragmentary and uncertain though information may be, its availability in one form or another is what makes the arms race possible.

ABORTIVE AND SUSTAINED ARMS RACES

An arms race may end in war, formal or informal agreement between the two states to call off the race, or victory for one state which achieves and maintains the distribution of power which it desires and ultimately causes its rival to give up the struggle. The likelihood of war arising from an arms race depends in the first instance upon the relation between the power and grievances of one state to the power and grievances of the other. War is least likely when grievances are low, or, if grievances are high, the sum of the grievances and power of one state approximates the sum of the grievances and power of the other. An equality of power and an equality of grievances will thus reduce the chances of war, as will a situation in which one state has a marked superiority in power and the other in grievances. Assuming a fairly equal distribution of grievances, the likelihood of an arms race ending in war tends to vary inversely with the length of the arms race and directly with the extent to which it is quantitative rather than qualitative in character. This section deals with the first of these relationships and the next section with the second.

An arms race is a series of interrelated increases in armaments which if continued over a period of time produces a dynamic equilibrium of power between two states. A race in which this dynamic equilibrium fails to develop may be termed an abortive arms race. In these instances, the previously existing static equilibrium between the two states is disrupted without being replaced by a new equilibrium reflecting their relative competitive efforts in the race. Instead, rapid shifts take place or appear about to take place in the distribution of power which enhance the willingness of one state or the other to precipitate a conflict. At least one and sometimes two danger points occur at the beginning of every arms race. The first point arises with the response of the challenged state to the initial increases in armaments by the challenging state. The second danger point is the reaction of the challenger who has been successful in initially achieving his goal to the frantic belated efforts of the challenged state to retrieve its former position.

The formal beginning of an arms race is the first increase in armaments by one state—the challenger—caused by a desire to alter the existing balance of power between it and another state. Prior to this initial action, a pre-arms race static equilibrium may be said to exist. This equilibrium does not necessarily mean an equality of power. It simply reflects the satisfaction of each state with the existing distribution of power in the light of its grievances and antagonisms with the other state. Some of the most stable equilibriums in history have also been ones which embodied an unbalance of power. . . .

For the purposes of analysis it is necessary to specify a particular increase in armaments by one state as marking the formal beginning of the arms race. This is done not to pass judgment on the desirability or wisdom of the increase, but simply to identify the start of the action and reaction which constitute the race. In most instances, this initial challenge is not hard to locate. It normally involves a major change in the policy of the challenging state, and more likely than not it is formally announced to the world. The reasons for the challenging state's discontent with the status quo may stem from a variety of causes. It may feel that the growth of its economy, commerce, and population should be reflected in changes in the military balance of power (Germany, 1898; United States, 1916; Soviet Union, 1946). Nationalistic, bellicose, or militaristic individuals or parties may come to power who are unwilling to accept an equilibrium which other groups in their society had been willing to live with or negotiate about (Germany and Japan, 1934). New political issues may arise which cause a deterioration in the relationships of the state with another power and which consequently lead it to change its estimate of the arms balance necessary for its security (France, 1841, 1875; England, 1884).

Normally the challenging state sets a goal for itself which derives from the relation between the military strengths of the two countries prior to the race. If the relation was one of disparity, the initial challenge usually comes from the weaker power which aspires to parity or better. Conceivably a stronger power could initiate an arms race by deciding that it required an even higher ratio of superiority over the weaker power. But in actual practice this is seldom the case: the gain in security achieved in upping a 2:1 ratio to 3:1, for instance, rarely is worth the increased economic costs and political tensions. If parity of military power existed between the two countries, the arms race begins when one state determines that it requires military force superior to that of the other country.

. . .

In many respects the most critical aspect of a race is the initial response which the challenged state makes to the new goals posited by the challenger. In general, these responses can be divided into four categories, two of which preserve the possibility of peace, two of which make war virtually inevitable. The challenged state may, first, attempt to counterbalance the increased armaments of its rival through diplomatic means or it may, secondly, immediately increase its own armaments in an effort to maintain or directly to restore the previously existing balance of military power. While neither of these responses guarantees the maintenance of peace, they at least do not precipitate war. The diplomatic avenue of action, if it exists, is generally the preferred one. It may be necessary, however, for the state to enhance its own armaments as well as attempting to secure reliable allies. Or, if alliances are impossible or undesirable for reasons of state policy, the challenged state must rely upon its own increases in armaments as the way of achieving its goal. In this case a sustained arms race is likely to result. . . .

If new alliances or increased armaments appear impossible or undesirable, a state which sees its superiority or equality in military power menaced by the actions of another state may initiate preventive action while still strong enough to forestall the change in the balance of power. The factors which enter into the decision to wage preventive war are complex and intangible, but, conceivably, if the state had no diplomatic opportunities and if it was dubious of its ability to hold its own in an arms race, this might well be a rational course of behavior.[7] . . .

At the other extreme from preventive action, a challenged state simply may not make any immediate response to the upset of the existing balance of power. The challenger may then actually achieve or come close to achieving the new balance of military force which it considers necessary. In this event, roles are reversed, the challenged suddenly awakens to its weakened position and becomes the challenger, engaging in frantic and strenuous last-ditch efforts to restore the previously existing military ratio. In general, the likelihood of war increases just prior to a change in military superiority from one side to the other. If the challenged state averts this change by alliances or increased armaments, war is avoidable. On the other hand, the challenged state may precipitate war in order to prevent the change, or it may provoke war by allowing the change to take place and then attempting to undo it. In the latter case, the original challenger, having achieved parity or superiority, is in no mood or position to back down; the anxious efforts of its opponent to regain its military strength appear to be obvious war preparation; and consequently the original challenger normally will not hesitate to risk or provoke a war while it may still benefit from its recent gains.

. . .

The danger of war is highest in the opening phases of an arms race, at which time the greatest elements of instability and uncertainty are present. If the challenged state neither resorts to preventive war nor fails to make an immediate response to the challenger's activities, a sustained arms race is likely to result with the probability of war decreasing as the initial action and counteraction fade into the past. Once the initial disturbances to the pre-arms race static equilibrium

[7]On the considerations going into the waging of preventive war, see my "To Choose Peace or War," *United States Naval Institute Proceedings*, LXXXIII (April, 1957), pp. 360-62.

are surmounted, the reciprocal increases of the two states tend to produce a new, dynamic equilibrium reflecting their relative strength and participation in the race. In all probability, the relative military power of the two states in this dynamic equilibrium will fall somewhere between the previous status quo and the ratio-goal of the challenger. The sustained regularity of the increases in itself becomes an accepted and anticipated stabilizing factor in the relations between the two countries. A sustained quantitative race still may produce a war, but a greater likelihood exists that either the two states will arrive at a mutual accommodation reducing the political tensions which started the race or that one state over the long haul will gradually but substantially achieve its objective while the other will accept defeat in the race if this does not damage its vital interests.... While generalizations are both difficult and dangerous, it would appear that a sustained arms race is much more likely to have a peaceful ending than a bloody one.

QUANTITATIVE AND QUALITATIVE ARMS RACES

A state may increase its military power quantitatively, by expanding the numerical strength of its existing military forces, or qualitatively, by replacing its existing forms of military force (normally weapons systems) with new and more effective forms of force. Expansion and innovation are thus possible characteristics of any arms race, and to some extent both are present in most races. Initially and fundamentally every arms race is quantitative in nature. The race begins when two states develop conflicting goals as to what should be the distribution of military power between them and give these goals explicit statement in quantitative ratios of the relative strengths which each hopes to achieve in the decisive form of military force. The formal start of the race is the decision of the challenger to upset the existing balance and to expand its forces quantitatively. If at some point in the race a qualitative change produces a new decisive form of military force, the quantitative goals of the two states still remain roughly the same. The relative balance of power which each state desires to achieve is independent of the specific weapons and forces which enter into the balance. Despite the underlying adherence of both states to their original ratio-goals, however, a complex qualitative race produced by rapid technological innovation is a very different phenomenon from a race which remains simply quantitative.

. . .

A qualitative arms race is more complex than a quantitative one because at some point it involves the decision by one side to introduce a new weapons system or form of military force. Where the capacity for technological innovation exists, the natural tendency is for the arms race to become qualitative. The introduction of a new weapons system obviously is normally desirable from the viewpoint of the state which is behind in the quantitative race.

. . .

In general . . . technological innovation favors, at least temporarily, the numerically weaker power. Its long-run effects, however, depend upon factors other than the currently prevailing balance of military strength. . . .

The problem which technological innovation presents to the quantitatively superior power is somewhat more complex. The natural tendencies for such a state are toward conservatism: any significant innovation will undermine the usefulness of the current type of weapons system in which it possesses a superiority. What, however, should be the policy of a superior power with respect to making a technological change which its inferior rivals are likely to make in the near future?

. . .

The very incentive which an inferior power has to make a technological innovation is reason for the superior power to take the lead, if it can, in bringing in the innovation itself. The British Dreadnought debate of 1904-05 had its parallels in the problem confronting the American government in 1949-1950 concerning the construction of a hydrogen bomb. Like the British, the Americans possessed a superiority in the existing decisive type of weapons system. As in the British government, opinion was divided, and the arguments pro and con of the technicians and military experts had to be weighed against budgetary considerations. As with the Dreadnought, the new weapons system was pushed by a small group of zealots convinced of the inevitability and necessity of its development. In both cases, humanitarian statesmen and conservative experts wished to go slow. In each case, the government eventually decided to proceed with the innovation, and, in each case, the wisdom of its policy was demonstrated by the subsequent actions of its rival. In an arms race, what is technically possible tends to become politically necessary.

Whether an arms race is primarily quantitative or primarily qualitative in nature has a determining influence upon its outcome. This influence is manifested in the different impacts which the two types of races have on the balance of military power between the two states and on the relative demands which they make on state resources.

Qualitative and Quantitative Races and the Balance of Power. In a simple quantitative race one state is very likely to develop a definite superiority in the long run. The issue is simply who has the greater determination and the greater resources. Once a state falls significantly behind, it is most unlikely that it will ever be able to overcome the lead of its rival. A qualitative race, on the other hand, in which there is a series of major technological innovations in reality consists of a number of distinct races. Each time a new weapons system is introduced a new race takes place in the development and accumulation of that weapon. As the rate of technological innovation increases each separate component race decreases in time and extent. The simple quantitative race is like a marathon of undetermined distance which can only end with the exhaustion of one state or both, or with the state which is about to fall behind in the race pulling out its firearms and attempting to despatch its rival. The qualitative race, on the other hand, resembles a series of hundred yard dashes, each beginning from a fresh starting line. Consequently, in a qualitative race hope springs anew with each phase. Quantitative superiority is the product of effort, energy, resources, and time. Once achieved it is rarely lost. Qualitative superiority is the product of discovery, luck, and circumstance. Once achieved it is always lost. Safety exists only in numbers. While a quantitative race tends to produce inequality between the two competing powers, a qualitative race tends toward equality irrespective of what may be the ratio-goals of the two rival states. Each new weapon instead of increasing the distance between the two states reduces it. The more rapid the rate of innovation the more pronounced is the tendency toward equality.... A rapid rate of innovation means that arms races are always beginning, never ending. In so far as the likelihood of war is decreased by the existence of an equality of power between rival states, a qualitative arms race tends to have this result. A quantitative arms race, on the other hand, tends to have the opposite effect. If in a qualitative race one power stopped technological innovation and instead shifted its resources to the multiplication of existing weapons systems, this would be a fairly clear sign that it was intending to go to war in the immediate future.

Undoubtedly many will question the proposition that rapid technological innovation tends to produce an equality of power. In an arms race each state lives in constant fear that its opponent will score a "technological breakthrough" and achieve a decisive qualitative superiority. This anxiety is a continuing feature of arms races but it is one which has virtually no basis in recent experience. The tendency toward simultaneity of innovation is overwhelming. . . . The logic of scientific development is such that separate groups of men working in separate laboratories on the same problem are likely to arrive at the same answer to the problem at about the same time. Even if this were not the case, the greatly increased ratio of production time to use time in recent years has tended to diminish the opportunity of the power which has pioneered an innovation to produce it in sufficient quantity in sufficient time to be militarily decisive.

· · ·

The Domestic Burden of Quantitative and Qualitative Races. Quantitative and qualitative arms races have markedly different effects upon the countries participating in them. In a quantitative race the decisive ratio is between the resources which a nation devotes to military purposes and those which it devotes to civilian ones. A quantitative race of any intensity requires a steady shift of resources from the latter to the former. As the forms of military force are multiplied a larger and larger proportion of the national product is devoted to the purposes of the race, and, if it is a race in military manpower, an increasing proportion of the population serves a longer and longer time in the armed forces. A quantitative race of any duration thus imposes ever increasing burdens upon the countries involved in it. As a result, it becomes necessary for governments to resort to various means of stimulating popular support and eliciting a willingness to sacrifice other goods and values. Enthusiasm is mobilized, hostility aroused and directed against the potential enemy. Suspicion and fear multiply with the armaments.

· · ·

Eventually a time is reached when the increasing costs and tensions of a continued arms race seem worse than the costs and the risks of war. Public opinion once aroused cannot be quieted. The economic, military and psychological pressures previously generated permit only further expansion or conflict. The extent to which an arms race is likely to lead to war thus varies with the burdens it imposes on the peoples and the extent to which it involves them psychologically and emotionally in the race. Prolonged sufficiently, a quantitative race must necessarily reach a point where opinion in one country or the other will demand that it be ended, if not by negotiation, then by war. The logical result of a quantitative arms race is a "nation in arms," and a nation in arms for any length of time must be a nation at war.

A qualitative arms race, however, does not have this effect. In such a race the essential relationship is not between the military and the civilian, but rather between the old and the new forms of military force. In a quantitative race the principal policy issue is the extent to which resources and manpower should be diverted from civilian to military use. In a qualitative race, the principal issue is the extent to which the new weapons systems should replace the old "conventional" ones. In a quantitative race the key question is "How much?" In a qualitative race, it is "How soon?" A quantitative race requires continuous expansion of military resources, a qualitative race continuous redeployment of them. A qualitative race does not normally increase arms budgets, even when, as usually happens, the new forms of military force are more expensive than the old ones. The costs of a qualitative race only increase significantly when an effort is made to maintain both old and new forms of military force: steam and sail; ironclads and wooden walls; nuclear and nonnuclear weapons. Transitions from old to new weapons systems have not normally been accompanied by marked increases in military expenditures. . . .

Quantitative and qualitative arms races differ also in the interests they mobilize and the leadership they stimulate. In the long run, a quantitative race makes extensive demands on a broad segment of the population. A qualitative race, however, tends to be a competition of elites rather than masses. No need exists for the bulk of the population to become directly involved. In a quantitative arms race, the users of the weapons—the military leaders—assume the key role. In a qualitative race, the creators of the weapons—the scientists—rival them for preëminence. Similarly, the most important private interests in a quantitative race are the large mass production industrial corporations, while in a qualitative race they tend to be the smaller firms specializing in the innovation and development of weapons systems rather than in their mass output.

While the rising costs of a quantitative race may increase the likelihood of war, they may also enhance efforts to end the race by means of an arms agreement. Undoubtedly the most powerful motive (prior to the feasibility of utter annihilation) leading states to arms limitations has been the economic one. . . .

In summary, two general conclusions emerge as to the relations between arms races and war:

1. War is more likely to develop in the early phases of an arms race than in its later phases.

2. A quantitative race is more likely than a qualitative one to come to a definite end in war, arms agreement, or victory for one side.

ARMS RACES, DISARMAMENT, AND PEACE

In discussions of disarmament, a distinction has frequently been drawn between the presumably technical problem of arms limitation, on the one hand, and political problems, on the other. Considerable energy has been devoted to arguments as to whether it is necessary to settle political issues before disarming or whether disarmament is a prerequisite to the settlement of political issues. The distinction between arms limitation and politics, however, is a fallacious one. The achievement of an arms agreement cannot be made an end in itself. Arms limitation is the essence of politics and inseparable from other political issues. What, indeed, is more political than the relative balance of power between two distinct entities? Whether they be political parties competing for votes, lobbyists lining up legislative blocs, or states piling up armaments, the power ratio between the units is a decisive factor in their relationship. Virtually every effort (such as the Hague Conferences and the League of Nations) to reach agreement on arms apart from the resolution of other diplomatic and political issues has failed. Inevitably attempts to arrive at arms agreements have tended to broaden into discussions of all the significant political issues between the competing powers.[8] On the other hand, it cannot be assumed that arms negotiations are hopeless, and that they only add another issue to those already disrupting the relations between the two countries and stimulating passion and suspicion.[9] Just as the problem of armaments cannot be settled without reference to other political issues, so is it also impossible to resolve these issues without facing up to the relative balance of military power. . . .

While arms limitation is seldom possible except as part of a broader political settlement, it is also seldom possible if the scope of the arms limitation is itself too broad. One of the corollaries of the belief that arms races produce wars is the assumption that disarmament agreements are necessary to peace. Too frequently it has been made to appear that failure to reach a disarmament agreement

[8]See Clyde Eagleton, *Analysis of the Problem of War* (New York, 1927), pp. 19-21.
[9]For this line of argument, see Merze Tate, *The United States and Armaments* (Cambridge, 1948), p. 5.

leaves war as the only recourse between the powers. In particular, it is false and dangerous to assume that any disarmament to be effective must be total disarmament. The latter is an impossible goal. Military force is inherent in national power and national power is inherent in the existence of independent states. In one way or another all the resources of a state contribute to its military strength. . . .

The narrower the scope of a proposed arms limitation agreement, the more likely it is to be successful. Disarmament agreements seldom actually disarm states. What they do is to exclude certain specified areas from the competition and thereby direct that competition into other channels. The likelihood of reaching such an agreement is greater if the states can have a clear vision of the impact of the agreement on the balance of power. The more restricted the range of armaments covered by the agreement, the easier it is for them to foresee its likely effects. In general, also, the less important the area in the balance of power between the two states, the easier it is to secure agreement on that area. . . .

Successful disarmament agreements (and a disarmament agreement is successful if it remains in force for a half decade or more) generally establish quantitative restrictions on armaments. The quantitative ratio is the crucial one between the powers, and the quantitative element is much more subject to the control of governments than is the course of scientific development. Furthermore, a quantitative agreement tends to channel competition into qualitative areas, while an agreement on innovation tends to do just the reverse. Consequently, quantitative agreement tends to reduce the likelihood of war, qualitative agreement to enhance it. In the current arms race, for instance, some sort of quantitative agreement might be both feasible, since the race is primarily qualitative in nature, and desirable, since such an agreement would formally prohibit the more dangerous type of arms race.[10] On the other hand, a qualitative agreement between the two countries prohibiting, say, the construction and testing of intercontinental ballistic missiles, might well be disastrous if it should stimulate a quantitative race in aircraft production, the construction of bases, and the multiplication of other forms of military force. In addition, the next phase in the arms race, for instance, may well be the development of defenses against

---

[10]Cf. Tate, *United States and Armaments*, p. 19, for the opposing argument that quantitative agreements are fruitless because they do not prevent qualitative competition.

ballistic missiles. A qualitative answer to this problem, such as an effective anti-missile missile, would, in the long run, be much less expensive and much less disturbing to peace than a quantitative answer, such as a mammoth shelter construction program, which would tax public resources, infringe on many established interests, and arouse popular concern and fear. Continued technological innovation could well be essential to the avoidance of war. Peace, in short, may depend less upon the ingenuity of the rival statesmen than upon the ingenuity of the rival scientists.

The balancing of power in any bipolar situation is inherently difficult due to the absence of a ' balancer."[11] In such a situation, however, a qualitative arms race may be the most effective means of achieving and maintaining parity of power over a long period of time. The inherent tendency toward parity of such a race may to some extent provide a substitute for the missing balancer. In particular, a qualitative race tends to equalize the differences which might otherwise exist between the ability and willingness of a democracy to compete with a totalitarian dictatorship. The great problem of international politics now is to develop forms of international competition to replace the total wars of the first half of the twentieth century. One such alternative is limited war. Another is the qualitative arms race. The emerging pattern of rivalry between the West and the Soviet bloc suggests that these may well be the primary forms of military activity which the two coalitions will employ. As wars become more frightening and less frequent, arms races may become longer and less disastrous. The substitution of the one for the other is certainly no mean step forward in the restriction of violence. In this respect the arms race may serve the same function which war served: "the intensely sharp competitive *preparation* for war by the nations," could become, as William James suggested, *"the real war,* permanent, unceasing. . . ."[12] A qualitative race regularizes this preparation and introduces an element of stability into the relations between the two powers. Even if it were true, as Sir Edward Grey argued, that arms races inevitably foster suspicion and insecurity, these would be small prices to pay for the avoidance of destruction. Until fundamental changes take place in the structure of world politics, a qualitative arms race may well be a most desirable form of competition between the Soviet Union and the United States.

[11] Friedrich, *Foreign Policy in the Making,* pp. 129-130; Wright, *Study of War,* II, pp. 763-64.

[12] *Memories and Studies* (New York, 1912), p. 273.

Warfare in
the Nuclear Age
Morton H. Halperin

Changes in military technology and the subsequent impact of these changes on international politics have aroused much attention, particularly among students of international politics. This interest has produced new terminology and new concepts that help explain the role of military power in the nuclear age.

The most pervasive notion is that of "deterrence": that the primary function of military force should be to prevent the use of military force by one's opponents. The great destructive power of nuclear weapons has forced students of international politics to take more seriously the possibility of eliminating or substantially reducing the likelihood of war and, in particular, of large-scale thermonuclear war. The recognition that conflict is likely to remain a part of the international political scene, coupled with the belief that thermonuclear war would be so devastating as to be unacceptable, has led to the development of a typology of warfare and to an emphasis on the possibilities and problems of limiting war.

SOURCE: From Morton H. Halperin, *Defense Strategies for the Seventies.* Copyright © 1971 by Little, Brown and Company (Inc.). Reprinted by permission of the author and publisher.

The first attempt to categorize wars came with the distinction between "limited" wars and "total" wars. A *limited war* was viewed as a conflict that would not involve the homelands of the United States or the Soviet Union and that would be limited both in objectives and in the means used. A *total war* was a war involving attacks on the homelands of the United States and the Soviet Union. It was assumed that in such a war there would be no limit on either objectives or the means employed.

Recently analysts have felt the need to use the terms "general" and "local" to distinguish wars. A *general war* is a war involving attacks by the United States and the Soviet Union on each other's homelands. A *local war* is a war in which the United States and the Soviet Union see themselves on opposite sides but in which no attacks are made on the homelands of the two superpowers. Both a local war and a general war could be a "limited" war—limited in objectives or in the means used and targets attacked.

GENERAL WAR

Beginning about 1964, the world finally entered the missile age that had been heralded at least since 1957. By the middle of the 1960's the major strategic offensive nuclear forces of the United States and the Soviet Union were ballistic missiles. Missiles had become part of the arsenals of both countries in the late 1950's, but until the mid-1960's the airplane remained the dominant mode for delivery of nuclear weapons. The smaller payload of missiles and their potential for greater control over operations have raised the possibility of controlling a general nuclear war, should one occur. Analysis of the possibilities for limitation in general nuclear war suggests three kinds of wars involving the use of strategic attacks on the homelands of the United States and the Soviet Union.

Spasm War. Throughout the 1950's American statements and planning seemed to be based upon the assumption that a general nuclear war between the United States and the Soviet Union would be an all-out, or "spasm," war. It was believed that a general nuclear war could not be limited, and thus if a general nuclear war was started, each side would fire all its nuclear weapons at the other side as quickly as possible in a spasm reaction to the beginning of war. In such a war each side would presumably fire all its strategic forces at military and population targets in the other's homeland. In fact, the Soviet Union continues to talk publicly about general nuclear war in spasm-war terms.

Controlled Response. If one recognizes that the all-out, uncontrolled use of nuclear weapons by both superpowers would lead to substantial destruction of the population and industry of the two countries, then clearly both sides might attempt to limit a general nuclear war, should one take place. Even a large-scale nuclear war might be limited in terms of the targets attacked: each side might refrain from bombing the other's major cities and might concentrate instead on military targets. In addition, each side might not use all its strategic forces, holding some in reserve to threaten the destruction of its opponent's cities. However unlikely such restraints would be in the event of nuclear war, both the United States and the Soviet Union have taken such possibilities into account in designing their forces.

Limited Strategic Strikes. At the opposite extreme from spasm war is the proposal that strategic nuclear weapons be used in limited numbers. The possibilities of this kind of war range from the bizarre notion of one side's destroying one or several of its opponent's cities to the somewhat more likely possibility of engaging in limited strategic strikes at military or industrial targets far from the centers of population. Such strikes might be used either to influence the course of a local war that is in progress or to demonstrate a willingness to go to large-scale general nuclear war if necessary.

Motivations for War Initiation. A general nuclear war may be a *deliberate war*—that is, a war consciously and deliberately initiated by one of the two superpowers while that superpower is fully cognizant of its option to avoid such a war. Without being able to rule out entirely the possibility of a deliberate nuclear war, most analysts contend that *inadvertent war* is more likely, given the relative destruction that would occur to both countries. An inadvertent war would occur because one or both sides come to the conclusion that whatever the intentions of the two superpowers, general nuclear war has for some reason become inevitable. In this situation, the leadership that begins the war does so believing that the choice is not between general nuclear war or no general nuclear war but rather between general nuclear war that it has initiated or general nuclear war initiated by its adversary. In this situation the motive for war is simply the belief that war will occur and that it is better to strike first or at least be a close, rather than a distant, second.

Triggers of Nuclear War. The destructive power of nuclear weapons and the inability of the bureaucracy in the United States or the Soviet Union to guarantee to the top leadership that destruction would be kept to tolerable levels, even with a first strike, has minimized the probability of a deliberately initiated general nuclear war. However, there are certain situations in which one side or the other might be tempted to launch a deliberate strike.

If one of the superpowers believed it could escape substantial retaliation because of a lack of diligence on the part of its opponent in developing strategic systems capable of surviving an attack and penetrating active defenses, it might be tempted to launch a strike. However, even if calculation suggested that there would not be substantial retaliation, political leaders might find it difficult to believe the calculations. And even if they believed them, they would not necessarily decide to begin war. In the late 1940's the United States had a monopoly that would have enabled it to strike the Soviet Union with nuclear weapons without fear of retaliation. Although it is possible that, in the same position, the Soviet Union would not pass up such an opportunity, it is perhaps more likely that it would attempt to exploit the situation for political purposes rather than actually carry out a deliberate nuclear strike. Nevertheless, while analysts assert that the probability of a deliberate nuclear strike is extremely low, governments on both sides have felt obliged to spend a great deal of money and devote a lot of time to making sure that their opponent will never come to the conclusion that a successful first strike is possible.

A deliberate strike might also be carried out if the leadership in one country believed that the consequences of not starting a nuclear war were even more devastating than the outcome of a nuclear war. For example, the Soviet leaders *might* resort to all-out nuclear war if Communist control of Eastern Europe appeared to be threatened and if they believed that there was no other way of preventing the establishment of regimes friendly to the West. During the Cuban missile crisis of 1962, the United States threatened to initiate a general war if the Soviet Union or Cuba fired from Cuban territory a single missile that landed anywhere in the Western Hemisphere.

Finally, at least in principle, one cannot rule out complete irrationality—that is, a decision to launch general nuclear war for reasons unrelated to the direct consequences of the outcome of the war, perhaps involving personal, psychological impulses. The governments of both the United States and the Soviet Union have taken steps to ensure that irrational action below the top level of government could not lead to a general war. Though it is difficult to evaluate the effectiveness of these steps, they appear to be reliable and to reduce to the barest minimum the possibility of a war triggered by the irrationality of a subordinate. Irrationality of the top leadership is, of course, more difficult to prevent by formal institutional means, and it should not be forgotten that Stalin demonstrated some tendencies of a mentally unbalanced person, although probably not those that might have led him to launch a general nuclear war.

Much more likely than the triggering of a deliberate nuclear war is the triggering of an inadvertent general nuclear war. However, the two dangers interact with each other: the higher the probability of a deliberate attack, the greater the danger of an inadvertent general nuclear war. In order for an inadvertent war to take place, there must be, first, a belief in the high probability of war and, second, a perceived value of striking first if war occurs. A reduction in either of these would substantially reduce the possibility of a general nuclear war.

The perception that general nuclear war is impending depends on, in turn, a conducive setting and some triggering event. Neither the leadership of the United States nor that of the Soviet Union is likely to conclude in a period of international calm that the probability of general nuclear war is so high that it is necessary to strike first. Only during an intense political crisis, as has occurred from time to time over Berlin and over Cuba, or in a setting of local war, as in Korea and Indochina, might the superpowers be inclined to feel that a general nuclear war is imminent. The triggering event that then precipitates the general nuclear war may be one of several incidents. It may literally be an accident—that is, the detonation of a nuclear weapon or the firing of a missile because of mechanical or human failure. Another possibility—although remote—is an attempt by a country other than the United States or the Soviet Union to simulate the beginning of a nuclear war, perhaps by exploding a nuclear device. Finally, the trigger may simply come from the expansion of the local war or crisis: the war may become so intense that one side resorts to general nuclear war.

Even if the probability of general nuclear war seems high, the occurrence of an inadvertent war depends on the perception of a great value in striking first should war occur. During the early 1960's the world passed through a period in which both sides appeared to believe that in the event of nuclear war, there was a high value in striking first. This was partly because neither side had paid sufficient attention to developing forces able to survive a first strike but also because, in the period of transition from airplanes to missiles, a small number of missiles seemed capable of destroying a large number of airplanes in a surprise first strike.

During the 1960's first the United States and then the Soviet Union paid greater attention to the *vulnerability* of strategic forces to a surprise first strike. Both sides have developed relatively invulnerable forces—that is, forces difficult to destroy in a first strike and designed to ride out the first strike of the opponent. This relative invulnerability is developed in three ways: concealment, hardening, and mobility. The Soviets relied for several years on concealment of the location of their strategic forces. However, improvements in intelligence capacities, particuarly satellites, rendered this method of developing relative invulnerability comparatively ineffective. American *Minuteman* missiles and the newer Soviet ICBMs are in hardened underground sites protected by concrete silos. Mobility gives relative invulnerability to the American and Soviet missile-firing submarines, which keep in constant motion under the vast oceans. As strategic forces have become relatively invulnerable, the United States at least has come to the conclusion that if it is confronted with a Soviet first strike, it should not launch its weapons until after a significant number of Soviet missiles have landed on American territory. The United States has tried to make it clear to the Soviet Union that it has adopted this position which should substantially reduce the probability of an inadvertent general nuclear war launched by either power. By removing fear of an American inadvertent strike, the Soviet need to strike first should be diminished. The United States has also stated that its policy is not to seek the capability of destroying Soviet strategic forces.

Despite the intensive efforts of both sides to develop invulnerable forces, technology in the early 1970's created the danger that the incentive to strike first would reappear. The deployment of highly accurate MIRVs, which would enable one missile to destroy several opposing missiles on the ground, coupled with large ABM systems, could by the late 1970's generate renewed fears of preemptive attack.

LOCAL WAR

Analysts have attempted to distinguish general strategic nuclear war from local war. A local nuclear war is by definition limited in that it excludes the homelands of the two superpowers. However, a number of other limits have been observed in local wars that have taken place in the postwar period. It is important to remember that although analyses of general nuclear war must proceed simply on the basis of theoretical analysis, discussion of local non-nuclear war can draw on relevant historical examples as well as on theory.

If we look at the history of local war since World War II, we discover four limitations that have apparently been of great importance in keeping a local war from becoming a general nuclear war. The first of these involves the geography of the area in which the fighting is taking place. Not only have the homelands of the two superpowers been spared in all warfare, but so has much of the rest of the world. Each of the local wars that has taken place has been confined to a relatively small geographic area: the Taiwan Straits, Korea, Indochina, Cuba and its surrounding waters, and others.

Perhaps the most important limit that has been observed in local war in the postwar period has been the reluctance to use nuclear weapons. Neither of the two superpowers, when engaged in military action, has employed those weapons that, even at the tactical level, are judged to be most effective.

Another limitation observed in many local wars but violated or ignored by the United States in Cuba and more recently in Vietnam is the sanctity of supply lines beyond the area of battle. American action in Cuba was spectacular in that the United States sought for the first time since World War II to interfere with the movement of materiel into the area of potential conflict. Later in Vietnam the United States again ignored the "sanctuary" of North Vietnam and began to destroy supply lines moving into the area of battle and in 1970 moved against the enemy supply lines in Cambodia. However, even at the height of United States bombing raids on North Vietnam some limits were observed. The port of Haiphong was not mined and rail lines to China were not bombed.

The fourth major limitation is the level of participation of various countries in the local war. The two superpowers and China have been concerned with avoiding a direct confrontation of the troops of two of the countries. There has, of course, not been any direct confrontation of Soviet and American formal military forces. Even in Korea, where American and Chinese troops clashed, American troops were disguised as part of a United Natons command and Chinese troops as volunteers. American actions in Vietnam in the 1960's demonstrate clearly the spectrum of roles that a superpower can play in relation to a local war. The United States began the decade providing diplomatic and economic support for the government of South Vietnam. It moved from that to providing military equipment and limited amounts of training on the ground in South Vietnam through a series of other steps leading up to the use of American combat troops. In 1968 the United States began to reverse the process.

How important the territory being fought over is to the superpowers is another key factor in determining the outcome and consequences of a local war. Some territories are more important to one of the superpowers than to the other. For example the United States recognized the greater Soviet interest in Hungary and Czechoslovakia and greater Chinese interest in Tibet, while the Soviets at least in the end, recognized the greater American interest in Cuba.

Although the interests and intentions of the superpowers are likely to be important determinants of the outcome of any local conflict, of equal or perhaps greater importance will be the local situation and the local political and military balance. Some wars, of course, start and end because of local conditions, and the superpowers never become involved. Even wars that turn out to be major confrontations between the United States, China, and the Soviet Union frequently begin because of local conditions and local pressures. The various conflicts in Vietnam and Laos, for example, were the result of pressures within Vietnam—some of them emanating from Indochinese Communists, but others, such as conflicts in Laos in 1962–1963, apparently resulting from the restlessness of neutralists under the leadership of Captain Kong Le. Other local conflicts erupt from the deliberate decision of leaders in Peking or Moscow. This appears to have happened in the Korean War and in various crises in the Taiwan Straits. Finally, we cannot exclude the possibility of the launching of a local war by the United States or another Western power, as was the case in the Suez crisis of 1956 and the Bay of Pigs invasion of Cuba in 1962.

We are concerned about local wars partly because the outcomes of these wars may have important consequences for the future of international politics but also because of the possibility that a local war may turn into a general nuclear war. The word frequently used to express this danger is "escalation," which has now "escalated" into everyday vocabulary from the more technical vocabulary of the strategic analyst. Notice, however, that "escalation" is ambiguous and refers actually to two different processes that may come about as a local war grows in size. The first of these, *explosion,* involves the sudden occurrence of general nuclear war during the local war. This explosion into general nuclear war can take place at any time during a local war situation, even if the local war appears to be at a low level. However, it is more likely to occur after *expansion* (the second process implied by "escalation") of the local war—that is, the growth in size of a local war. Expansion may be deplored or applauded precisely because it increases the danger of general nuclear war: one side may want to show its determination by engaging in action that consequently increases the risk of an explosion into general war. An expansion of a local war may also be aimed at influencing the outcome of a local military battle.

· · ·

Guerrilla Warfare
in Theory
and Policy
Samuel P. Huntington

1. WARS AND WARFARE

Guerrilla warfare has assumed a new importance in American military policy. The phrases "paramilitary operations," "unconventional war," "irregular warfare," "internal war," and "guerrilla warfare" have all blossomed forth in recent discussions of strategy. No doubt each term serves some purpose, although one cannot help but feel that semantics has perhaps outstripped theory. Whether or not the resurgence of interest in guerrilla warfare has any lasting basis depends upon the roles which it may play in world politics. These can only be understood in terms of a general theory of armed conflict. A key element in such a theory is the distinction between *types of war* and *forms of warfare.*

A war is a violent interaction between two organized political groups (governments or otherwise). Types of war are types of inter-

SOURCE: From Franklin M. Osanka (ed.), *Modern Guerrilla Warfare.* Copyright © 1962 by the Free Press, a Division of The Macmillan Company. Reprinted by permission of the author and The Macmillan Company.

action. They may be defined in terms of the nature of the participants, the nature of their goals, the efforts they make to achieve those goals, and, broadly speaking, the resources they employ. Four types of war seem peculiarly relevant to world politics today.

1. *Total war* is a struggle between governments in which at least one aims at the destruction of the other and uses all the means at its disposal to achieve that aim. Under present conditions total war between major powers would involve the use of thermonuclear weapons.
2. *General war* is a struggle between governments in which at least one aims at the complete destruction of the other but does *not* use all the means at its disposal. Under present conditions general war between major powers could not involve extensive use of thermonuclear weapons. World War II was a total war; if it occurred again, it would be a general war.
3. *Limited war* is a struggle between major or minor powers in which each has a restricted goal and in which each employs only a portion of its resources, usually within a defined geographical area. The Korean War was a limited war for the United States and Communist China.
4. *Revolutionary war* is the struggle between a nongovernmental group and a government in which the latter attempts to destroy the former by some or all the means at its command, and the nongovernmental group attempts by all the means at its command to replace the government in some or all of its territory. The post-World-War-II struggles in Indochina, Malaya, and Algeria were revolutionary wars.

The boundary lines between these types of war are not necessarily precise. In theory, however, the four types are mutually exclusive. Each type encompasses the sum total of the military interactions between the participants. A form of warfare, on the other hand, is one variety of military activity involving particular military forces, weapons, and tactics. It need not encompass the complete pattern of military interaction between the opposing parties. A naval blockade, a "conventional" ground forces campaign, strategic air bombardment, are forms of warfare carried out by specialized types of military forces, but they are not types of war. They may appear in more than one type of war. The types of war thus set the contexts in which the forms of warfare are employed.

Guerrilla warfare is clearly a form of warfare and not a type of war. Its current significance derives from its relevance to all four types of war possible in world politics today. This relevance derives from its distinctive character. *Guerrilla warfare is a form of warfare by which the strategically weaker side assumes the tactical offensive in selected forms, times, and places.* Guerrilla warfare is the weapon of the weak. It is never chosen in preference to regular warfare; it is employed only when and where the possibilities of regular warfare have been foreclosed. Guerrilla warfare is decisive only where the anti-guerrilla side puts a low value on defeating the guerrillas and does not commit its full resources to the struggle. Except in these instances, guerrilla warfare is never self-sufficient. To achieve victory in most wars, guerrilla warfare must be accompanied by other forms of warfare. Guerrilla warfare is resorted to (1) after regular (i.e., stronger) forces have been defeated, (2) before they have been created, and (3) where they are unable to operate. All three possibilities of guerrilla warfare exist among the types of war that are likely today.

If the regular forces of one side have been defeated, or if they never existed in the first place, that side may turn to guerrilla warfare to continue the struggle as long as possible. Having lost the ability to conduct regular operations, this side resorts to guerrilla warfare in the hope that outside help may materialize or that prolonged resistance through this lesser form of warfare may induce the victorious side to accept more lenient peace terms. The term "guerrilla" itself was first applied to the bands of Spanish soldiers fighting the Napoleonic armies in Spain. This was a spontaneous development in the absence of any regular Spanish forces. Analogously, the Boers shifted to guerrilla warfare after the British had destroyed their ability to wage regular warfare. The British had to make a major new effort to break the back of the guerrilla resistance. As one Englishman observed at the time,

> *If there is one certain education to be drawn from past experience it is that guerrilla tactics, when carried out by a resourceful and persistent enemy, have invariably led to a protracted struggle, during which the invading armies against which they have fought have suffered a series of minor disasters and "regrettable incidents."* . . .[1]

At about the same time the United States Army was having similar difficulties in quelling the Philippine insurgents under the leadership of Aguinaldo.

[1] B. Firth, "The Guerrilla in History," *Fortnightly Review,* 70 (1901), 803.

Guerrilla warfare is possible in the later phases of a future total war. Such a war presumably would begin with an air-missile exchange of nuclear explosives. If one side emerged dominant from this exchange and the other side was unwilling to accept the peace terms proposed by the strategic victor, then the strategic victor might well attempt to occupy the enemy's country with its military forces. In such circumstances, the last resort of the defeated country would be guerrilla warfare. Such warfare might succeed in enhancing the defeated power's bargaining position, but it could never succeed in defeating the victorious power. Only outside intervention with new sources of power and regular military strength would reopen the prospects of victory for the defeated country. If such intervention is impossible, eventual suppression of the guerrillas is inevitable. George Kennan's proposals that the West should rely on "paramilitary" formations to defend Europe are, consequently, an argument for defeat.[2] If he assumes that such formations could by themselves dislodge the Russians from Western Europe, his assumption is false. If he assumes that they could not and that another massive invasion of Western Europe by the United States would be necessary, then his policy is pernicious.

Guerrilla warfare may also be undertaken by a side that is too weak at the opening of a war to engage in regular operations. Guerrilla warfare then becomes a way of harassing and wearing down the enemy while developing one's own strength. Unless the enemy has little interest in the struggle, the weaker side must eventually shift from guerrilla operations to regular warfare in order to achieve victory. If the weaker side is unable to develop regular forces and if the enemy is relentless in its pursuit of the conflict, the weaker side will be eventually overwhelmed. Guerrilla warfare plays a preliminary role in revolutionary war. It is not, however, identical or coextensive with revolutionary war. Guerrilla warfare may be employed in other types of war than revolutionary war, and a successful revolutionary war requires other types of struggle than guerrilla warfare. All of this is made very plain in the writings of the principal theorist of revolutionary war, Mao Tse-tung. The key problem in revolutionary war is to calculate the timing and the means for the shift from guerrilla warfare to regular warfare. Too early a shift invites a defeat; too late a shift postpones victory.

Guerrilla warfare may also be employed as a supplement to regular operations in areas where one side is weak and the other side is strong. In these situations the importance of guerrilla warfare to a

[2] See George F. Kennan, *Russia, the Atom, and the West* (Harper, 1957), p. 63.

side usually varies inversely with the strength of that side. In a "regular" war both sides may organize supplementary guerrilla operations to harass the enemy's rear. Usually, the stronger a side is, the less the proportion of its total effort, however, that will be allocated to guerrilla warfare. A side that is completely confident of its ability to secure victory in regulare warfare usually has little interest in or need for guerrilla warfare. A side that is dubious of its ability to secure victory through regular warfare will place a greater emphasis on guerrilla warfare. Similarly, in a regular general or limited war, guerrilla warfare will normally play a more important role in the operations of the side that suffered defeats in the early stages of the war than in the operations of the side that was initially successful. In World War II, Allied guerrillas played significant roles in Western Europe, Yugoslavia, Russia, and Burma. In the Korean War, Communist guerrillas also played an important role behind Allied lines in South Korea. In any future general or limited war, guerrilla warfare undoubtedly will be a significant supplement to regular operations.

II. GUERRILLA WARFARE AND THE GUERRE DE COURSE

The distinctive character of guerrilla warfare and of counterguerrilla warfare can be fully understood only if they are viewed in connection with their naval counterparts. Guerrilla warfare is to land war what the *guerre de course* is to sea war. Originally conceived by Fench naval officers in the eighteenth century, the idea of the *guerre de course* was further developed by the *Jeune École* of the 1880's. It was the means by which an inferior continental naval power attempted to counterbalance the naval supremacy of Great Britain. Its weapons were the frigate and privateer in the eighteenth century, the torpedo boat and cruiser in the nineteenth century, and the submarine in the twentieth century. Yet the tactics of the *guerre de course* remained essentially the same. They are also the tactics of guerrilla warfare. Each is the offensive of the weaker against the stronger. The employer of each attempts to avoid the enemy's military forces and to strike at his supply lines and communications. The motto of the *Jeune École* is also the motto of the guerrilla: "Shamelessly attack the weak, shamelessly fly from the strong."[3] Mobility, concealment, and surprise are the allies of both. Both employ the tactics of hit-and-run. The security that the guerrilla

---

[3]Quoted in Theodore Ropp, "Continental Doctrines of Sea Power," in Edward Mead Earle (ed.), *Makers of Modern Strategy* (Princeton, 1943), p. 450.

The Roles of Warfare in Wars

Forms of Warfare	Types of War			
	Revolutionary	Limited	General	Total
Guerrilla warfare	Dominant in early phase	Supplementary role	Supplementary role	Probable after nuclear exchange
"Conventional" land warfare	Dominant in later phase	Of major importance	Major role	Secondary role
Tactical nuclear warfare	No role	Possible but unlikely	Possible	Supporting role
Naval warfare	Peripheral	Minor to important role	Very important	Secondary, except for strategic bombardment
Strategic nuclear warfare	No role	No role	Possible on small scale	Decisive

finds in rugged terrain and a friendly populace the commerce raider finds in the empty reaches and lower depths of the ocean. In both, the psychological effects of the military action often outweigh the military effects. Both attempt to spread uncertainty, panic, and disorder. The successful operation of both involves small units— guerrilla bands or individual ships—loosely coordinated and directed by a superior authority. In each case these forces must put first priority on preserving their own existence. Neither can risk a dubious battle. Each puts a premium upon daring, imaginative, resourceful leadership of these small units: Paul Jones and Gunther Prien had all the essential characteristics of a successful guerrilla. Each form of warfare eschews heavy armament. Each is relatively inexpensive to engage in and very expensive to combat. To a large extent, the success of both is measured by the resources which the enemy has to divert to defend itself against them.

The requirements of effective counterguerrilla warfare closely resemble those employed to combat the *guerre de course*. The antisubmarine warfare men of the Navy and the counterguerrilla forces of the Army are confronted with similar problems. The most effective counterthrust is to destroy the base areas from which the guerrillas operate and the naval bases from which the submarines operate. A second form of counteraction is to create strong points that can defend themselves against surprise attack. In counterguerrilla warfare, this means fortifying key supply and transportation centers and the resettlement of peasants in areas where they can be protected. In antisubmarine warfare it means resort to convoys. A third tactic is to attempt to search out and destroy the elusive raiders. In counterguerrilla warfare this requires mobile columns equipped with cross-country vehicles, helicopters, and light weapons. In antisubmarine warfare, it means hunter-killer groups of fast aircraft carriers and destroyers. Finally, in each case, it is at times possible, within limits to set a thief to catch a thief. Guerrillas can assist in the detection and elimination of guerrillas; submarines can assist in the detection and elimination of submarines. In each case, intelligence plays a critical role in the successful operations. The guerrillas and the submarines must be found before they can be destroyed. Sonar and radar are to antisubmarine warfare what spies and scouts are to counterguerrilla warfare.

The strengths and limits of the *guerre de course* are the strengths and limits of guerrilla warfare. As a supplementary weapon the *guerre de course* served its progenitors well. Some members of the *Jeune École* hoped, however, that through the *guerre de course* they could achieve a cheap victory without destroying the military strength of the enemy. They deceived themselves in thinking that they could make it more than a harassing device. Mahan easily exposed the shallowness of their arguments and the futility of their dreams. In 1916 the Germans thought that the submarine had now made possible the defeat of a superior naval power dependent upon extensive overseas commerce. But again commerce raiding failed to be decisive. In World War II a much larger German effort came closer to success, in part because the British were suffering from overconfidence derived from their World War I victory.[4] Between 1939 and 1944 the U-boats effectively tied up Allied resources in the battle of the Atlantic just as Allied guerrillas pinned down a score of Axis divisions in the Balkans. The battle was hard and close, but again commerce destruction alone was unable to tip the scales. In contrast, the American submarine campaign in the Pacific did make a

---

[4] For an excellent brief summary, see Bernard Brodie, *A Guide to Naval Strategy* (Princeton, 1958; 4th ed., Naval War College Edition), pp. 136-152.

significant contribution to the defeat of Japan because it was a supplement to rather than a substitute for command of the sea. The Napoleonic Wars, the War of 1812, and two World Wars reveal the potentialities and, more especially, the limitations of the *guerre de course*.

Similarly, today, it would be a mistake to overdramatize the threat or the opportunities of guerrilla warfare. At the appropriate moment in revolutionary war, limited war, general war, and total war, the guerrilla may have a major role to play; but he cannot play it for long alone and unaided. The guerrilla can destroy but he cannot conquer. God remains on the side of the bigger battalions—and guerrilla battalions are always small. Guerrilla warfare makes the most of small battalions, but guerrilla troops are no more a substitute for superior conventional forces than the torpedo boats of the *Jeune École* were a substitute for the line of battle of the Royal Navy.

III. GUERRILLA WARFARE IN AMERICAN POLICY

The most immediate problem posed by guerrilla warfare for American policy is in connection with revolutionary war. Other types of wars are possible, but they seem less likely to occur than revolutionary wars.[5] Khrushchev himself has rejected total war and limited war but has endorsed "wars of national liberation." All revolutionary wars move through a guerrilla phase. Timely and appropriate counteraction may prevent them from moving out of that phase. Communist guerrillas in Malaya, Greece, and the Philippines were effectively squelched. The strategy of both the revolutionary and the counterrevolutionary forces in a revolutionary war, however, involves far more than guerrilla warfare. A doctrine of counterguerrilla warfare is a necessary but not a sufficient doctrine in the struggle against revolutionary forces. Doctrines of guerrilla warfare and counterguerrilla warfare, moreover, may be derived from the experiences of World War II and other wars where guerrilla warfare played a supplementary role. In revolutionary war, the tactics of guerrilla warfare remain the same, but its strategic role and implications differ. Revolutionary war is a distinctive type of war, as different from the traditional interstate limited war as the Korean War was from World War II. To win a revolutionary war, it is necessary to carry on a prolonged campaign for the support of a

[5]See my *Instability at the Non-Strategic Level of Conflict* (Institute for Defense Analyses, Study Memorandum Number 2, October 6, 1961), pp. 10-16.

crucial social group.[6] Guerrilla warfare and counterguerrilla warfare must be directed to this goal. Thus, the immediate problem of the United States is to develop a doctrine of counterguerrilla warfare as one element in a broader politico-military strategy of counter-revolutionary war.

What role does guerrilla warfare itself have in American strategy? At the moment undoubtedly its place is a minor one.[7] At some time in the future, however, guerrilla warfare could become an important instrument of American policy. For this to happen will require major innovations in American strategic doctrine. Guerrilla warfare has not been an American *forte*. Guerrillas played a significant role in our eighteenth-century revolutionary war, when we were the underdog and the intervention of an outside power was necessary to secure victory. They also played a somewhat less important role on the southern side in the Civil War. In most of its wars, however, the United States has not had to rely upon guerrilla warfare. American experience with guerrilla warfare has been limited by the strength of American arms. The United States has been able to mobilize over-whelming economic and military power and to bring it to bear directly on the enemy, attacking him not where he was weakest but where he was strongest, because we were stronger still. American military doctrine has reflected this experience. It has followed the pattern of what Churchill called "the American clearcut, logical, large-scale, mass-production style of thought." British strategy, on the other hand, has traditionally followed an intermediate path. Less liberally endowed with resources and manpower, the British have relied upon what Sir Julian Corbett called a "maritime strategy" and Liddell Hart "the strategy of the indirect approach." This is one step away from the American theory of the steamroller offensive toward a strategy of the weaker.

In the future the United States may find itself forced to act in areas and in ways in which it can no longer bring to bear over-whelming military force. It may find itself forced to lead from weakness rather than from strength, its military power caught in the twin fetters of political exigency and mutual deterrence. In such situations the United States could have occasion to resort to guerrilla warfare, the classic strategy of the weaker. This is not, perhaps, a happy prospect, but it may well be one of the many adaptations that Americans will have to make in their struggle for survival in a world that they can neither escape nor dominate.

[6]See my "Patterns of Violence in World Politics," in *Changing Patterns of Military Politics* (Free Press, 1962), pp. 17-50.

[7]See Peter Paret and John Shy, *Guerrillas in the 1960s* (Praeger, 1961), chap. V.

chapter ten
ECONOMIC PROCESSES

Foreign Aid, Intervention and Influence

David A. Baldwin

Foreign aid can be "related" to intervention in many ways. Some argue, with Senator J. W. Fulbright, that aid tends to precede intervention and to increase the probability of intervention.[1] Others would say that aid follows intervention, contending, for example, that American aid to Vietnam was evidence of a prior diplomatic commitment. Still others see aid as an alternative to intervention—if we give aid now we are less likely to have to intervene in the future.

SOURCE: From *World Politics*, Vol XXI, No. 3 (1969). Copyright © 1969 by Princeton University Press. Reprinted by permission of the author and Princeton University Press.

*This is a revised version of a paper delivered at the Conference on Intervention and the Developing States sponsored by the Princeton International Law Society, November 10-11, 1967. The author has benefited from comments on earlier drafts by Howard Bliss, Charles Frank, Christian Potholm, Laurence Radway, Richard Sterling, and W. Howard Wriggins.

[1] J. William Fulbright, *The Arrogance of Power* (New York 1967), 232-37.

Another group would contend that the aid-giving process may *constitute* intervention.[2] It is with the views of this last group that most of this article deals. In examining them, we shall focus on three topics: (1) the links between foreign aid and influence; (2) the links between particular types of aid and what is often called intervention; and (3) the possibility of functional equivalents for aid that do not involve intervention. There are some conceptual problems, however, that we must address first.

I. THE CONCEPT OF "INTERVENTION"

Conceptual difficulties abound in thinking about the relationship of aid to intervention.[3] Although much has been written about intervention and "dollar diplomacy," most of these writings have employed a traditional concept of intervention that is too limited for use today. This traditional concept shares legalistic and military connotations with many other terms in the standard vocabulary of the student of international politics. The old definitions of intervention in terms of illegal military infringement of national sovereignty are simply inadequate at a time when non-military techniques of statecraft are becoming increasingly important. Spokesmen for the developing states have found it frustrating to try to describe twentieth-century phenomena with a nineteenth-century vocabulary. They have resorted to such terms as "neo-colonialism," "economic imperialism," and the like, in an attempt to overcome some of these semantic obstacles.

How, then, should we proceed in a discussion of foreign aid and intervention? One way is to equate "intervention" with "influence."[4] This would have three advantages. First, almost everyone's definition of intervention would be included, since there is widespread agreement that intervention is a type of influence.

[2] James N. Rosenau, "Pre-Theories and Theories of Foreign Policy," R. Barry Farrell, ed., *Approaches to Comparative and International Politics* (Evanston 1966), 27-92. See also Andrew M. Scott, *The Functioning of the International Political System* (New York 1967).

[3] A thoughtful series of essays on the concept of intervention is found in the *Journal of International Affairs*, XXII, No. 2 (1968).

[4] "Influence" is defined by Robert Dahl as "the ability of A to get B to do something he would not otherwise do." For elaboration on the use of this definition, see Robert A. Dahl, *Modern Political Analysis* (Englewood Cliffs 1963), 39-54.

Second, normative arguments that are unlikely to lead to agreement would be avoided. The breakdown in the consensus regarding what kinds of influence are legitimate and what kinds illegitimate often mires discussions of intervention in fruitless arguments over values. A third advantage of equating "intervention" with "influence" is that it helps us understand what the developing states are really complaining about. Reasonable and responsible leaders from developing nations have applied the label of "intervention" to almost every conceivable form of influence during the last twenty years. Only a very broad definition of intervention will allow us to discuss the matter in a way that is relevant to the concerns of these nations.

II. FOREIGN AID AND INFLUENCE

Although few would deny the connection between aid and influence, there is very little agreement on the precise nature of this connection or on analytical methods to be used in studying the problem. Some general questions about the aid-influence relationship need to be asked: What does it mean to say that aid is "political"? How can donors "control" their aid? Must aid be given in order to constitute intervention? Who wants this kind of intervention? Does the sword of intervention through aid cut two ways?

Political Aid

Since the proposition that foreign aid is "political" is not self-explanatory, we would expect those who state it to explain it. Unfortunately, they rarely do. Lucian Pye, for example, alleges that Americans wrongly view their aid program as "inherently 'non-political.' "[5] He neglects to tell us precisely what this means, however.[6] Perhaps the most common meaning given to the proposition is that aid donors are motivated by self-interest, which in turn is usually equated with a desire to acquire power. Defining political aid in terms of motivation, however, can lead us to overlook important dimensions of the problem of intervention through aid. Must intervention be motivated by a desire to intervene or by other ulterior motives? The elephant who dances among the chickens may be

[5] Lucian W. Pye, "Soviet and American Styles in Foreign Aid," *Orbis*, IV (Summer 1960), 168.
[6] For similar examples, see David A. Baldwin, "Analytical Notes on Foreign Aid and Politics," *Background*, X (May 1966), 66-90.

accused of intervention regardless of his intentions. Likewise, many of the complaints of the developing states concern the effects of big powers' actions rather than the motivation for such actions. In the eyes of many developing states, the big powers intervene in their affairs simply by existing.[7]

Many of those who believe that foreign aid is political have in mind consequences rather than motivations of the donors' actions. Given the importance of wealth as a power base, it would be difficult to imagine a foreign aid transaction that did not change the distribution of influence both within and among nations with respect to several issues.

In addition to those who would focus on the motivation or consequences of foreign aid are those who define its political nature in terms of the process by which it is given. Political processes, according to Quincy Wright, involve groups of people seeking to advance their purposes against the opposition of other groups.[8] The foreign-aid transaction process clearly qualifies as "political" in this sense. Within any aid-giving nation there are groups who disagree as to the priority that should be given to foreign aid relative to alternative ways of using the resources, and who attempt to get their views accepted as government policy. Although we may not be able to name him, we may reasonably assume that Otto Passman has a Russian counterpart. More directly relevant to foreign intervention is the existence of conflicts between aid-donors and recipients. Such conflicts may concern amounts, repayment terms, fiscal policy, land reform, or myriad other issues.

Foreign aid may constitute intervention in terms of motivation, consequences, process, or all three simultaneously. Fruitful discussion of foreign aid and influence, however, requires us to differentiate among these three plausible meanings of the statement that "aid is political."

Controlling Aid

If we are to recognize effective intervention, it helps to have some idea of how donors can control the impact of their aid. As an example of a "penetrated political system" Rosenau has suggested "the operation of any foreign aid program in which the aiding

[7] On this point, see Scott, 23, and Herman Kahn and Anthony J. Wiener, *The Year 2000* (New York 1967), 365.

[8] Quincy Wright, *The Study of International Relations* (New York 1955), 130-32.

society maintains some control over the purposes and distribution of the aid in the recipient society."[9] A clear understanding of what constitutes "control" of aid is required before we can identify such a situation in the real world.

Three methods are frequently suggested as "controls" for foreign aid—auditing the books, setting up formal coordinating machinery, and furnishing aid in the form of commodities. None suffices as evidence that control is actually being exercised by the donor. Measuring effective control requires an estimate of the extent[10] to which things are different in the recipient society from what they would have been in the absence of aid. The world's most efficient auditors can go over the books of the donor nation and learn nothing about the actual impact of the donor's aid. Earmarking aid shipments for bookkeeping purposes and controlling the impact of aid are two different operations.

Likewise, elaborate, fully-staffed aid missions in the recipient nation may not exercise control. If they participate in the making of decisions that would have been made even without their participation, they are not controlling much of anything. On the other hand, to the extent that they participate in decisions that would not have been made in their absence, they are exercising some control.[11]

Similarly, providing aid in the form of particular goods fails to ensure that the donor controls the impact of his aid. Food aid does not necessarily feed people; nor does aid in the form of tanks necessarily bolster military forces. If the recipient of tanks reduces its own military budget by an offsetting amount and spends the saved money on housing, the effect of the tanks has been to build houses.

The point is that some alleged "controls" on distribution of aid may not be intervention at all. Some strings constitute intervention; others do not. A string that asks the recipient to do what it would have done anyway can hardly be considered intervention. On the other hand, control may be taking place without many outward

[9] Rosenau, 66. Rosenau defines a "penetrated political system" as one "in which nonmembers of a national society participate directly and authoritatively, through actions taken jointly with the society's members, in either the allocation of its values or the mobilization of support on behalf of its goals." 65.

[10] The word "extent" is somewhat misleading. We might be interested in at least three important dimensions of control: (1) scope, (2) weight, and (3) domain. Cf. Harold Lasswell and Abraham Kaplan, *Power and Society* (New Haven 1950).

[11] Cf. Dahl, 53.

appearances. If the donor can accurately estimate how the potential recipient would allocate its resources[12] in the absence of aid, he is then in a position to exercise tight control over the use of his aid-funds without many of the formal trappings of control. In short, intervention may be real but not apparent, or apparent but not real.

"Non-Aid" as Influence

There is more to the aid-influence relationship than controlling the use of aid actually given. At least as important, in both theory and practice, is knowing how and when *not* to give aid. This is not just a matter of playing with words. Although much has been written about how to give aid, very little has been written about how not to give it. There are several possible ways to say "no"—as every woman and every political candidate knows—and there are several possible ways not to give aid. Some of the more common ways to say "no" to a request for foreign aid include: (1) "My government would like to help you, but we have no (time, money, etc.)." (2) Ignore the request or pigeonhole it. (3) Interpret the request to mean what the party saying "no" wants the request to mean. (4) "My government will study your request and let you know." (5) "Not at this time—come back next (month, year, decade, century, etc.)." (6) Say "no" in advance by establishing well-publicized policies. (7) "How dare you make such an outrageous request! Such behavior raises questions about your good sense and may affect my evaluation of your future requests." (8) No. (9) *No.* (10) NO! Although each method says "no," political influence is likely to vary from one method to another. How one says "no" does matter.

Suppose the United States wants to encourage developing states to be more hospitable to private foreign investors. Suppose, also, that American policy-makers believe that the attitudes of governments in developing states toward private foreign investors depend in part on their expectations regarding alternative sources of funds. In such a situation, the United States might adopt a tactic that game-theorists call the "commitment." "In bargaining, the commitment is a device to leave the last clear chance to decide the outcome with the other party, in a manner that he fully appreciates; it is to relinquish further initiative, having rigged the incentives so that the other party must choose in one's favor."[13] Thus, the United States government may try to commit itself not to provide an alternative source of funds for

---

[12]These "resources" can be political as well as economic.

[13]Thomas C. Schelling, *The Strategy of Conflict* (Cambridge, Mass. 1960), 37.

developing states, in a way that they fully appreciate, in order to leave the developing states with the last clear chance to avert disaster. The United States would thus be using "non-aid" to get developing states to do something they would not otherwise do—i.e., be nicer to private foreign investors.

It is one thing to cite a hypothetical example; it is another to show counterparts in the real world. Has non-aid ever been seriously proposed as a technique for influencing the developing states? Yes, responsible members of the governmental, business, and academic communities have all argued for non-aid as a technique for influencing these states. During the preliminary planning for the Bretton Woods institutions, Secretary of the Treasury Morgenthau expressed the hope that the International Bank would *"scrupulously* avoid undertaking loans that private investors are willing to make on reasonable terms."[14] Now, there is a great difference between not making loans for which private capital is available and "scrupulously avoiding" such loans. The difference, in terms of bargaining theory, is that between neglect and blackmail. Similarly, the "General Policy Statement of the Export-Import Bank of Washington" in 1945 included a special section devoted to outlining what the Bank would *not* do.[15] The Randall Commission Report in 1954 exhorted the government to make it "abundantly clear to prospective borrowers"[16] that American public lending would not be a substitute for private investment. Such abundant clarity was supposed to remove the uncertainty about American aid policies that the Commission believed affected "the willingness of foreign countries to accept private capital from abroad."[17] Using similar logic, the Clay Report in 1963 advocated "judicious withholding of funds" in order to encourage "internal reform" in developing nations.[18]

The American business community has also advocated non-aid. Perhaps the clearest statement of this position was made in 1951 by the National Foreign Trade Convention. In bargaining terminology the following excerpt is clearly a call for the American government to

[14]*New York Times*, November 24, 1943, 9. Italics added.

[15]*Department of State Bulletin*, September 23, 1945, 443.

[16]Commission on Foreign Economic Policy, *Report to the President and the Congress* (Washington 1954), 23.

[17]*Ibid.*, 18.

[18]Committee to Strengthen the Security of the Free World, *The Scope and Distribution of United States Military and Economic Assistance Programs* (Washington 1963), 13. (Hereafter cited as the "Clay Report.")

364 The International Political System

try to influence foreign governments by increasing the credibility of the promise not to provide aid to foreign governments:

> *It cannot be expected that economic environments conducive to the investment of American private capital will be established in these foreign lands so long as the governments concerned have reason to believe—as they do have reason to believe—that they will continue to be the beneficiaries of the hand-outs our own Government has given them for so long. They have every right to assume, on the evidence afforded, that this profligate practice will continue to be the order of the day. It is clear why this is so: our own Government, conscious of the fact that economic development abroad is highly desirable, has proceeded on the unfortunate assumption that private enterprise is unwilling or unable to undertake the task, and that, in consequence, the free provision of Government funds for the purposes in view is the only course open. This attitude has been seized upon by foreign governments as justification for their refusal to do the things they would otherwise find it necessary to do in order to attract the private capital they need. The dilemma is one which cannot be resolved until our Government brings itself to announce, as a fundamental element of our foreign economic policy, that we look upon industrial development abroad as the particular function of private enterprise, and that, until the receptive and cooperative attitudes called for are shown, no United States Government funds will be made available for any purpose except those of the most exigent military or humanitarian nature.*[19]

Similar logic appears in a thorough and clearly reasoned study prepared by academics and presented to Congress in 1957, entitled "American Private Enterprise, Foreign Economic Development, and the Aid Program."[20]

Although strategic use of non-aid has been an important means of influencing developing states, its significance is rarely recognized. Even foreign-aid experts can look directly at this phenomenon and

[19]*Report of the Thirty-Eighth National Foreign Trade Convention* (New York 1952), XXXII.

[20]American Enterprise Association, "American Private Enterprise, Foreign Economic Development, and the Aid Program," *Foreign Aid Program: Compilation of Studies and Surveys*, 85th Cong., 1st sess., S. Doc. 52 (Washington 1957), 539-618, esp. 548, 558-59.

fail to understand it. Witness the following statement by a veteran aid administrator:

> *During the 1950's, U.S. aid policy was dominated by the curious notion that aid should be denied countries that are potentially attractive to U.S. investors. Latin America was considered capable of attracting all the foreign capital it needed from private sources; aid was considered to be a palliative that discouraged countries from creating appropriate conditions to attract foreign investors.*[21]

Why should this be regarded as a "curious" situation? It is precisely the kind of behavior we should expect from a nation for which avoidance of competition with private capital is one of the basic guiding principles of its aid program. After we grow accustomed to thinking of non-aid as a technique of statecraft, there is nothing at all puzzling about the situation described. It was clearly United States policy to withhold aid from certain countries in order to force (encourage?) them to rely on foreign private investment. The same author notes that since the ten states that harbor two-thirds of all U.S. private investment in developing areas have received less than 7 percent of U.S. postwar economic aid, the United States cannot be accused of allocating its aid funds so as to further the interests of its private investors.[22] Precisely the opposite conclusion can and should be drawn. For twenty years American private investors have been exhorting the government to withhold aid funds from areas where they might compete with private capital. Official policy statements have repeatedly committed the government to comply with this exhortation. The empirical evidence is consistent with an American aid policy designed to help private investors, that is, designed to use non-aid to influence foreign investment climates. If we are to understand the relationship between foreign aid and intervention in developing states, we cannot afford to overlook the significance of non-aid.

Desired Intervention?

Analysis of aid and intervention is further complicated by the difficulty of determining whether intervention is being resisted. Nations are not the monolithic corporate entities that we often imply they are. Within the government of an aid-recipient there are

[21] Jacob J. Kaplan, *The Challenge of Foreign Aid* (New York 1967), 179.
[22] *Ibid.*, 179-85.

usually many groups with a variety of opposing views on policy matters. "To 'intervene,' " says Schelling, "is usually to encourage or support one part of the government rather than another, or one political force rather than another."[23]

Sometimes the intervention might be on behalf of the government vis-à-vis domestic political pressures. For example, the government might want to adopt measures to control inflation but might fear that it would thereby lose domestic popularity. Intervention by an aid donor on behalf of an anti-inflationary policy would strengthen the hand of the government by giving it a scapegoat on which to blame the unpopular measures. It is rumored that the International Monetary Fund has played the role of scapegoat on several occasions. The point here is that the desires of the donor and the recipient government may actually coincide even though they appear to conflict. Politics defined as group conflict may be more apparent than real.

Two-Way Intervention

Karl Deutsch has pointed out that a nation can increase its autonomy in two ways. Either it can break its linkages with the outside world or it can reverse the flow of influence while maintaining the links.[24] This second possibility is rarely acknowledged in discussions of foreign aid. Although intervention of the donor in the recipient's affairs comes up often, we almost never find references to the converse situation. Even though they may not use the vocabulary of intervention, many American Negro leaders have made it quite clear that they think the plight of their people has been worsened by the activities of Marshal Ky and his countrymen.

This is not to say that Vietnam exercises more influence vis-à-vis the United States than the United States does vis-à-vis Vietnam. It is to say that Vietnam now has more influence on American affairs than it would have had if the United States were not injecting massive aid into Vietnam. We live, as one study put it, in "the era of reciprocal involvement."[25]

---

[23]Thomas C. Schelling, "American Foreign Assistance," *World Politics*, VII (July 1955), 623. On this point, see also George Liska, *The New Statecraft* (Chicago 1960), 126-83.

[24]Karl W. Deutsch, "External Influences on the Internal Behavior of States," *Approaches to Comparative and International Politics*, 10-12.

[25]Maxwell Graduate School of Citizenship and Public Affairs, *The Operational Aspects of United States Foreign Policy*, Senate Committee on Foreign Relations, Committee Print, 86th Cong., 1st sess. (Washington 1959), 17.

III. TYPES OF AID AND INTERVENTION

It is often suggested that particular types of foreign aid involve more intervention in the recipient's affairs than do other types. Let us examine four types that are frequently mentioned in this context: (1) loans as opposed to grant aid; (2) economic as opposed to military aid; (3) multilateral as opposed to bilateral aid; and (4) private as opposed to public capital.

Grants vs. Loans

During the 1950's a frequently suggested means for eliminating intervention by aid donors in recipients' affairs was a shift from grants to loans. Loans were often described as a more "businesslike" way to provide aid. Loans allocated on the basis of "strictly economic" considerations were alleged to be politically sterile. Such a contention, however, cannot withstand even cursory analysis. In the first place, it is impossible to judge the credit-worthiness of a nation without reference to broad considerations of fiscal and monetary policy, the probability of internal civil disorders, and the overall role of the government in the economy. "In a world where governments can expropriate property, manipulate exchange rates, and control the currency supply, it is nonsense to speak of evaluating the economic soundness of a project without reference to governmental behavior."[26] Raymond Mikesell has described "political factors" as "the most fundamental consideration in the determination of credit worthiness."[27]

The implication of the necessity for taking political factors into account in evaluating loan applications is that potential borrowers may have to take politically significant steps in order to qualify as credit-worthy. Controlling inflation, for example, is not a purely economic matter. Basic changes in the institutional structure of the society are involved. Joseph Schumpeter has described inflation as "one of the most powerful factors that make for acceleration of social change."[28] In spite of this, neither the International Monetary Fund nor the World Bank has hesitated to advise developing states to

[26]David A. Baldwin, "The International Bank in Political Perspective," *World Politics*, XVIII (October 1965), 69.
[27]Raymond F. Mikesell, "Problems and Policies in Public Lending for Economic Development," Raymond F. Mikesell, ed., *U.S. Private and Government Investment Abroad* (Eugene, Ore. 1962), 325.
[28]Joseph A. Schumpeter, *Capitalism, Socialism, and Democracy* (3rd ed., New York 1950), 421.

control inflation in order to qualify for loans on the basis of purely "economic considerations."

In addition to the argument that loans can be allocated by strictly economic criteria is the contention that loans provide "no excuse" for donors to interfere in the affairs of the recipient states. "So long as the payments of interest and repayments of principal are made in full on the due dates, as stipulated in the terms of the loan, the details of how it is spent are no concern of the creditor. The independence of the borrowing country remains inviolate."[29] This does not apply to grants, argues Frederic Benham. "A country which makes grants is entitled to make sure that they fulfill their purpose and are not frittered away in corruption and waste."[30]

Do loans provide no excuse for intervention by the lenders? The bank that lent me money to buy a car seems to think that it has a right to tell me how much insurance I should carry on that car. Likewise, foreign-aid lenders have often cited an outstanding debt as reason enough for them to take an extraordinary interest in the domestic affairs of a debtor. The World Bank maintains a "close relationship with its borrowers throughout the life of each loan" and claims the right to give "continuing attention throughout the life of each loan to the general economic and financial conditions in the borrowing country" in order to "ensure that the maintenance of service on Bank loans is not jeopardized by the emergence of conditions which might be prevented."[31]

It would seem that we could make a fairly good case for the proposition that loans provide more opportunity for intervention than do grants. A grant transaction is unlikely to extend over a time-span as long as a typical foreign aid loan-agreement—ten to fifty years. Thus, the apparatus for administering the repayment of the loan may provide a conduit for influence over a considerable period of time. A loan-agreement is not just an excuse for interesting oneself in another's affairs; it is an eminently respectable excuse. Also, a one-time grantor is in a very weak position to intervene. Although he may be "entitled" to make sure that his grant is not wasted, the recipient has no incentive to allow such intervention. It is the expectation of the next grant that provides this incentive. Similarly, the

---

[29] Frederic Benham, *Economic Aid to Underdeveloped Countries* (London 1961), 104.

[30] *Ibid.*

[31] International Bank for Reconstruction and Development, *Policies and Operations of the World Bank, IFC, and IDA* (Washington 1962), 42.

hope of getting future loans acts as an incentive for a borrower to let his creditors examine his books.

During the early 1950's there was one aspect of American grant-aid that strengthened the argument for loans as a means of reducing intervention. It was customary for the United States to require a recipient of grant-aid to place an "equivalent" amount of its own currency in a "counterpart fund." This fund was owned by the recipient government but could be used only by joint agreement between the governments. "The exercise of American influence over the use of counterpart funds inevitably raised the question of interference with the internal affairs of countries in receipt of assistance."[32] Counterpart funds and grant aid were gradually replaced by soft loans repayable in inconvertible local currency during the later 1950's.[33] This resulted in a rapid build-up of enormous amounts of American-owned foreign currencies and even greater fears about intervention than had been generated by the counterpart funds.[34] Once again the advantages of loans over grants proved to be illusory.

The most obvious weakness in the argument that loans do not involve intervention is that loans are not just an "excuse" for intervention; they are a *means* of intervention and have been advocated as such. One writer speaks of the desire to place aid on a loan basis "for the benefit of superior discipline";[35] another refers to "our efforts to employ loan assistance as a means of influencing or compelling economic reforms in developing countries."[36] Perhaps the single most frequently heard argument in favor of placing the American aid program on a loan basis was that of the desirability of ensuring that the funds would be used economically.[37] Other control devices

[32] William Adams Brown and Redvers Opie, *American Foreign Assistance* (Washington 1953), 188.

[33] The evolution of this process is traced in David A. Baldwin, *Economic Development and American Foreign Policy: 1943-1962* (Chicago 1966).

[34] On this point, see Consultants on International Finance and Economic Problems, *The Problem of Excess Accumulation of U.S.-Owned Local Currencies: Findings and Recommendations Submitted to the Under Secretary of State*, April 4, 1960.

[35] Thomas C. Schelling, "American Aid and Economic Development: Some Critical Issues," *International Stability and Progress* (New York 1957), 157.

[36] Raymond F. Mikesell, "Capacity to Service Foreign Investment," *U.S. Private and Government Investment Abroad*, 406.

[37] It should be noted that the repayment requirement provides an incentive to allocate aid resources to *financially* remunerative projects, not necessarily to *socially* remunerative ones, such as feeding babies.

would be unnecessary because the necessity of repayment would provide the discipline needed to prevent waste.

One final aspect of the loan-grant debate deserves attention. If loans do not involve less intervention than do grants, how do we explain the expressed preference for loans by several developing states during the 1950's? There are at least two plausible explanations that do not depend on an expected reduction of intervention. The first is that governments in developing states might not want to appear in the eyes of their domestic public as dependent on foreign charity. It might be good domestic politics to refuse grants— regardless of the real merits of grants as opposed to loans. A second explanation is in terms of Friedrich's "rule of anticipated reactions."[38] The growing preference of the American Congress for loans as opposed to grants during the 1950's was no secret. Yet, writers on foreign aid rarely consider the possibility that potential recipients decided to ask for loans not because they preferred them but simply because they thought they were more likely to get them.[39]

In sum, loan aid appears to offer at least as much opportunity for the donor to intervene in the recipient's affairs as does grant aid.

Economic vs. Military Aid

Those who want to limit intervention through aid often point to military aid as an especially odious type. Economic aid, on the other hand, is supposed to involve less intervention. The weakness in this line of reasoning stems from a failure to distinguish between the commodities actually financed by the aid and those to which the aid is tied in a bookkeeping sense. As we noted earlier, aid in the form of tanks does not necessarily add to military strength; it may, in fact, buy milk for babies. If the recipient nation had intended to allocate one million dollars of its own funds for tanks in the absence of aid, and if it then received the equivalent of one million dollars worth of tanks as aid, it would be free to take the one million dollars that it had intended to spend on tanks and spend it some other way. If it used the money for a school lunch program, the "military aid" would actually have financed a school lunch program. We can tell little or nothing about the net impact of aid by looking at its

[38]Carl J. Friedrich, *Constitutional Government and Democracy* (Boston 1941), 589-91.

[39]For some evidence that this was indeed the case, see Baldwin, *Economic Development and American Foreign Policy.*

commodity content as described by the bookkeepers. Instead, we must estimate how the recipient would have allocated its resources in the absence of aid and then compare this with the actual allocation after aid has been given. Only thus can we tell whether the military sector of the economy is really being strengthened by what is often called "military aid."[40]

Measuring allocation of economic resources, however, is not the only way to measure influence. It may be that there are side effects of a military aid program that could be considered intervention. The administration of the program by military men may increase their ability to influence people in the recipient nation. In addition, a donor who gives aid labeled "military" may be perceived as giving a stamp of approval to the military establishment in the recipient nation, thereby bolstering its prestige. It is easy to see how reasonable men could describe either of these side effects as intervention.

One particular type of economic aid is often alleged to be especially free from overtones of intervention—technical assistance. To suggest that technical assistance may involve as much intervention as do other types of aid is to tread on what many consider to be sacred nonpolitical ground. Without repeating the previous discussion of military aid, it should be obvious that technical assistance is merely another way of labeling the commodity-content of aid; and it is no more indicative of the actual impact of the aid than is the label of military aid.

The technical-assistance label is a very useful public-relations device. A primary source of political opposition to foreign aid had always been the business community, who had traditionally feared and resisted government intervention in the economy. Use of the technical-assistance label was supposed to reassure private foreign investors that the government did not intend to compete with them. In fact, technical assistance did compete with private investment in at least two ways. First, the services provided under technical-assistance programs could and would have been provided by private firms if the price had been high enough. Second, indirect competition was given to potential direct investors. For example, surveys of investment opportunities might provide the government with enough information to enable it to establish a public enterprise instead of relying on private enterprise. The point is that investigating

[40]On this point, see Charles Wolf, Jr., *Foreign Aid: Theory and Practice in Southern Asia* (Princeton 1960), 159-62, 187-89, 258, 417-19.

investment opportunities has always been one of the services offered
at a price by potential direct investors, even though we are un-
accustomed to describing their activities this way. Describing this aid
as "technical" was a way of making it sound as if it were something
other than "capital" assistance. The United Nations Special Fund's
"pre-investment surveys" are merely an extreme form of the attempt
to make technical aid sound noncontroversial. Using technical
language to divert attention from controversial issues is an old
political tactic, one that has worked well in the case of technical
assistance.[41] The technical-assistance label implied a qualitative
difference between this type of aid and other types. It implied that
technical assistance involved services that the private investment
community would be unwilling to provide *at any price*. It also
benefited from the vague widespread feeling that the technical and
the political are two mutually exclusive realms. Those who would
understand the relationship between aid and influence, however,
should not overlook technical assistance.

Multilateral vs. Bilateral Aid

Perhaps the most frequently heard proposal for political sterili-
zation of aid giving is to multilateralize it.[42] In this context it has
been argued that multilateral aid is (1) non-political, (2) stringless,
(3) more acceptable to recipients, and (4) insulated from the foreign
policies of donor nations. These arguments will be examined in turn.

Is multilateral aid political in any of the three ways referred to
earlier? It is difficult to see how the process of distributing multilateral aid could be anything but political in the sense of involving
group conflict. Even if various nations could be effectively coordinated from the lending side, it is inconceivable that recipients
and donors would agree on the amount of aid needed by the
recipient. Given the limited amounts of aid likely to be channeled
through international agencies and given the almost limitless needs of
the poor nations, conflict seems inevitable. Some sort of impact on
the distribution of political influence within and among nations also

[41]Cf. Scott, 210, and James Patrick Sewell, *Functionalism and World Politics*
(Princeton 1966), 43-44.

[42]For a useful review of the arguments for multilateral aid, not all of which
concern intervention, see Robert E. Asher, "Multilateral Versus Bilateral Aid:
An Old Controversy Revisited," *International Organization*, XVI (Autumn
1962), 697-719. On international organizations and non-intervention see Scott,
208-11.

seems to be a necessary concomitant of multilateral aid. Thus, international aid would be political in this sense also. Whether multilateral aid would be politically motivated is more difficult to determine. Although it is doubtful that a desire for power as an end in itself would be an important motivating factor, it is highly probable that some attempt would be made to get recipients to do things that they would not otherwise do. The experience of the World Bank provides many examples of just such behavior.[43]

It is sometimes argued that multilateral aid does not carry with it the strings associated with bilateral assistance. The lending pattern of the Inter-American Development Bank gives some credence to this argument. Its funds are apparently earmarked in advance for allocation to specific countries, thus eliminating competition for funds and making it fruitless for the Bank to attach many strings. It does not follow, however, that multilateral aid necessarily involves fewer strings. It is interesting to note that some advocates of multilateral aid see it as a way of increasing the effectiveness of intervention in recipient nations. One proponent of multilateral aid, for example, sees the relevant question as "to what extent and in what ways the United Nations may provide a better channel for such intervention than bilateral programs of economic assistance."[44] International agencies, so the argument goes, are less likely to be accused of intervention and are thus freer to intervene. Multilateral aid, then, has been proposed as a means of both impeding and facilitating intervention. Channeling aid through international agencies does not guarantee fewer or weaker strings; in fact, aid through the World Bank complex is likely to involve a limited number of very strong strings—perhaps even ropes.[45] Those who want stringless aid should be wary of proposals for channeling more aid through the IBRD and its affiliates.

The argument for multilateral aid is often bolstered by the statement that such aid, with or without strings, is more acceptable

[43] See Baldwin, "The International Bank," 68-81.

[44] Benjamin Higgins, *United Nations and U.S. Foreign Economic Policy* (Homewood, Ill. 1962), II. For similar statements advocating multilateral aid as a means of facilitating intervention, see the following: Kaplan, 350; Advisory Committee on Private Enterprise in Foreign Aid, *Foreign Aid Through Private Initiative* (Washington 1965), 12; Clay Report, 15-16; Henry Cabot Lodge, "Mutual Aid Through the United Nations," *Department of State Bulletin*, April 4, 1960, 525.

[45] For a description of the strings used by the World Bank, see Baldwin, "The International Bank," 75-79.

to developing states.[46] There is some evidence, however, that this may not be true. John Lewis has described a pronounced shift from bilateral to multilateral operations as "one of the last things the government of India wants."[47] He notes that the existence of several bilateral aid channels permits India to fend off intervention by playing off one benefactor against another. The Indian government, according to Lewis, "is no readier to surrender to the World Bank or the United Nations than it is to the United States or the Soviet Union."[48] The acceptability argument usually carries an implicit assumption that multilateral aid involves no increase in the amount of intervention in the recipient's affairs. Thus, it is usually implied that, "other things being equal," multilateral aid is more acceptable. Other things, however, may not remain equal. The centralized co-ordination that would probably accompany a massive shift to multi-lateral aid would make intervention by the international donor much easier than it is now for an individual donor nation. If the World Bank, for example, were the only major source of development aid, its bargaining position vis-à-vis borrowers would be enormously strengthened.

A fourth argument for multilateral distribution of aid holds that it prevents individual donor nations from using such aid as a tool of national policy. Henry Cabot Lodge, for example, describes such programs as "obviously insulated against political manipulations" by donor states.[49] Does channeling aid through international agencies neutralize it as a tool of national policy? An influential RAND Corporation study is based on the assumption that those interested in foreign aid as an instrument of United States foreign policy need not concern themselves with the activities of the International Bank.[50] There are three reasons to doubt the wisdom of this assumption, however. First, a donor nation may choose to distribute its aid through international agencies purely on the basis of its calculations of its own national interest. The United States, for example, "may seek the comparative anonymity of multilateralism when the recipient regime or local opposition suspect 'strings' or other undue

[46] For examples, see Benham, 105; and Lodge, "Mutual Aid," 525.

[47] John P. Lewis, *Quiet Crisis in India* (Washington 1962), 263.

[48] *Ibid.*, 264. Jacob Kaplan contends that the "only instance of the expulsion of a Western aid mission for pressing unwelcome advice is that of the World Bank advisor who was resident in Turkey in the early 1950's." 361.

[49] "Mutual Aid Through the United Nations," 525.

[50] Wolf, 80 n.

influence by the donor."[51] Such a move would not mean political neutralization, however. "To seek a measure of anonymity," Liska rightly observes, "is not to suspend the primarily political character of aid; it is merely to adopt a politically more proficient method in situations where direct involvement may be onerous for either the donor or the recipient."[52]

A second reason for skepticism about the degree to which multilateral aid is insulated from national policy is that some donors exercise extraordinary influence on the activities of international aid agencies. The United States, for example, wields over one-fourth of the voting power in the World Bank, an institution that has always had an American president. When the United States diverts some of its funds from bilateral channels to the World Bank complex, it is not giving up as much influence over aid-distribution policies as it seems to be. Likewise, when the United States gives aid to the Inter-American Development Bank, it does not lose as much control over distribution of funds as the formal arrangements would indicate. Although Latin American nations can outvote the United States in the Inter-American Development Bank, their hope for future funds gives them an incentive not to do so. In Friedrich's terms, they are anticipating the reactions of the United States and acting accordingly. Note that the Inter-American Development Bank has never made a loan to which the United States specifically objected. Anticipated reactions are far more important as a link between aid and influence than are formal voting arrangements.

There is a third reason for rejecting the hypothesis that multilateral aid cannot be a tool of national statecraft. To the extent that any nation can predict the aid-distribution pattern of an international agency, it can use that agency as a tool of its foreign policy. That is, it can frame its foreign policy so as to allow for the activities of the international agency. Thus, if there is reason to suspect that Ruritania will be successful in getting a loan from the International Development Association to finance a dam that the United States had intended to finance, the United States may decide to take the funds it had earmarked for financing the dam and use them to promote some other foreign policy goal. Successful use of this foreign policy technique depends on one's ability to predict accurately the aid-distribution patterns of international agencies. Doing this permits one to identify those projects that will probably

[51] Liska, 217.
[52] *Ibid.*

be financed anyway and those that are on the margin. By confining its aid to marginal projects, a nation can strengthen its bargaining position vis-à-vis aid recipients.[53] A former AID administrator's description of the American negotiating process indicates that the United States does try to strengthen its bargaining position in this way: "Before even a tentative program is put together, the resources available from other countries, the United Nations specialized agencies, and foreign private business must be estimated. . . . Only at this stage does it become relevant to look at the resources available from the United States."[54]

In conclusion, there are several reasons to doubt Henry Cabot Lodge's assertion that multilateral aid programs are "obviously insulated against political manipulations" by individual states. Channeling aid through international agencies will not necessarily reduce the intervention in developing states; it may even increase it.

Private vs. Public Channels

One of the great American myths is that the private sector of the economy is "nonpolitical." It is not surprising, therefore, to encounter the argument that private "nonpolitical" investment would involve less intervention in developing states than does "political" public foreign aid.[55] The following discussion will focus on two questions: First, is private capital "political" in the three ways mentioned earlier? Second, in what ways is private investment linked to foreign policies?

The motivation of private businessmen is usually described in terms of a desire for profit. Without denying the importance of the profit motive, we may point out that profit can be pursued in various ways by different organizations. The rationale that typically underlies a description of business as nonpolitical implies the existence of numerous small firms obedient to impersonal market forces.

[53]On the importance of this, see Thomas C. Schelling, *International Economics* (Boston 1958), 443-44.

[54]Frank M. Coffin, *Witness for AID* (Boston 1964), 14-15. See also Agency for International Development, *Loan Terms, Debt Burden, and Development* (April 1965), 23.

[55]For examples, see Cleona Lewis, *The United States and Foreign Investment Problems* (Washington 1948), 277; American Enterprise Association, "American Private Enterprise, Foreign Economic Development, and the Aid Programs," *Foreign Aid Program: Compilation of Studies and Surveys*, 592; Clair Wilcox, *A Charter for World Trade* (New York 1949), 145; and John Pincus, *Trade, Aid and Development* (New York 1967), 344.

Such a rationale ignores one of the most important economic institutions in the world today—the giant corporation. We are only beginning to perceive the far-reaching political and economic implications of this form of social organization.[56] It is clear, however, that these firms are not the slaves of the market envisioned in the model of pure competition. Many of them own more assets than the annual GNP in several developing states. It is these giant corporations that account for most of the American direct investment abroad. Roughly one-third of this investment is in the petroleum industry, which is so well organized that it has been described as a private world government.[57] Pursuing power and pursuing profit are not necessarily mutually exclusive undertakings.

Regardless of the motivations of private foreign investors, it is difficult to deny the political impact of their actions. The provision of forty million dollars in revolving credit to South Africa by a group of American banks has a profound effect on the distribution of influence within the recipient nation and among various nations. This same group of banks is unlikely to extend similar credit to Cuba in the near future. This is not to imply any sort of devious plan by bankers to promote racism or any other ideology. The point is that in making judgments about what constitutes a "safe" investment they tend to favor certain social systems. This link between private international capital flows and particular social institutions was identified by Eugene Staley in his classic study, *War and the Private Investor*: "Indeed, the export of capital to countries previously untouched by capitalistic industrialism necessitates the simultaneous "export" of specialized governmental forms and institutions, such as commercial law, and specialized economic institutions, such as the wage system. Out of this fact . . . a deep and inevitable conflict emerges between capital-importing and capital-exporting countries when their social institutions are radically different."[58]

Is international private investment a political process in the sense that it involves conflict among groups? There are at least two reasons to think that it is. First, many of the developing states, rightly or wrongly, associate private foreign investors with their former colonial masters. As long as these attitudes persist, friction between developing states and private foreign investors is to be expected.

[56]On this point see John K. Galbraith, *The New Industrial State* (Boston 1967); Adolph A. Berle, Jr., *Power Without Property* (New York 1959); and Michael D. Reagan, *The Managed Economy* (New York 1963).
[57]Robert Engler, *The Politics of Oil* (New York 1961).
[58]Eugene Staley, *War and the Private Investor* (Garden City 1935), 142.

Second, a substantial degree of group conflict in the process of transferring capital from the developed to the developing states should be expected even if there were no colonial heritage to stigmatize foreign investors. Staley sees such conflict as inevitable: "The process of international investment establishes between a capital-importing and a capital-exporting country a relatively permanent capital-labor conflict, a creditor-debtor conflict, a conflict of vested interests with groups interested in social reform or revolution, not to speak of cultural conflicts unleashed by the industrialization which accompanies capital investment."[59]

It is quite possible for private foreign investment to be political in all three ways mentioned above and still be insulated from the foreign policies of the government in the lending country. Although we often hear allegations that foreign policy is molded to suit private investors, we rarely hear private investment described as a "tool" of foreign policy. The United States government, however, has clearly tried to use private foreign investment to promote some of its foreign policy goals in developing states. It has used diplomacy, investment guarantees, propaganda, and non-aid to stimulate the flow of private capital to developing areas.[60] The Advisory Committee on Private Enterprise in Foreign Aid recently pointed out that "private institutions may be far more effective instruments of national policy in some situations than government institutions."[61] The committee report went on to describe private investment abroad as an effective way to exert "pressure" on the developing states to adopt the kind of pluralistic social system that the authors of the report believe exists in the United States.[62] The report made it clear that the authors viewed private capital as a means of intervening in the affairs of developing states.

After examining several types of aid, we conclude that none of them offers much hope to those who oppose any and all intervention in the recipient's affairs. Each of them can serve, and has served, as a mechanism for intervention. Although there may be types of foreign aid that cannot be used by the donor to intervene, they are not among those examined here.

[59] *Ibid.*, 367. See, also, Leo Model, "The Politics of Private Foreign Investment," *Foreign Affairs*, XLV (July 1967), 639-51.

[60] For details on the United States use of these techniques for promoting private foreign investment, see Baldwin, *Economic Development and American Foreign Policy.*

[61] *Foreign Aid Through Private Initiative*, 5.

[62] *Ibid.*, 6-8.

IV. TRADE, NOT AID: A WAY OUT?

A commonly suggested substitute for aid might be thought to provide a way out for those interested in preventing donors from influencing recipients. "Trade, not aid" has been a slogan heard intermittently for the last twenty years. Preferential treatment of developing countries in their trade relations with the developed ones could serve as a functional equivalent for aid, at least to some extent. The United Nations Conference on Trade and Development in 1964 proposed a variety of ways to cloak foreign aid in the guise of special trading arrangements.[63] If this could be done, would donors still be able to intervene? There would be no need for annual Congressional appropriations, no negotiating for each project, and no need for aid missions. It would appear that many opportunities for intervention by donors would thus be foreclosed.

Appearances can be deceiving, however. International trade can also be an instrument of national foreign policy. Implicit in all trade among nations is the potential threat of each trading partner to terminate the trade.[64] Three potential sources of intervention are obvious: (1) actual termination of trade by a rich country, (2) threatened termination, and (3) actions by developing states anticipating potential reactions by the developed states. One cannot make an *a priori* judgment as to which nations would be in the strongest bargaining positions with regard to terminating or threatening termination of trade. Other things being equal, however, nations gaining the most from the trade would have the most to lose and would thus be more vulnerable to threats to end the trade. It is interesting to note, in this respect, that several of the Unctad proposals involve measures to increase the developing nations' gains from trade with the rich nations. We are presented with the irony of a situation in which the developing states ask the rich nations to do many of the same things that Hirschman views as ways to maximize a nation's potential influence over its trading partners.[65] The Unctad proposals may be worthwhile, but developing states are deluding themselves if they think that implementation of the proposals will necessarily insulate them from intervention by rich nations.

[63] For a description and analysis of the UNCTAD proposals, see Harry G. Johnson, *Economic Policies Toward Less Developed Countries* (Washington 1967).

[64] On this point, see Albert O. Hirschman, *National Power and the Structure of Foreign Trade* (Berkeley and Los Angeles 1945).

[65] *Ibid.*, 34-35. See also Pincus, 44.

V. CONCLUSION

The preceding discussion focused on three major topics: (1) the links between aid and influence, (2) the links between particular types of aid and intervention, and (3) the links between trade and intervention. The section on aid and influence was devoted to highlighting some of the less obvious aspects of the relationship and to noting a variety of analytical problems that confront the student of foreign aid. The examination of several types of aid revealed that all were likely to involve significant amounts of intervention in the developing states. The third section held out some hope, but not much, for minimizing intervention by the functional equivalent of special trading arrangements.

We did not discuss the question of whether certain types of intervention are desirable—by whatever standard. The preceding analysis will seem to have isolationist policy implications only for those who refuse to recognize that the doctrine of nonintervention was "fashioned for a world in which nations were set apart in space and did not interact significantly; a world in which there were no countries so much more powerful than others that they 'intervened' simply by being and acting . . . a world that has ceased to exist."[66] To increase economic well-being and to ensure world peace, some types of intervention are probably useful, even necessary. We live in a highly interdependent world and might as well make the best of it. As a Syracuse University study pointed out several years ago: "We cannot undertake any significant action without becoming involved in some nation's internal affairs, either in technical assistance, in economic planning, or in military training. . . . The appropriate attitude toward this new role of ours is acceptance of involvement, or joint participation, as a permanent part of our international life and on this basis to participate as intelligently and usefully as we can."[67]

[66]Scott, 23.

[67]Maxwell Graduate School, *The Operational Aspects of United States Foreign Policy*, 17.

chapter eleven
PSYCHOLOGICAL PROCESSES

Psychological Warfare

Terence Qualter

The disintegration of German morale in the last months of 1918 convinced the Great Powers that propaganda was an effective and relatively cheap weapon of war. Among the Allied leaders the value of propaganda was noted and filed away for future reference while the propaganda agencies themselves were disbanded as part of a general disarmament ushering in the new era of peace. But in Germany, the General Staff, in an attempt to excuse the military defeat, grossly exaggerated the part played by Crewe House and the Committee on Public Information. The Commander in Chief, Erich von Ludendorff, repeatedly declared that the German armies were victorious, but had stopped fighting because civilian morale had been destroyed by Allied propaganda. Stress on the "corruption of the German soul" inspired German sociologists and army psychologists to undertake extensive research into the military possibilities of

SOURCE: From Terence Qualter, *Propaganda and Psychological Warfare*. Copyright © 1962 by Random House, Inc. Reprinted and abridged by permission of the author and Random House, Inc.

propaganda. From this and from the experiences of the Russian revolution emerged the modern study of psychological warfare.

It is not to be supposed, of course, that psychological warfare is an invention of German sociologists. The paint and feathers of the Cherokee Indians, the *clamor* or battle cry of the Roman soldiers, and the *auto-da-fé* of the Spanish Inquisition were all forms of psychological warfare. All that is new is the attempt to replace the occasional acts of a few exceptional leaders, or the habitual behavior of warlike peoples, by a continuing coördination of political, military and economic decisions with psychological principles founded on a scientific study of human motivations.

Psychological warfare is more than propaganda. It is propaganda tied in and coördinated with military, political and economic strategy and policy. Psychological warfare is based on the knowledge that the chances of success of a military operation are heightened by the demoralization of the enemy, the realization that while screamers attached to bombs will not add to the material destruction they will undermine the "will to resist." And while psychological tricks may increase military effectiveness, so may a military operation supplement a propaganda campaign. News and pictures of Germany's ruthless destruction of Polish cities were invaluable aids to German propagandists trying to persuade other powers that resistance was not the wisest policy. Military victory can be achieved by the destruction of the enemy's material resources, but the amount of destruction necessary to force the enemy to admit defeat depends upon his will, his determination and his perseverance, all of which can be affected by propaganda.

Psychological warfare may precede or supplement a military campaign, "softening" opposition, sowing discord, doubt, and confusion, preparing the way for the armies. It is in this sense, "... an offensive war waged with intellectual and emotional 'weapons' to destroy the power of moral resistance in the enemy's army and civilian population and to diminish enemy prestige in the eyes of neutrals."[1] In our own age, with the world divided into nuclear-armed camps, psychological warfare has assumed new dimensions. It has become a substitute for military action and the only form of warfare which the great powers can afford to wage.

Covering as it does such a wide range of activities, psychological warfare is recognizable only in terms of its objectives. Words and

[1] F. Bertkau and H. Franke, "Geistiger Krieg," (1938), quoted by L. Farago, *German Psychological Warfare* (New York: Committee for National Morale, 1941), p. 142.

deeds that, by corrupting the morale of the enemy, weaken his willingness to fight; that sow discord in the enemy camp and foster suspicion of the motives of the enemy in his own territory and among neutrals; that, if unable to enlist the active support of neutrals, at least keep them sympathetic and neutral; or that foster resistance movements in territories occupied by the enemy, are all part of what is now termed psychological warfare and anything that promotes any of these ends is a weapon of psychological warfare. Successful waging of psychological warfare demands the combined talents of many specialists including, in addition to writers, broadcasters, and artists, some competent to maintain close liaison with the political and military leaders of their own country, others well versed in the language, culture, and politics of the target country, and still others with training in such fields as psychology, anthropology, and political science.[2]

. . .

GROWTH OF PSYCHOLOGICAL WARFARE IN THE WEST

Even a superficial survey of the political influences at work in a democratic society leads to the obvious conclusion that propaganda is being disseminated from a thousand sources through every media of communication. The press, the educational system, the motion picture and the theater, radio and television, books and periodicals, the graphic arts, and all other propaganda techniques are used in all countries, either by government agencies or private institutions, for the furthering of political causes.

But although it might be impossible to identify techniques as characteristic of democratic or non-democratic propaganda, it is still obvious that the character of propaganda in a democracy differs from that in a dictatorship. The precise nature of the difference is not, however, quite so obvious. No one seriously disputes the fact that in a modern dictatorship propaganda plays a much larger role as a deliberate instrument of official policy than it does in a democracy. Yet there is probably a greater volume of propaganda in the United States today than there ever was in Hitler's Germany. It is less dominating, however, less overpowering and therefore less evident, because it originates not in one source, but in hundreds. It is

[2]See P. M. Linebarger, *Psychological Warfare* (New York: Duell, Sloan & Pearce, 1954), pp. 99-101, for a more detailed treatment of the qualifications for psychological warfare.

disseminated by political parties, trade unions, churches, business houses, newspaper owners, government departments, politicians, societies, clubs, professional associations, and individuals. It is at this level that the difference between democratic and non-democratic propaganda becomes apparent. The average citizen in a democracy seems to have no objection to political propaganda as such, and seems to regard as legitimate almost any method of political persuasion short of direct corruption and intimidation, provided, however, that it is not done by the government. This last point is all important. In a dictatorship all propaganda is government propaganda; in a democracy there is great reluctance to allow the government to enter into the propaganda field at all.

This distrust of government propaganda explains the pressure on any democratic country to withdraw from the propaganda field as soon as the immediate crisis of war is over. But because, in the years imm.diately following the end of World War II, the United States government demobilized its wartime psychological warfare facilities,[3] it had to build up a completely new organization to cope with the Cold War. Remobilization followed as the Western world began to appreciate the changed character of postwar international politics. Beginning slowly in 1948, and speeding up after the outbreak of the Korean conflict in 1950, the United States government has now established a complex organization for international psychological warfare.

The Department of State, through its Bureau of Public Affairs (Office of News) provides, through all the major media of communication, a world-wide news coverage of the activities of the United States government in foreign affairs, and generally announces and explains the foreign policy of the country. More specifically in the realm of international propaganda is the United States Information Agency established in 1953. Guided by the decisions of the Department of State and the National Security Council, its function is "to submit evidence to the peoples of other nations by means of communications techniques that the objectives and policies of the United States are in harmony with and advance their legitimate aspirations for freedom, progress and peace."[4] Outside the United

---

[3]The Office of War Information (OWI) ceased independent existence at the end of August, 1945, although it continued to function in a limited way under the control of the State Department. The companion organization, Office of Strategic Services (OSS) was broken up by an Executive Order of September 20, 1945.

[4]United States, Office of the Federal Register, *United States Government Organization Manual*, 1960-61, p. 519.

States, the Agency's offices, integral parts of the various American embassies and consulates, are known as the United States Information Service (USIS). There are now USIS offices in more than eighty countries, all charged with interpreting and explaining the policies of the United States government, countering "hostile attempts to distort or frustrate the objectives and policies of the United States,"[5] and generally presenting a picture of the life and culture of the American people that will facilitate understanding of American policies and objectives.

The official psychological warfare of the Western powers is generally tactically sound, for the propagandists have taken to heart a lesson from the First World War: the principle that all good propaganda must be factually true, that one should never make statements that might later be refuted. And it is important that material should not only be true, it should also be credible. M. F. Herz, who was for a time working with the combat propaganda team attached to the Fifth Army in Italy during World War II, recalls the disastrous effects of American propaganda leaflets in which it was mentioned that prisoners in American P.O.W. camps received eggs for breakfast. This, although perfectly true, seemed so preposterous to the enemy that they rejected it and so were inclined to disbelieve the rest of the message. The leaflets had to be withdrawn.[6]

Another important lesson, more fully appreciated by those engaged in psychological warfare than by those voting the money for it, is that psychological warfare is not just large-scale advertising. International persuasion is a complex matter requiring an understanding of the attitudes of those whose attention is sought, and the advertising techniques, which work so well in the American marketplace, are not necessarily appropriate in countries with different standards of values. "What sells soap in Indiana can unsell democracy in India." A successful psychological warfare campaign requires a detailed background study of the aspirations and values of the country concerned. It is necessary to know the attitudes of the country towards the United States, the other Western countries, the Soviet Union, and the neutral countries; and the factors, favorable and unfavorable, that would affect United States propaganda activities. These would include the source, nature, and strength of other influences on public opinion, the communication channels

[5] *Ibid.*

[6] Cited by M. F. Herz, "Some Psychological Lessons from Leaflet Propaganda in World War II," *Public Opinion Quarterly*, XII (1949), p. 472.

available, and the nature and causes of differences of opinion within the country.

It is useless to dwell on the virtues of free private enterprise in underdeveloped lands where the doctrines of laissez faire have never taken root. Little advantage is gained by providing economic aid, unless there is tight control of associated publicity. The propagandist must know his foreign country. Too often American generosity has failed to achieve its purpose because Soviet propagandists have been able to create the image of "sinister dollar imperialism," the "underwriting of the forces of reaction," or of American duplicity in using the small nations as pawns in the struggle against the Soviet Union. The United States has not always been quick or effective in replying to these charges.

Many mistakes are made in psychological warfare, by anti-democratic forces as well as by the West, through a misinterpretation of audience reaction. An American radio station, for example, might receive enthusiastic reports of a program beamed to a Russian-occupied country, but there would be grave danger in placing too much reliance on such reports without first "weighing" them. That is to say, the opinion of right-wing opponents of a Communist regime is not of much value in assessing the effectiveness of propaganda aimed at Communist sympathizers. Propaganda should be directed at the "marginal" man, "the man who does not believe everything we say, but who is interested in our message because he does not believe everything our opponents say either."[7] American propaganda makes little, or no, impact on the dedicated Communist and for the convinced anti-Communist the effort is unnecessary. Its target is, or should be, the waverer. The enthusiasm with which it is received in the anti-Communist camp is usually a poor measure of its accuracy in hitting that target.

THE "COLD WAR"

Psychological warfare was specifically developed as an aid to military action, to make victory more certain and to reduce the cost of armed conflict. Since 1945, however, psychological warfare has undergone a transformation. It has continued unabated, perhaps even at times intensified, but as a substitute for, rather than an auxiliary to, military engagement.

It is, however, an oversimplification to think of the Cold War as just the latest in history's apparently endless series of conflicts,

[7]M. F. Herz, *op. cit.*, p. 475.

differing only in that conventional arms have been replaced by psychological weapons. The Cold War is being conducted between two ideological divisions, one of which regards conflict as the normal state of affairs between nations. To the Communist "the history of all hitherto existing society is the history of class struggles," struggles which can cease only when the class basis of society is itself eliminated. From this basic assumption, axiomatic to all good Communists, it follows that, unlike earlier wars, there can be no agreed cessation of hostilities in the Cold War, no compromise solution for the maintenance of the status quo. According to Marxist theory, the continuation of class conflict is the status quo. If the West is to survive, it must recognize that the Cold War will continue; for it can end only with the final victory of one side, which seems unlikely in any foreseeable future, or in a shooting war, a nuclear war, in which there may be no victor.

For a brief period after the armistice in 1945, it seemed possible that the good will and fellowship of the military alliance might continue; but within a year all illusions, except among a number of naïve idealists, were destroyed. With its rejection of the Baruch plan for the control of atomic weapons in June, 1946, the Soviet Union made it clear that it was not going to cooperate with the West. Instead, the Soviet Union initiated a policy of fomenting discord and encouraging revolutionary Communist movements in all countries outside the direct control of Russia. The ruthlessness and determination with which this policy was conducted finally roused the West to take counteraction and, beginning in March, 1947, a combination of military aid, economic support, and moral encouragement checked Soviet advances in Greece and halted further expansion in the Balkans.

The assumptions on which Soviet psychological warfare is based, when applied to the formulation of foreign policy, demand first of all that the Soviet Union become strong enough to safeguard the revolution from external enemies. Second, it is also necessary that the Soviet Union continue to harry and confuse the West, lending its aid to any movement or group which embarrasses or threatens Western unity, probing and enlarging upon any divisions or discords that may arise among the non-Communist states, and seeking to discredit the major Western powers in Asia, Latin America, and Africa, in the belief that it can thereby weaken the West and hasten the collapse of capitalism. Third, in pursuance of this same policy, the Soviet Union must aid and abet the establishment and continuance of Communist movements and "front" organizations, the "seeds of revolution," whenever and wherever they are likely to be valuable. And finally, in order to preserve unflinching unity of purpose, the Soviet Union insists on rigid "doctrinal purity," launching the bitterest of attacks on those who, while professing to be Communists, deviate from the Moscow line.

Yet a psychological warfare campaign will have the desired effect only if the assumptions on which it is based are themselves soundly established. And for a long time the assumptions on which Soviet policy was based were not founded in fact. With a less dogmatic approach to politics, they could have been recognized as false. It was, for example, assumed that the postwar withdrawal of United States troops from Europe signaled America's return to isolationism. This inspired the attempts to frighten the small powers of Europe into accepting Russian domination, but the actual result was that the United States renounced isolationism and took over the leadership of the Western alliance. It was also taken for granted that the shift of the American economy from a war to a peace basis would be followed by a major economic collapse. This led the Russians to a serious underestimation of the extent to which the United States could assist European economic recovery and the extent to which she could use economic aid as an anti-Communist weapon in under-developed countries. The failure to appreciate the resilience of the American economy led further to overconfidence about the role of native Communist parties in exploiting the discontents of the victims of economic crisis. Finally, the Russians believed that British-United States relations would be characterized by increasingly bitter rivalry and took this to mean that organizations such as NATO would be rendered ineffectual and unstable by the antagonisms of the principal members. Frequent attempts by the Soviet Union to exploit natural differences between the two nations have almost inevitably resulted in even closer ties between Britain and America.[8]

In turning now to the Western approach to psychological warfare, we can begin by recalling the reluctance with which democratic societies permit their governments to use official funds and resources for propaganda. Although this is particularly true of domestic party politics, or what might be interpreted as party politics, the same fear of official propaganda extends into the field of international psychological warfare. The great handicap which the West has had to overcome has not been one of moral scruple about the kind of tactics which should be adopted, but the jealousy of private agencies which

[8]See E. W. Barrett, *Truth is Our Weapon* (New York: Funk & Wagnalls, 1953), p. 189, for a discussion of these assumptions of Soviet policy.

have been unwilling to give to governments the powers necessary to wage psychological warfare.

The Soviet Union gained tremendous initial advantages in the Cold War because the United States government, unable to convince a parochial and unimaginative Congress of the values of psychological warfare, was for several years unable to obtain the funds necessary to launch any large-scale reply to Soviet claims. In July, 1950, during a Soviet campaign to portray the United States as the aggressor in Korea, President Truman asked Congress "to implement his call for a 'great campaign of truth' by granting a supplemental appropriation of $89 million for foreign information activities."[9] This appropriation was drastically cut by Congress to the extent that the regular and supplemental appropriation totaled only $94 million. Partly explainable in terms of the traditional congressional distrust of the State Department and partly a product of a system of government which sets Congress up as a check on administrative spending, these reduced appropriations reflect, even more, an unwillingness of Congress to invest money in schemes having such intangible objectives as "a more sympathetic attitude to the United States and its policies."

Attacks on the United States psychological warfare campaigns have come therefore from three sources: those who have a vested interest in defeating or obstructing United States policy, the unimaginative and the anti-intellectuals who do not appreciate the potency of psychological warfare and who distrust those engaged in it, and the laissez faire extremists, the determined opponents of any extension of governmental power, who deny the right of the administration to engage in propaganda. These three forces, otherwise so far apart, together hindered for several years the American attempt to compete on equal terms with Soviet propaganda in the international field. The United States did not a first have the resources, nor were those engaged in psychological warfare given sufficient control over policy to ensure consistency in their campaigns.

Much of this initial disadvantage has now been overcome and the West now has financial and technical resources which could be used to overcome an initial disadvantage. It is important to remember this, for there is a tendency to assume that because the West started late in the propaganda struggle, because it has undoubtedly made

[9] B. W. Patch, "Non-Military Weapons in Cold War Offensive," in R. E. Summers (ed.), *America's Weapons of Psychological Warfare* [Reference Shelf 23 (4)] (New York: Wilson, 1951), p. 32.

blunders in Cold War strategy, and because it lacks the tireless persistence of the Soviet bloc, the West must always be defeated. To counter this pessimism it is well to recall that the West won the first really big trial of strength. When the Russians clamped down the blockade on Berlin on April 1, 1948, they clearly thought they could force the West to give up the city. The West replied with the air lift which continued from July, 1948, until the Russians lifted the blockade in May, 1949. The air lift was more than a superb technical achievement; it was evidence of the determination of the Western powers not to be intimidated by Russia. It was the first major setback suffered by the Soviets and it effectively destroyed the myth of their invincibility. The heartening effect of the air lift was followed by a series of treaties and military alliances, from NATO to ANZUS, that refuted Russian charges that the Western countries would soon tear each other to pieces.

In retrospect it would seem that, as long as Soviet Cold War strategy was dominated by Stalin's inflexible dogmatism, the West had a fair chance of victory, but that advantage has for a time slipped away. Soviet policy became more realistic, more adaptable to changing circumstances, while American policy, possibly as a product of McCarthyism, became infected with an anti-Communist hysteria that led the Americans to commit a number of tragic blunders. The principal mistakes of United States Cold War strategy have stemmed from the failure in some high places to understand that the people of Asia and Africa, and even of Europe, see neither communism nor the free enterprise "American way of life" as these might be seen by the right wing of the Republican party or by the Daughters of the American Revolution. When, for example, in January, 1954, John Foster Dulles announced his policy of "massive retaliation to deter aggression," it appeared from European comment that he had scared his Allies more than he had scared the Russians.

Again, it must be pointed out that the successes are not all one-sided, that the Russians have no special magic which ensures that every victory will be theirs. One has only to recall the tremendous blow to Russian prestige that followed the savage and inept handling of the Hungarian uprising and the inability of the Russians to halt the flow of defections from the occupied countries to the West. The wall that divides Berlin is a monument to the failure of Communist propaganda. So long as the democracies continue to exploit every weakness and failure of the Russian dictatorship, the Cold War can be turned to the advantage of the Western powers.

One cannot leave the subject of American psychological warfare without mentioning the extent to which officially-sponsored campaigns are supplemented, but sometimes also frustrated, by private ventures. Unlike the dictatorships, where all public communication is government communication, the United States is the home of hundreds of organizations anxious to have their say in converting the world to the "American way of life," a phrase which does not mean the same thing to all Americans everywhere. One of the most influential and well established of these groups is the American Committee for Liberation, founded in 1951 by "American individuals deeply concerned for the future of the Soviet peoples."[10] The major enterprise of the Committee is *Radio Liberation* which maintains a twenty-four-hour-a-day program to the Soviet Union from nine "national desks"—Russian, Ukrainian, Armenian, Azerbaijanian, Byelorussian, Georgian, North Caucasian, Tatar-Baskir and Turkestani. *Radio Liberation*'s headquarters are in Munich and it has transmitters in both Europe and the Far East. "Each desk endeavors to speak from the point of view of its own people in support of the common cause."[11] Another private venture into international broadcast propaganda is *Radio Free Europe,* and a parallel organization, *Radio Free Asia.* These are, as one writer has expressed it, "dedicated to broadcasting those things which the State Department finds it impolitic to put on the air."[12] The traditions of international protocol impose certain limits on the sort of thing the officials of one government may say about the officials of another, but *Radio Free Europe* has no need to feel inhibited by such traditions. It has sometimes been suggested that the State Department does not object to the existence of *Radio Free Europe* and that, perhaps, there is a measure of unofficial cooperation.

American magazines with a wide foreign circulation, magazines such as *Time, Life, Saturday Evening Post,* and *Reader's Digest* are an obvious medium for American propaganda, but at least as important as the editorial and feature material, which often overstates the case, are the advertisements. These, designed primarily for the American consumer, present to less fortunate peoples an image of sybaritic abundance. The articles may be discounted as "mere propaganda," but the advertisements will impress because they give a "real" picture of the American way of life. This impression of easy luxury is reinforced in the overseas offices of American corporations and official

[10] From a pamphlet, *A Fresh Look at Liberation,* issued by the Committee in 1957.
[11] *Ibid.*
[12] P. M. Linebarger, *Psychological Warfare* (New York: Duell, Sloan, & Pearce, 1954), pp. 273-74.

agencies. I have myself spent many afternoons in the USIS Library in London, not only because it was an excellent library, but because on a winter's day it seemed to be one of the few places where one could be sure of being warm.

All this amounts to a massive anti-Communist campaign greatly in excess of anything the government can hope to do and it certainly does much to redress the disadvantages the United States government must suffer in dealing with a totalitarian regime. But these private ventures themselves have one great, insoluble, and perhaps even fatal weakness. By their very nature they are uncoördinated. They frequently contradict each other, they attack communism for a variety of not always consistent reasons, and they often damage United States policy by destroying the image which the government is trying to create, especially in some neutral or uncommitted nation. Those right-wing extremists, for example, who vie with each other in spying out Communists in the most unlikely places, dangerously undermine America's status in Europe as an honest, free democracy, opposed to the Soviet Union not only because it is a rival military and economic power, but because the existence of communism is a threat to political liberty, which America genuinely values.

While in the Cold War all the familiar devices of psychological warfare continue to be used: oral and written propaganda of every kind, winning friends and influencing people through economic or military aid, "front" organizations and the encouragement of friendly movements, and the various tricks and stratagems of international negotiation, there has been one substantial new development. All psychological warfare is based on the determinist theories and conditioning experiments conducted by Pavlov.[13] This much is fairly obvious, but there has been more recently a "refinement" in the techniques of "conditioning" and an extension of their use. This new technique, which has been given the name of "brainwashing," consists first of all of a softening-up process in which the resistance of individuals is broken down by "hunger, fatigue, tenseness, threats, violence," and in extreme cases, drugs and hypnotism.[14] This is followed by an indoctrination process through which the victim is persuaded that he has been let down and betrayed by his former

---

[13]In *The Rape of the Masses* (London: Labour Book Service, 1940), S. Chakotin devotes a whole chapter to the relation between conditioned reflexes and propaganda.

[14]United States Congress, House of Representatives, Committee on Un-American Activities, *Communist Psychological Warfare, (Brainwashing)*, Consultation with Edward Hunter, March 13, 1958, p. 15.

friends, and that his persecutors are in reality the only ones he can trust, the ones who will protect him from further betrayal, his only "true" friends. The horror of brainwashing is its effectiveness in destroying the mind of the individual. The harrowing accounts in Koestler's *Darkness at Noon* or Orwell's *1984* are not purely fictional. They are not unlike the actual treatment of some American prisoners of war in Korea.

There is some evidence that brainwashing tactics can succeed in special cases. Although after the Korean conflict the number of American prisoners who declined to return to the United States was small (one report states that there were only twenty-one out of a total of more than seven thousand who had been captured), this was the first time American prisoners of war had refused to return home.[15] These numbers, of course, fade into insignificance compared with the thousands who have defected from East to West, and although they show that brainwashing can have some impact, they demonstrate even more clearly its limitations. In evidence before the House Committee on Un-American Activities, Edward Hunter made the point that brainwashing succeeds best with those whose intelligence is high, but whose education is low, those whose "heads were like a good, solid, but empty bucket, only waiting to be filled."[16] According to Hunter, the Communists were able to impose their version of American action in Korea because the American forces on the whole lacked any other information about American policy towards communism. He illustrated the types of pressure that could be put on a prisoner by recounting the experiences of one Air Force officer who had been subjected to alternating periods of brutality and care until, to quote the officer, when finally the brutality ceased, ". . . you are grateful to them for saving your life. You forget that they are the people who almost killed you."[17]

Although the Communists have had notable success in psychological warfare, especially among the "propertyless, resentful, politically unenfranchised, frustrated, mentally underdeveloped masses of mankind,"[18] it is easy to overestimate their ability, a misjudgment almost as dangerous to the West as the complete disregard of the psychological struggle. In giving too much stress to Soviet Cold War victories, there is a tendency to overlook those

[15] *N. Y. Times*, January 6, 1957.
[16] United States Congress, *Communist Psychological Warfare,(Brainwashing)*, p. 17.
[17] *Ibid.*
[18] W. Albig, *Modern Public Opinion* (New York: McGraw-Hill, 1936), p. 307.

Communist advances which are due, not to propaganda, but to skillful deployment of force, careful party organization, and the determination to make the most of every opportunity. With great skill the Russians have managed to seize the popular role of "apostle of peace," forcing the West into the embarrassing position of refusing to take part in "peace movements" and having to condemn all peace campaigns as Communist fronts. The extent to which "peace" became a Communist monopoly was illustrated by a cartoon by Giles of the London *Daily Express*. In the picture, one little urchin is chalking something on the sidewalk, the other is yelling at the top of his voice, "Mum, Cyril's wrote a wicked word." The "wicked word" is PEECE.[19] But this type of triumph is rare. Much Russian propaganda is characterized by a battering-ram technique and a crude repetition of dull, meaningless dogmatism.

Against this intellectual strait jacket of Marxism the democracies have many advantages. Their message, properly presented, offers greater hope and greater respect for human dignity and individual well-being. The Western powers, apart from a few embarrassing allies whose only virtue is a determined anti-communism, have an impressive record of social and material progress. In most there is a substantial body of human rights and freedoms, reasonably well protected by law and custom. The major Western powers have also the advantage of an abundant supply of raw materials that, combined with a highly advanced technology, ensure both a material standard of living and a war-making potential that would not easily be challenged. The West has thus a good case to make in the Cold War, and access to a network of communications for presenting this case to the world. All that is required is an awareness of the nature of the Cold War and its near-permanent character, and a sense of determination to continue it. Given these there is no reason to suppose that the West must lose nor that it need abandon its own values in fighting that war.

[19] *Daily Express*, November 14, 1950.

part four

Setting
of the International
Political System

Introductory Note

The concept "environment" or "setting" grows out of system. A system is a set of variables abstracted from all others, presumably because they merit special attention. Setting merely refers to those variables from which the special set was selected. Every system, with the single exception of the Universe, exists—physically, behaviorally, or both—in a setting. It is, of course, possible to be intellectually oblivious to a system's environment, choosing instead to regard it in isolation. This technique is common in the physical sciences. Experience suggests that, in international politics, to ignore setting is to pass over the possible source of explanation of much that occurs. Part Four is organized into three chapters, each of which centers around one dimension of the setting that political scientists regard as important.

Of the various segments of the international system's environment, none is more pervasive in its influence than domestic political systems. It is often only with great difficulty that we can separate them, even in the abstract, so continuous and tightly woven is the

397

social fabric that joins them. Professor James Rosenau provides a short introduction to Chapter Twelve that touches upon the nature and extent of that relationship. In a balanced and thoughtful essay, Professor Carl Friedrich proposes a "three-level theory of democratic foreign policy" which explains many of the discontinuities in foreign policy by reference to the societal level at which the policy is made. The critical variable in his discussion is the degree to which a particular issue arouses widespread public sentiment.

International law and morality are not usually thought of as part of setting. It is more common to think of them as active parts of the political process. Such a perspective usually suffers from a tendency to equate national and international law. Except for nomenclature, the two are quite dissimilar. In domestic politics, the output of the struggle is normally law; the victors do not usually administer their law directly, but entrust that task to generally recognized institutions which hold a monopoly or quasi-monopoly of force. In international politics, the terms of the victory are enforced directly by the victors without the mediating stage of law, and the shroud of hypocrisy that usually accompanies it. International law, far from being the specific outcome of political processes, is more like the general moral norms that inform a society's conception of right and wrong.* It tends to reflect international consensus on such matters as the nature of conflict and proper use of force. By placing international law and morality in the environment, we are not automatically downgrading its importance or suggesting that it does not influence the political process.

The selections of Chapter Thirteen generally reflect this orientation. Professor Stanley Hoffmann's discussion is largely a catalogue of the functions of international law from the point of view of the policy maker, and in terms of the establishment and maintenance of world order. The argument offered by Professor William Coplin is that instead of a set of coercive norms, international law is a device for "communicating to the policy makers of various states a consensus on the nature of the international system." It might be added that the author finds more ambiguity than consensus in the present system. Professor Werner Levi attempts to isolate international morality to determine the extent to which it has actually affected actors' behavior—his results are expectedly pessimistic.

*In their failure to administer international law in all but the most trivial cases, proto-international institutions like the World Court supply indirect support for this thesis.

The most obvious, although not necessarily most important dimension of setting is the physical or geographic. Geography, however, cannot be separated from technology since the latter conditions the former. Oceans were meaningful barriers only in an era before intercontinental ballistic missiles. This is the theme of the first article in Chapter Fourteen by Harold and Margaret Sprout. Change is the keynote of Professor Bruce Russett's article, which ranges from the factors that affect trends to the difficulties involved in predicting future states of the international environment. The final article, by Professor Ernst Haas, urges us to adopt a more positive attitude toward controlling our environment, and suggests means by which this might be achieved.

chapter twelve
DOMESTIC SETTING

The Domestic Sources
of Foreign Policy:
Introduction

James N. Rosenau

As your Secretary of State I wish to talk to you about foreign relations. Let me start with a simple remark which I earnestly hope you will never forget: Foreign policy is about you. It is about your home, your community, your safety, your well-being, your chance to live a decent life and to prepare a better world for your children. Foreign policy is not a game played by "those people in Washington" with other players from far-off distant places. It is as close to you as the members of your family, or the neighbor's boy, in uniform . . . as close as the taxes you pay to sustain the struggle for freedom, as close as the prices and the markets for what you produce. Even more personal, it is as close as your highest hopes, your puzzled concern that man can be both so good and yet so evil, your own impulse to do something to build a better world, your own private and personal search for the answer to the ageless question: "What is the chief end of man?"[1]

SOURCE: From James N. Rosenau (ed.), *Domestic Sources of Foreign Policy.* Copyright © 1967 by The Free Press, a Division of The Macmillan Company. Reprinted by permission of the author and The Macmillan Company.

[1] Dean Rusk, address to the Farmers Union Grain Terminal Association, St. Paul, Minnesota, December 10, 1963.

However else they may be interpreted, these exhortations succinctly illustrate both the underlying premise and the main dilemma of this book. The premise is that domestic sources of foreign policy are no less crucial to its content and conduct than are the international situations toward which it is directed. The dilemma is that the links between the domestic sources and the resulting behavior—foreign policy—are not easily observed and are thus especially resistant to coherent analysis.

Perhaps never before have the domestic sources of foreign policy seemed so important and been the focus of so much discussion. The intense controversy in the United States over the struggle in Vietnam has dramatized anew the fact that the foreign policy of governments is more than simply a series of responses to international stimuli, that forces at work within a society can also contribute to the quality and contents of its external behavior.

However, it is one thing to believe that a nation's foreign policy reflects its way of life and quite another to back up such a conviction conceptually and empirically. It is one thing for an official to tell citizens, "Foreign policy is about you," but is quite another for the scholar to identify the causal processes implied in such an assertion.

In other words, greater recognition of the wellsprings of foreign policy does not necessarily lead to greater clarity of thought about it. On the contrary, as the discussion of why states behave the way they do widens, so does reliance on crude and oversimplified explanations. Explaining foreign policy has become a popular sport and everyone seems to have a pet theory about who caused what event or what event caused whom to respond. The crudest of these, of course, are the "devil theories," in which the course of events is attributed to a power-hungry individual or to a conspiratorial group. These theories are especially attractive to people in times of international or domestic tension, such as a war abroad or an election at home. It is much easier to fix on a single culprit as the cause of undesirable events than to treat such events as the culmination of many factors, each of which is a necessary, though not a sufficient, cause. Devil theories thus provide a simple and quick explanation for complexity, enabling their holders both to take a position and to cope with anxiety.

Yet clarity is hardly a distinguishing feature of many of the more sophisticated approaches that do not rely on the devil for coherence. Theories which concede that events are not caused by single factors are numerous, but all too often holders of these theories reorganize them so as to make the complex of factors consistent with other values. Thus, for example, many Democrats who are impressed by a Johnson or a Kennedy will, in the case of decisions they applaud, ascribe primary causation to the presidency and secondary causation to public opinion and the mass media, but they will reverse the strength of the factors in the case of decisions they deplore. When a Republican enters the White House, such theorists will rearrange the factors again and blame the President for events they regret, but will treat his actions as merely responses to public demands in the case of trends they approve.

Nor are professional inquiries into such matters models of clarity. How the various sources of foreign policy combine to produce various forms of behavior under various kinds of conditions is neither the subject of extensive research nor the focus of systematic theorizing. Most scholarly treatments of foreign policy are either case studies or institutional analyses; that is, they are concerned either with the effects of many sources in a particular situation or with the effect of a single source in a variety of situations. Rare is the work that traces and assesses the relative contribution made by many sources in many diverse situations.[2] Moreover, like the case studies and institutional analyses, those few inquiries that do attempt to generalize across both sources and situations tend to minimize the domestic sources of foreign policy and to stress the processes of governmental decision-making, the events abroad with which officials must contend, and the nonhuman realities—such as geographic position, resource availability, and military or economic capacity—which limit or enhance their choices. Although such inquiries usually pay lip service to the idea that events and trends within a society also impinge upon the deliberations of its officials, the literature is short on works that consider a wide range of nongovernmental variables and estimate how their interaction shapes the contents and conduct of foreign policy.[3] Occasionally, to be sure, inquiries will focus di-

---

[2] For an elaboration of this point, see James N. Rosenau, "Pre-Theories and Theories of Foreign Policy," in R. Barry Farrell (ed.), *Approaches to Comparative and International Policies* (Evanston: Northwestern University Press, 1966), pp. 27-92.

[3] Some possible exceptions are Gabriel A. Almond, *The American People and Foreign Policy* (New York: Frederick A. Praeger, 1960), and Karl W. Deutsch and Lewis J. Edinger, *Germany Rejoins the Powers* (Stanford: Stanford University Press, 1959).

rectly on the connection between public opinion and foreign policy,[4] but, since they deal exclusively with public opinion, these are also single-factor analyses rather than systematic attempts to link basic societal processes to the behavior of officialdom.

There are, of course, good reasons for this disparity between the recognition that foreign policy springs from domestic sources and the scant treatment paid these sources in research. One is that events abroad, nonhuman realities, and governmental decision-making processes *are* the primary determinants of foreign policy and, on balance, they may well be more crucial than any and all domestic sources. In the rare instances when politicians cannot prevent the requirements of external and internal situations from coming into direct conflict, the former are likely to prevail in virtually every society.[5] So it is understandable that analysts have been inclined to concentrate on the international, nonhuman, and governmental sources of foreign policy.

However, domestic factors may be of considerable significance even if they are not primary sources of foreign policy, and on some issues they may well be dominant. It is instructive to note, for example, how McGeorge Bundy, himself a leading student of foreign

---

[4]See, for example, Douglas H. Mendel, Jr., *The Japanese People and Foreign Policy: A Study of Public Opinion in Post-Treaty Japan* (Berkeley: University of California Press, 1961) and William A. Scott and Stephen B. Withey, *The United States and the United Nations: The Public View* (New York: Manhattan Publishing Co., 1958).

[5]Such a conflict occurred in the United States on May 15, 1965. The Johnson administration, concerned about academic criticism of its policies in Vietnam, had previously agreed that one of its top foreign policy decision-makers, McGeorge Bundy, would participate in a nationally televised "teach-in" devoted to the issue on that day. As the time for the debate neared, however, a crisis in the Dominican Republic became so acute that a choice had to be made as to whether Mr. Bundy's time should be devoted to the external or the internal scene. And apparently it was an inescapable choice: to have Bundy participate in the teach-in was to remove a key adviser from a fast-moving and critical situation, but to fail to appear at the teach-in was to risk further antagonism of a critical group in the society. Unable to hedge, the administration decided that Mr. Bundy would attend to the Dominican Republic rather than Academe and sent him on a mediating mission to the strifetorn island. To interpret his trip as a ruse for avoiding the teach-in, as some ardent critics did, is to minimize the extent to which internal considerations must give way to external ones when the two cannot be accommodated to each other.

policy before becoming a presidential adviser, responded to an interviewer's query about "What was different in the actual conduct of American diplomatic affairs from how it had seemed to be from the safety of Harvard Yard?" According to the interviewer, "Bundy thought that three things stood out. The first was his recognition of the powerful place of domestic politics in the formulation of foreign policies . . ."[6]

Another reason for the disparity, and one that goes farther in accounting for it, must be noted. Upon reflection, the number of nongovernmental factors that can shape a society's foreign policy is staggering and, accordingly, the task of piecing them together into a coherent whole is extraordinarily complex. Many analysts may have a sense that the structure of a society is somehow related to the way in which its officials cope with the international environment, but translating this insight into meaningful research propositions presents a theoretical challenge that few have dared to confront. What aspects of societal structure affect what kinds of official behavior? Exactly how and under what circumstances are the forces at work in society—the shared values, the unresolved conflicts, the irrational drives, the memories of the past, the ever-changing dynamics of group life, the shifting composition of cities and classes, the ups and downs and changing structure of production and trade, the profound alterations in work and leisure patterns induced by technology— articulated in the actions of decision-makers? Through the latters' conscious perceptions of such forces? Through their prior socialization and training, which has made them unconsciously sensitive to societal tendencies? Through the resource opportunities and limitations that derive from societal structure and that serve as parameters within which effective choices can be made by officialdom? Through intervening institutions such as elections, mass media of communications, and organized interest groups?

. . .

[6] Henry F. Graff, "How Johnson Makes Foreign Policy," *The New York Times Magazine*, July 4, 1965, p. 17.

Intranational Politics and Foreign Policy in Developed (Western) Systems

Carl J. Friedrich

Foreign and domestic policy in developed Western systems constitutes today a seamless web.[1] The former sharp division which expressed itself in such principles as the primacy of foreign over domestic policy is no longer tenable and has not been for some time. These principles, never fully operative, were not merely descriptive

SOURCE: From R. Barry Farrell (ed.), *Approaches to Comparative and International Politics.* Copyright © 1966 by Northwestern University Press. Reprinted and abridged by permission of the author and Northwestern University Press.

[1] I am not going to take up the Soviet Union, the Fascist dictatorships, and related totalitarian regimes, though some of them no doubt constitute developed systems. The problems they present are too different, and our knowledge of the impact of internal party politics on foreign relations is too fragmentary. Cf. Zbigniew K. Brzezinski, *The Soviet Bloc,* rev. ed. (New York, Frederick A. Praeger, 1961), esp. Chaps. 6-8, for some essentials. Characteristically, however, Merle Fainsod in his magistral *How Russia Is Ruled,* rev. ed. (Cambridge, Mass., Harvard University Press, 1964), while noting that "domestic and foreign policy are intimately interrelated" (p. 597), discusses foreign policy in a brief three pages (342-45) under the heading of "goals of the Soviet leadership." Cf. also Friedrich and Brzezinski, *Totalitarian Dictatorship and Autocracy,* rev. ed. (Cambridge, Harvard University Press, 1965), Chap. 27 and pp. 357 ff.

but contained expedient normative propositions; now they have become utopian.[2] The division remains, of course, but it resembles that between agricultural and fiscal policy, calling for a distinct organization and a separate set of specialists, but certainly not calling for a separate kind of political theory. It is the more curious that just such a theory has been demanded in recent years by very able writers in the field of international relations.[3] Such demands seem to spring from a certain lack of theoretical framework in the study and teaching of international relations and foreign policy. Nor can there be any question that the field of foreign relations raises distinctive issues which call for treatment within the context of a general theory of politics.[4] But these distinctive issues, or at least some of them, bear close resemblance to patterns and processes characteristic of other kinds of political relations, e.g., negotiation, employment of violence, compacts. Some of these have been explored in the interesting papers on behavior.[5] As a matter of fact, the intermeshing of domestic and foreign policy is so intricate that it has even become difficult to define foreign policy satisfactorily. For what is genuinely foreign in a world shaped by a great variety of international organizations? Even if we draw reasonably neat lines between such organizations as the Council of Europe, on the one hand, and the European Community of the Six, operative as ECSC, EEC, and Euratom, on the other, they are apt to become blurred once the details are taken into account.[6] Hence such terms as "international

[2] Cf. my *Foreign Policy in the Making* (New York, W. W. Norton and Co., 1938), Chap. 3, and a later article "Das Ende der Kabinettspolitik," in *Aussenpolitik*, I (1950), pp. 20 ff., and the critical reply by Hans Rothfels, *ibid.*, pp. 274 ff.

[3] Stanley Hoffmann, ed., *Contemporary Theory in International Relations* (Englewood Cliffs, N.J., Prentice-Hall, 1960), esp. the editor's own comments, and Raymond Aron, "The Quest for a Philosophy of Foreign Affairs," as well as the latter's *Paix et guerre entre les nations*, rev. ed. (Paris, Colmann-Lévy, 1962), esp. pp. 16 ff. These *prises de position* are focused in terms of the "autonomy" of an academic "discipline" of international relations, but such a discipline must necessarily be part of political science when theoretically considered.

[4] I have dealt with some of these in *Man and His Government* (New York, McGraw-Hill, 1963), esp. in Chaps. 27, 30-32, and 35.

[5] See the papers by K. Deutsch and J. Rosenau in this volume and the literature cited there, and Deutsch, *The Nerves of Government* (London, Free Press of Glencoe, 1963), esp. Chap. IV and pp. 205 ff.

[6] Stanley Hoffmann made a valiant effort in this direction in the paper entitled "Discord in Community" which he contributed to *The Atlantic Community—Progress and Prospects*, ed., Francis O. Wilcox and H. Field Haviland, Jr. (New York, Praeger, 1963). Cf. for contrast the paper by Haviland.

federalism" have come into vogue,[7] and the protests against "community" are not likely to halt the internalization of international politics.

In considering the impact of intranational (domestic) politics on international affairs, we are confronted with a host of widespread prejudices and stereotypes. At the outset, some of these deserve mention in order to set the stage for the analysis. For one, the people are seen as desiring peace and are therefore presumed to render a country's foreign policy more pacific—if granted greater influence, either directly or through their representatives. Experience suggests that while the premise is correct, the deduction is in error; for the general public, uninformed about the complexities of foreign relations, often insists upon the very policies which make for conflict. In this connection, some of the specific dynamics of democratic politics, such as the predominant impact of the well-organized group, are frequently neglected. The notion, often advanced by well-meaning persons and by no means only academic ones, that it is possible to cope with these difficulties by education has little support in actual experience.

The history of the development of democratic politics shows that democracies were not organized to deal with foreign affairs. The classic theorists of democracy, John Locke and Jean-Jacques Rousseau, paid slight attention to the issues. "What matters principally to every citizen," Rousseau wrote, "is the observance of the laws internally, the maintenance of private property, and the security of the individual. As long as all goes well with regard to these three points, let the government negotiate and make treaties with foreign powers. It is not from this quarter that the dangers will come which are most to be feared."[8] The rise of totalitarian dictatorship in the twentieth century, intimately linked to crises growing out of the misconduct of foreign affairs, provides an eloquent rebuttal to such illusionism. But the notion persists in generally held views upon which such approaches as isolationism, neutralism, and other forms

[7] Cf. the collective volume, ed. E. Plischke, entitled *Systems of Integrating the International Community* (Princeton, N.J., Van Nostrand, 1964), and my own paper therein, "International Federalism in Theory and Practice." The latter was elaborated for the IPSA Round Table on Federalism, Oxford, 1963 (published in *Politische Vierteljahrsschrift*, 1964.) Cf. also fn. 38.

[8] Rousseau, *Contrat Social.* Cf. also Locke, *Second Essay on Civil Government*, Section 147: "What is done in reference to foreigners . . . must be left in great part to the prudence of those who have this power committed to them," the reason being that this power is "much less capable to be directed by antecedent, standing, positive laws."

of escapism are based.[9] How to structure the process of foreign-affairs decision-making in a nation which is democratically organized so as to insure an effective conduct of its foreign policy is an unsolved problem. Numerous eloquent appeals have been made, especially in the United States, but the Republic stumbles along, muddling through crisis after crisis as best it can.

Another common assumption is compounded of the two notions that a country should have an integrated foreign policy and that this foreign policy should be animated by active, if not aggressive, concern with some kind of central purpose, usually described as "national interest." Actually, an integrated foreign policy is a rare and marginal case even in the history of autocratic regimes (Charles V, Richelieu, Bismarck, and other "masters") and is typically based upon some central aggressive and/or imperialist design; its closest parallels in our time are the world-revolutionary thrusts of totalitarian foreign policy. The United States has not had such an integrated foreign policy. The foreign affairs of the United States and other democracies (as well as many other states) have been a pragmatic patchwork of a plurality of policies,[10] dealing with particular issues as they arise and inspired by some general defensive notions related to specific areas and defined in terms of concrete advantage and disadvantage, symbolized by a tariff reduced or a military involvement avoided. In his path-finding study on the national interest,[11] Charles Beard years ago showed how this patchwork is woven by officials, special interests, and occasional outbursts of popular concern. Let us therefore agree that we are not talking about foreign policy but about foreign policies, and accept as a working hypothesis that such a pragmatic and reactive approach to foreign affairs may work as well in the long run as any grand designs.

[9] *Foreign Policy in the Making, op. cit.*, Chap. 2, gives some illustrations of this notion. Recently, G. J. Mangone has published interesting findings, *Foreign Policy and Onandaga County* (1964).

[10] The volume edited by Joseph E. Black and Kenneth W. Thompson, *Foreign Policies in a World of Change* (New York, Harper & Row, 1963), while organized in terms of the foreign policy of various countries, actually serves to prove what is said in the text.

[11] Charles A. Beard, *The Idea of the National Interest—An Analytical Study in American Foreign Policy* (New York, Macmillan Co., 1934), esp. Chap. XII. For an approach based upon the assumption that the "national interest" is more or less self-evident, see Hans J. Morgenthau, *In Defense of the National Interest—A Critical Examination of American Foreign Policy* (New York, Alfred A. Knopf, 1951).

Let me turn, then, to the so-called principle of the primacy of foreign affairs—that is to say, the principle that foreign policy considerations take precedence when they clash with those of internal politics, or that they ought to do so. For as usual in politics, the existential and the normative are intermingled (and confused). It is readily apparent that to the extent that foreign and domestic issues can be distinguished, there is no such principle at work, as far as the actual conduct of foreign affairs is concerned. In all democratic countries the dynamism of popular participation in foreign affairs produces in the mind of all politicians a continuous balancing of foreign and domestic concerns, with now one, now the other in the ascendancy. That is the reason why a democracy's foreign policy is rarely more than a hodgepodge of separate policies, propagated and in turn opposed by various groups and organizations. Though it may be urged by informed observers[12] that those in charge of foreign policy should not allow internal issues to determine the course of foreign policy, how are these makers of foreign policies to escape the constellations in party and parliament that bring about such determination? Admittedly the British parliamentary system is better able to withstand the pressures of Parliament and the general public, but only at the expense of being more vulnerable to those within the governing party; the American situation is just the reverse. It stands to reason that a system which expressly proclaims that all power stems from the people will be subject to the people's preoccupations; it is found to be so in all democratic states—but not only in the democratic ones. Totalitarian governments, while somewhat freer from a general public opinion and its gyrations, are demonstrably subject to the push and pull of party divisions.[13] Hence in both democratic and totalitarian regimes the people may force a bad policy, they may prevent a good policy from being adopted, they may allow special interests to deflect national policy, and they may

[12]Joseph-Barthélemy, *La Conduite de la politique extérieure dans les démocraties* (Paris, Publications de la Conciliation Internationale, 1930). The same view has often been voiced since, notably in the book by Morgenthau cited in the previous note. See also the books in note 16.

[13]Merle Fainsod, *How Russia Is Ruled*, rev. ed. (Cambridge, Mass., Harvard University Press, 1964); Z. Brzezinski, *The Soviet Bloc*, rev. ed. (New York, Praeger, 1961), Chaps. 1-7. For the belief system which provides the framework for the shifts, that is to say, the guiding continuity, see Nathan Leites, *A Study of Bolshevism—An Analysis of Soviet Writings to Find a Set of Rules Governing Communist Political Strategy* (Glencoe, Ill., The Free Press, 1953). Despite the changes depicted by Brzezinski, these rules still largely apply.

even provide the government with ready excuses for a policy which is unpalatable to other powers.[14] Communist theory explicitly acknowledges the interdependence of domestic and foreign policy and rejects the principle of the primacy of foreign policy in favor of a primacy of domestic policy. This principle is, however, in flagrant contradiction to the world revolutionary goals of the Communist ideology, and a detailed examination of Soviet foreign policy in no way supports the contention that domestic policy has precedence over foreign policy.[15]

Overall appraisal of recent experience forces one to the conclusion that the formation of foreign policy is part of the continuous process of policy formation, responding in kaleidoscopic fashion to the interaction of a great number of interests and viewpoints. Foreign policy will dominate the decisions only to the extent to which the interests active in a particular foreign area successfully press for adequate concern and/or the general public happens to respond. One view or another may dominate for a time, and considerable uncertainty may surround particular policies.

This last observation leads me to comment briefly upon another "principle" of cabinet-style foreign policy, that of the so-called continuity of foreign policy. It too has been stated both as norm and as fact with some measure of empirical evidence to support it. The idea that foreign policy is or ought to be continuous has clearly some factual basis; yet like many expediency norms, continuity depends upon circumstances, and a sharp alteration in the situation ought obviously to elicit a rapid alteration and adaptation in policy. The principle that foreign policy is and ought to be continuous applies, therefore, only *rebus sic stantibus,* other things being equal, and only on the basis of the further understanding that "continuity" means steady and gradual transformation of policy to adapt it to evolving conditions. The principle is intended to exclude the discontinuity of sudden reversals, gyrations, and oscillations. How such a principle is to be made operative in a regime based upon a system of parties, geared to sharply antagonistic conceptions of policy, is the problem. It has become the more perplexing as foreign and domestic policy have become increasingly intertwined. One answer has been bipartisan foreign policy, but while that conception works for short

---

[14]Beard, *op. cit.,* Chap. IX. For the role of the party in integrating foreign-interest diversities, cf. W. Y. Elliott, ed., *United States Foreign Policy* (New York, Columbia University Press, 1952), pp. 133 ff.

[15]Cf. the paper by Vernon V. Aspaturian in this volume.

periods of national emergency, it is so contrary to the very spirit of party politics that it cannot be the answer for long. The American situation is deceptive in this respect, because of the fact that the real operative party division in international affairs cuts across traditional party lines, the true division being between internationalists and nationalists (formerly isolationists).[16]

Neither in England nor in the Federal Republic of Germany has a bipartisan foreign policy conception found favor with the opposition party. And rightly so, because too many vital issues are bound up with international affairs to make such an approach workable if there is to be a real opposition. To the extent, then, that party outlook and ideology impinge upon foreign policy, it will necessarily be discontinuous. This means in terms of our overall problem, of course, that intranational politics molds the handling of international affairs. A very striking instance of the resulting discontinuity occurred in connection with British Prime Minister Macmillan's efforts to bring Britain into the European Common Market. Space forbids a review of the case in its complex totality, but we may note that the party cleavage became very pronounced, some Labour politicians going so far as to indicate that they would not honor a treaty bringing Britain into the Common Market but would take her out again. It is not possible to know to what extent these vigorous hints at radical discontinuity influenced President de Gaulle's judgment in declaring himself against British entry. They are likely to have been a factor, since they suggested a fairly widespread disinclination among the British public to join the Community of the Six.[17] Democratic politics is party politics, and hence the progress of democratization has brought about an emphasis upon alternative lines of foreign policy. There are, of course, certain basic guide lines to a national policy which are said to escape the immediate impact of party

[16]See H. Bradford Westerfield, *Foreign Policy and Party Politics—Pearl Harbor to Korea* (New Haven, Yale University Press, 1958), for richly documented case studies; James A. Robinson, *Congress and Foreign Policy-Making* (Homewood, Ill., Dorsey Press, 1962), speaks of the "secondary role" of Congress in international relations. He attributes this decline to (1) the need for large amounts of technical information, (2) short decision time, and (3) financial cost. While true, it in fact reinforces what is said in the text.

[17]*Foreign Policy in the Making*, Chap. 4. The case of Britain's entry into the Common Market was most interestingly analyzed by Roland Young and James A. Robinson, "Parliamentary Decision-Making in Great Britain—The Case of the Common Market," paper delivered at APSA meeting, 1962. For a vivid, if biased, account see Drew Middleton, *The Supreme Choice—Britain and Europe* (London, Lecher & Warburg, 1963).

conflict, but it is doubtful that any such basic issues are really immune. The British case just cited touches the very core of British foreign policy. What could be more central to German foreign policy than reunification? Yet the three German parties differ considerably on how to approach it. The solidarity of the Americas as expressed in the Monroe Doctrine was believed to be sacrosanct, but did it really remain beyond party and intraparty controversy, even before the Cuban revolution put the entire doctrine in jeopardy? It has from time to time been suggested that one might deal with the problem by distinguishing the goal, such as reunification, from the means or way to achieve it. While such a distinction may at times be useful, it is often seen on closer inspection that the agreement on the goal is merely verbal and that behind the common formula there are hidden very important differences in substance. Thus reunification may mean a good many things to different people in Germany, and the same is true of Britain's joining the Common Market and of the Monroe Doctrine.[18]

The possibilities which merely verbal agreement offers for achieving an appearance of unity and continuity, where it does not in fact exist, have led to the development of formulas as a method of democratic foreign policy. Such formulas are often expressed under the heading of "doctrines." Monroe, Truman, Eisenhower, as well as Hallstein and others have been credited with such doctrines concerning highly controversial fields of foreign policy. Those doctrines introduce a certain degree of continuity into democratic foreign policies, although they tend at the same time to "rigidify" specific areas and thereby to contribute to the lack of unity of such policies. They possess, however, the very distinct advantage that they can be made the focal point of official efforts to commit the general public and a majority of the representative bodies (parliament) to a particular line. They may be compared to brand names, which allow a comparable concentration of advertising efforts. In other words, such formulas allow a party to "sell" its approach in a particular field of foreign policy. At the same time they provide a convenient facade

---

[18] For Britain, see U. W. Kitzinger, *The Politics and Economics of European Integration—Britain, Europe, and the United States* (New York, Praeger, 1963), Chaps. V-VII, and Royal Institute of International Affairs, *Britain in Western Europe* (London, New York, 1956); for the United States, see Dexter Perkins, *A History of the Monroe Doctrine*, rev. ed. (Boston, Little, Brown, 1955); on Germany, see James H. Wolfe, *Indivisible Germany—Illusion or Reality?* (The Hague, M. Nijhoff, 1963), and Wilhelm G. Grewe, *Deutsche Aussenpolitik der Nachkriegszeit* (Stuttgart, Deutsche Verlags-Anstalt, 1960), esp. pp. 169 ff.

behind which policy can be evolved and adapted to changing circumstances. While the American people and Congress remained committed to the Monroe Doctrine, American policy toward Latin America underwent a steady evolution from protectorate to partnership.[19] It would seem that such formulas give foreign policy an ideological slant, and like ideologies they are subject to elaborate manipulation.[20]

Party-conditioned discontinuity (including the intraparty conflicts over the party line) is said to be transcended by those factors determining foreign policy which operate regardless of human preferences and decisions. Among these factors (if we exclude the elusive and highly stereotyped "national character") geography has been urged recurrently as a permanent determinant of foreign policy. Not only the discredited exponents of *Geopolitik* but many others have taken the view that "the geographical position of a nation is the principal factor conditioning its foreign policy."[21] But mountains, lakes, and rivers determine policy only after its objectives have been set by peoples or rulers; or, to put this proposition more accurately, they do not determine, but condition, foreign policy. Geography does not play the role of fate; it merely does or does not present obstacles, when a government pursues a policy of expansion, or of protection if the policy is one of defense. A body of water illustrates the point; it can become a sea lane for attack as well as an obstacle assisting in the defense. Similar comments may be made about such matters as mineral resources, climate, and the rest of geographical givens. They inject a persistent conditioning factor into national foreign policy, but they do not determine it or provide it with genuine continuity.

A comparable, though slightly more flexible, situation is presented by the existence of national cultural minorities within the boundaries of a national state, especially if such minorities are regionally distributed in fixed and historically well-established habitats. The situation ought not to be confused with that in the United States, where such groups are widely scattered and most of them have recently arrived, being composed of immigrants with a determined will to become American citizens. Even here pressure groups of such

[19] Cf. Dexter Perkins, *op. cit.*, pp. 314-70.

[20] *Man and His Government*, Chap. 4; *Totalitarian Dictatorship and Autocracy* (1956), Chap. 9 (with Z. Brzezinski).

[21] Jules Cambon, in his discussion of French foreign policy, contained in a collective volume issued by the Council on Foreign Relations entitled *The Foreign Policy of the Powers* (New York, Harper and Brothers, 1935). This view is no longer prominent in the volume cited above, note 10.

minorities have been a continuing problem of American foreign policy makers, who have, however, been traditionally inclined to pay as little attention to their pressure as the democratic process will allow.[22] In Europe, by contrast, these minorities were, after World War I, given explicit protection by the peace treaties and under the League of Nations. This protection proved rather feeble, but the impact of these situations on foreign policy was nonetheless considerable. The existence of such cultural minorities is a serious challenge to the homogeneity and equality of all citizens which democratic theory presupposes.[23] In Europe such minorities have tended to reinforce the idea of an over-arching, supranational European community, especially since quite a few of them are survivals from an older European order containing supranational communities of language, religion, and so forth. In the period between the two world wars such minorities, often with distinct political aspirations, constituted almost 10 per cent (32 million) of the European population. The vast migrations following World War II have considerably reduced this figure, and the totalitarian structure in Eastern Europe has further reduced the problem.[24] Even so, the problem remains a serious one.

At the present time ideological issues arising from the worldwide Communist movement are often claimed to be the true factor of continuity. As long as the world-revolutionary ideology and the thrust toward world conquest continue, the foreign policy of all those states which are in the posture of defending themselves against this thrust is rendered continuous to that extent. But this continuity obviously depends upon the continuance of the threat. Such constellations have existed in earlier times and undoubtedly account in part for the principle itself. At the same time they reveal it as somewhat tautological; no separate principle of continuity is required for explaining the persistence of ideological orientations or for the response to them on the part of those who are threatened by such ideological expansionism. The apparent continuity is deceptive. In fact, periods of great revolutionary upheaval have usually been accompanied by a pronounced lack of continuity in foreign policy. The impact of revolutionary ideas is itself the primary factor making

[22]Cf. Bradford Westerfield, *op. cit.*, pp. 77-78; 227-39.

[23]Heinz O. Ziegler, *Die Moderne Nation: Ein Beitrag zur politischen Soziologie* (Tübingen, Mohr, 1931); Hans Kohn, *The Idea of Nationalism—A Study in its Origins and Background* (New York, Macmillan Company, 1944).

[24]For the situation about 1930, cf. Wilhelm Winkler, *Statistisches Handbuch der Europäischen Nationalitäten* (1931), pp. 153 ff.

for lack of continuity. Attempts to delineate and interpret Soviet foreign policy in terms of tsarist foreign policy have ended in failure, even though some common traits and parallel problems can be shown to prevail. To the extent that all regimes, even the most autocratic ones, depend upon a limited measure of popular approval and general consensus, continuities springing from persistent factors in a nation's location and tradition are likely to be operative. But there is no need to look upon such continuities as norms of expedience; they may even constitute distinct disvalues and cause permanent handicaps, such as Poland's wide-open frontiers. On the other hand, the discontinuities caused by party conflict in developed political orders are a positive advantage, especially because of the continuous vigorous criticism which such conflict engenders.

In this connection a relatively free and competitive press such as is found in developed democratic societies deserves brief mention. Not only does such a press provide a continuous flow of information gathered by self-reliant correspondents and reporters, although this information is undubitably of vital importance in the shaping of foreign policies. Such a press also continually scrutinizes a country's foreign policy and provides suggestions and at times directives to the policy-makers.[25] It is difficult to know precisely what the degree of impact may be and whether it currently goes beyond mild irritation. There can be no question that writers like Walter Lippmann, Raymond Aron, and James Reston, to mention only three eminent examples, have at times occasioned more or less "agonizing reappraisals" of particular policy lines and specific decisions. By molding public opinion and arousing parliamentary and congressional attention, such writers may affect the conduct of foreign policy in subtle and devious ways. It is uncertain, but nonetheless probable, that the British press, notably *The Times* and its editor, Geoffrey Dawson, had a good deal to do with British appeasement policy.[26] Since these writers and the press are part and parcel of the national political scene, their minds provide some of the most interesting

[25] Cf. the bibliography given by Ralph O. Nafziger, *International News and the Press* (New York, H. W. Wilson Co., 1940), *passim*, and such special studies as Eber M. Carroll, *French Public Opinion and Foreign Affairs, 1870-1914* (New York, London, The Century Co., 1931), which concentrate on the press.

[26] Martin Gilbert and Richard Gott, *The Appeasers—The Decline of Democracy from Hitler's Rise to Chamberlain's Downfall* (London, Weidenfeld and Nicholson, 1963), pp. 66 ff. See also B. Granzow, *A Mirror of Nazism—British Opinion and the Emergence of Hitler—1922-1933* (London, Gollancz, 1964).

transmission channels for intranational political issues and for their projection upon the international level of policy conflict. This sort of projection has had some of its most deleterious effects during wartime, when journalistic interest in particular stereotypes fitting the emotional state of war, especially prejudicial views on the national character of the enemy, may serve to fix lines of policy which prevent the making of peace.[27]

The role of the press, the absence of continuity, and the subordination of foreign to domestic issues have, along with other related studies and observations, suggested what I have called the three-level theory of democratic foreign policy.[28] It seems that part of the complexity and discontinuous opaqueness of contemporary foreign policy is due to the fact that in increasingly democratized political regimes foreign policy decisions occur on three distinct levels: (1) the technical and bureaucratic level of professional diplomacy, (2) the one-sided level of particular interest groups, and (3) the emotional level of broad popular participation. Marked deviations occur as policy decisions move from the first level to the second and from the second to the third. The first level, continuously involved in the day-to-day decisions of state department and foreign office, is distinguished by its careful attention to detail, by its reference to specific advantage or disadvantage defined in relation to the particular adversary at hand, by its operative relation with comparable technicians working for the other powers—whether partners, friends, neutrals, or enemies—and by its acceptance of a general code of conduct, called the rules of diplomacy (still a potent factor, even though considerably changed by the world-revolutionary situation).[29]

[27] Harold Nicolson, *Peacemaking—1919* (Boston and New York City, Houghton Mifflin Co., 1933); also his *Sir Arthur Nicolson, Bart., First Lord Carnock; A Study in the Old Diplomacy* (London, Constable & Co., Ltd., 1930); John L. Snell, *Wartime Origins of the East-West Dilemma over Germany* (New Orleans, Hauser Press, 1959).

[28] Carl J. Friedrich, "Die öffentliche Meinung Amerikas in der Krise," *Aussenpolitik*, VII, 1956, pp. 502 ff. Gabriel Almond, *The American People and Foreign Policy* (New York, Harcourt, Brace and Company, 1950), distinguishes four levels which he calls the general public, the attentive public, the policy and opinion elites, and the legal and political policy leadership, pp. 138-39. He does not relate these to the policy process in quite the way I have, but rather elaborates the classification of elites, pp. 140 ff.

[29] Harold C. Nicolson, *Diplomacy*, 2nd ed. (London, New York, Oxford Press, 1958). For a more personal approach, cf. Charles W. Thayer, *Diplomat* (New York, Harper, 1959).

The second level is reached when an issue of foreign relations vitally affects a particular interest group, or several such groups, so that it is induced to mobilize its resources for influencing both the experts and the popular representatives, as well as the general public, especially the press. Under this pressure the technician may retreat into inaction, he may fight back, or he may adopt the interested position in whole or in part.[30]

The third level heaves into view at those infrequent intervals when the general public becomes aroused. Such occasions may arise in connection with a threat to peace, a flagrant aggression, or some other overt act touching profound national sensibilities. When on these occasions the general public—the people's voice of old—is heard, both technicians and special interests are apt to respond by adapting themselves to the mass reaction. It is here that some of the most dramatic turns and even reversals of foreign policy have occurred. It takes extraordinary mastery, such as was displayed by John F. Kennedy at the time of the Cuba crisis, to avoid rash and irrevocable errors. This sort of third-level decision may occur after a previous technical or interested decision has been reached, as in the case of British policy after Suez, or it may be the decisive stimulant in the first place, as was true at the time of the outbreak of hostilities in Korea and again at the time of the stand-pat rejection of Soviet demands regarding Berlin in 1958.[31]

[30] Perhaps the most interesting of the older studies is the well-documented story of oil politics by Alfred Vagts, *Mexico, Europa und Amerika unter besonderer Berücksichtigung der Petroleumpolitik* (Berlin-Grunewald, W. Rothchild, 1928); my *American Policy Toward Palestine* (Washington, Public Affairs Press, 1944) shows another pressure group at work; cf. also Frank Manuel's more recent *The Realities of American-Palestine Relations* (Washington, Public Affairs Press, 1949). The oil politics in the Middle East are discussed by George Kirk, *The Middle East, 1945-1950* (London, New York, Oxford University Press, 1954), who also discusses Palestine within the general context of Mideastern international relations.

[31] W. Phillips Davison, *The Berlin Blockade: A Study in Cold War Politics* (Princeton, N.J., Princeton University Press, 1958), esp. pp. 149 ff., while sound on the leaders, fails to take into account the popular support which made Truman's and Clay's position viable. The curious lack of corresponding action in the summer of 1961 when the Berlin sector boundary was sealed off has never been satisfactorily explained; cf. Hans Speier, *Divided Berlin—The Anatomy of Soviet Political Blackmail* (New York, Praeger, 1961); there is little doubt that the public would have supported action corresponding to the airlift, if the U.S. government had taken it. Davison has also given a general analysis of the German

Since the three levels interact in various ways, the distinctions between them ought not to be exaggerated, but an inspection of, say, American policy in the Middle East proves the value of drawing attention to the dependence of international relations upon these factors. They suggest why the extent of the dependence of the foreign policies of developed constitutional systems upon *intra*-national politics allows of no facile generalizations. It very much depends upon whether the issue involves a response on the first, second, or third level.

The foregoing sketch does no more than indicate some of the basic issues. Many others deserve treatment, such as the role of minorities in affecting foreign policy in the regimes we have considered, the special problems presented by such interest groups as churches and trade unions, and the difficulties arising from the built-in propensity of democratic regimes to minimize the role of foreign affairs through such devices as isolation, neutrality, and the transfer of responsibility to supranational groupings, whether regional or worldwide.

Even more significant is the range of issues presented by the framework of political theory and its propositions that was mentioned at the outset. Power, rule, and influence, authority, legitimacy, and the problem of justice, equality, and freedom, as well as the problems of decision-making, negotiating, arbitrating, and fiscal control are part of the problem of intranational politics and the formulation and execution of foreign policies by developed (open) systems.[32] The extensive literature on these and other related issues of foreign policy-making has added much to our knowledge in all these fields. And yet very sizable research tasks loom ahead. Apart from the relatively limited, though important, areas in which

position in his two chapters contributed to the volume he edited with Speier, entitled *West German Leadership and Foreign Policy* (Evanston, Ill., Row, Peterson, 1957); this study also contains interesting analyses of other aspects of the German democracy's problems in foreign relations, with pressure groups producing various policies in specific contexts. For France, see Jean-Baptiste Duroselle's interesting chapter in Stanley Hoffmann, et al., *In Search of France* (Cambridge, Mass., Harvard University Press, 1963), pp. 305 ff., and the same author's *De Wilson à Roosevelt, Politique Extérieure des Etats Unis, 1913-1945* (Paris, A. Colin, 1960).

[32] See *Man and His Government* (New York, McGraw-Hill, 1963), *passim;* and Raymond Aron, *Paix et guerre entre les nations* (Paris, Colman, Levi, 1962). An interesting general theory was put forward by the late Eugen Fischer-Baling, *Theorie der Auswärtigen Politik* (Köln, Westdeutscher Verlag, 1960).

quantitative studies are becoming possible, in none of the developed systems of government today is the dynamics of foreign policy determination adequately known and understood. It is clear that foreign affairs are not being conducted as they once were in the bygone days of cabinet policy fashioned and directed by small cliques of insiders, whether aristocratic or bureaucratic. Yet there are at present so much experimentation and innovation, so many failures as well as successes in a variety of terms of reference that research has been able to cope with only a limited part of the whole. The rapidly increasing areas of international federalism pose a whole set of new questions, as the interdependence of domestic and foreign policies is further complicated by their conduct on two or more territorial levels.[33] Boundaries are becoming problematic as it appears increasingly uncertain what is *intra* and what not.

A functional approach to policy processes will therefore (1) treat foreign policy as part of the policies of developed political systems, seen as an interdependent collection of approaches to concrete problems having both a domestic and a foreign dimension, and (2) understand foreign affairs not only as the external aspect of self-contained systems but also as the internal aspect of supranational (regional and worldwide) systems of policy formation and control.[34] Such a treatment will enrich the understanding of intranational politics, by building an awareness of the continuous interaction between domestic and foreign issues—an interaction which is increasing steadily as the political community grows beyond the boundaries of national states.

. . .

In conclusion, it deserves to be repeated that foreign policy in mature democratic societies is closely interwoven with domestic policy without either always having precedence or always being subordinated to it. It all depends upon the extent to which the particular issue of foreign policy touches the sentiments of the public

[33]Besides the work cited in note 6, see *Systems of Integrating the International Community*, ed. Plischke (Princeton, N.J., Van Nostrand, 1964).

[34]The clashes and conflicts between politics and morals, often stressed in connection with foreign policy, e.g., K. W. Thompson, *Christian Ethics and the Dilemmas of Foreign Policy* (Durham, N. C., Duke University Press, 1959), are peculiar neither to Christianity nor to foreign policy. Cf. my *Constitutional Reason of State* (Providence, R.I., Brown University Press, 1957), for the basic issues in Western developed systems of constitutional government.

at large. In matters which profoundly arouse the people, all considerations of domestic and party politics are apt to be swept aside; in more limited matters considerations of party politics may seriously affect the outcome. Where nationalities intertwine, the passions are especially apt to be engaged, and hence democratic foreign policy becomes especially unreasonable and difficult to manipulate in the interest of peace and international cooperation. In any case, the international relations of mature and sufficiently large-scale constitutional democracies are apt to be congeries of distinctive policies suitable for particular areas rather than to constitute any "grand design." And the task of the chief policy-maker, whether president, prime minister, or secretary of state, is likely to be the most difficult and politically the most unrewarding.

chapter thirteen
LEGAL-MORAL SETTING

The Functions of
International Law

Stanley Hoffmann

The student of international law who examines its functions in the present international system and in the foreign policy of states will, unless he takes refuge in the comforting seclusion from reality that the pure theory of law once provided, be reduced to one of three attitudes. He will become a cynic, if he chooses to stress, like Giraudoux in *Tiger at the Gates,* the way in which legal claims are shaped to support any position a state deems useful or necessary on nonlegal grounds, or if he gets fascinated by the combination of cacophony and silence that characterizes international law as a system of world public order. He will become a hypocrite, if he chooses to rationalize either the conflicting interpretations and uses of law by states as a somehow converging effort destined to lead to some such system endowed with sufficient stability and solidity, or else if he endorses one particular construction (that of his own statesmen) as a privileged and enlightened contribution to the achievement of such a system. He will be overcome by consternation, if he reflects

SOURCE: From Lawrence Scheinman and David Wilkinson (eds.), *International Law and Political Crisis.* Copyright © 1968 by Little, Brown and Company (Inc.). Reprinted by permission of the author and Little, Brown and Company (Inc.).

upon the gap between, on the one hand, the ideal of a world in which traditional self-help will be at least moderated by procedures and rules made even more indispensable by the proliferation both of states and of lethal weapons, and, on the other hand, the realities of inexpiable conflicts, sacred egoisms, and mutual recriminations.

Recent efforts to bridge the growing distance between international law and political science have underlined rather than eased the predicament. On the one hand, the analysis of international law as part of the national decision-making process (in which law, i.e., the making of authoritative and controlling decisions, aims at realizing certain values through the selection of a preferred policy alternative) has the merit of diverting the student's attention from the misleading notion of law as a set of rigid commands somehow independent from and superior to the political processes of statecraft. But it has had the disastrous effect, not only of obscuring the differences between law as an instrument of policy and other, less solemn political and administrative techniques, but also encouraging the second kind of hypocrisy deplored above—that which puts a legal-universalist coating on decisions that are essentially self-serving. On the other hand, the study of the role international law actually plays in the foreign policy process and in foreign policy decisions provides political scientists at last with empirical reasons for examining a body of material which, due to the combined impact of behavioral approaches and of so-called realism, they had tended to leave disdainfully to the lawyers; but such study may actually feed the very cynicism which the realists have displayed.

Most of the authors in this book are political scientists; their conclusions are stark and, on the whole, pessimistic. Their case studies provide the reader with a perceptive analysis of the functions international law performs for the policy-maker, and with a trenchant view of the reasons why international law plays a minor part not only in the policy process but also in the establishment and maintenance of world order.

1. Some of the functions of international law constitute *assets both for the policy-maker and from the viewpoint of world order,* i.e., of providing the international milieu with a framework of predictability and with procedures for the transaction of inter-state business.

    (a) International law is an instrument of *communication.* To present one's claims in legal terms means, one, to signal to one's partner or opponent which "basic conduct norms" (to use Professor Scheinman's expression) one considers relevant or essential, and two, to indicate which procedures one intends to follow and would like the other side to follow. At a time when both the size of a highly heterogeneous international milieu and the imperatives of prudence in the resort to force make communication essential and often turn international relations into a psychological contest, international law provides a kind of common language that does not amount to a common code of legitimacy yet can serve as a joint frame of reference. (One must however remember, one, that communication is no guarantee against misperception and, two, that what is being communicated may well determine the other side's response to the message: if "we" communicate to "them" an understanding of the situation that threatens their basic values or goals—like our interpretation of the war in South Vietnam as a case of aggression—there will be no joint frame of reference at all, and in fact the competition may become fiercer.)

(b) International law affords means of *channeling conflict*—of diverting inevitable tensions and clashes from the resort to force. Whenever there have been strong independent reasons for avoiding armed conflict—in an international system in which the superpowers in particular have excellent reasons for "managing" their confrontations, either by keeping them nonviolent, or by using proxies—international law has provided statesmen both with alibis for shunning force, and with alternatives to violence. The case studies of the Berlin airlift crisis and of the Cuban missile crisis establish this point forcefully. In Berlin, both the Soviets and the West shaped their moves in such a way as to leave to the other side full responsibility for a first use of force, and to avoid the kind of frontal collision with the other side's legal claim that could have obliged the opponent to resort to force in order not to lose power or face. Thus, today as in earlier periods, law can indeed serve as an alternative to confrontation whenever states are eager or forced to look for an alternative.

2. International law also plays various useful roles in the policy process, which however do not *ipso facto* contribute to world order. Here, we are concerned with *law as a tool of policy* in the competition of state visions, objectives and tactics.

(a) The establishment of a network of rights and obligations, or the resort to legal arguments can be useful for the *protection or enhancement of a position:* if one wants to give oneself a full range of means with which to buttress a threatened status quo (cf. the present position of the West in Berlin; this is also what treaties of alliance frequently are for); if one wants to enhance one's power in a way that is demonstrably authorized by principles of international law (cf. Nasser's claim when he nationalized the Suez Canal, and Sukarno's invocation of the principle of self-determination against Malaysia); if one wants to restore a political position badly battered by an adversary's move, so that the resort to legal arguments becomes part of a strategy of restoring the *status quo ante* (Western position during the Berlin blockade; Kennedy's strategy during the Cuban missile crisis; Western powers' attempts during the first phase of the Suez crisis; Soviet tactics in the U.N. General Assembly debates on the financing of peacekeeping operations).

(b) In all those instances, policy-makers use law as a way of putting pressure on an opponent by *mobilizing international support* behind the legal rules invoked: law serves as a focal point, as the tool for "internationalizing" a national interest and as the cement of a political coalition. States that may have political misgivings about pledging direct support to a certain power whose interests only partly coincide with theirs, or because they do not want to antagonize another power thereby, may find it both easier and useful to rally to the defense of a legal principle in whose maintenance or promotion they may have a stake.

(c) As professor Gerberding points out, a policy-maker who ignores international law leaves the field of political-competition-through-legal-manipulation open to his opponents or rivals. International law provides one of the numerous *chessboards* on which state contests occur.

3. Obviously, this indicates not only that to the statesman international law provides an instrument rather than a guide for action, but also that this tool is often *not used,* when resort to it would hamper the state's interest as defined by the policymaker.

(a) One of the reasons why international law often serves as a technique of political mobilization is the appeal of reciprocity: "you must support my invocation of the rule against him, because if you let the rule be violated at my expense, someday it may be breached at yours; and we both have an interest in its preservation." But *reciprocity cuts both ways:* my using a certain legal argument to buttress my case against him may encourage him, now or later, to resort to the same argument against me; I may therefore be unwise to play on a chessboard in which, given the solemn and abstract nature of legal rights and obligations, I may not be able to make the kind of distinction between my (good) case and your (bad) one, that can best be made by resort to ad hoc, political and circumstantial evidence which is irrelevant or ruled out in legal argumentation. Thus, Professor Gerberding points out that during the Cuban crisis, when the United States tried to distinguish between Soviet missiles in Cuba and American ones in Turkey, in order to build its case and get support, America's use of the OAS Charter as the legal basis for its "quarantine" established a dangerous precedent which the Soviets could use some day, against the U.S. or its allies, on behalf of the Warsaw Pact. And in the tragicomedy of the battle over Article 19 of the U.N. Charter, one reason why the U.S. finally climbed down from its high legal horse and gave up the attempt to deprive the Soviets of their right to vote, unless they paid their share, was the growing awareness of the peril which the principle of the exercise of the U.N. taxing power by the General Assembly could constitute some day for the United States if it lost control of the Assembly.

(b) One of the things that international law "communicates" is the solemnity of a commitment: a treaty, or a provision of the Charter, serves as a kind of tripwire or burglar alarm. When it fails to deter, the victim and third parties have a fateful choice between upholding the legal principle by all means, at the cost of a possible escalation in violence, and choosing to settle the dispute more peacefully, at the cost of *fuzzing the legal issue.* For excellent political reasons, the latter course is frequently adopted, either in the form of dropping any reference to the legal principle at stake (cf. the U.S. retreat from Article 19) or in that of a *repli* on a less explosive or more procedural legal argument (cf. the U.N. organs' preference for invoking Chapter VI instead of VII, analyzed by Professor Miller with reference to Kashmir).

(c) The very *ambiguity* of international law, which in many essential areas displays either gaping holes or conflicting principles, allows policy-makers in an emergency to act as if international law were irrelevant—as if it were neither a restraint nor a guide. Professors Friedmann and Collins' analysis of the Suez crisis (second phase), and their comparison of Britain's and France's behavior with that of the U.S. and the Soviet Union in similar circumstances, are particularly eloquent in this respect. So are Professor Gerberding's conclusions about the small role played by legal considerations in the minds of President Kennedy and of his top advisers in October, 1962.

However, precisely because there is a legal chessboard for state competition, the fact that international law does not, in a crisis, really restrict one's freedom of action, does not mean that one will forgo legal rationalizations of the moves selected. Here we come to the last set of considerations about the role of law:

4. The resort to legal arguments by policy-makers may be *detrimental to world order and thereby counterproductive for the state* that used such arguments.

(a) In the legal vacuum or confusion which prevails in areas as vital to states as internal war or the use of force, each state tries to justify its conduct with legal rationalizations. The result is a kind of *escalation of claims and counterclaims,* whose consequence, in turn, is both a further devaluation of international law and a "credibility gap" at the expense of those states who have debased the currency. America's rather indiscriminate resort to highly debatable legal arguments to support its Vietnam policy is a case in point. The unsubtle reduction of international law to a mere storehouse of convenient *ex post* justifications (as in the case of British intervention at Suez, or American interventions in Santo Domingo and Vietnam) undermines the very pretense of contributing to world order with which these states have tried to justify their unilateral acts.

(b) Much of contemporary international law authorizes states to *increase their power.* In this connection, Nasser's nationalization of the Suez Canal Company was probably quite legal, and those who accept the rather tortured argument put forth by the State Department's legal advisers to justify the Cuban "quarantine" have concluded that this partial blockade was authorized by the OAS

Charter and not in contradiction with the U.N. Charter. Yet it is obvious that a full exploitation by all states of all the permissions granted by international law would be a perfect recipe for chaos.

(c) *Attempts to enforce or to strengthen international law,* far from consolidating a system of desirable restraints on state (mis)behavior, may actually *backfire* if the political conditions are not ripe. This is the central lesson of the long story of the financing of U.N. peace-keeping operations. American self-intoxication with the importance of the rule of law, fed by misleading analogies between the U.N. Charter and the U.S. Constitution, resulted ultimately in a weakening of the influence of the World Court (which largely followed America's line of reasoning), and in an overplaying of America's hand during the "non-session" of the General Assembly in the fall of 1964 and winter of 1965.

These are sobering considerations. But what they tell us is not, as so many political scientists seem to believe, that international law is, at best, a farce, and, at worst, even a potential danger; what they tell us is that *the nature of the international system condemns international law to all the weaknesses and perversions that it is so easy to deride.* International law is merely a magnifying mirror that reflects faithfully and cruelly the essence and the logic of international politics. In a fragmented world, there is no "global perspective" from which anyone can authoritatively assess, endorse, or reject the separate national efforts at making international law serve national interests above all. Like the somber universe of Albert Camus' Caligula, this is a judgeless world where no one is innocent.

One may, however, find the picture presented too gloomy for two different reasons. First, one could point out that the cases studied here are all within one corner of the international arena—the darkest: they all deal with tests involving the use or the threat of force, or the consequences of a resort to force. In other words, they deal with breakdowns of order; they do not deal with the innumerable placid instances in which the national policy process is permeated with international law, in which international law, reflecting a reciprocity of concerns or a community of tasks, plays an uncontroversial and accepted role as a restraint on and harness of state interests, as an almost seamless web of stability and predictability. Two, one could argue that a study of policy decisions in crisis situations would have led exactly to the same conclusions as this one, had it dealt with 19th century examples instead of with the period since the end of

World War Two; and yet the 19th century was a golden age for international law.

Neither argument is convincing, for reasons that I have developed elsewhere at greater length.[1] One, it is the problem of war and peace that is both the distinctive feature of international politics, and the test of any legal system. A legal system that breaks down in the area of greatest importance for its subjects is like a house without foundations. The solidity, scope and intensity of regular legal transactions is dependent on the preservation of moderation at the higher level of the states' essential interests. Two, what makes the weakness of international law at that level particularly dangerous today is the difference between the present international system and past ones: this one seems to breed more tests of will, i.e., to provide more cases of breakdown, in circumstances that leave little room for complacency.

What produces periodic crises is, first, the very complexity of an international system that covers the whole planet and includes a bewildering variety of units, regimes, ideologies, economic systems and class structures, with countless opportunities for conflict over territory, principles of legitimacy, or resources. Secondly, the new conditions of the use of force incite states to prudence in the resort to large-scale violence, but create a grave danger of escalation when violence breaks out, and also contribute to a recurrence of violence precisely because of the greater difficulty of settling disputes in a world teeming with causes of conflicts. These conflicts stay unresolved due to the very restraints on war, which used traditionally to be the most expeditious way of settling conflicts: hence lasting centers of trouble, such as the Middle East, Kashmir, Berlin, Indochina. It is the nature of the present international system which makes competitive attempts at building rival systems of law and at multiplying legal tripwires both inevitable and perilous. It is the nature of the system which makes premature worldwide attempts at regulating behavior through legal norms positively dangerous, yet keeps "informal" agreements and habits of restraint tactical and shifting, and insures that the grand principles or values that are invoked by most, and are of moral-political significance rather than of a legal nature, remain stakes in a contest for legitimacy and power.

---

[1]See my contribution to: S. Hoffmann and Karl Deutsch (eds.), *The Relevance of International Law* (Cambridge: Schenkman Publ. Co., 1968, forthcoming); also, *The State of War* (New York: Praeger, 1965), Chaps. 4–5.

The permanent plight of international law is that, now as before, it shows on its body of rules all the scars inflicted by the international state of war. The tragedy of contemporary international law is that of a double divorce: first, between the old liberal dream of a world rule of law, and the realities of an international system of multiple minidramas that always threaten to become major catastrophes; second, between the old dream and the new requirements of moderation, which in the circumstances of the present system suggest a *down playing* of formal law in the realm of peace-and-war issues, and an *upgrading* of more flexible techniques, until the system has become less fierce. The interest of international law for the political scientist is that there is no better way of grasping the continuing differences between order within a national society and the fragile order of international affairs than to study how and when states use legal language, symbols and documents, and with what results. One can only hope that case studies such as these, by showing at what points in the political process international law becomes relevant, will allow both students and statesmen to overcome consternation or sarcasm and to think of ways in which statecraft could combine the defense of national interests and the interest in world order, make the state's material power serve both, and harness both to that strategy and ethics of prudence that Raymond Aron has called for.

International Law
and Assumptions
about the State
System

*William D. Coplin**

Most writers on international relations and international law still examine the relationship between international law and politics in terms of the assumption that law either should or does function only as a coercive restraint on political action. Textbook writers on general international politics like Morgenthau,[1] and Lerche and Said,[2] as well as those scholars who have specialized in international

SOURCE: From *World Politics*. Vol. XVII, No. 4 (1965). Copyright © 1965 by Princeton University Press. Reprinted and abridged by permission of the author and Princeton University Press.

*I want to thank Dr. Robert W. Tucker of the Johns Hopkins University and Richard Miller of Wayne State University Law School for their constructive criticism of the first draft of this article.

[1] Hans J. Morgenthau, *Politics Among Nations* (New York 1961), 275-311. The entire evaluation of the "main problems" of international law is focused on the question of what rules are violated and what rules are not.

[2] Charles O. Lerche, Jr., and Abdul A. Said, *Concepts of International Politics* (Englewood Cliffs, N.J., 1963), 167-87. That the authors have employed the assumption that international law functions as a system of restraint is evident from the title of their chapter which examines international law, "Limitations on State Actions."

434

law like J. L. Brierly[3] and Charles De Visscher,[4] make the common assumption that international law should be examined as a system of coercive norms controlling the actions of states. Even two of the newer works, *The Political Foundations of International Law* by Morton A. Kaplan and Nicholas deB. Katzenbach[5] and *Law and Minimum World Public Order* by Myres C. McDougal and Florentino P. Feliciano,[6] in spite of an occasional reference to the non-coercive aspects of international law, are developed primarily from the model of international law as a system of restraint. Deriving their conception of the relationship between international law and political action from their ideas on the way law functions in domestic communities, most modern writers look at international law as an instrument of direct control. The assumption that international law is or should be a coercive restraint on state action structures almost every analysis, no matter what the school of thought or the degree of optimism or pessimism about the effectiveness of the international

[3]J. L. Brierly, *The Law of Nations* (New York 1963), I. Brierly defines international law as "the body of rules and principles of action which are binding upon civilized states in their relations. . . ."

[4]Charles De Visscher, *Theory and Reality in Public International Law* (Princeton 1957), 99-100.

[5]Morton A. Kaplan and Nicholas deB. Katzenbach, *The Political Foundations of International Law* (New York 1961), 5. In a discussion of how the student should observe international law and politics, the authors write: "To understand the substance and limits of such constraining rules (international law), it is necessary to examine the interests which support them in the international system, the means by which they are made effective, and the functions they perform. Only in this way is it possible to predict the areas in which rules operate, the limits of rules as effective constraints, and the factors which underlie normative change." Although the authors are asking an important question—"Why has international law been binding in some cases?"—they still assume that international law functions primarily as a direct restraint on state action. For an excellent review of this book, see Robert W. Tucker, "Resolution," *Journal of Conflict Resolution*, VII (March 1963), 69-75.

[6]Myres S. McDougal and Florentino P. Feliciano, *Law and Minimum World Public Order* (New Haven 1961), 10. The authors suggest that if any progress in conceptualizing the role of international law is to be made, it is necessary to distinguish between the "factual process of international coercion and the process of authoritative decision by which the public order of the world community endeavors to regulate such process of coercion." This suggestion is based on the assumption that international law promotes order primarily through the establishment of restraints on state actions.

legal system.[7] With an intellectual framework that measures international law primarily in terms of constraint on political action, there is little wonder that skepticism about international law continues to increase while creative work on the level of theory seems to be diminishing.[8]

Therefore, it is desirable to approach the relationship between international law and politics at a different functional level, not because international law does not function at the level of coercive restraint, but because it also functions at another level. In order to illustrate a second functional level in the relationship between international law and politics, it is necessary to examine the operation of domestic law. In a domestic society, the legal system as a series of interrelated normative statements does more than direct or control

[7] There are a few writers who have tried to approach international law from a different vantage point. For a survey of some of the other approaches to international law and politics, see Michael Barkun, "International Norms: An Interdisciplinary Approach," *Background*, VIII (August 1964), 121-29. The survey shows that few "new" approaches to international law have developed beyond the preliminary stages, save perhaps for the writings of F. S. C. Northrop. Northrop's works (e.g., *Philosophical Anthropology and Practical Politics* [New York 1960], 326-30) are particularly significant in their attempt to relate psychological, philosophical, and cultural approaches to the study of law in general, although he has not usually been concerned with the overall relationship of international law to international political action. Not mentioned in Barkun's survey but important in the discussion of international law and politics is Stanley Hoffmann, "International Systems and International Law," in Klaus Knorr and Sidney Verba, eds., *The International System* (Princeton 1961), 205-38. However, Hoffmann's essay is closer in approach to the work by Kaplan and Katzenbach than to the approach developed in this article. Finally, it is also necessary to point to an article by Edward McWhinney, "Soviet and Western International Law and the Cold War in a Nuclear Era of Bipolarity: Inter-Bloc Law in a Nuclear Age," *Canadian Yearbook of International Law*, I (1963), 40-81. Professor McWhinney discusses the relationship between American and Russian structures of action, on the one hand, and their interpretations of international law, on the other. While McWhinney's approach is basically similar to the one proposed in this article in its attempt to relate international law to politics on a conceptual level, his article is focused on a different set of problems, the role of national attitudes in the contemporary era on ideas of international law. Nevertheless, it is a significant contribution to the task of analyzing more clearly the relationship between international law and politics.

[8] See Richard A. Falk, "The Adequacy of Contemporary International Law: Gaps in Legal Thinking," *Virginia Law Review*, L (March 1964), 231-65, for a valuable but highly critical analysis of contemporary international legal theory.

the actions of its members through explicit rules backed by a promise of coercion. Systems of law also act on a more generic and pervasive level by serving as authoritative (i.e., accepted as such by the community) modes of communicating or reflecting the ideals and purposes, the acceptable roles and actions, as well as the very processes of the societies. The legal system functions on the level of the individual's perceptions and attitudes by presenting to him an image of the social system—an image which has both factual and normative aspects and which contributes to social order by building a consensus on procedural as well as on substantive matters. In this sense, law in the domestic situation is a primary tool in the "socialization"[9] of the individual.

International law functions in a similar manner: namely, as an institutional device for communicating to the policy-makers of various states a consensus on the nature of the international system. The purpose of this article is to approach the relationship between international law and politics not as a system of direct restraints on state action, but rather as a system of quasi-authoritative communications to the policy-makers concerning the reasons for state actions and the requisites for international order. It is a "quasi-authoritative" device because the norms of international law represent only an imperfect consensus of the community of states, a consensus which rarely commands complete acceptance but which usually expresses generally held ideas. Given the decentralized nature of law-creation and law-application in the international community, there is no official voice of the states as a collectivity. However, international law taken as a body of generally related norms is the closest thing to such a voice. Therefore, in spite of the degree of uncertainty about the authority of international law, it may still be meaningful to examine international law as a means for expressing the commonly held assumptions about the state system.

The approach advocated in this article has its intellectual antecedents in the sociological school, since it seeks to study international law in relation to international politics. Furthermore, it is similar to that of the sociological school in its assumption that there is or should be a significant degree of symmetry between international law and politics on the level of intellectual constructs—that is, in the way in which international law has expressed and even shaped ideas about

---

[9] See Gabriel A. Almond and James S. Coleman, eds., *The Politics of the Developing Areas* (Princeton 1960), 26-31, for an explanation of the concept of socialization.

relations between states. It is hoped that this approach will contribute to a greater awareness of the interdependence of international
law and conceptions of international politics.

Before analyzing the way in which international law has in the
past and continues today to reflect common attitudes about the
nature of the state system, let us discuss briefly the three basic
assumptions which have generally structured those attidues.[10] First,
it has been assumed that the state is an absolute institutional value
and that its security is the one immutable imperative for state action.
If there has been one thing of which policy-makers could always be
certain, it is that their actions must be designed to preserve their
state. Second, it has been assumed that international politics is a
struggle for power, and that all states seek to increase their power.
Although the forms of power have altered during the evolution of
the state system, it has been generally thought that states are
motivated by a drive for power, no matter what the stakes. The third
basic assumption permeating ideas about the international system has
to do with maintaining a minimal system of order among the states.
This assumption, symbolized generally by the maxim "Preserve the
balance of power," affirms the necessity of forming coalitions to
counter any threat to hegemony and of moderating actions in order
to avoid an excess of violence that could disrupt the system.

. . .

I. CLASSICAL INTERNATIONAL LAW
AND THE IMAGE OF THE STATE SYSTEM

Almost every legal aspect of international relations from 1648 to
1914 reinforced and expressed the assumptions of the state system.
State practices in regard to treaties, boundaries, neutrality, the

[10]The following discussion of the assumptions of the state system is brief,
since students of international politics generally agree that the three assumptions
listed have structured most of the actions of states. This agreement is most
complete concerning the nature of the "classical" state system. The author is
also of the opinion that these assumptions continue to operate today in a somewhat mutated form. (See his unpublished manuscript "The Image of Power
Politics: A Cognitive Approach to the Study of International Politics," chaps. 2,
4, 8.) Note also the agreement on the nature of classical ideas about international politics in the following: Ernst B. Haas, "The Balance of Power as
Guide to Policy-Making," *Journal of Politics*, XV (August 1953), 370-97;
Morton A. Kaplan, *System and Process in International Politics* (New York
1957); 22-36; and Edward Vose Gulick, *Europe's Classical Balance of Power*
(Ithaca, N.Y., 1955).

occupation of new lands, freedom of the seas, and diplomacy, as well as classical legal doctrines, provide ample illustration of the extent to which the basic assumptions of the state were mirrored in international law.

The essential role of treaties in international law reflected the three assumptions of the state system. First, treaty practices helped to define the nature of statehood. Emanating from the free and unfettered will of states, treaties were the expression of their sovereign prerogatives. Statehood itself was defined in part as the ability to make treaties, and that ability presupposed the equality and independence usually associated with the idea of the state. Moreover, certain definitive treaties, like those written at the Peace of Augsburg (1515) and the Peace of Westphalia (1648), actually made explicit the attributes of statehood. The former treaty affirmed the idea that the Prince had complete control over the internal affairs of the state, while the latter emphasized that states were legally free and equal in their international relationships.[11]

. . .

Treaty law also contributed to the evolution of the classical assumption regarding the maintenance of the international system. Both explicitly and implicitly, treaties affirmed the necessity of an international system. Whether or not they contained such phrases as "balance of power," "just equilibrium," "universal and perpetual peace,"[12] "common and public safety and tranquillity,"[13] "public tranquillity on a lasting foundation,"[14] or "safety and interest of Europe,"[15] the most important treaties during the classical period affirmed the desirability of maintaining the international system.[16] Also, many treaties reaffirmed earlier treaty agreements, contributing to the idea that the international system was a continuing, operative unity.[17] Therefore, treaties usually reminded the policy-maker that the maintenance of the international system was a legitimate and necessary objective of state policy.

[11] For the effects of the two treaties, see Charles Petrie, *Diplomatic History, 1713-1939* (London 1949), III; David Jayne Hill, *A History of Diplomacy in the International Development of Europe* (New York 1924), 603-6; and Arthur Nussbaum, *A Concise History of the Law of Nations* (New York 1961), 116.

[12] *Treaty of Ryswick*, Article I, in *ibid.*

[13] *Barrier Treaty of 1715*, Article I, in *ibid.*, Vol. X.

[14] *Treaty of Vienna, 1713*, in *ibid.*, Vol. VIII.

[15] *Treaty of Quadruple Alliance, 1815*, in *ibid.*, Vol. XI.

[16] Leo Gross, "The Peace of Westphalia, 1648-1948," *American Journal of International Law*, XLII (January 1948), 20-40.

[17] For a treaty which expressed the necessity of keeping prior obligations, see *Treaty of Aix-la-Chapelle, 1748*, in Browning, ed., Vol. X.

Finally, treaties affirmed the necessity and, in part, the legality of the drive for power. The constant juggling of territory, alliances, and other aspects of capability was a frequent and rightful subject of treaty law. Treaties implicitly confirmed that power was the dynamic force in relations between states by defining the legal criteria of power and, more important, by providing an institutional means, subscribed to by most of the members of the system, which legalized certain political transactions, such as territorial acquisition and dynastic exchange.

A second state practice which contributed to the classical assumptions about the state system was the legal concept of boundaries. Inherent in the very idea of the boundary were all three assumptions of the classical system. First, the boundary marked off that most discernible of all criteria of a state's existence—territory.[18] A state was sovereign within its territory, and the boundary was essential to the demarcation and protection of that sovereignty. Freedom and equality necessitated the delineation of a certain area of complete control; the boundary as conceptualized in international law was the institutional means through which that necessity was fulfilled. Second, the boundary was essential for the preservation of the international system.[19] After every war the winning powers set up a new or revised set of boundaries which aided them in maintaining order by redistributing territory. More important, the boundary also provided a criterion by which to assess the intentions of other states. Change of certain essential boundaries signified a mortal threat to the whole system, and signaled the need for a collective response.[20] Finally, the legal concept of boundaries provided a means through which the expansion and contraction of power in the form of territory could be measured. Since the boundary was a legal means of measuring territorial changes, international law in effect reinforced the idea that the struggle for power was an essential and accepted part of international politics. All three assumptions of the state system, therefore, were mirrored in the classical legal concept of boundaries.

Another international legal concept which reflected the assumptions about the state system was the idea of neutrality. The primary

[18]See John H. Herz, *International Politics in the Atomic Age* (New York 1962), p. 53, for a discussion of the role of territory in the classical state system and the international legal system.

[19]See Hoffmann, 212, 215, for a discussion of the way in which territorial settlements in treaties aided stability within the system. He calls this function part of the law of political framework.

[20] E.g., the English and French attitude toward Belgium.

importance of neutrality law lay in its relation to the classical emphasis on the preservation of the international system. The practice of neutrality was an essential element in the mitigation of international conflict because it provided a legitimate means of lessening the degree of violence in any given war (by reducing the number of belligerents) and also made those involved in a war aware of the possibility of hostile actions from outside should the conflict weaken the participants too greatly. In short, the legal concept of neutrality implied that the actions of states must remain moderate and flexible in order to preserve the state system.[21]

There were other aspects of international legal practice which substantiated the assumptions of the state system. For instance, since the sixteenth century the law pertaining to the occupation of new lands and to freedom of the high seas constituted a vital aspect of international law, and provided "legitimate" areas in which the struggle for power could take place.

From the outset, most of the non-European areas of the world were considered by the great powers to be acceptable arenas for the struggle for power. International legal practice made it easy for states to gain control of land overseas by distinguishing between the laws of occupation and the laws of subjugation. This distinction made it easier for powers to extend control over non-European territorial expanses because it enabled states to "occupy" territory legally without actually controlling it.[22] Through the laws of occupation, international law confirmed the assumption that colonial expansion was part of the struggle for power.

The law of the high seas also contributed to the idea of the struggle for power. The expansion of trade, military power, and territorial domain was, throughout almost the entire history of the state system, greatly dependent upon the free use of the high seas. The laws of the sea were designed so that maximum use could be made of this relatively cheap mode of transportation. Like the laws of occupation of non-European territory, sea law helped to keep the distribution of power among European states in continuous flux.[23]

---

[21] For a discussion of the role of neutrality in the balance of power system, see McDougal and Feliciano, 391-413.

[22] L. Oppenheim, in H. Lauterpacht, ed., *International Law* (New York 1948), I, p. 507.

[23] The attempt to control a "closed sea" was sometimes a bid by a powerful state to freeze the *status quo*—e.g., Portugal's control of the Indian Ocean in the sixteenth and seventeenth centuries (Nussbaum, Ill).

Therefore, both the laws of the seas and the laws governing the occupation of new lands were instrumental in "legalizing" areas for conflict. Given the assumption that states always maximize their power, a free sea and the easy acquisition of non-European lands provided the fluidity needed for the states to struggle for power. Moreover, both sets of laws removed the area of conflict from the home territory, thus enabling states to increase the scope of their struggle without proportionately increasing its intensity.[24]

. . .

Although the norms of classical international law sometimes went unheeded, the body of theory and of state practice which constituted "international law as an institution" nonetheless expressed in a quasi-authoritative manner the three assumptions about international politics. It legalized the existence of states and helped to define the actions necessary for the preservation of each state and of the system as a whole. It reinforced the ideas that vigilance, moderation, and flexibility are necessary for the protection of a system of competing states. And finally, international law established a legalized system of political payoffs by providing a means to register gains and losses without creating a static system. In fact, this last aspect was essential to the classical state system. With international law defining certain relationships (territorial expansion, empire-building, etc.) as legitimate areas for political competition, other areas seemed, at least generally in the classical period, to be removed from the center of the political struggle. By legitimizing the struggle as a form of political competition rather than as universal conflict, international law sanctioned a form of international system that was more than just an anarchic drive for survival.

II. CONTEMPORARY INTERNATIONAL LAW AND THE ASSUMPTIONS OF THE STATE SYSTEM

As a quasi-authoritative system of communicating the assumptions of the state system to policy-makers, contemporary international law no longer presents a clear idea of the nature of international politics.

[24]Analysts have argued over whether colonialism reduced or exacerbated international antagonism. Without settling the argument, it seems safe to say that the struggle for colonies was a more spectacular and relatively less dangerous system of conflict than was competition for European land.

This is in part a result of the tension, within the structure of contemporary international law itself, between the traditional legal concepts and the current practices of states. International law today is in a state of arrested ambiguity—in a condition of unstable equilibrium between the old and the new. As a result, it no longer contributes as it once did to a consensus on the nature of the state system. In fact, it adds to the growing uncertainty and disagreement as to how the international political system itself is evolving. The following discussion will attempt to assess the current developments in international law in terms of the challenges those developments make to the three assumptions of the state system. It is realized that the three assumptions themselves have already undergone change, but our purpose is to show where contemporary international legal practice and theory stand in relation to that change.

The Challenge to the State and the System

The current legal concept of the state is a perfect example of the arrested ambiguity of contemporary international law and of the threat that this condition represents to the assumptions of the state system. . . . Certain contemporary developments contrast sharply with the traditional territory-oriented conceptions of international law.[25] With the growth of international entities possessing supranational powers (e.g., ECSC), the legal idea of self-contained units based on territorial control lacks the clear basis in fact that it once enjoyed. Many of the traditional prerogatives of the sovereign state, such as control over fiscal policy,[26] have been transferred in some respects to transnational units. While the development of supranational powers is most pronounced in Europe, there is reason to believe, especially concerning international cooperation on technical matters, that organizations patterned on the European experience might occur elsewhere.

. . .

[25] For a survey of current challenges to traditional international law, see Wolfgang Friedmann, "The Changing Dimensions of International Law," *Columbia Law Review*, LXII (November 1962), 1147-65. Also, see Richard A. Falk, *The Role of the Domestic Courts in the International Legal Order* (Syracuse 1964), 14-19, for a discussion of the fact that while there is a growing "functional obsolescence" of the state system, the assumptions of the state system continue to operate for psychological and political reasons.

[26] E.g., Articles 3 and 4 of the *Treaty Establishing the European Coal and Steel Community* (April 18, 1951).

Other developments in contemporary international law represent, theoretically at least, a challenge to the assumption that the state and its freedom of action are an absolute necessity for the state system. Most noticeable has been the attempt to develop an international organization which would preserve a minimal degree of order. Prior to the League of Nations, there had been attempts to institutionalize certain aspects of international relations, but such attempts either did not apply to the political behavior of states (e.g., the Universal Postal Union) or did not challenge the basic assumptions of the state system (as the very loosely defined Concert of Europe failed to do). As it was formulated in the Covenant and defined by the intellectuals, the League represented a threat to the assumptions of the state system because it sought to settle once and for all the tension between the policy-maker's commitment to preserve his state and his desire to maintain the state system by subordinating his state to it through a formal institution.

Proponents of the League saw it as a means to formalize a system of maintaining international order by committing states in advance to a coalition against any state that resorted to war without fulfilling the requirements of the Covenant. If it had been operative, such a commitment would have represented a total revolution in the legal concept of the state as an independent entity, since it would have abolished the most essential of all sovereign prerogatives, the freedom to employ coercion. However, the ideal purpose of the League, on the one hand, and the aims of politicians and the actual constitutional and operational aspects of the League, on the other, proved to be quite different. . . .

Like the League, the United Nations was to replace the state as the paramount institutional value by establishing a constitutional concert of powers. However, it has succeeded only in underscoring the existing tension between the drive to maintain the state and the goal of maintaining the system. In the Charter itself, the tension between the state and the system remains unresolved.[27]   Nor does the actual operation of the United Nations provide a very optimistic basis for the hope that tension will be lessened in the future.

In terms of international law, regional organizations constitute a mixed challenge to the traditional relationship between the state and the system. Although certain organizations represent an attempt to transcend the traditional bounds of their constituent members on

[27]Compare Articles 25-51, or paragraphs 2-7 in Article 2, for the contrast between system-oriented and state-oriented norms.

functional grounds, this does not necessarily mean that those members have rejected the state as a political form. In reality, if regional organizations represent any transformation at all in the structural relationship between the state and the system, they constitute an attempt to create a bigger and better state, an attempt which is not contrary to the traditional assumptions of the state system. . . .

A more serious challenge, but one somewhat related to the challenge by regional organizations, is the changing relation of the individual to the international legal order. In the classical system, international law clearly relegated the individual to the position of an object of the law. Not the individual, but the state had the rights and duties of the international legal order.[28] This legal formulation was in keeping with the classical emphasis on the sanctity of the state. Today, however, the development of the concepts of human rights, international and regional organizations, and the personal responsibility of policy-makers to a higher law not only limit the scope of legally permissible international action but, more important, limit the traditional autonomy of the leaders of the state over internal matters.[29] The idea that the individual rather than the state is the unit of responsibility in the formulation of policy has a long intellectual tradition;[30] however, it is only recently that the norms associated with that idea have become a part of international law.

. . .

The Challenge to the Concept of Power

One of the most significant developments in international law today relates to the assumption that states do and should compete for power. In the classical period, international law, through the legal concepts of neutrality, rules of warfare, occupation of new lands,

[28] See Corbett, 53-56, for a discussion of the place of the individual in classical international law.

[29] Most modern writers have noted that the individual no longer stands in relation to international law solely as the object (e.g., Corbett, 133-35, or Friedmann, 1160-62), though they are agreed that, to use Friedmann's words, "the rights of the individual in international law are as yet fragmentary and uncertain."

[30] According to Guido de Ruggiero, *The History of European Liberalism* (Boston 1959), 363-70, the liberal conception of the state has always assumed that the individual was the absolute value, though this idea has not always been operative.

rules of the high seas, and laws of diplomacy, reinforced the idea that a struggle for power among states was normal and necessary. Today, many of these specific legal norms still apply, but the overall permissible range of the struggle for military power[31] has been limited by the concept of the just war.

The idea of the just war is not new to international law. Most of the classical writers discussed it, but they refused to define the concept in strict legal terms and usually relegated it to the moral or ethical realm.[32] The nineteenth-century positivists completely abandoned the doctrine with the formulation that "wars between nations must be considered as just on both sides with respect to treatment of enemies, military arrangements, and peace."[33] However, with the increased capability of states to destroy each other, a movement has grown to regulate force by legal means.

. . .

The concept of the just war directly challenges the assumptions of the state system, because it implies that the military struggle for power is no longer a normal process of international politics. No longer does international law legitimize the gains of war, and no longer do policy-makers look upon war as a rightful tool of national power.[34] This is not to say that states do not use force in their current struggles or that the doctrine of the just war would deter them in a particular case. However, the doctrine does operate on the conceptual level by expressing to the policy-makers the idea that the use of force is no longer an everyday tool of international power politics. In terms of the traditional assumption about the state's natural inclination to maximize power, the contemporary legal commitment to the just-war doctrine represents a profound and historic shift.

[31] Although the military struggle today is considered to be only one aspect of the struggle for power, it is the one most closely related to the problem of order in both the classical and the contemporary system, and therefore the most crucial in the relationship between law and politics.

[32] See D. W. Bowett, *Self-Defense in International Law* (Manchester 1958), 156-57 and Nussbaum, 137, 153-55, 171.

[33] See Nussbaum, 182-83. Also see Ian Brownlie, *International Law and the Use of Force by States* (Oxford 1963), 15-18.

[34] Certainly, technological developments have been primarily responsible for the rejection of war as a typical tool of international power. In this case, as in most, international legal doctrine mirrors the existing attitudes and helps to reinforce them.

III. INTERNATIONAL LAW AND THE REALITY OF CONTEMPORARY INTERNATIONAL POLITICS

Contemporary international legal practice, then, is developing along lines which represent a threat not only to traditional concepts of international law but also to the assumptions of the state system. The sporadic developments in international and regional organizations, the evolving place of the individual in the international legal system, and the doctrine of the just war are manifestations of the transformation occurring today both in the structure of international law and in attitudes about the state system. Actually, of course, the traditional conceptions of international law and the classical assumptions about international politics are not extinct.[35] Rather, there is in both international law and politics a perplexing mixture of past ideas and current developments. The only thing one can be sure of is that behind the traditional legal and political symbols which exist today in a somewhat mutated form, a subtle transformation of some kind is taking place.

. . .

In order to understand more fully the relation of international law to world politics, it is necessary to do more than examine law merely as a direct constraint on political action. The changes in the conceptual basis of international law that are manifested in current practice and, to a lesser extent, in current legal theory are symptomatic of a series of social and institutional revolutions that are transforming all of international politics. To conclude that international law must adjust to political reality, therefore, is to miss the point, since international law is part of political reality and serves as an institutional means of developing and reflecting a general consensus on the nature of international reality. In the contemporary period, where the international legal system is relatively decentralized, and international politics is subject to rapid and profound development, it is necessary to avoid a conceptual framework of international law

[35] As in the past, international lawyers are still concerned with definitions and applications of concepts of territorial integrity, self-defense, and domestic jurisdiction, and policy-makers are still motivated by the traditional ideas of state security and power. However, the traditional political and legal symbols have been "stretched" to apply to current conditions. For a development of this position see Coplin, chaps. 4 and 8.

which breeds undue pessimism because it demands too much. If international law does not contribute directly and effectively to world order by forcing states to be peaceful, it does prepare the conceptual ground on which that order could be built by shaping attitudes about the nature and promise of international political reality.

The Relative Irrelevance of Moral Norms in International Politics

Werner Levi

THE UNVERIFIED ASSUMPTIONS

There exists a widespread belief that the absence of common moral norms among the peoples of the world is largely responsible for the hostilities and the violence characteristic of international relations. The hopeful assertion is made that cooperative behavior and a more peaceful solution of international conflicts would be assured if only the nations could agree on common moral norms. The reasoning is, more or less, that moral norms prescribe the propriety of action. When the use of violence in human affairs is morally condemned and the maintenance of peace is elevated to a high moral value, people who adhere to these norms can always come to an agreement on whether they should or should not behave in a certain manner. In any case, acceptance of these norms would make it very

SOURCE: From *Social Forces*, Vol. XLIV, No. 2 (1965). Copyright © 1965 by the University of North Carolina Press. Reprinted and abridged by permission of the author and the University of North Carolina Press.

difficult for either side in a conflict to engage in evil action toward the other. Ideally, these moral norms would become so embedded in international institutions and become so much part of the decision-makers' social environment, that interests and goals incompatible with these norms would never be allowed to reach the acute stage in which their realization would be attempted. They would be discarded as soon as they were conceived. Swords may be beaten into plowshares.[1]

This belief may be considered an oversimplified and specialized aspect of the theory that the foundation of any integrated society is the normative structure of a common value-orientation among its members.[2] So broadly stated, that is when all values are included, this theory can be justified at least on the grounds that if all the members of a society had differing and conflicting values, there could hardly be cohesion of any kind. The real problem in discovering the role played by values in maintaining a relatively peaceful society is to determine which values are relevant and in what manner they are relevant. Of special interest here is the somewhat narrower question whether moral norms are relevant and why and how?

A slightly different, though related theory is that the possession of common values is a community building factor.[3] This is presumably true because almost anything people have in common has such a propensity. Common values would then contribute to the integration—and therewith possibly peacefulness—of a community not because they are values or because of their substance, but because they are something shared by the members. Their effectiveness would rest on the same basis that the flag as a common symbol to

---

[1] For some examples see F. Ernest Johnson (ed.), *World Order: Its Intellectual and Cultural Foundation* (New York: Harper & Bros., 1945), p. 22; Thomas Merton *et al. Breakthrough to Peace* (Norfolk, Va.: New Directions, 1962), p. 29; Arthur I. Waskow, *The Worried Man's Guide to World Peace* (New York: Doubleday & Co., 1963), p. 49.

[2] E.g., Talcott Parsons and Edward A. Shils (eds.), *Toward a General Theory of Action* (New York: Harper & Row, 1962), pp. 159-189; Talcott Parsons, *The Social System* (Glencoe, Ill.: The Free Press, 1951), pp. 41-42.

[3] Rudolf Smend, *Verfassung und Verfassungsrecht* (München: Duncker & Humblot, 1928), pp. 34-45; Karl W. Deutsch *et al., The Political Community and the North Atlantic Area* (Princeton, New Jersey: Princeton University Press, 1957), p. 123; Philip E. Jacob and James V. Toledano, *The Integration of Political Communities* (Philadelphia: J. B. Lippincott Co., 1964), pp. 209-246; Werner Levi, *Fundamentals of World Organization* (Minneapolis: University of Minnesota Press, 1950), p. 21.

the enjoyment of a national sport could contribute to integration. Whether also the content, the substance of moral norms would have the effect of producing more peaceful behavior leads exactly to the crux of the hopeful 'assertion that common moral norms would produce a peaceful society.

The assumption that they do implies an extraordinary confidence in the ability of moral norms to work as determinants of behavior. They would not merely be the rules and precepts according to which all behavior ought to be shaped, they would be expected, in fact, to shape behavior. They are envisaged as the checkpoint through which all decisions to act have to pass successfully. The moral norms would represent a superstructure over all social behavior, controlling it in its totality. An even furtive look at international behavior throughout the ages would raise serious doubts about the effectiveness of such a control or else raise serious doubts about the nature of moral norms applying to the international society. On this last point, the answer can quickly be provided that, at least as far as public confessions everywhere are concerned, the basic moral norms alleged to apply to international behavior are the same as are presumably to apply to any behavior. This reduces the scope of this investigation to the effectiveness of moral norms as controls in international behavior. In its pursuit a distinction can usefully be made between moral norms and interests.[4] Both are classes of values and motivators of behavior. But they are psychologically and functionally different. Moral norms are evaluative. They are the rules according to which behavior ought to be shaped and, as long as they remain untranslated into law, their enforcement is a matter of conscience. Their function is to maintain the individual in coexistence with his fellow individuals in a society. Interests are the wants and desires of an essentially non-ethical-normative nature. They relate to—usually—material needs, directly or indirectly, and they function to produce behavior intended to satisfy these needs. The relationship between moral values and interests is hierarchical, with interests, or at least their realization, subordinated to morality.[5] One of the most striking features of international behavior is the obvious disturbance in this hierarchy. Wherein may lie its causes—whether in the nature of international politics or in the

---

[4] For examples of the discussion of this vexing problem see Vernon Van Dyke, "Values and Interests," *American Political Science Review,* 56 (September 1962), pp. 567-576; Jacob and Toledano, *op. cit.,* pp. 224-225.

[5] The important point here is not to state a final definition of morality and interests as different types of values. It is, rather, to emphasize that they differ as motivational forces of behavior.

nature of moral norms or in a combination of both—is the object of this investigation. For, if it should turn out that the influence of moral norms on international behavior is nonexistent or very limited, the acceptance of common norms by the nations as the remedy of international ills would not be very helpful; respectively, the prevailing ills must be due to other causes than the absence of common norms.

THE EMPIRICAL EVIDENCE

History provides at best an inconclusive answer to the question. There is evidence that in the course of time men have attempted to humanize their relations. There is the counter-evidence also that they have treated each other with increasing dishonesty and cruelty. The same civilization which raised the status of the common man has also perfected his destruction. Still, until that destruction takes place, from time to time statesmen appear to find it increasingly necessary to justify their international acts in moral terms. The records of international agencies abound in moral appeals and in moral justifications of international actions. The content of international law reflects more and more the improvement of international methods of coexistence from a moral viewpoint. Charitable impulses can be discovered behind grants of mutual aid. Those who look desperately for a greater moralization of the international society may find some hope in this development. But they should not be under any illusion that the order of things is becoming very favorable for the ascendancy of moral norms. There have been statesmen who have shaped their foreign policy according to moral prescriptions, which has all too often earned them the derogatorily meant sobriquet of "idealist" or "dreamer." The evidence is overwhelming that in making their decisions most statesmen have asked, first, what needed to be done to preserve the interests of the country, and only second, if ever, what the moral thing might be to do. When there was incompatibility in the answers, the interests almost always carried the day. Mostly for reasons of expediency or to satisfy public demands for moral behavior, the interests may have been reformulated or adjusted, but most rarely changed and never abandoned—unless different interests, judged higher, but interests nevertheless, made it advisable to adhere to moral norms in the given instant. Such indirect tribute to moral norms may be a compliment to the public and better than none. It may eventually lead to institutions which have the "sober and tried goodness of the ages, the deposit, little by little, of what has been found practicable in the wayward and transient outreaching of human idealism."[6] But this is not the ruling influence of morality that those have in mind who hope for a better world from the predominance of common norms. There may be this minimal moral influence, but the hierarchy is reversed, with the interests commanding the moral values. Perhaps it may be said, to use a metaphor of Max Weber's, that the moral norms have acted as switchmen to affect no more than the tracks along which the interests were running.[7]

"The deposit" which the normative system prevalent in a society may leave "little by little" in the social institutions becomes an integral part of the social environment in which those participating in the making of foreign policy decisions—from statesman to the man in the street—live. They are in part the product of this environment and "the deposit" will affect the frame of reference within which they judge their situations and make their decisions.[8] Moral norms through some process of absorption, and socialization thus gain some influence upon decisions, regardless of whether in any given case or in general a person deliberately and consciously evaluates his actions by moral standards. This is a very imponderable influence. It hardly justifies the optimistic belief that knowledge of the norms "opens the way to identifying with considerable precision one major distinguishable and vital element in the determination of human behavior."[9] Such knowledge may be helpful when normative standards have been deliberately applied to a decision. But there are many cases where this is not true of individuals; and there are overwhelming numbers of cases—as will be seen—where this is not true in collective decisions on foreign policy.

Even granting, as one obviously must, that moral norms are instrumental, together with many other forces in shaping social institutions, there still remains the question in what manner they are effective. This refers not only to the intensity of the influence but to its substance. Uncertainty exists on both counts. On the first, because moral norms have to compete with many other forces in

[6]Charles H. Cooley, *Social Organization* (New York: Schocken Books, 1962), p. 322.

[7]H. H. Gerth and C. Wright Mills, *From Max Weber, Essays in Sociology* (New York: Oxford University Press, 1946), p. 63.

[8]Muzafer Sherif, *The Psychology of Social Norms* (New York: Harper & Bros., 1936), pp. 25, 66, 85, 142.

[9]Jacob and Toledano, *op. cit.*, p. 220.

shaping behavior. On the second, because in the translation of the norms into behavior a vast choice of actions becomes possible. As these points are examined, it will become evident that there are reasons why the influence of moral norms in general, as it has just been discussed, and in the sense of directing behavior toward the assumed high standards of the norms, are likely to be quite insignificant in international politics. Unfortunately for those who are hoping for great improvements in the international society from commonly accepted moral norms, the reasons for this insignificance are more abundant as well as more cogent than those permitting the assumption of some vague, moral influence upon internationally important decisions.

The evidence, not conclusive but revealing, to be culled from the memoirs and occasional statements of statesmen indicates that they felt the foremost consideration in shaping foreign policy must be and was the interests of the nation. The deliberate application of moral standards to foreign policy decisions has usually been on second thought, if it took place at all. In security measures to guarantee a nation's survival, there is little room for moral considerations, as alliances between the strangest ideological bedfellows or the manufacture of the H Bomb clearly show. In a balance of power policy, the most widely accepted and practiced of all policies, moral considerations must be deliberately avoided, as its manipulators fully realize. To quote Sir Winston Churchill: the balance of power "has nothing to do with rulers or nations." It is "a law of public policy which we are following, and not a mere expedient dictated by accidental circumstances, or likes and dislikes, or any other sentiment."[10] The principle underlying the idea that "Great Britain has no permanent friends, Great Britain has no permanent enemies, Great Britain has only permanent interests" becomes, sooner or later, the guideline in the formulation of any nation's foreign policy. Mr. John Foster Dulles expressed this in his defense of the State Department, whose task, he said, was not to make friends for the United States, but to take care of her interests. Even the newest nations, while still seized by their nationalistic fervor, in a righteous mood, and quite idealistic about their future and mission in the world, very quickly recognize the need to be coldblooded and coolheaded about the preservation of their interests on the international scene. With all his moralizing about foreign policy, Mr. Nehru, for instance, reminded his Parliament on every occasion that interests are the

[10]Winston S. Chruchill, *The Second World War*, Vol. I, *The Gathering Storm* (Boston: Houghton Mifflin Co., 1948), pp. 207-208.

dominant determinants of a nation's foreign policy. Hopefully, and presumably as a result of that vague influence of moral norms on social institutions, a nation's interests may be formulated to avoid a clash with prevailing moral norms, or may be reconciled with them through some process of rationalization. And quite possibly, the conception of the interests or, where these are fairly rigidly given through the international system, the conception of the means and methods to realize these interests, are in some not easily definable manner affected by the residue of the moral norms embedded in the social structure. All this, however, is a far cry from the image of moral norms as the superstructure forcing all behavior into its allegedly clearly visible framework.

THE FUNCTION OF MORAL NORMS

The rank order given by statesmen to interests and moral norms in the making of foreign policy is not a matter of cynicism or immorality, nor is it alone a result of the international system which forces each nation to guarantee its own survival. It is, to some extent, the hardly avoidable consequence of the way in which most moral norms must function. With a few exceptions (e.g., the precept to engage in charitable action) which rarely apply to international politics anyway, moral norms are qualifiers, not initiators or ends of behavior.[11] Honesty, reliability, trustworthiness, neighborly love cannot be established or demonstrated in the abstract. They need an apropos. They can only find expression as qualities of behavior aiming at some other goal. Moral norms are not ends in themselves. Nations do not act to translate moral norms into reality. A treaty is not signed to demonstrate trustworthiness, nor a transaction undertaken to prove honesty. Instead, these actions are engaged in to pursue some interest, and moral norms can then be applied to the pursuit or the interest. Ralph Barton Perry pointed out that the "solid meaning" of morality lies in "doing good."[12] Morality is related to behavior, and (rational) behavior is end oriented, an end most of the time not moral per se, though subject to judgment by moral standards. This kind of end and behavior represent the bulk in international relations. The usual sequence: defining the interest first, choosing the behavior to realize it second, examining both in the

[11] This is to be distinguished from moral norms motivating certain types of behavior, a behavior which has been stimulated or initiated by other forces.
[12] Ralph Barton Perry, *One World in the Making* (New York: A. A. Wyn, 1945), p. 45.

light of morality third (assuming that all three processes are deliberate) creates itself a tendency to give interests primacy over morality. This becomes truer the stronger the interest. And there are no more compelling social interests than those called national interests. Moral norms would have to be extraordinarily powerful to match their strength and overcome them. There are no such to be seen. The rule not to kill is probably more strongly held and less equivocally held than any other. Even it gave way to "just wars" in defense of national interests.

This degradation of moral norms to serve rather than master interests is enhanced by their social function. This function is to be effective as a social control and thereby contribute to the preservation of the society. By accepting and internalizing the set of moral norms, the members of the society are expected to act in solidarity and unison, giving the society cohesion, solidity, integration, and permanence. It can happen that social change produces needs for the perpetuation of the society which cannot be filled or are actually contravened by the prevailing behavior. The norms supporting such behavior then become dysfunctional and, as the behavior adjusts to new needs, devoid of social significance. Such norms, if they last, become "survivals" whose nature cannot be explained by present utility, but only by their historical function in the past.[13] International relations provide abundant examples of changes in behavior which are not easily reconcilable with traditional norms. One only has to think of the numerous activities taking place in international agencies in contravention of the nationalistically influenced norms implied in the concept of sovereignty and its demands for the untouchability of "domestic" or "internal" affairs, or of the fate of women and children in warfare with modern weapons. As in this case so in all others. When norms and necessary social practice move so far apart that tension is created in the society, either the norms or the practice has to give. Almost invariably, because of the pressure of interests and for other reasons (soon to be demonstrated) the norm passes into oblivion or, if it is strongly embedded in institutions and consciences, is being reinterpreted to suit new interests, as it has to be if it is to remain socially useful.

The assertion that the function of moral norms is to produce and support behavior useful for the perpetuation of the society in which they exist may appear contradicted by the apparent general and universal validity of these norms. For the needs of a given society are usually specific while the norms are formulated in broad terms. But

---

[13]Sherif, *op. cit.*, pp. 199-200 and W. H. R. Rivers quoted there.

this is a surface appearance. There are several reasons for this kind of formulation, though none interferes in practice with the specific purpose of the norm for specific societies. The general formulation improves the functionality of the norm for the same reason that a broadly worded national constitution is more serviceable and enduring than a specific one. Secondly, certain fundamental norms (e.g., you shall not kill) are essential to the maintenance of any society. Thirdly, the formulation of norms in universal terms aims at strengthening their appeal. Finally, the unpredictability of situations in which the norms must exercise their controling influence upon behavior on the one hand, and the advisability of having the norm internalized in advance of the situations on the other, make it mandatory to state the norm in general terms. It must also not be forgotten that for purposes of international propaganda broadly stated norms lend themselves nicely to nationalistic missionary activity.

It is, however, clearly evident from the practice of nations that in specific application and interpretation, the social norms are geared to the preservation of the national society. So much so that they permit the subordination and, if need be, disturbance and destruction of the international society. Since most of the citizens cherish the preservation of their nation as their highest interest, their social moral norms are made to function, or more correctly are intended to function in support of the nation. They cannot at the same time function also in support of the wider international society, since the peoples of the world are interested in its maintenance only insofar as this may serve the higher interest of maintaining their own nations.[14]

Leaving aside for a moment the question of the efficiency of moral norms, an interesting conclusion emerges from the general formulation and the specific application of moral norms for those who hope for a better world from commonly held norms. The most fundamental norms designed to support a society are mostly held in common across the globe already—of necessity so because of the basically similar characteristics and requirements of human societies. Almost everywhere, they are formulated in general terms, unrestrained by national considerations. The rule is that you shall not kill, regardless of the victim's nationality. On the international scene, the evidence is in article 38 of the Statute of the International Court of Justice empowering the Court to decide cases in accordance with

[14]Werner Levi, "On the Causes of Peace," *Journal of Conflict Resolution,* 8 (March 1964), pp. 30-31.

the "general principles of law recognizcd by civilizcd nations," which represent a part of a moral, normative system. Thus, the responsibility for the much criticized state of international relations and politics can hardly be placed upon the absence of commonly held norms. Instead, it appears more justifiable to put the blame upon the manner in which the norms are interpreted and applied. Not common norms must be postulated, but their interpretation and application must be in such a manner as to produce potentially the desired result.And since these are related to the function the norms are intended to perform, that is to say: since the interpretation and application are dependent upon the interests the norms are designated to safeguard, the call should really go out for a growing community of interests and for an emphasis upon common interests already established as the key factor in the integration toward a peaceful international society.[15] Once there is awareness of common interests, the norms already accepted by most nations in their abstract form will be specified to assist these interests and may perform their socially beneficial functions—inasmuch as they may do so at all—for the international society. Whether they do so is now to be considered further.

. . .

INTERESTS AS DETERMINANTS OF MORAL NORMS

The total picture emerging from this analysis in regard to the influence of moral norms on international behavior can not be very encouraging to those whose hope for a more peaceful world is largely based upon the power of morality. Statesmen are inclined to give moral norms secondary consideration in making policy decisions or to use morality expediently. Interests have chronological precedence over norms in the shaping of national behavior. National interests overpower morality. Norms support rather than produce institutions. Finally, the nature of norms and of norm systems permits widely differing interpretations, the selection of expediently useful norms from the total system, and the suppression of inconvenient and not too intensely held norms. Each of these factors permits a great variety of behaviors, which is further increased by the combination of these factors. It is likely therefore that the influence of moral

[15]*Ibid.*, pp. 31-32.

norms is mostly to permit behavior along a vast range, but short of extremes which cannot be rationalized in the terms of the norms. The extermination of millions of people in Germany in the 1930's and 1940's, for instance, seemed to have gone beyond the points to which ordinary German norms could be stretched so that the whole theoretical structure of a "super race" with new moral norms had to be built before the act of killing could be justified.

The wide choice of behavior available under moral norms raises the question of what determines the choice. The answer may be easier for international than for individual behavior because of the overwhelming strength of national interests and the endeavor of official decision-makers to act—in accordance with their estimation of these interests—for the realization of the national interests. The behavior of nations indicates that most of the time interests, judged generally apart from and sometimes in deliberate disregard of moral norms, have been decisive in shaping behavior. It could hardly be otherwise, if the foregoing analysis is reasonably close to the truth. Mostly for reasons of public acceptance of foreign policies, international propaganda, and others related to psychological warfare, have the choices based on interests been cloaked in the language of morality. But this, in some cases demonstrably, has been an afterthought and moral norms served, to use Jeremy Bentham's expression, as "fig leaves of the mind." When, historically, international behavior conformed to moral norms, there may have been no conflict, or else it is more likely that interests and ulterior motives demanded such conformity than that the force of morality produced it.

This analysis could also help to explain why it is so difficult to discover the influence moral norms, as compared to interests, may have on national behavior on the international scene. The interpretability, flexibility, and selectivity of moral norms and moral systems makes it possible to find a moral justification for almost any national behavior. Hence the familiar phenomenon that statesmen can claim, and often rightly so, to act in accordance with moral norms, and accuse their opposites for failing to do the same. Under the circumstances, commitment by nations to common norms, as postulated and, indeed, as already existing to some extent, does not hold out the hoped-for great promise of more peaceful international relations. These are more likely to come with the growth and awareness of common interests. Thucydides recognized over two thousand years ago that "identity of interests is the surest bond, whether between states or individuals."

chapter fourteen
PHYSICAL-
TECHNOLOGICAL
SETTING

Geography and International Politics in an Era of Revolutionary Change[1]

Harold and Margaret Sprout

The earth is the stage upon which mankind enacts the drama of life. From time immemorial men have speculated regarding the relations of this earthly stage to human undertakings and accomplishments. Almost every aspect of human affairs has been linked to the distribution and arrangement of things upon and close to the surface of the earth.

Students of that aspect of human affairs which we call "international politics" have long regarded the physical earth as a basic datum of their subject. Every nation-state has a territorial base, a spatial section of the earth's surface in the idiom of geographic science. Territory is one of the absolute requisites of statehood. In

SOURCE: From *Journal of Conflict Resolution*, Vol. IV, No. 1 (1960). Copyright © 1960 by the University of Michigan Press. Reprinted and abridged by permission of the authors and the University of Michigan Press.

[1]This paper is one of the fruits of a program of study and research on the interrelations of geography and politics, supported jointly by Princeton University and the Rockefeller Foundation, neither of which, of course, bears any responsibility for judgments and conclusions expressed herein.

nearly all international transactions involving some element of opposition, resistance, struggle, or conflict, the factors of location, space, and distance between the interacting parties have been significant variables. This significance is embodied in the maxim, "Power is local." That is to say, political demands are projected through space from one location to another upon the earth's surface. Such operations involve expenditure of energy and consumption of other resources. A state's access to resources may decisively affect its ability to impose its demands on other nations and, conversely, to resist demands, pressures, and attacks made on it. In ways both obvious and obscure, the factors of climate—air termperature, relative humidity, air circulation, barometric pressure, etc.—also appear to have directly and indirectly affected the distribution of political capabilities over the earth. Awareness of these various non-human factors, and notions as to their limiting effects, have commonly entered into the deliberations of national statesmen and appear on many occasions to have affected significantly the substance of policy decisions.

Today the relations between man and his non-human environment are decidedly in flux. As a result of revolutionary advances in technology and other social changes no less revolutionary, such relationships are probably more unstable than in any previous historical period. There are indications, moreover, that recent huge strides toward the conquest of nature may be altering in fundamental ways the patterns of human existence upon our planet. The function of this discussion is to examine certain aspects of this possibility. The discussion is limited to the phenomena commonly called "international relations" and, more precisely, "international politics." And we shall deal chiefly with the changing international significance of non-human factors of environment, with geographical configuration in particular, and to a lesser degree with distributions of economic resources and climate.

. . .

FACTORS AND RELATIONSHIPS

Environmental factors, whether constant or variable, can affect human affairs in only two ways. Such factors can be perceived, interpreted, and taken into account by the human actors under consideration. In this way, and in this way only, can environmental factors "influence" attitudes and decisions. The relation of environmental factors to performance and accomplishment (i.e., their relation to the operational consequences of decisions) is quite different. Such factors comprise a sort of matrix, figuratively speaking, which limits the execution of decisions. Limitations on performance and accomplishment are not necessarily dependent on the actor's perception. *Such limitations may be operative irrespective of whether or how the limiting factors are perceived in the process of reaching decisions.*

As we have emphasized on previous occasions, what matters in the explanation of decisions and policies is how the actor *imagined* his environment to be, not how it actually was, whereas what matters in the explanation of accomplishments is how the environment actually was, not how the actor imagined it to be. By suitable change of tense and substitution of assumptions (where necessary) regarding the future state of the environment, the same two propositions differentiate the prediction of policy decisions from the estimation of capabilities. Consistent observance of this simple distinction—between the relation of environmental factors to attitudes and decisions, on the one hand, and to accomplishments and capabilities, on the other—would help to avoid the confused and footless disputation which has characterized so much of the discussion of man-environment relationships (12, 13).

The Earth as a Concept in Men's Minds. An important corollary flows from the first of the two propositions just above. It is that, with reference to attitudes and decisions, *erroneous* geographical conceptions may be just as "influential" as notions that do correspond to the "facts" of the "real world."

Any number of examples could be cited to illustrate this proposition. The queen of Spain financed Columbus to sail westward across the Atlantic to "discover" Asia, in ignorance of the geographic facts that rendered the undertaking impossible to carry out as planned. . . .

Frequently important misconceptions arise not from ignorance of the layouts themselves but from ignorance or neglect of their political significance. The great British naval base upon the island of Singapore was designed on the mistaken assumption that swamps, jungles, and other natural obstacles would prevent any hostile approach across the nearby mainland of Malaya. Englishmen still speak of "going to Europe" when they ferry or fly the twenty to sixty miles across the Channel. Many Americans still behave as if the wide oceans protected their country as in the early days of the Republic, even though scores of planes traverse these oceans daily in a few hours, and every American city lies within range of Russian ballistic missiles.

Discrepancies between the earth as it is and as men have imagined it to be are characteristic of all peoples. In a passage of great eloquence and insight, the great British geographer Sir Halford Mackinder observed:

> *The influence of geographical conditions upon human activities has depended . . . not merely on the realities as we now know them to be and to have been, but in even greater degree on what men imagined in regard to them. . . . Each century has had its own geographical perspective. . . . To this day . . . our view of the geographical realities is colored for practical purposes by our preconceptions from the past. In other words, human society is still related to the facts of geography not as they are, but in no small measure as they have been approached in the course of history [9, pp. 28-30].*

These words, written over forty years ago in the final days of World War I, have a continuing relevance today as we struggle to readjust our geographical ideas to the realities of the nuclear age.

. . .

IMPLICATIONS OF ENVIRONMENTAL CHANGE

At any given time and place there is usually some range of fruitful choice with reference to a given sphere of human interest and activity. There may be choice among ends and choice among alternative means to desired ends. The range of fruitful choice is constantly changing. In some historical periods it changes slowly; in others, more rapidly, depending upon the nature and rate of changes among the non-human and social components of the environment. We are living through a period in which change is rapid and far-reaching and in which the political implications of change are probably more revolutionary than is generally appreciated.

With reference to the non-human environment, change presents two facets: changes in the non-human factors themselves, and changes in social factors which in turn alter the political properties or meaning of relatively stable non-human factors. Let us consider first the changes that take place in the non-human factors themselves.

Some of these changes, we may note in passing, arise from physical processes of nature: earth slipping, volcanoes erupting, rocks falling, water flowing and freezing, wind blowing, plants, animals, and microorganisms reproducing, multiplying, or dying out, etc. Sometimes these "natural" processes produce human catastrophes such as earthquakes, floods, famines, and epidemics; occasionally, such catastrophes have affected in some degree the patterns of international politics.

Alongside these natural phenomena—and probably more important in the context of international politics—are changes in the earth wrought by the hand of man. Let us examine some of these briefly. With advancing technology—that is, with more effective tools and skills—men have increasingly changed the physical structure of the earth itself. They have dug canals and changed the course of rivers. They have built harbors and tunneled through mountains. They have cut down forests and planted new ones. They have depleted the soil and sometimes restored its fertility. They have made deserts bloom and have turned verdant landscapes into deserts. They have pumped irreplaceable oil and natural gas from underground reservoirs. They have consumed underground water faster than it could accumulate. They have smashed atoms and fused them. They have created new elements and transmuted matter into energy. In these and many other ways, men have altered at ever accelerating rate the structure of their earthly habitat.

Such structural changes have affected in greater or lesser degree the economic and military capabilities of nations and their political relations in peace and in war. A good historical example is the opening of the Suez Canal in 1869. That engineering feat cleared a shipway across the desert which had separated the Mediterranean Sea from the Indian Ocean. The canal cut several thousand miles from voyages between European ports and the ports of southern and eastern Asia. It soon became one of the most heavily used trunk lines of *international* commerce. But the canal also became the strategic axis of the *internal* communications system of the British Empire. This led within a few years to British occupation of Egypt and British military domination of the canal. Thus it is probably no exaggeration to conclude that the opening of the Suez Canal altered the strategic geography of the British Empire and affected Britain's political relations with nearly every state and region.

As another example, consider the international implications of the heavy and progressive depletion of North American forests, soils, mineral fuels, ores, and other natural resources. This depletion has been going on for well over a century. The rate of depletion has turned sharply upward in recent decades. Consumption of natural resources reached record levels during World War II. It is climbing to still higher peaks in our time. These alterations of the physical geography of North America have various political implications. Not the least of these is the increasing dependence of the United States on imported iron ore and other basic raw materials in a period of continuing change in the international political relations of all states and regions.

The international consequences of man-made changes in the earth's surface and subsurface have been great in the past and seem likely to be even greater in the future. But, great as these changes have been, they are overshadowed and probably outweighed in their political effects by other changes—especially advances in science and engineering—which, while not actually altering the basic structure of the earth's surface substantially, have given new meanings and values to such geographic features as location, distance, terrain, climate, and natural resources.

Consider, for example, the changes which have taken place in the military properties of oceanic space during the last sixty or seventy years. Theories of sea power which appeared, in 1900, to be as permanent as the ocean themselves have become progressively obsolescent during the intervening years. Yet the oceans and connecting seas (one set of environmental factors) have remained approximately constant in terms of this particular development. Their size and shape have not changed significantly. But the activities which men can carry out upon the oceans and connecting seas have changed profoundly. Ships now have power plants designed to cruise greater distances without refueling. Methods for refueling at sea have been perfected for naval vessels. Submarines with automotive torpedoes have become formidable instrumentalities with which to challenge the passage of vessels upon the surface. Special ships have been designed for landing troops and heavy equipment on hostile open beaches. Aircraft have become powerful factors in the control of the sea and the lands beyond the seas. Submarines propelled by nuclear engines can remain beneath the surface for months at a time. Rockets with nuclear warheads can be launched from beneath the water's surface. These and many other technological advances have radically modified and continue to modify the military properties of oceanic space.

It would be difficult to exaggerate the importance of the giant and ever lengthening strides with which modern science and engineering are conquering space. Man has speeded up and enormously increased the capacity of transport and communications. He has created more and ever more deadly weapons systems with which to threaten, if not actually to destroy, his fellow men and all their works. He has made astounding advances in medicine, sanitation, weather forecasting, climatic adaptation, agriculture, metallurgy, and other branches of engineering and technology.

These achievements affect in many ways the range of fruitful choices open to the statesmen. Sometimes the effect has been narrowing; more often it has been broadening. In order to understand and appreciate the impact of these developments, the political properties and meanings of geographic facts have to be reconsidered in the light of technological and other social changes. If attention is directed to one set of environmental factors—oceanic space, in the example above—the change in the range of possible performance and accomplishment appears as an adaptation to a stable environment. But such adaptation appears, from a different perspective, to consist of alterations in another set of environmental factors—modes of transportation and design of weapons, in the example—alterations which change the social meaning, or properties, or implications of environmental factors which themselves may not have undergone significant structural change.

This interaction between human activities and the non-human environment has been going on ever since man emerged as a tool-inventing and tool-using creature. But, until a century or so ago, the rate of technological change was slow. Today the rate is rapid and seems to be still accelerating. The unsettling effects of new tools and new techniques on the political, military, and economic meaning of geographic layouts and configurations, climatic variations, and the distributions of useful earth materials have great and varied significance for the student of international politics.

It is out of the question, within the limited compass of this discussion, to undertake any comprehensive inventory of these effects. The most that we can do in the remaining pages is to raise a few issues and suggest some hypotheses both tentative and controversial.

Changing Significance of Geographical Configuration. At the close of the lecture to the Royal Geographical Society (8, pp. 421-44), in 1904, in which Mackinder outlined his geopolitical interpretation of history and advanced his hypothesis of the future predominance of the Eurasian "Heartland," one member of his audience rose to challenge the whole conception. This man was Leopold S. Amery, a name virtually unknown to most Americans despite his subsequent long career in the British public service.

Amery contended that a "great deal of this geographical distribution must lose its importance" with future advances in the means of transportation on land, upon the sea, and in the air. "The successful powers" of the future, he predicted, would be "those which have the greatest industrial basis." It would "not matter whether they are in the center of a continent or on an island; those people who have the industrial power and the power of invention and science will be able to defeat all others" (1).

Events of the past half-century have clearly gone some way toward confirming Amery's prediction. Naval forces can now refuel and carry out even major repairs at sea. This has reduced the military value of permanent oversea bases. Submarines, bombing planes, and ballistic missiles have eroded the former defensive strength of islands, peninsulas, promontories, and remote ports on coasts protected by mountains, deserts, or jungles. Airplanes have "shrunk" the widest oceans and continents and have surmounted refractory barriers of terrain and distance. Pipe lines, motor vehicles, and still expanding railway and highway grids have enormously increased the mobility of overland transport. These and other changes in weapons and transport have profoundly altered the relative political and military values of heartlands, marginal lands, and islands.

The physical layout of lands and seas, as emphasized above, has not changed substantially. The deserts, mountains, and prairies, the configuration of coast lines, and other physical dimensions of our planet remain substantially unchanged. What has changed, and changed radically, is the political and military value of these geographic facts—changes resulting in large measure from the revolutionary advances of modern engineering and technology.

Changing Character of Environmental Limitations. Americans, Russians, and others display understandable pride in the part which their respective nationalities have played, and are playing, in the massive twentieth-century assault on the non-human environment. From pride in achievement it is only a step to imagining that the world is "our oyster." Yet as the late Isaiah Bowman pungently observed, over twenty-five years ago, "For all his independence and ingenuity [man] can never wholly escape from his environment. He cannot move mountains without floating a bond issue. . . . Man conforms to many defective layouts because it would cost him too much to alter them" (2, pp. 3-4).

What Bowman seems to be suggesting—and it is even more true today than in the 1930's—is that the problem of overcoming the limitations of the non-human environment has become more economic than purely technological. In the technically advanced countries at least, sufficient engineering knowledge is available to accomplish a great deal more than is actually undertaken. More railroads and highways could be built and more airlines established. More ores could be mined and refined, and more synthetic substitutes for scarce natural resources could be produced. More people could be more adequately fed. More and better medical service could be provided. More buildings could be cooled in hot, damp climates. More swamps could be drained. Sea water could be desalted and more deserts irrigated. Explorations of outer space could be speeded up. Weapons could be further improved and military establishments generally strengthened. Industries could be relocated to make them less vulnerable to airborne nuclear attacks.

When such projects are contemplated, the issue is rarely one of technical capacity alone. The issues are rather: How much will it cost? What projects should have priority? Who is going to pay for it? Money spent on television sets, new motorcars, expensive vacations, and other ingredients of a high standard of living cannot be spent on fallout shelters, industrial relocation, or other projects designed to strengthen a country's defenses. Tolerance for austerity varies widely from one country to another. Sensitivity of politicians to public demands also varies from one political system to another. That is to say, limitations on public policy that are imposed by the social order have become in general more important—and in some countries very much more important—than limitations imposed by space, adverse climate, or any other set of non-human factors.

This is not to argue that technology has erased differentials in opportunities and limitations among nations. It is certainly true that many more units of energy are required to heat buildings in winter and to keep them tolerably cool in summer in the savage mid-continental climate of the American Middle West than in the milder climates of Britain and France. It is likewise true that greater expenditure of energy is required to haul ores and other heavy freights across the vast continental space of the Soviet Union than is required for similar tasks in a small compact country like Britain.

Every country has "natural" advantages and disadvantages in comparison with any other. Technological advances may narrow these differences, provided certain other conditions prevail. In any case, the consequence of achieving a higher level of productivity per capita is that this enables a people to pay a higher price for overcoming "natural" obstacles which, at a lower economic and technological level, were insurmountable. The more efficient a people's equipment, and the greater their skills, the greater becomes their potential capacity to master the limitations of the non-human environment—and do so at a price compatible with their conception of a tolerable standard of living.

From this perspective, one queries writings which attribute a certain absoluteness to the limitations set by the non-human environment. An example of this is a little book entitled *How Strong Is Russia?* by George Cressey (4), of Syracuse University. In this book, published in 1954, Cressey seems to us to come very close to arguing that the non-human environment of the Soviet Union presents permanently disabling obstacles to successful Soviet competition with western Europe and the United States. Cressey writes:

> *Geography has imposed permanent limitations on the develop-ment of the Soviet Union. Man can do much, but the restrictions of great distances, remoteness from the ocean, terrain, short growing seasons, inadequate and variable rainfall, and con-tinentality will always remain. . . . The geographic potentials are very large, but the geographic limitations are formidable. . . . Premier Stalin gave his country the task "to overtake and surpass the capitalist world." From the standpoint of geography this does not appear possible. Limitations of location, climate, scattered resources, and continentality combine to create land-scapes which no amount of planning can fully surmount. Whatever its government, Russia can never become a truly great world power [4, pp. 29, 98, 120].*

If these quotations accurately summarize Cressey's conclusions, it seems to us that he has seriously underestimated the implications of rapid technological advance and of differences in national political systems. No one could quarrel with the premise that every nation pays a price for its accomplishments and that the price tag may be higher or lower depending on the country's location, area, con-figuration, climate, mineral bodies, and other resources. But a de-duction, from this premise, that a state with greater "natural" obstacles to overcome cannot allocate more goods and services to the pursuit of political objectives, or play as influential a role as states more favorably endowed by "nature," would appear to be tenable only on one or both of the following assumptions: (1) that the period of rapid technological advance is drawing to a close and (2) that similar values and principles govern the allocation of goods and services in the Soviet Union as in other great states.

Neither of these assumptions is sound, in our judgment. All evidence known to us indicates that further technological break-throughs are in prospect in such fields as nuclear fuels, climate control, plant breeding, etc. Such advances are likely in the future, as in the past, to diminish the handicaps of distance, area, location, or other non-human factors. Furthermore, governmental policies deter-mining who gets what and how much vary widely from one political system to another. As already emphasized, values and demands vary, tolerance for austerity varies, sensitivity of politicians to public demands varies, ability of politicians to mold public opinion varies, and so do many other features of national political systems. This brings us back to our major conclusion in this section—that one of the consequences of rapid and continuing technological advance is to make limitations imposed by the social order relatively more significant politically than "natural" obstacles present in the non-human environment.

Environmental Limitations and Social Catastrophe. A rather different sort of environmental limitation on the modern state has been argued by Harrison Brown (3, chap. vii), of the California Institute of Technology. Brown emphasizes that the enormous and still rising consumption of mineral ores and fuels in recent years has depleted most of the more accessible and easily worked sources of non-renewable raw materials. From here on out, it will require deeper mines and oil wells, and more complicated industrial installations and processes, to reach and utilize the poorer-grade raw materials upon which industrial societies will have increasingly to depend.

Such dependence is all very well, Brown argues, so long as no nuclear war or other social catastrophe destroys the complicated installations and disrupts the increasingly complex and delicate industrial processes and interrelations. But he advances the profoundly disturbing thesis that, once destroyed, our fragile industrial civilization could never make a successful fresh start with the low-grade ores and more inaccessible fuels which would remain available.

This thesis is manifestly controversial. But it rests upon solid facts and should be carefully examined. Above all, its international political implications should be explored. If Brown's thesis is accepted, the conclusion follows that our conquest of nature, of which twentieth-century man is so proud and boastful, is viable only in a universe from which total war fought with nuclear weapons is permanently excluded. A further implication latent in Brown's thesis is that nuclear war would probably disable countries in proportion roughly to their level of industrialization and to the geographical concentration of their industrial conurbations. In plain English, a reasonable inference from Brown's thesis is that a future general war would wipe out the densely inhabited industrial countries of western Europe, damage the United States and Soviet Union probably beyond recovery, and turn over the management of the earth to the Chinese Communists and other emerging nations of Asia and Africa.

Modern Arms and the Territorial State. We come finally to the most controversial hypothesis of all. This hypothesis, put forward by

John Herz (6), of City College, New York, holds that modern weapons systems are inexorably eroding the foundations of the territorial state itself. The point at issue is whether the territorial state, which for several centuries has been the basic unit of the international system, can much longer perform the supreme function for which it evolved—the function of providing a reasonable degee of safety for the person and property of its members.

Various hypotheses have been advanced to explain the integration of medieval towns and feudal communities into larger political-territorial units. At least one of the necessary conditions for this development seems to have been the "gunpowder revolution." The invention and improvement of firearms made castles and walled towns increasingly less defensible, that is to say, more easily penetrable by force. The same development, combined with some improvement in roads and haulage, made it possible to mobilize larger forces to defend larger geographical areas. More efficient weapons and communications likewise enlarged the geographical area which could be effectively policed and administered from a single capital. Thus the large-area state, in the words of Herz, "came finally to occupy the place that the castle or fortified town had previously held as a unit of impenetrability."

In the centuries that followed the formation of modern territorial nation-states, the prime function of statecraft was to make and to keep the country's geographical boundaries as impenetrable as possible. In pursuit of this objective—the direct antecedent of today's expanded concept of national security—much attention was given to achieving strong "natural boundaries." Among the coveted kinds of natural boundaries seacoasts ranked high, and a state that was wholly insular came to be regarded as fortunate indeed. Other forms of strong natural boundaries included rivers, mountains and other rough terrain, deserts, and jungles. Economic goods and services were poured into frontier fortifications, military roads, and other installations designed to strengthen "weak" and vulnerable boundaries.

Geographical space—between the state's boundaries and its vital centers of population and economic production—was likewise regarded as a strategic asset. Where space was deemed inadequate, a buffer zone of protected states—we would call them "satellites" today—might be created to absorb the shock of invasion. As late as 1918, Sir Halford Mackinder (9) outlined such a project to keep partially defeated Germany and Revolutionary Russia physically apart and to provide a security zone for western Europe. This project envisaged establishing a tier of small states in eastern Europe all the way from the Baltic to the Black Sea. The Peace Conference of 1919 did create such a buffer zone—with results that are well-known history.

By the end of World War I there was considerable evidence that developments in weapons were undermining the security of the territorial state. A long sequence of inventions had greatly increased the per capita firepower of military forces. Railroads, better roads, and motor vehicles had given greater overland mobility to this growing firepower. The development of mines, automotive torpedoes, and submarines provided more effective instruments with which to sink cargo shipping and to blockade marine frontiers. Aircraft, though still primitive, provided more than a hint of the possibility of over-leaping even the most strongly fortified frontiers.

Subsequent development of air power transformed the hint into fearsome reality. For the first time in history it has become possible to project terrific firepower over great distances to attack the complex industrial conurbations upon which modern military power depends—and do so without blasting a path across fortified land frontiers or storming ashore on hostile open beaches. In the seesaw struggle between offensive and defensive weapons systems, the offense has decisively outrun the defense. There are rumors of anti-missile missiles and other defensive innovations around the corner. Such a development might conceivably restore in some degree the shattered impenetrability of the territorial state. But it is noteworthy that many leading scientists and engineers are pessimistic of achieving any really effective defense against missile-borne nuclear explosives.

In 1957 the British Government candidly recognized this state of affairs. Perhaps the most important sentence in its statement on defense that year was the frank admission that "there is at present no means of providing adequate protection for the people of this country against the consequences of an attack with nuclear weapons" (11).

Some reactions within the United States to this British candor were characteristic of the seeming inability of so many of us Americans to come to terms with the technological revolution in which we are caught. One comment, more or less typical of many others, was that the Western Allies ought to "work and plan hopefully toward an effective defense against hydrogen weapons rather than proclaiming and thus encouraging a sense of hopelessness among the people" (10). Certainly, such efforts will continue. But is it safe to ignore the opposite possibility—which may, indeed, be the more probable of the two—that no really effective defense can be perfected to protect nations against devastating airborne attacks with thermonuclear explosives?

If the latter turns out to be the case, future historians from the perspective of the twenty-first century (if somehow the ultimate catastrophe is avoided and if there are historians left to interpret the past) may well conclude that the combination of thermonuclear explosives, long-range bombing planes, and ballistic missiles made the territorial nation-state as unviable as the medieval castle became after the development of artillery.

These speculations all point to the conclusion that the technological revolution and other social changes taking place in our time are affecting the international political significance of location, distance, space, terrain, climate, and natural resources. Broadly speaking, the geographical layout of lands and seas and the configuration of the lands have lost much of the military-political value once attached to these factors. Insularity has less protective value. Commanding positions, athwart the trunk lines of international commerce—such as Gibraltar, Malta, Suez, and Singapore—no longer provide the leverage they formerly did. Outlying military installations become progressively less tenable, not only in a strictly military sense, but also because of the attitudes and policies of the new nations within whose territory many of them are located. Mountain passes, river valleys, and other "natural pathways" have likewise lost most of their political and military significance. The study of boundaries has changed in the main from analysis of military strength and weakness to analysis of transition zones where one culture merges into another. Attempts to achieve national "self-sufficiency" continue sporadically, but that struggle too is a lost cause, what with the progressive depletion of easily accessible resources and the extended list of materials required at the more advanced levels of economic development.

When all is said, countries and regions still differ, and these differences have political significance. They differ in stage of industrialization and urbanization and, consequently, in degrees of vulnerability to bombardment with nuclear weapons. Differences in economic development mean differences in ability to provide goods and services for military or other political purposes as well as to satisfy general consumer demands. Such differences still depend in some degree upon limitations implicit in the non-human environment; but, increasingly, they depend more on limitations imposed by the technological level and by the structure and operation of the national social order.

Nations still differ in attitudes, aspirations, and expectations as well as in their capacity to translate aspirations into solid accomplishments. Notions of what is desirable and what is possible, what should be supported and what should be resisted, are deeply rooted, as Mackinder emphasized, in each people's geographical and other preconceptions from the past. Time lag between environmental change and general awareness of such change and the consequences thereof is not a new phenomenon. But, because of the nature and rate of technological and other changes taking place today, the gap between image and reality seems to be both wider and more dangerous than in any period since the formation of the modern international system.

REFERENCES

1. Amery, Leopold S. Discussion of H. J. Mackinder, "The Geographical Pivot of History," *Geographical Journal*, XXIII (1904), 439-41.

2. Bowman, Isaiah. *Geography in Relation to the Social Sciences*. New York: Charles Scribner's Sons, 1934.

3. Brown, Harrison. *The Challenge of Man's Future*, New York: Viking Press, 1954.

4. Cressey, G. B. *How Strong Is Russia?* Syracuse, N. Y.: Syracuse University Press, 1954.

5. Cumming, W. P. *The Southeast in Early Maps*. Princeton, N. J.: Princeton University Press, 1958.

6. Herz, J. H. "Rise and Demise of the Territorial State," *World Politics*, IX (1957), 473-93.

7. Hoar, G. F. *Autobiography of Seventy Years*. New York: Charles Scribner's Sons, 1903.

8. Mackinder, H. J. "The Geographical Pivot of History," *Geographical Journal*, XXIII (1904), 421-44.

9. _____ *Democratic Ideals and Reality*. Rev. ed. New York: Henry Holt & Co., 1942.

10. Reston, James. Article in the *New York Times*, April 5, 1957.

11. Sprout, Harold. "Britain's Defense Program," in *Britain Today: Economics, Defense and Foreign Policy*, pp. 57-76. Princeton, N. J.: University Conference, May, 1959.

12. Sprout, Harold and Margaret. *Man-Milieu Relationship Hypotheses in the Context of International Politics*. Princeton, N. J.: Center of International Studies, 1956.

13. _____ "Environmental Factors in the Study of International Politics," *Conflict Resolution*, I (1957), 309-28.

The Ecology
of Future
International
Politics*

Bruce M. Russett

THE RANGE AND PROBABILITY OF
FUTURE OUTCOMES

The prediction of future world events is frequently an exercise in political sociology. Or perhaps more accurately, it is a problem in political ecology, one concerned with the relationship between the political system and its social and physical environment.

A statement that nothing will change over the next few decades would hardly be credible, and anyway it would be boring. On the other hand, to quote one of my favorite books on prediction, "If a

SOURCE: From *International Studies Quarterly*, Vol. XI, No. 1 (1967). Copyright © 1967 by Wayne State University Press. Reprinted and abridged by permission of the author and Wayne State University Press.

*An earlier version of this paper was given as an address to the Annual Meeting of the American Sociological Association at Miami Beach, August 29, 1966. Marc Pilisuk, J. David Singer, Harold Sprout, and Guy E. Swanson offered valuable comments. I wrote the paper while Visiting Research Political Scientist at the Mental Health Research Institute, University of Michigan, and am grateful for its stimulating environment.

476

man predicts large but not very large changes, the public will regard him as a man of imagination; but if he predicts extremely large changes, his audience will replace imagination by phantasy."[1] I would like, in this paper, to avoid both extremes. In any case, my recent menus have offered neither sheep livers nor chicken entrails, so I am unable to engage in prophecy. I will not attempt to foretell a specific event on a specific occasion, nor to paint a detailed picture of a particular political future. But I am a restrained believer in the outlook aptly labelled by Charles Burton Marshall as "the limits of foreign policy."[2] Without getting into the determinist-free will debate—which in the still youthful state of our sciences is largely irrelevant anyway—we can, I think, agree generally with the idea that political prediction is best concerned with the future state of the *milieu* within which decisions have to be made. In this context we are interested in *negative* prediction—we aspire to narrow the range of possibilities, to eliminate some events as unlikely, and to produce a range of outcomes within which future developments will lie.[3]

In effect, we want to do what we do as scientists when generalizing from our samples to larger populations; we want to make a prediction that states both a *range* of possibilities—the confidence interval—and the probability, or *significance level,* that we attach to the likelihood that the true value will fall within that range. If we give as a "best guess" some point within that interval, we recognize that it is really only shorthand for a much more complicated statement. I think this is true whether we are making explicitly

[1] H. Thiel, *Economic Forecasts and Policy* (Amsterdam: North Holland, 2nd edition, 1961), p. 156.

[2] Charles Burton Marshall, *The Limits of Foreign Policy* (New York: Henry Holt, 1954).

[3] See Harold and Margaret Sprout, *The Ecological Perspective on Human Affairs* (Princeton, N.J.: Princeton University Press, 1965), pp. 180, 199. See also Thiel, *op. cit.*, ch. 1; and Nicholas Rescher, "Discrete State Systems, Markov Chains, and Problems in the Theory of Scientific Explanation and Prediction," *Philosophy of Science*, 30 (1963), pp. 325-45; and, for a similar if less rigorous and overly cautious statement, Saul Friedlander, "Forecasting in International Relations," in Bertrand de Jouvenel, ed., *Futuribles: Studies in Conjecture*, II (Geneva: Droz, 1965), p. 99. On the difficulties of predicting particular events, relevant comments include those by Wilbert E. Moore, *Social Change* (Englewood Cliffs, N.J.: Prentice-Hall, 1963), pp. 3-4; and Kenneth E. Boulding, "Expecting the Unexpected: The Uncertain Future of Knowledge," in Edgar Morphet and Charles Ryan, eds., *Conference on Designing Education for the Future*, Denver, Colo., July 1966.

quantitative statements, such as the number of people who would be killed in a nuclear war, or whether we are talking about apparently discrete events, such as whether or not "war" will occur. We may simplify our analytical models to talk about war *vs.* peace, but we know that there are many shades and varieties of each, and that in *many* respects the "war" we refer to is less a step-level jump from previous states than the mode of a distributional curve. We have learned this well from our recent experiences with civil unrest and insurgency. All of us know too about the problem of subjective probabilities and the inappropriateness of assigning a probability to a unique event; when we make a prediction that is not based on a sample from a known universe we are beyond the limits within which the assignment of precise probability levels is permissible. Yet without some such effort, however crude and subjective, the analysis is incomplete and misleading.

. . .

RIGOR, INFORMATION, AND IMAGINATION

. . .

One way to make political and social predictions is by the extrapolation of apparent growth rates, yet even a sensible-appearing use may go very far wrong.[4] Upward trends do *not* go on forever, but at some point, for some reason, level off, oscillate, or go into a downturn. A child doubles in height between the ages of 2 and 18—but he won't (I trust) double his height again before he is 35. Political history is full of examples of failures to anticipate the system break, the turning point, when what used to be appropriate is no longer so. Generals' alleged preparedness to fight the last war is just such an instance. A national population policy which stressed producing large numbers was appropriate for an era when the number of soldiers a state could field was a major basis of

[4]One of the most forceful statements about the utility of prediction *via* extrapolating exponential growth curves is Hornell Hart, "Predicting Future Trends," (New York: Appleton-Century-Crofts, 1957), pp. 455-73, and a good argument for caution, trying instead to anticipate jumps and quantum leaps, is Gardner Murphy, "Where is the Human Race Going?" in Richard E. Farson, ed., *Science and Human Affairs* (Palo Alto, Calif.: Science and Behavior Books, 1965), pp. 7-17. A more general treatment of how exponential growth rates change is Daniel Bell, "Twelve Modes of Prediction: A Preliminary Sorting of Approaches in the Social Sciences," *Daedalus*, 93, 3 (1964), pp. 845-80.

its power; some countries, like Italy, carried that policy over into an age when per capita wealth was equally important as a power base. Political goals, as well as political methods, must be adapted to changes in the social and technological environment. Perhaps we have reached a period when the simple goal of maximizing the "national interest"—whatever that is—has become inappropriate in a world where heavy symbiosis and cooperation are unavoidable. We also must have sufficient discrimination to know which growth rates are important to us. By 1870 there was, within the British government, a clear awareness that Germany's growing steel production would intersect with Britain's before the end of the nineteenth century. For another decade, however, they thought that the country they had to worry about, for political reasons, was France, not Germany. Here then, are still a variety of crucial roles for imagination.

This is the kind of thing to which I want to devote the rest of this article: to examining some of the features of the environment of the international political system that have undergone very rapid change in recent years, suggesting what the prospects are for their continued growth, and what their political consequences may be. There are at least four possible ways in which a smooth, continuous rate of growth in something may eventually have a discontinuous effect on other aspects of the system, producing what may be called step-level change or system transformation.[5]

CROSSING A THRESHOLD

One is an increase which crosses a threshold, a rate of growth that continues until, on reacting with some other aspect of the social or political system, it produces a discrete change. A given equilibrium may be unstable. In forest ecology, forms of life, adapted to their environment, grow and develop in an area, but in so doing they modify their environment until it has changed so that they are no longer adapted to it. Hardwood trees, for instance, first become established in sunny, relatively open areas. But as they grow up and mature over many decades, they shade the ground beneath them, and in the shade young conifer trees thrive better than new hardwoods. In time, as the large hardwoods die out they are replaced by conifers, which in turn create even deeper shade that prevents the growth of any more hardwoods. The resulting "climax" forest is then in a static

[5] An early use of this approach in political science is, of course, Morton Kaplan's *System and Process in International Politics* (New York: Wiley, 1957).

equilibrium, and will maintain itself indefinitely except for exogenous change introduced by the activities of man, fire, or other natural disaster. An obvious political example is the slow growth of a voting bloc that, on passing the 50 per cent mark, is able then to effect a sharp change in policy.[6] Even here the change may not be all that discontinuous—some political change is likely to occur in response to the pressure of any large bloc, and some further change will arise in anticipation of its majority status as it approaches the half-way mark. But the principle, even though not entirely un-ambiguous in most empirical examples, is clear enough.

If in the future we have a world government, with effective authority over its member states or over individuals, this example might be of more importance for international politics than it now seems to be. Already the poor states (those with a per capita income of less than $300 a year) form more than a majority in the United Nations, and actually they have the two-thirds majority which is required for issues defined as "important." If they were able to enforce their collective will they doubtless would expand United Nations assessments many times over, spreading the new revenues around for economic development. But though for years they have had the votes necessary to pass this assessment—and have been able to band together to defeat the rich powers on other occasions—they have not done so with the tax rate. It is one thing to assess taxes, quite another, in the current state of international organization, to collect them. So for the present they avoid a show of parliamentary strength that would merely expose their executive weakness.

Another example of this phenomenon which might have more immediate effect is provided by relative power relationships in the Middle East. Despite Israel's numerical inferiority to her neighbors (on the order of one to twenty) her wealth, organization, and external assistance, plus the divisions among the Arabs, allow her to remain militarily equal to her antagonists. But a sustained growth in income and organizational efficiency in Egypt could over the long run tip that balance in the Arabs' favor. The notion of a sharp system change or step-level jump is an over-simplification, but at least sub-jectively, if not objectively, Egypt could reach a point where its leader could decide that from then on he had the power to crush Israel. Whether he really was able to do it, whether he miscalculated and was beaten again, or whether Israel changed the whole threat

[6]Bertrand de Jouvenel, "Political Science and Prevision," *American Political Science Review*, 59, 1 (1965), p. 34.

system by going nuclear, the effect would nevertheless be of a slow and smooth change in one parameter that had, at some pretty clearly identifiable point, produced a discrete change in the system.

More generally, something of this sort has happened in the international system as a whole. Kenneth Boulding has adapted from economics what he calls the "loss of strength gradient," or the rate at which a nation's power declines with distance from its borders.[7] For the major industrial powers this gradient has been steadily pushed outward since the Napoleonic Wars, as fewer and fewer states have remained "unconditionally viable." (He calls a nation unconditionally viable if it can prevent foreign imposition of a drastic change of political or social organization inside its own borders.) The ability of one nation to coerce another even at a great distance was strengthened first by social changes (such as the *levée en masse,* the aggregation of large nation-states, and revolutionary ideology), and then technological innovation (the steamship, tanks, aircraft, and finally the atomic bomb). For many years this meant that only six or so great powers were viable against any opponent, and that these great powers could conquer even far away small states.

The cumulative effect of these trends, however, produced a dramatic system-change at the end of World War II, when only the two superpowers could dependably resist the domination of any other state. The erosion of all other nations' unconditional viability is in effect what we mean by the transformation of the international system in the early postwar years.

And the bipolar system as we knew it only a decade ago has itself become transformed by the maintenance of the very same trends that first produced it. Continuing technological change, moving from atom bombs and manned bombers to thermonuclear weapons and intercontinental missiles, has removed the sanctuaries that the superpowers used to enjoy in their homelands. Thus there has been a limited revival in the independence of the middle powers, as the great powers can no longer provide such a credible deterrent umbrella. Yet though smaller states are not now so dependent on the big powers for protection—not dependent simply because they are not so confident in it—they still could never hope to *defeat* a superpower. Thus we are somewhere between a bipolar situation and a balance of power world with many foci of more or less equal strength.

Changes in transportation and destructive capacities produced fairly discontinuous changes in the political system, first by cutting the

[7]Kenneth E. Boulding, *Conflict and Defense* (New York: Harper, 1960).

number of great powers to two, and then by restoring to those at the middle level *some* of the independence they had possessed before bipolarity. The elimination of *all* states from the "unconditionally viable" category makes the need for new political forms for the international system more pressing than ever. We hear less about this now than a few years ago when the balance of terror was thought to be unstable, but I think the passing of extreme bipolarity *increases* the long-run requirement for political change.

Possibly these trends will have further sharp effects on the international system. The most likely way would be if technology were for a while to favor strongly the defender, especially in the development of an anti-ballistic missile system for continental defense. Apparently such development has progressed a good bit farther than most of us would have expected a couple of years ago, and an effective anti-ICBM defense no longer seems utterly out of the question for the two big and rich powers.[8] If successful, and if not merely outflanked by chemical or bacteriological weapons, it would return its possessor to the unconditional viability of the good old days. But at the moment that still seems to be a long shot, and I suspect we must look in other directions for new ecological influences on the political system.

DEMAND AND SUPPLY AS LIMITS
TO GROWTH

The previous example was of a smooth trend that, on reacting with some other characteristics, produced a marked change in the system. There are in addition several possibilities for trends to stop moving along at their previously established rates—the growth stops, or at least is drastically modified. Our *second* class, then, is of a development that reaches a so-called "logical" ending point, where it stops because of a change in the needs, perception, and behavior of men, because the *demand* which initiated it has essentially been fulfilled. One such is probably in the destructiveness of modern weapons that I alluded to a moment ago. During the century preceding World War II the destructive radius of the biggest weapons then available grew at a doubling rate faster than every 10 years, with the perfection of explosive chemicals and the development first of

[8]See Jeremy J. Stone, *Containing the Arms Race* (Cambridge: M.I.T. Press, 1966), pp. 224-32, and Bruce M. Russett, "The Complexities of Ballistic Missile Defense, *Yale Review*, Spring 1967.

large cannons and finally of blockbuster bombs. The explosion of the first atomic bomb marked a certain discontinuous jump here, and in the two decades following it the doubling period shortened, to about every four years, culminating in the 100 megaton weapon that can collapse an ordinary frame house within 30 miles of its explosion point. But there is an obvious limit to the destructiveness of modern weapons—the size of anything worth destroying. At the doubling rate of four years, another twenty would be quite sufficient for a weapon capable of obliterating an entire continent; less than a decade more would produce a doomsday machine with a destructive radius exceeding that of the globe. More than that would appear to be a waste of scarce resources. Weapons development and improvement might well continue, but along other dimensions like reliability, discrimination (as between men and structures in the neutron bomb), and "cleanliness."[9]

Many of the characteristics of what has been termed the "mobiletic" revolution are likely also to fall into this category, and also rather soon. Mobiletics is a slightly inelegant but useful term coined to cover the whole range of movement—of things, of energy, and of information.[10] One of its components is the transportation of men and other high value-per-unit-volume goods. In the nineteenth century the speed at which men could travel over transcontinental or intercontinental distances doubled more or less every 25 years. It began at the speed of the sailing ship or horse and carriage (depending on the medium), which was hardly more than five miles an hour over sustained distances in the early 1800's. This progressed through the perfection of clippers, the steamship and the railroad. After the Wright brothers this rate speeded up, with a doubling about every ten years, reaching around 600 miles an hour in the late 1940's and the 2000-mile-an-hour bomber in the early 1960's. The built-in limits to the trend are fuzzy but fairly obvious, at least on this small earth. Something like a man-carrying intercontinental rocket is the top; 5000 mile missiles make the entire trip from point to point in under 30 minutes or roughly 10,000 miles per hour. Extrapolation of the 10-year doubling rate since the turn of the century would bring us to this limit sometime in the 1980's. Since the 2000-mile-per-hour

---

[9]The data in this and the following paragraph are from Bruce M. Russett, *Trends in World Politics* (New York: Macmillan, 1965), ch. 1.

[10]Bertram E. Gross, *Space-Time and Post-Industrial Society* (Syracuse, N.Y.: Syracuse University, Maxwell School of Citizenship and Public Affairs, 1966, mimeo.), p. 4.

airliner is not expected to be operational until after 1970 this projection for the rocket seems rather over-optimistic, and the social demand for human travel at 10,000 miles per hour instead of 200 miles per hour is not likely to be so great as to require that the "schedule" imposed by extrapolating past changes be kept. In the longer run faster speeds for manned travel to the planets and beyond are to be expected, but even here the extrapolation to 30,000 miles per hour in the year 2000 is, give or take a few years and tens of thousands of miles, about as long as current rates of growth can go unabated. According to most scientific authorities, by then there would appear to be more payoffs in suspended animation, or interstellar travel by colonies that would reproduce themselves en route. The real upper limit to man's travel capabilities may be only at the speed of light, but it is unlikely to be approached at the current high rates of increase. This, then, is another rate of change that will, within the lifetimes of some of us, slow down drastically.

With the advent of the telegraph, communication became virtually instantaneous, at the speed of light plus processing time, over short distances. The changes are not so orderly that any simple exponential growth curve can be fitted to this one, but modern improvements have concentrated on eliminating the need for fixed channels of communication such as wires, on lengthening the distance that could be covered, and on providing facilities for transmitting a wider variety of messages, from electrical impulses that had to be translated from Morse code into letters, to impulses that could be made into faithful reproductions of sound and sight. When these developments culminate, as they will shortly, in the installation of a world-wide system of satellite relays to carry television impulses around the earth within two seconds, the most important dimension of the communication revolution will be completed.[11] Further work will be left to clean up the quality and variety of transmission possibilities and to proliferate transmitters and receivers. These mobiletic changes, therefore, are now approaching their natural completion. Probably they will pick up again on some now hardly imaginable dimensions,[12] but it is unlikely that in the next fifty years or so they will again produce such a sudden change in the environment of international politics as they have just put us through.

[11]See John R. Platt, "The Step to Man," *Science,* 149 (August 6, 1965), p. 608.

[12]Sometimes this mutation and revival is called "escalation." See Gerald Holton, "Scientific Research and Scholarship: Notes Towards the Design of Proper Scales," *Daedalus,* 91, 2 (1962), pp. 369-99.

These are growth rates that will slow down essentially as the *demand* is satisfied. Making an effective decision to speed up or slow down their growth is not always within the capabilities of our social and political systems, but at least the growth is not so autonomous that we need anticipate any particular difficulties when the "natural" slowdown points approach. This is by no means universally the case with rapidly growing social phenomena, so we are led to a *third* category—growth rates that come to a halt because the *supply* of some basic commodity is exhausted.

Behind all the changes just listed has been the explosion of science and technology. Since the eighteenth century the number of scientists in the world at large has doubled approximately every 15 years; in the United States alone the doubling rate has been faster, roughly every 10 years. This clearly can't go on. The number of scientists and engineers has now reached almost one per cent of the total population,[13] and if one eliminates the temperamentally and intellectually unfit (eliminates them only for analytical purposes), they amount to possibly one fifth of those who have the capacities to become productive scientists. Even if we forget about leaving high-IQ individuals for commerce, administration, and the arts, it is clear that this exponential growth curve has a built-in ceiling. We will see the end of it well before the century is out; it will affect our professional lives and especially those of our graduate students. Some mitigation may be in sight; for instance, utilizing the brain-drain of high-IQ people from underdeveloped countries, a reservoir that may not dry up for another fifty years or so; or extremely sophisticated computer usage; or hiring more secretaries; or improving information retrieval; or various ways of relieving scientists of the substantial drudgery that still remains in their work. Yet this kind of relief only postpones the day when surgery will be necessary. Federal obligations for research and development in the United States doubled roughly every four years between 1950 and 1964.[14] But for the past three years they have levelled off at about three per cent of national income. This is nearly a third of what we now spend on defense, and even allowing for growth in real national income (perhaps a doubling

[13]This is from a projection and adaptation of figures for 1962-64 in U.S. Bureau of the Census, *Statistical Abstract of the United States, 1966* (Washington, D.C.: U.S. Government Printing Office, 1966), pp. 547-48. I am assuming that the potential talent pool includes all those of working age with an IQ of at least 120.

[14]*Ibid.*, p. 544, and *Statistical Abstract of the United States, 1959*, p. 539. The figures are not fully comparable, but the general pattern is unmistakable.

every 20 years at an annual rate of about four per cent) it is hard to see how science spending can grow very much more. Depending upon how it is handled, the levelling-off of this trend could lead to a period of regrouping and digestion in science, as better means are perfected for making us aware of other people's research and avoiding some of the duplication that is currently so prevalent. In the world at large, it is conceivable that a levelling-off of the growth in science could slow down some of the more wasteful and dangerous aspects of international technological competition. In any case, the levelling has already begun.

THE SOCIAL CONTROL OF GROWTH

This leads us to a distinction which ushers in our *fourth* class of growth patterns—between growth rates that are brought to a halt only by resource limitations, and rates that are controlled, short of the physical limits, by deliberate social policy.[15] John Platt's fascinating essay in "The Step to Man" also mentions some of the growth curves I have detailed, and forecasts their orderly levelling-off.[16] But orderly transition may be the exception. A growth rate may reach its ceiling and, in the absence of social control or an escalation that picks up again on some other dimension, bump along the ceiling. In effect this is oscillation around the equilibrium level, and I will illustrate it with the outcome foreseen for the population explosion according to one model.

Imagine an island with no foreign trade and where there is neither emigration nor immigration—a closed system. The area of agricultural land is fixed, and for some time it has supported a population, growing at a constant rate, that has not yet required all of the

[15] I distinguish between this *planned diminution* and the simple relatively autonomous slackening of demand discussed as the second category. Note too that the first and third categories apply to environmental limitations that act regardless of human cognition, whereas the second and fourth operate only as a consequence of perceptions. This useful distinction between different environmental effects is made by Sprout and Sprout, *op. cit.*

[16] Platt, *op. cit.* An initially exponential curve that bends over smoothly in an S-shape is the logistic curve. An early example in demographic prediction is Lowell J. Reed, "Population Growth and Forecasts," *Annals of the American Academy of Political and Social Science*, 188 (November, 1936), pp. 159-66. The logistic curve may have looked applicable to U.S. population in the 1930's, but it does not fit later developments. The article is nevertheless useful as an explicit answer to the projection of exponential rates to infinity.

available land. As land utilization reaches 100 per cent and the level of technology remains constant, the population will approach the maximum that the island can support. But if technology is evolving, as it has been in the Western world over the past several centuries, the ceiling may continually be pushed upward and the population may continue to grow at its exponential rate. Let us assume, however, that at some point the local farmers' ingenuity gives out and they exhaust all methods for substantially increasing the yield of their land. When this point is reached the population of the island will have attained its ceiling. Growth may not stop absolutely short in its tracks, for there may be some belt-tightening possible. But it must stop soon, and not necessarily as a simple levelling-off to a smooth plateau. On the contrary, after the first steps of belt-tightening the next consequence is likely to be a disease epidemic in a population made vulnerable by malnutrition, or there may occur a natural disaster which drastically cuts food production in a situation where there is no margin to spare. Instead of simply levelling-off, the population will drop sharply in response to the sudden rise in death rates. But after this immediate disaster is past, there will again, at the advanced technological level achieved, be a surplus of land relative to population. So, for a short period, unless reproductive habits have been changed, the population will again shoot upward, at the previous rate, until the gap is filled once more. And again, the population will become vulnerable to disease or nature, will fall once again, and so on. Here is the classic Malthusian trap in which population is forced into equilibrium with limited productive resources. The pattern, however, is one of violent oscillations to and from a ceiling imposed by "nature."[17]

Such a perpetual unhappy fate is nevertheless not the only possible denouement to the exponential growth curve. If, instead of allowing resource limitations to determine the situation, it is subjected to human volition and social control, a better solution is feasible. If the birth rate is brought down fairly quickly and made

[17]A good example of thinking that hitting the ceiling is the only probable outcome to such demographic pressures is Sir Charles Darwin, "Forecasting the Future," in Edward Hitchings, Jr., *Frontiers in Science* (New York: Basic Books, 1958), pp. 100-116. Richard L. Meier, *Modern Science and the Human Fertility Problem* (New York: Wiley, 1959), pp. 53-63, forecasts something much like this happening in certain areas of the world, notably the island of Mauritius. For a similar result with a different mechanism (the stress syndrome) see Hudson Hoagland, "Mechanisms of Population Control," *Daedalus*, 93, 3 (1964), pp. 812-29.

equal to the death rate before the ceiling is reached, the curve can be made to taper off smoothly and culminate in an even plateau without wild oscillation. Presumably there will be some fluctuation for a while, as the social controls are perfected and the right mix is found to depress the birth rate just to, and not beyond, the equilibrium level. But in principle the proper procedures could be worked out.

Going from the abstract model of the isolated island to the current world demographic situation brings, I would guess, substantial cause for optimism. Many sociologists and economists are more expert on demographic matters than I, and I will not try to encroach on their territory. It appears to me, however, that this represents a growth rate that is on the verge of being brought under control, at least sometime before the end of the century. I doubt very much that the world will look like our mythical island, or even like Hong Kong. For what is, by comparison with the funds expended for military research and development, a very modest investment, we have come up with a variety of extremely promising methods for population control, and have still more in the works. Even a cosmic pessimist would have to admit that the technical side of this problem is being licked before our eyes. The social side—how to bring about widespread acceptance and use—is not so easy, but with the new attitudes in developed and underdeveloped countries alike, it does not seem so formidable as it did only a few years ago. I should perhaps say these things in a still small voice, since I am assuming a high degree of public awareness and determination to defeat the threat, a degree that has not yet been reached and must be maintained for decades if any prediction is to come true. It could, if it makes us complacent, become a self-defeating prophecy. And I am aware that the details of solving this problem could yet be very difficult, and that the quality of life on earth may well depend less on *whether* the demographic revolution is brought to its thermidor, than on how quickly. A delay of a generation will mean almost twice as many people to accommodate, and give us some very serious economic and political crises throughout Asia—crises that may be partly avoided by more rapid action. Thus I am very much in sympathy with those who are in a hurry. But this is nevertheless a promising area. With some luck, determination, and dedication, it may become an example of how a social pattern, an exponential growth rate of enormous import, was brought under control before it reached its built-in ceiling and burdened mankind with its oscillations.

Here then is a prediction, imbued with I think only a small component of over-optimism, for the turn of the coming century. The population explosion will be, at least for macro-purposes, ended.

We may not have reached the state of equal birth and death rates and hence a stable population, but the rate of growth should be much reduced. The world food crisis will have been met and surmounted. (Notice, however, that I did *not* say avoided. I do not think we will get off that easily. Before population control takes full effect we will have had to deal with mass famine in Asia.) The problem of economic development will still be with us, and perhaps in even more pressing form. But it will be in *different* form, for rapid population growth will no longer be a major brake on the developmental process, demanding heavy inputs of capital investment just to stay in place. The major problems instead will be in the areas of organization, determination, and the difficulties of controlling the social and political unrest that is associated with the middle stages of economic development. How to cope with rising expectations, with wants that increase even faster than growing satisfactions, will not be an easy question. The last stages of the mobiletic revolution, in bringing to even the poorest members of world society images of how foreign and domestic rich live, will enormously exacerbate problems we can already see.

THE END OF STABLE CHANGE

For the past century men in the Western world, and more recently over the rest of the globe, have lived in a period when change was the usual state of affairs. Though the change has been exciting, disruptive, and demanding for the individuals undergoing it, all of us have become accustomed to it; our parents with some head shaking, our children in a way that takes space travel and other wonders in stride as normal and utterly expectable events. Prediction of the ecology of international politics has been difficult primarily because for most of the time we have been so ignorant about the precise magnitudes of change and its predictable regularities. Had we before us accurate information about past experience, and courage enough to extrapolate, much of the present situation could have been predicted merely by expecting more of the same that had prevailed—not the same levels, but the same change rates. Relatively speaking, *political* prediction would have been easy (given today's data sources and theoretical achievements). Persistence forecasting, or the extrapolation of mildly sloping trends, would have been accurate. But until recently much of the necessary quantitative information simply had not been assembled, and since one can hardly extrapolate a trend without knowing what the trend is, we have a clear example of a case where neither imagination nor rigor were, by themselves, sufficient for adequate forecasting. Where precise data are still lacking, the normal difficulties of forecasting have been compounded recently by the rapid changes implied in the high levels now reached on many of the exponential growth curves, where a doubling in eight years instead of twelve can make a very great difference in the absolute changes with which society must cope.

Some of these problems will remain in future years, but as more and better data become available, and as social science develops greater rigor and a better understanding of our environment, they are being eased. For a brief period prediction may have great success in a world of rapid but dependable change. It will soon be shaken, however, by the system brakes that can be discerned in the not so distant future. Then new qualities of imagination will be required, both to *predict* and to *determine* what the world will be like. Much of the future will depend upon which growth rates change first, and whether by orderly deliberate control that brings them to a plateau with a minimum of oscillation, or whether they bump up and down against a ceiling imposed by the environment. Doubtless we all would prefer a world where population growth was brought to a regulated halt, rather than one where Malthus reigned supreme and the population rose and fell with epidemics and bad harvests. And because many of these growth rates are interrelated, an uncontrolled change in one is likely to have far-ranging effects.

For several generations we have been living in an era of transition between great system changes. That era is now coming to a close, and a period of instability is ahead. We have a limited amount of time to break loose from habit, inertia, and administrative routine, to decide which trends we most need to control, and to devise ways of doing it. Without adopting a naive eighteenth-century faith in the omnipotence of science, it is nonetheless true that when a social need is strongly felt *some* solution is often found, even though no one could have predicted in advance precisely what that solution would be.[18] On the whole, I am hopeful that the necessary social and technological innovations can be found under pressure, although the

---

[18]See Bell, *op. cit.*, and John R. Platt, *The Excitement of Science* (Boston: Houghton Mifflin, 1962), ch. 4, for good discussion of how this may be true, and also L. B. Slobodkin, "On the Present Incompleteness of Mathematical Ecology," *American Scientist*, 53, 3 (1965), pp. 347-59. It is important, however, to distinguish between what an *observer* might diagnose as social needs, and effective social *demands.*

time is short and the margin for error not at all wide. The population control experience is a good omen here. Only ten years ago one could not have said which, if any, of the possibilities then being explored might pay off; now we find unanticipated degrees of freedom. Maybe something of the sort will arise for international politics and world order. Right now no one can produce a scheme for the year 2000 that really looks workable, but as the pressure comes on, ingenious men may be able to develop something.

While trying to improve our predictive powers we must, at the same time, avoid *depending* on a high level of predictive success. We must maintain a pluralist approach so as to be able to adapt to the unexpected; we must have several possible alternatives and "keep our options open." It is worth recalling a statement by Alfred North Whitehead that is even more appropriate now than when he wrote it forty years ago:

> *We must expect that the future will be dangerous. It is the business of the future to be dangerous, and it is among the merits of science that it equips the future for its duties. . . . The middle class pessimism over the future of the world comes from a confusion between civilization and security. In the immediate future there will be less security than in the immediate past, less stability. . . . There is a degree of instability which is inconsistent with civilization. But, on the whole, the great ages have been unstable ages.*[19]

[19] Alfred North Whitehead, *Science and the Modern World* (New York: Macmillan, 1925), p. 291.

Toward Controlling
International Change:
A Personal Plea

Ernst B. Haas

In the world of Isaac Asimov the computer programmer is God: he selects the facts and relationships between facts from which as yet unknown correlations flow; thus he rules the world by predicting and manipulating change, and thus he maintains stability.

In our world the programmer has not yet achieved divine status; statesmen and scholars still select facts and deduce relationships from them; their correlations are far from exhaustive and the changes produced by them are intractable to clear prediction or effective manipulation. Of stability there is no trace.

Each of these two worlds possesses certain attractions. That of science fiction—but how much longer will it be fictitious?—assures a minimum of security because it controls change; but it has sacrificed freedom to the conformity which flows from the computer. Our present world offers little security and sacrifices generously to the Mammon of cumulative innovation which approaches hyperbolic

SOURCE: From *World Politics*, Vol. XVII, No. 1 (1964). Copyright © 1964 by Princeton University Press. Reprinted and abridged by permission of the author and Princeton University Press.

chaos; but freedom, of a sort, remains with us as long as the forces of innovation are able to compete fiercely.

Perfect prediction reaffirms the self-fulfilling prophecy: the certainty that a given choice will produce a desired result induces us to adopt that choice, and since no competing predictions are programmed, the desired result becomes history. The imperfect art of forecasting in which our generation of social scientists still indulges need not cause us to fear this outcome as yet, because the very grossness of its procedures assures that lack of certainty which enables us to envisage alternative outcomes.

If, as I shall argue, cumulative innovation is intolerable for a minimal stability in our environment, the means for making it bearable, at least, are still varied enough and the perspectives which define them sufficiently pluralistic to encourage the hope that we may attempt some control over our environment without falling victim to the benign totalitarianism of electronics. If I have cast Asimov's Hari Seldon in the shape of a god, I have deliberately substituted a deterministic future for a probabilistic one. The rule of electronics need not be totalitarian, to be sure, but it sharpens our perceptions to keep the possibility in mind. In any event, my concern is with the probabilistic aspects of the future world environment. As the argument proceeds I shall make my peace with the computer as one promising means for making the future a bearable one.

I

The stability for which many of us yearn is only partly represented by the hope that the major ideological and political chasms of international relations can somehow be contained. Clearly, the forces competing in Vietnam and Berlin, Katanga and Cuba, in Geneva and on the East River, can hardly be considered as giving order and certainty to our lives. Political ideology with religious fervor when also organized into opposing military blocs with thermonuclear toys is hardly a stabilizing factor. Yet I suggest that this kind of tension and uncertainty may be tolerable and comprehensible as compared with the challenge to order which is associated with the cumulative innovation resulting from technology, science, and the economic and social pursuits linked to them. In time the cross-pressures flowing from the nexus of technological possibility, exaggerated human expectations, and frantic efforts at meeting them may capture the instability of the cold war and subsume it. The continuation of cumulative innovation when blindly exploited by the forces of the cold war may yet create a world scenario in which the electronic philosopher-king will be greeted as the savior. Hence I shall address myself to the major technological factors which may make the international environment unlivable in our generation and explore the possibilities for stabilizing them.

Let me present some of these factors. In a perspective of unlimited progress and a better life for the developed as well as the underdeveloped nations, they all appear desirable and praiseworthy. Bearing in mind, therefore, the remaining possibilities of envisaging alternative outcomes, I wish deliberately to explore the conceivably disastrous implications of these factors in our focus of stability and change.

Thus technology, in principle, seems capable of meeting the demands of the revolution of rising expectations. But what happens if in the underdeveloped countries the expectations outstrip the capacity of the political and social system to meet them? What happens in the developed nations when "objective" needs of sharing affluence with the needy in order to head off their revolt against the West—whether under Communist or some other aegis—meet a pervasive and democratically legitimate insistence on husbanding affluence at home and investing it in the domestic revolution of still higher expectations, the hopes for a third and fourth car, for the split-level ranch house and the mountain cabin? Is more leisure time a force making for contentment or frustration, for do-it-yourself ceremonies or stormtrooper rites? It is certainly possible that the diffusion of nuclear knowledge will enable energy-poor countries to achieve industrialization at a faster rate; but what is to prevent the same countries from investing this knowledge first in less wholesome pursuits?

It is sometimes suggested that scientific breakthroughs in the field of motivation research, conditioning, teaching, and the not always gentle arts of communication will give us the techniques for making premodern people capable of assimilating, utilizing, and understanding at an ever-faster rate the tools of industrialism and mass consumption. Teaching machines may take the place of human technical assistance. Chemical inducements to "reenforce motivation" (we might call it "positive brainwashing") may eliminate the habits of nepotism, corruption, and status security which presently militate against speedy economic development. Progress in psychology can thus act as a link between the surge of technology and the lagging of societies and attitudes. But what is to guarantee us that the resulting balance will yield international stability rather than chemically, genetically, or verbally induced race hatred, envy, or greed? I suggest that at the moment no group, agency, or government knows how to direct scientific possibilities into politically stabilizing channels.

We might add other disturbing technological forces. In the future it may be possible to control the climate and the rhythm of agricultural production. Would the resulting changes in rural life be stabilizing to the international environment? Successful programs of public health have given us the amply familiar pattern of gigantic population growth before the advent of the industrial revolution and ahead of the completion of the urbanization process. The result is a tendency toward famine, migration, and stagnation in terms of per capita improvements in welfare despite growth in total production. Areas in Asia, Latin America, and Africa in which industrialization has been most rapid have also displayed the greatest amount of political dissatisfaction and social frustration. Is indiscriminate economic development a stabilizing factor? Certainly not in the short run, and—as Keynes assured us—in the long run we will all be dead. To complete this catalog of woe, let us bear in mind that while the industrialization process covers the globe, the older industrial nations tend to "progress" at a still faster rate. Soon we may have synthetics for all the major raw materials. Controlled photosynthesis and chemically manipulated genetics may yield economic results that will make national autarky a very simple matter. What, under such conditions, happens to world trade? Do we retrain the entire manpower of the jute industry, the middle-class elements who exist on the processing and sale of coffee? We may have to resort to teaching machines in order to induce these groups to settle down and accept their fate without harassing world stability.

In a dispassionate survey of these trends, the Stanford Research Institute noted that "Scientific developments in the next decade will give rise to or intensify many problems that must engage the attention of foreign policy planners. Scientific developments will also help solve foreign policy problems. But the outlook is that the progress of science and technology will do more to create or intensify than to ameliorate such problems, *unless deliberate policy measures are taken.*"[1] It is not a conflict between C. P. Snow's two

---

[1] *Possible Nonmilitary Scientific Developments and Their Potential Impact on Foreign Policy Problems of the United States*, A Study Prepared at the Request of the Committee on Foreign Relations, U.S. Senate, 86th Congress, 1st Session (Washington, GPO, 1959), I (emphasis supplied).

cultures, the humanistic and the scientific, which produces this instability. Rather, the destabilizing tendency of technological innovation is more accurately described by Ogburn's notion of cultural lag: as the rate of innovation increases because of the telescoping of research and development time, and as innovation becomes cumulative with the application of new approaches in one field to problems in another, human organization and thought patterns, hallowed values, and formal ideologies cannot keep up, even though they may be willing to undergo change as well. The result may be a wider gap between what world society is able to accomplish in terms of physical or biological knowledge and what it is capable of accommodating in terms of its values.

If the gap remains wide, then indeed cumulative innovation spells hyperbolic international chaos. The problem is compounded by the growth of planned innovation, unmatched by planned human adaptation. Some philosophers of science, like Michael Polanyi, argue that the unplanned forces of unfettered and unsubsidized scientific genius produce the greatest advances because the scientific equivalent of the free market guides their progress. If there were anonymous competition in scientific and technological innovation, we might derive a breathing spell from this condition; but the fact is that monopolitistic competition, at best, characterizes the process, in that governments, foundations, and giant corporations guide and direct the areas in which breakthroughs will be scored. Therefore innovation becomes the more terrible because it has acquired a systematic as well as a cumulative character. Can nations singly, or in concert, "plan" to adapt themselves to this trend? Can they assimilate innovation that corresponds to certain values professed by their citizens while also controlling it so as to protect other and equally fervently held values? Can they reconcile the competing values so as to avoid civil strife, mass frustration, new imperialisms, and uncharted anxieties? To this question we now turn.

II

One currently fashionable attempt to close the gap can be described only as contemporary chiliasm. The not always complementary notions of immediate world federation with world law and of instantaneous and possibly unilateral disarmament provide cases in point. Sometimes these nostrums are held out as sufficient in themselves to get us beyond chaos. At best they seek to eliminate those aspects of technical innovation which relate to the waging of war, thus leaving untouched the disturbing aspects of change which might threaten us with instability even if only crossbows and poisoned darts were available.

More to the point is a psychiatric variety of chiliasm—as, for instance, that preached by Erich Fromm and Brock Chisholm. Fromm would cure us by introducing an intense personal creative life and the force of social love; Chisholm sees world federalism as a kind of mass psychotherapy designed to prod mankind toward adult maturity from its present infantile approach to international problem-solving. The more intractable the problem becomes—because childlike approaches toward its solution are adopted—the more regressive national anxieties and policies grow. If we were to grant—though I am very far from willing to do so—that all conflict is irrational and curable by proper therapy, then this approach would still not help us in our predicament because modern states plainly are not rest homes ruled over by omniscient psychiatrist-kings. For better or for worse, the political conflicts of nations which overlap with the technological threats are perceived as rational in the minds of the real kings. And the adaptation of international society with its diverse values to the challenge of technological and scientific chaos must therefore proceed within the vise of the values as perceived by these kings.

It has been suggested that our kings—the decision-makers—be subjected to intensive motivational research in order to weed out those plagued by personality factors which cannot adjust to pure problem-solving behavior. This would no doubt be feasible in terms of our growing knowledge of emotional manipulation. If we knew precisely what problem required solving and which underlying values were the most desirable, this kind of certainty would be as acceptable as that provided by the computer. Actually we should remind ourselves, that the innate political values of men and groups in society *have*—in a sense, spontaneously—displayed some remarkable adaptive tendencies. It seems to me that the actual adaptation to industrialism is much more rapid today in totalitarian as well as in free societies than it was during the onset of the industrial revolution. Still, the travail engendered by that social cataclysm, as described in Karl Polanyi's *The Great Transformation,* is hardly such as to make its imitation in the now-developing countries a desirable event; accounts of mass behavior in Calcutta and São Paulo suggest that social adaptation to modernity is far from smooth. Perhaps the cultural lag is growing shorter in the West, or perhaps negative reaction is only being delayed; but the specter of automation, for instance, seems kind as compared with the anguish caused by the spinning jenny. The nations of the West look so different today than they did in the 1930's and the victory of the welfare state is so complete as to suggest that national societies do learn to assimilate innovation. Values inimical to industrialism do yield, and aspects of the mass egalitarian society gain acceptance, in the sense that their opponents make reluctant peace with the new and still remain members of the society. If this is true at the national level, why cannot the same occur internationally? Can we not turn to action patterns of a non-chiliastic nature to eliminate cultural lag?

One way of doing this would be to continue to seek human adaptation to a changing international technology whose rate of progression remains unchecked. I do not know whether this is possible without serious schizophrenia, but the chiliasts as well as the actual historical pattern of adaptation suggest that, thus far, man has been malleable and technology rigidly demanding. To reverse the pattern would slow down economic and technical advance, but it would save us from the hyperbolic chaos to which unchecked innovation may lead. I therefore wish to look at the theoretical possibility of fore-shortening the cultural lag by controlling the rate of innovation. Wishing to avoid the tyranny of the computer and feeling encouraged by the demonstrated inability of many famous scientists to forecast the effects of their own discoveries, I shall try to see, in the words of Robert Heilbroner, "the future as history." I am under no illusion that I am engaging in precise forecasting. But I also have shed the illusion that we can rely on the automatic forces of some impersonal divinity of competition to sift the desirable in science from the undesirable, to arrive at peace by unplanned rivalry, or to achieve stability on the basis of unilinear international economic and social progress. It is too late for any unbounded optimism in yearning for a world corresponding somehow to liberal values. But perhaps it is not yet too late for the reasoned pessimism which hopes merely to avert the worst by the application of historically sanctioned planning.

Historically sanctioned planning seeks to exercise that modicum of freedom of the will available to man within the sluggish context of abstract historical development. In the classical terminology, it involves the strategic exercise of *virtù*—albeit of a rather unheroic character—in a setting of *necessità*. Evolutionary changes involving the uncontrolled revolution of rising expectations in the material sense, the upsurging resentment against poverty, inequality, and indignity based on race, the snowballing of civilian and military science and technology as well as the possibilities of successful mass manipulation—all these are natural consequences of earlier unplanned historical developments: they cannot simply be brought to a stop. All man can do is to envisage possible alternative outcomes, predict the worst, and seek to guard against it with the limited means free will gives him. Planning and control, therefore, are conceivable only *within* these surging forces. But the example of successful totalitarian-revolutionary societies teaches us—among other things—that a conscious direction of the development of economic and political pattern is possible. In the words of Robert Heilbroner, "The possibility posed by history is not that of denying the advent of planning, but of seizing control of it to assure the kind of collective economic responsibility we want. . . . The issue is not the simple and clear-cut one of a greater or lesser freedom. It is the difficult and clouded choice of a subservience to the necessities imposed by the forces visibly at work in our midst, or the perilous freedom of an exercise of historic control over ourselves."[2]

This approach to planning is as germane to the solution of our national and local problems as it is to the international environment. But we have more control over the national scene, both in terms of legal powers and because of a greater homogeneity of values. The true challenge to *virtù*, then, lies in the effort to address ourselves to the kind of international planning which is historically sanctioned, which is conceivable within the confines of the hostile material, ideological, and military forces besieging us. And in this manner we may possibly succeed in stemming some of the destabilizing factors which threaten the international scene with even more terror than the thermonuclear variety to which some of us are growing accustomed.

III

To the superficial observer, contemporary international organizations appear to be very frail institutions for stabilizing anything: their involvement in the exchange of propaganda broadsides and their failures in guaranteeing the firm military security of the member states receive such disproportionate attention. But if viewed against the backdrop of the fundamental changes which the international environment has undergone since 1945, the organizations which make up the United Nations system appear to be remarkably adaptive contrivances. If such organizations manage to survive drastic

[2] *The Future as History* (New York 1961), 188-89.

changes in the nature of their membership and in the demands which the members pose, they must, by definition, adapt themselves. Since few such organizations possess an organic self apart from and greater than the sum of their member states, this is another way of saying that an evolving environment tends to convince the nations that new tasks can and should be imposed on established international organizations. To the extent that they are adaptive, then, international organizations are themselves part of the historical process and can become institutions of self-conscious historically sanctioned planning. I urge this view of the United Nations in order to expose as analytically erroneous and morally vicious the position of the patriotic realist who either shrugs off or condemns international organizations as "idealistic" or "utopian." But I also urge it to call attention to the historical soundness of these contrivances in juxtaposing them to the chiliastic impatience of the world federalist who would deny the moral validity of the existing nation-state system.

But thus to assert the integral role of the United Nations in the modern world is not to prove its capacity to deal with the problem of cultural lag. The policies followed hitherto in that organization with reference to technical, scientific, and economic innovation, far from foreshortening the cultural lag, have in fact contributed heavily to its intensification. Technical and economic assistance programs, because of the poor coordination and lack of prescience which have accompanied their implementation, have piled innovation upon innovation without apparent regard for the possibilities of chaos which remain implicit in this pursuit. If we wish to slow down the process of innovation by central planning to bring it into harmony with the adaptive capacity of underdeveloped societies, we must first alert the member governments to the dangers of chaos.

Examples such as the desperate birth control campaigns and the desire to gear the rate of industrialization to the expansion of the agricultural sector in India suggest that some awareness of the chaotic implications of unchecked innovation already exists. The first need, therefore, is to reenforce this sense of danger and to call attention to the intensification of the cultural lag. This must be followed by efforts within the United Nations system to stress the possibilities of controlling the process of innovation insofar as it is influenced by United Nations programs. Essentially this involves an effort to persuade the member nations to negotiate among themselves the kind of agreements which would subordinate development to planning, crass innovation to ordered evolution.

There is no more effective way of doing this than to follow the standard method adopted by the specialized agencies and regional economic organizations in launching major new programs. A general conference of the membership must be called; this, because of the heterogeneity of its composition and the complexity of the subject matter, will yield only the most general consensus; it will then be followed by meeting of experts, loosely and permissively instructed, aided by totally uninstructed experts from the international secretariats involved. Provided the recommendations of these experts address themselves to a problem experienced in common by all the member states, there is every reason to believe that not even the major ideological tensions of our period can block their adoption in some form. Once this much is accomplished, it would be a relatively small matter to bend the policies of such established international institutions as the Special Fund and the International Bank in the direction of controlling rather than accumulating innovation.

From an initial basis of field-by-field *ad hoc* consultations, there may emerge a modest international brain trust for the general planning of innovation. Composed of eminent scientists and philosophers and representing East, West, and neutrals, it would take as its task the review of all technical and scientific inventions in order to assess their probable impact on society. When persuaded that, if used properly, a given invention would conduce to orderly progress, this panel of reviewers could then license the invention for general application; the unlicensed utilization of inventions would become punishable. I can live with the idea of new drugs capable of controlling heredity and able to shape individual motivation only if their use is subjected to this kind of scrutiny; I am emboldened to think that adherents of mutually antagonistic ideologies would feel the same if they suspected that the enemy might otherwise possess a weapon favorable to himself.

While this review should be applied to all kinds of inventions, its efficacy is suggested, in fact, by the existing international system of control over narcotic drugs. Ideological differences have prevented its proposed application to the field of disarmament. But I suggest that a shared awareness of uncharted chaos resulting from scientific developments not yet consummated is a more potent source of shared fears than the existence of weapons to which we have, for better or for worse, adapted ourselves.

. . .